PSYCHIATRIC MEDICINE

Previously Published Volumes from
The American College of Psychiatrists

Psychiatric Medicine

Edited by
GENE USDIN, M.D.

Clinical Professor of Psychiatry and Behavioral Sciences
Louisiana State University School of Medicine (New Orleans)

BRUNNER/MAZEL, *Publishers* • New York

Library of Congress Cataloging in Publication Data

American College of Psychiatrists.
   Psychiatric medicine.

   Proceedings of the annual meeting of the American College of Psychiatrists, held Feb. 1977 in Atlanta.
   Includes bibliographical references and index.
   1. Medicine, Psychosomatic—Congresses.   2. Psychiatric consultation—Congresses.   I. Usdin, Gene L.   II. Title. [DNLM: 1. Psychiatry.   2. Psychosomatic medicine.   3. Social environment. WM100
P9785]   RC49.A416   1977   616.8'9   77-10139
ISBN 0-87630-151-0

Published by
BRUNNER/MAZEL, INC.
19 Union Square
New York, New York 10003

THE AMERICAN COLLEGE OF PSYCHIATRISTS

Officers

Program Committee for 1977 Annual Meeting

Publications Committee

Contributors

W. ROBERT BEAVERS, M.D.
Associate Clinical Professor of Psychiatry, Southwestern Medical School

H. KEITH H. BRODIE, M.D.
Professor and Chairman of Psychiatry, Duke University Medical Center

NED H. CASSEM, M.D.
Associate Professor of Psychiatry, Harvard Medical School

MAURICE H. GREENHILL, M.D.
Professor of Psychiatry, Albert Einstein College of Medicine

THOMAS P. HACKETT, M.D.
Professor of Psychiatry, Harvard Medical School

CHASE PATTERSON KIMBALL, M.D.
Professor of Psychiatry and Medicine, University of Chicago

JERRY M. LEWIS, M.D.
Director of Research and Training, Timberlawn Psychiatric Research Foundation, and Associate Professor of Psychiatry, Southwestern Medical School

PETER A. MARTIN, M.D.
Clinical Professor of Psychiatry, University of Michigan Medical School, and Adjunct Professor of Psychiatry, Wayne State University

CAROL R. NADELSON, M.D.
Associate Professor of Psychiatry, Harvard Medical School

MALKAH T. NOTMAN, M.D.
Associate Professor of Psychiatry, Harvard Medical School

MORTON F. REISER, M.D.
> Professor and Chairman of Psychiatry, Yale School of Medicine

ROBERT L. ROESSLER, M.D.
> Professor of Psychiatry, Baylor College of Medicine

HERBERT WEINER, M.D., Ph.D.
> Professor of Psychiatry and Neuroscience, and Chairman of the Department of Psychiatry, Albert Einstein College of Medicine

JOHN K. WING, M.D. Ph.D.
> Professor of Psychiatry and Director of Medical Research Council, Social Psychiatry Unit, Institute of Psychiatry, London, England

Contents

ix

PART III

THE FAMILY

PART IV

THE STANLEY R. DEAN AWARD LECTURE

Preface

This publication of the American College of Psychiatrists continues the pattern of presenting the papers delivered at the organization's annual scientific meeting, in this instance, the one held in February 1977 in Atlanta, Georgia. Each College meeting focuses on a particular theme and brings together experts to educate the College membership. The 1977 meeting and this volume come at a period in which psychiatry is reaffirming its close kinship with medicine—when psychiatrists are returning to the laboratory, studying and reviewing pertinent new developments in the basic sciences. With increased interest in the basic sciences, it might have been anticipated that the time was ripe for a stride forward in coming to grips with the relationship of stress to organic disease.

The papers presented approached psychiatric medicine from two different perspectives. One involved the rapidly expanding knowledge about underlying physiologic processes involved in a variety of diseases in which psychologic factors play an important role. The second perspective was the role of the psychiatrist in the general hospital. This publication, therefore, presents the reader with the opportunity to pursue the current state of knowledge and clinical skills in two important areas.

Rapid advances in technology have led to clarification of many of the underlying physiologic processes but there is resulting concern that those advances could lead to a diminution in the concern for the patient as person. With each advance in scientific understanding there is an associated need to re-emphasize the patient as an experiencing human—with fears, hopes, values, and a network of others who may either help or hinder the patient in dealing with his disease. The disease must be placed in the context of a patient with a unique personality, having a reaction at a specific time of life, in a specific environment, with particular relatives and friends, under certain defined socioeconomic circumstances, frequently being offered the latest of medical techniques and technology, and, quite importantly, reacting to the knowledge, skill, and personality of the treating physician.

Terms fall into disfavor, sometimes because of undefined boundaries which cause them to be used as catchalls. The diagnosis of psychopathic personality is an example. *Borderline personality* now seems to have this potential because of its dubiously specified boundaries. *Psychosomatic* has been criticized as a medical term, since it appears to commit the user to a classical Cartesian dualism; the papers in this volume may serve to revitalize the term psychosomatic as being appropriate to describe the conditions in which the psyche and soma especially interact.

Early work in the 1940's searching for specific psychodynamic patterns associated with the so-called seven classical psychosomatic diseases did not, for the most part, fulfill its promise. Several factors may have been involved, including the concept that there may be different underlying physiologic processes that can produce one such disease. It may be that psychodynamic variables are important but correlate with only certain physiologic processes and not other pathways to the same disease. Another factor that may prove to have been a confounding issue is the increasing realization that there may be psychologic influences that render the individual more susceptible to all disease and, until those are clarified, they may obscure the role of specific psychodynamic factors.

During the interval since the early work on psychosomatic disease, there has been a growth of knowledge regarding "illness behavior" —those psychologic responses to disease that often comprise a significant part of the patient's experiencing of disease. There has also occurred an increasing interest in the supportive or detrimental role that can be played by the patient's interactional systems—patient-doctor, family, and the interpersonal milieu of the hospital unit.

This volume brings the reader detailed coverage of a wide variety of these important issues. Part I reviews and analyzes topics that are basic to an understanding of *Psychobiology and Liaison Psychiatry*. In Part II the focus is on specific areas of special significance to the psychiatrist dealing with physical disease (psychosomatic medicine). Part III on *The Family* was prepared especially for this volume by two College members, leading researchers in the field of family functioning and dysfunctioning, in order to provide coverage of this increasingly important area. Another valuable addition for this volume is the overview in the epilogue by Peter Martin, president of the College at the time of the 1977 meeting.

The Stanley R. Dean Award lecture, "The Management of Schizophrenia in the Community," presented at the meeting by Dr. John K. Wing, is also included. With the increasing involvement and sophistication of nonpsychiatric physicians in the long-term management of chronic schizophrenic patients, Dr. Wing's chapter becomes pertinent and useful.

This, the ninth publication of the College, continues the pattern of early publication following the College meetings so that the material is current and, therefore, more useful for the reader. Acknowledgment of the cooperation of the publisher is appropriate. Likewise, the close, active working relationship between the Program and Publications Committees has been a cardinal factor in the editing process.

GENE USDIN, M.D.

PSYCHIATRIC MEDICINE

Part I

PSYCHOBIOLOGY AND LIAISON PSYCHIATRY

1

The Psychobiology of Human Disease: An Overview

Herbert Weiner, M.D., Ph.D.

Medicine may be the only discipline that does not have a comprehensive theory. Theories of physics, biology, history, art, sociology and psychology exist but we have no theory of health or disease. The only extant theory in medicine is the theory of infectious disease that can account for no more than 10 percent of all diseases. The theory of infectious disease is itself oversimplified, linear and restrictive.

We have, in fact, no complete explanation of the causes of most diseases. Most medical explanations of disease are functional in nature. They tell us about the relationship of a low cardiac output to pulmonary edema, but they do not tell us why at a particular point in time the heart failed. In other words, most explanations of the symptoms and signs of a disease (and the functional disturbances that they express) do not explain its antecedents. The disadvantage of an antecedent or historical explanation is that it is descriptive and not predictive—the variety of animal or plant species can, in part, be explained by a genetic mutation, but the theory does not predict when a new mutation will occur. A complete theory of disease would allow us to predict who is at risk for a particular disease and when and in what circumstances the predisposed person will develop it.

3

A complete theory of disease would need to be functional, historical and predictive.

A theory of disease should also incorporate a full statement of all the factors that predispose, initiate and sustain diseases. It should explain the rise or fall in incidence and prevalence of a disease over time and why some diseases occur more frequently in one society, culture or group than in another. Some diseases are age-dependent. Other diseases occur with greater frequency in one sex than in the other. A theory should account for the variable natural history of most diseases. It must also incorporate a theory of health.

Two major impediments stand in the way of the development of a comprehensive theory of disease: One is conceptual, and the other is methodological. The conceptual problem stems from the fact that some believe that all disease is a disease of cells, whereas others hold that only organisms have diseases. The methodological problem is due to the fact that we traditionally study diseases after their onset. At that time the factors that predispose to the disease tend to be confounded not only with those that initiate it but also with those that are brought into play to adapt to the pathogenetic process itself. (Arteriolar damage or adrenal cortical hyperplasia may be the result of longstanding high blood pressure.* Antibody formation designed to protect the body against antigen may at times culminate in anaphylactic shock and death.) Therefore, the first step to be taken in the development of a theory of disease is an empirical and methodological one. Persons must be studied before disease onset in order to determine the factors responsible for the maintenance of health and those that are responsible for disease.

Disease is a failure of adaptation; it is a biological phenomenon. Because it is a biological phenomenon, it deals with organisms in interaction with their natural, social and cultural environments. Disease is not merely a matter of a disturbance of the self-regulatory mechanisms within cells, or of any *one* single factor such as infection or nutritional deprivation.

---

* At other times adrenal cortical hyperplasia (aldosterinoma) may antecede high blood pressure.

The only branch of medicine that has a more comprehensive view of disease—in that it attempts to provide functional and historical explanations of disease—is (awkwardly) named psychosomatic medicine. Because psychosomatic medicine does not lay claim to any one disease or any group of diseases (or an organ such as the brain, or of a system such as the circulation), it is accorded little status in organized medicine. Its unstated (and possibly immodest) goal is the development of a comprehensive theory of health and disease. Its concerns have always been more with predisposition to, and the initiation of disease than with pathophysiology. Pioneer studies prior to the onset of disease have been carried out under its aegis (1, 2, 3). These studies have also shown that social, cultural, psychological, as well as genetic, physiological, biochemical and immunological factors should be accorded roles in the predisposition and inception of disease by those who use the psychosomatic approach (4).

This approach has an intellectual history of at least 4,200 years (5). The idea that emotional and environmental factors play a role in the inception of disease can be found in the writings of physicians—Hippocrates, Galen, Maimonides, Sydenham, Cabanis, Esquirol, Heinroth, Freud and Osler—and of philosophers—Plato and Descartes.

But we owe to Freud, Groddeck, Krehl, von Weizsäcker, Wittkower, Dunbar, Alexander and others the first observations in the 20th century that psychological and social factors play a role in the most frequent (as well as other) diseases to which mankind is prey.

These observations are predicated on the axioms that persons (not only cells or organs) have diseases—the domain of psychosomatic medicine—and that diseases occur in persons—the domain of liaison psychiatry.

If one ascribes to the axiom that persons have diseases, one needs to study persons and their human, social and cultural environments which they inhabit. The particular aspect of the person and his environment chosen for study will determine the data obtained and their conceptualization: We, therefore, have a variety of observations about diseased persons.

GENERAL FACTORS IN DISEASE

Predisposing Factors

1) In Groddeck's view (6), the lesion characteristic of a disease was a symbolic representation of a preexisting, unconscious, psychological conflict, in the same manner as a conversion symptom represented a sexual conflict. Groddeck also believed, therefore, that the conflict was pathogenetic. Today we are inclined to believe that a lesion may acquire a symbolic meaning for its owner (7) but that this meaning plays no role in the predisposition or initiation of the disease but it may help sustain it (8).

2) In Dunbar's opinion (9), particular character or personality traits were associated with particular diseases. For example, hypertensive patients were said to be shy, perfectionistic, reserved and self-controlled but given to "volcanic eruptions of feelings" when in conflict with authority. (Dunbar did, however, comment that beneath these traits smouldered anger and resentment.)

This point of view is now considered to be invalid because such traits, habits and attitudes are present in many healthy people and are not the outcome of any one factor. But it has recurred in the guise of the Type A personality—the driven, impatient, ambitious executive—who is prone to coronary artery disease if he is also biochemically and physically predisposed to it. (The physiological features consist of a higher blood platelet count in whole blood, a diminished tendency of platelet aggregation to norepinephrine during exercise, an increased beta- to alpha-lipoprotein ratio, and elevated mean serum cholesterol and triglyceride levels.)

3) In Alexander's work (10, 11) we find the point of view that specific, dynamic, unconscious constellations of conflicts characterized patients with the diseases he studied. These constellations were not, in his view, unique to those with these diseases—but they differed in persons with these different diseases and, therefore, were specific to the disease. The patient with a peptic duodenal ulcer has an unconscious wish to be fed and to receive of which he is ashamed and he becomes excessively independent. The patient with essential hy-

pertension has a fear of his own aggressive assertiveness which he inhibits or represses, often for fear of retaliation (12). The child with bronchial asthma wishes to be enveloped and protected by the mother. In some children that wish is expressed in a cry for the mother's protection but the cry is inhibited for fear that the mother will repudiate the child. In other children, the wish to be protected and enveloped is imagined to be dangerous; in these children the asthmatic attack can be averted by separating the child from its mother.

Alexander (10) also stated that there were psychological similarities between patients with different diseases—that at base all of the patients were dependent in their relationships.

4) Additional commonalities between patients with the diseases studied by Alexander have been described by Ruesch (13) and by McDougall (14), Marty and de M'Uzan (15), Nemiah (16, 17) and Sifneos (18). Reusch observed that most such patients displayed behavioral and psychological features that were "infantile"—that is, inappropriate to their age. These features included arrested and impaired social learning; a reliance on imitation; a tendency to express themselves in direct physical action or through bodily channels; dependency and passivity; childlike ways of thinking; rigid and self-punishing moral standards and ideals; high and unrealistic aspirations; difficulties in assimilating and integrating life experiences; a reliance on securing love and affection; and an inability to master changes in their lives or to learn new techniques for overcoming frustrations.

The other clinicians mentioned above have observed common cognitive ("alexithymic") characteristics in these patients: 1) They are unable to describe their feelings; 2) they cannot localize the physiological accompaniments of emotions in their bodies; 3) they cannot distinguish feelings from each other; 4) they have a paucity of conscious fantasies; 5) they are preoccupied with the minute details of external events; 6) they are stiff and wooden in their manner. Whether or not alexithymia is unique to patients with psychosomatic diseases is not clear.

We may conclude that patients with the diseases share certain common psychological characteristics. But they also differ in their psychologic characteristics as Alexander had stated. Since his time, much controversy has surrounded Alexander's formulations about specific psychological conflicts. While this controversy was raging, his other statements were forgotten. His concept of these diseases was actually tripartite: 1) The specific conflict predisposed patients to certain diseases but only in the presence of other (at that time, undetermined) genetic, biochemical and physiological (X-) factors; 2) in certain specific life situations to which the patient was sensitized by virtue of his key conflict, the conflict was activated and enhanced; 3) strong emotions accompanied the activated conflict; they were channeled by autonomic, hormonal or neuromuscular channels to produce changes in structure and function.

Alexander, therefore, made the most comprehensive statements about the several factors that play a role in the etiology and pathogenesis of disease. In the past 20 years it has become evident that all of the diseases he studied are heterogeneous (*vide infra*). Therefore, controversy about specific or non-specific conflicts are probably generated in part by the fact that populations of subjects are not homogeneous. Another development has occurred during this time. A great deal of emphasis has been placed on the setting of disease onset by a study of the psychological reactions to bereavement, life change, job loss and stressful occupations (19, 24), the manner in which they are coped with and the psychological reactions they promote (21, 25, 26). The evidence is that distressing events when adaptively coped with (by defenses) do not lead to disease. But when the event (such as a parting) is not coped with, it may lead to adaptive failure—for instance, to helplessness, hopelessness, giving-up and a state of having given up—and disease may ensue.

Thus the recent emphasis has been adaptational. Studies of adaptive success and failure have been accompanied by many studies of their physiological correlates. Implicit in such studies is that adaptive failure occurs in the setting of disease onset. Adaptive failure sets off pathogenetic mechanisms in the predisposed person.

Today we are able to specify with some accuracy the predisposing X-factors, which Alexander postulated were the predisposing companions of psychological conflict. These factors are social and experiential as well as genetic, immunological and hormonal.

Sociocultural, Economic, Historical and Political Factors in Disease

The influence of social and cultural factors in disease takes many forms. Diseases vary in incidence and prevalence in various societies and cultures. Some diseases are much more prevalent in one cultural subgroup than in another. Shifts in prevalence of a disease occur from one period in history to another. Socioeconomic and social class factors are powerfully correlated with prevalence of some diseases. Changes in economic conditions may even be (indirectly) reflected in physiological changes (27).

The importance of social class factors was attested to by the observation (28) that not all patients with peptic duodenal ulcer were excessively independent and drivingly ambitious as Alexander had claimed. Some, in fact, were overtly dependent, frequently alcoholic and often derelicts. Since then it has also become obvious that another group of patients was independent in some contexts and dependent in others (29). The reason for Alexander's (biased) findings is a simple one—he was studying patients who belonged to the upper or upper-middle social class.

The nature of the society in which a person lives may also have powerful influences in protecting or eliciting a disease. Societies or social groups that are traditional, stable and structured, and that promote felicitous social bonds tend to protect their members against coronary artery disease and the development of high blood pressure (Figure 1). The members of most societies tend to show an increase in blood pressure levels with age but, in some societies, blood pressure levels remain constant or may actually fall with age (30). In stable societies blood pressure levels do not rise with age. In those societies in which rapid social (value) changes occur that are fraught with strife, blood pressure levels rise.

Social strife, unstable marriages, police brutality and violence also correlate with the known fourfold prevalence of high blood

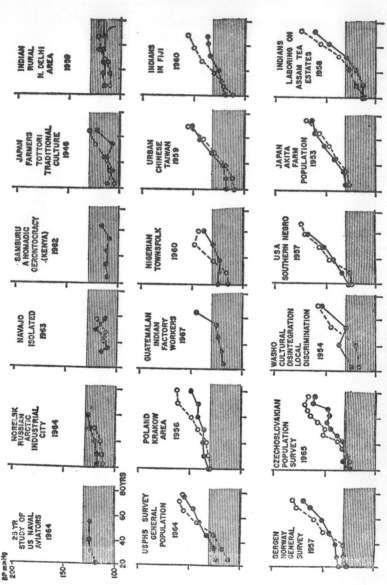

FIGURE 1. The increase in systolic pressure levels with age occurs both in men (closed circles) and women (open circles) in most societies but not all. The *rates of increase* vary markedly. (From Henry, J. P. and Cassel, J. *Am. J. Epidemiol.* 90:171, 1969).

pressure in black Americans when compared with their white compatriots (31).

The military occupation of countries by particularly violent and brutal conquerors may have a marked influence on the incidence and prevalence of hyperthyroidism. The effects of these social and political conditions may, however, be modified by nutrition. The incidence and prevalence of hyperthyroidism (both toxic diffuse and nodular goiter) rose 5 to 7 times in Denmark and 5 times in Norway from 1941-1945 during the German occupation (32, 33, 34). In 1934, the incidence and prevalence of hyperthyroidism began to fall in Norway at a time that the Germans systematically began to starve the Norwegians into submission. Beginning in 1940, the same regimen of starvation had been applied to the Dutch, who had a fall in the prevalence of hyperthyroid states during World War II (35). The Germans never tried to starve the Danes.

Therefore, one must conclude that social or political factors alone do not determine the changes in incidence and prevalance of a disease. Multiple factors play a role. The factors include a predisposition to a disease.

Today we know that in any population there is a pool of persons who are at risk for a certain disease. The risk is imparted to them by the presence of specific combinations of several predisposing factors that specify the disease. As social, political, economic, occupational and human changes occur in the environment, some predisposed members of the pool fall ill with the disease to which they are predisposed. Clearly, psychological factors alone do not predispose to disease.

The choice of a disease is, therefore, partially determined by several predisposing factors. Being predisposed to a disease does not mean that the disease will inevitably develop. No disease will develop if the person is not predisposed to it. The fluctuating incidence of disease suggests that in every population there are more persons predisposed to disease can develop it. As environmental conditions change, a certain number of persons develop the disease. The same exogenous source of the disease (such as a drug) does not inevitably produce the same morbid condition; it may produce different diseases in different persons. The specific disease produced by the drug depends on the person's predispositions to it.

The Role of the Family in Disease

Some of the burden of the ontogenesis of the psychological conflicts that characterize patients with some "psychosomatic" diseases has been borne by the mother. Throughout the literature on this topic one finds statements about the overprotective, domineering or directly rejecting behavior of mothers towards their children who develop bronchial asthma, rheumatoid arthritis or ulcerative colitis.

Studies of the mother-child relationship have been extended to studies of families. Such studies tend to be fraught with bias because the observer usually knows that one family member is ill. The meaning of the results of such studies is also hard to interpret. All of the diseases under discussion run in families—the population geneticist interprets the results to mean that genetic factors play a role in the disease, the student of families looks for family pathology. A third interpretation of the data is possible—a child may "learn" to have asthmatic attacks if exposed to the asthmatic attacks of his or her parents.

Nonetheless studies of asthmatic families have shown that no single pattern of family relationships exists. Mothers may be: 1) overprotective or oversolicitous; 2) perfectionistic and overambitious for the child; 3) overtly domineering, rejecting, punitive or cruel; 4) helpful and generatively maternal (36, 37). Furthermore, the attitudes of parents to their asthmatic child may be more accurately related to the social maladjustment of the child than to his asthmatic attacks (38, 39). When parents become more sympathetic and understanding, the child's invalidism and truancy from school may disappear.

Systematic studies of the families of patients with ulcerative colitis have been carried out by Jackson and Yalom (40). These families are described as having "pseudomutual" relationships that also characterize the families of schizophrenic patients. The incidence of psychotic illness is about seven times greater in patients with ulcerative colitis than in the normal population. Therefore, the tentative conclusion might be drawn that the "pseudomutuality" of the family relationship is related more to the predisposition to psychosis than to ulcerative colitis. But we do not know whether that conclusion is a valid one.

In any case, the systematic study of families is in its infancy. Until we have more information about families, any conclusions about the role of the family in predisposing to and initiating illness must remain tentative. In view of the fact that different kinds of relationships occur in the families of asthmatic and arthritic children, the present conclusion is that no one pattern of relationship is either necessary or sufficient to the etiology of the disease.

The Role of Genetic Factors in Disease

Genes express themselves through the formation of specific enzymes. Genetic disturbances may express themselves in a variety of forms: 1) the enzyme may be altered in structure; 2) the enzyme may not be formed at all, and is, therefore, absent; 3) the amount of enzyme formed may be depressed or increased; 4) new enzyme is continually formed in the absence of substrate; a) not because it is needed but because the mechanism controlling ("the repressor") the gene is defective; b) because the end product of its synthetic activities does not inhibit enzyme formation; or c) because of a disturbance in the interaction of "the repressor" and the gene area ("the operator") which regulates enzyme synthesis; 5) the enzyme may be chemically unstable.

We have also learned that disease may not occur despite a structural alteration in a gene. Abnormally composed genes may express themselves quantitatively, qualitatively, not at all, or only in interaction with environmental factors. For example, deficiency of the enzyme glucose-6-phosphate dehydrogenase (G-6PD) is expressed in a variety of ways. Eighteen different genetically determined varieties of the deficiency have now been identified (41). It is likely that each separate form of this deficiency is the product of a distinctive change in the structure of the protein, possibly due to the substitution of a single amino acid for the usual one at a single position in the poly-peptide chains of the enzyme.

In part, the manifestations of the structural defect are a product of the level of abnormal enzyme in red blood cells. One variant of G-6PD deficiency expresses itself only when the person is exposed to certain drugs, and another when he is exposed to fava beans. In some variants a chronic hemolytic anemia occurs "spontaneously"; in still other forms no clinical expression of the enzyme variation occurs.

Quantitative genetic factors also play a role by lowering the amount or level of an enzyme, or by causing its absence. For example, in the Lesch-Nyhan syndrome an abnormal gene on the X-chromo-some is apparently responsible for a virtual absence of the enzyme hypoxanthine-guanine phosphoribosyl transferase. (A partial defi-ciency of this enzyme has also been found in some patients with gout.) Not only may enzyme levels in such patients be markedly reduced but at least two forms of structural alteration of the enzyme itself are known. It is also worth noting that various structural alterations of this enzyme may express themselves in the same phenotype, i.e., as gout, but the virtual *absence* of the enzyme results in the Lesch-Nyhan syndrome, a very different disease from gout (41). To complicate the matter further, different forms of genetic variation may have the same phenotypic expression: In gout, purine biosynthesis is excessive, or uric acid secretion by the distal renal tubules is defective, or both defects are present, all leading to ele-vated serum uric acid and to gouty arthritis in some persons. How-ever, genetic variation may not be expressed phenotypically at all, for reasons that are still not understood: Only a small proportion of persons with elevated levels of serum uric acid develop clinical gout. Genetic variation may also account for the increased capacity to form pepsinogen (Figure 2) in the stomach, or for the occurrence of a unique pepsinogen isoenzyme. Excessive pepsinogen produc-tion may, on the other hand, merely be due to a quantitative pheno-menon in that it may stem from an increased size of the parietal cell mass, the origin of which is still unknown.

Genetic factors of a very specific kind probably play a predisposing

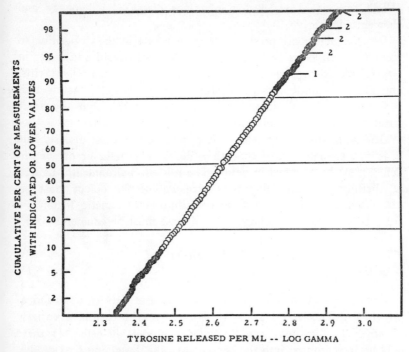

FIGURE 2: Distribution of blood serum pepsinogen concentrations: the frequency distribution of the logarithm of the concentration of the pepsinogen in the serum plotted on a probit scale. The subjects selected for special study were among those designated with closed circles. The numerals refer to individuals with duodenal ulcer. (Weiner, H., et al. *Psychosom. Med.* 19:1, 1957)

role in perhaps 10 percent or more of all patients with primary anorexia nervosa. Specifically, this subgroup of patients are placed at risk by having an XO chromosome or XO/XX mosaicism; they have Turner's syndrome (42). Such specific chromosomal abnormalities have not been found in the other major "psychosomatic diseases."

Patients with a virtual absence of gammaglobulin formation of the Bruton-type, which is presumably due to an enzymatic defect in

B-cells, are at high risk for infectious diseases, malignancy and rheumatoid arthritis.

Genetic factors are presumed to play a role in the disposition to form IgE antibodies in bronchial asthma, antithyroid antibodies in Graves' and other diseases, rheumatoid factors in rheumatoid arthritis, and anticolon antibodies in ulcerative colitis. Genetic factors also probably play a role in essential hypertension also, but the exact nature of that role is unknown.

Genetic factors do, therefore, play some role in most disease. But it is not enough to say that they do. The genetic or enzymatic defect must be specified in detail. The role of environmental factors in eliciting or neutralizing the expression of the defect must be explicated. Finally, the relative contribution of genetic factors in the predisposition or etiology of the disease must be enumerated.

The Role of Viruses in the Predisposition and Initiation of Disease

Viruses consist of a nucleoprotein (RNA or DNA) core and a protein capsule. They may be benign or cause disease in a variety of ways: 1) they may acutely damage or destroy cells; 2) they may be incorporated into the genome of cells, becoming part of the genetic apparatus: a) therefore, they can be transmitted vertically from one generation to the next to cause disease; b) they may alter or preempt the synthesis of enzymes and, therefore, cell (membrane) constituents. The altered constituents are then no longer "recognized" as belonging naturally to the host and stimulate the formation of (auto-) antibodies against them; c) they may depress certain quiescent genes, totally to alter the cell which then becomes malignant (43).

Viruses may play a role in autoimmune diseases such as juvenile diabetes mellitus and systemic lupus erythematosus. The suggestion has also been made that the autoimmune phenomena of Graves' disease, rheumatoid arthritis and ulcerative colitis are due to viruses, according to the principle outlined in 2b (above). Slow viruses may also play a predisposing role in many diseases.

The Role of Immune Phenomena in Disease

In 1950, Alexander could not have known about the role that immune, and in particular, autoimmune processes play in the etiology and pathogenesis of disease, except in the case of the allergic (extrinsic) form of bronchial asthma.

Immune processes may play a significant role in the etiology and pathogenesis of atopic eczema, allergic rhinitis, bronchial asthma, Graves' disease, regional enteritis, rheumatoid arthritis, ulcerative colitis and many other diseases. They may do so in several different ways (Figure 3).

1) The antibodies found in atopic eczema, allergic rhinitis and the allergic form of bronchial asthma are specific immunoglobulin-E (IgE) antibodies that are formed in response to specific allergens. The capacity to form IgE antibodies is inherited. Having the capacity to form them does not invariably lead to disease.

2) Some antibodies have the properties of hormones (44, 45). The capacity to form them is probably also inherited. They play a necessary but not sufficient role in Graves' disease. They are called the long-acting thyroid stimulator (L.A.T.S.), the L.A.T.S. protector and the human thyroid stimulator (H.T.S.). They act to stimulate uncontrolled thyroid hormone production. They are formed in response to an unknown stimulus.

Other (so-called autoimmune) antibodies occur in Graves' disease, myxedema and Hashimoto's thyroiditis. These autoimmune antibodies—the antithyroglobulin and thyroid antimicrosomal antibodies—are directed towards cellular components of the thyroid gland.

No agreement has yet been reached about the role of autoimmune antibodies in Graves' or other disease(s): whether in fact they damage cells, causing disease. Nor do we actually know whether they originate from genetic variation or they are formed in response to a change in components of a normal cell brought about by a virus, injury or mutation, or because the cell contains a chemical substance common to it and a bacterium.

3) Autoimmune autoantibodies play an important role in rheumatoid arthritis, regional enteritis, and ulcerative colitis. Immunoglo-

Disease	Antigen	Class of Immunoglobulin or Antibody (if known)	Type of Reaction	Action and Medic
Allergic Rhinitis Bronchial Asthma (allergic form) Atopic Eczema (Atopic Diseases)	Allergen (Pollen, Dust, Hair, Food)	IgE	Anaphylaxis	Release Chemical (Histamine, E.C.F. SRS-A)
Graves' Disease	A. Unknown	1. L.A.T.S. 2. L.A.T.S. protector 3 H.T.S.	Hormones	Stimulate T3 and production
✦ Myxedema, Hashimoto's Thyroiditis	B. Thyroid cell components	Antithyroglobulin Antithyroid microsomal	Autoantibody	?
Rheumatoid Arthritis	IgG IgG IgG	Normal IgA IgG IgM (Rheumatoid Factors)	IgG - IgA IgG - IgG IgG - IgM (Rheumatoid Complexes)	Tissue Deposition and Cellular Ingestion
Ulcerative Colitis (Regional Enteritis)	A. Unknown B Unknown	Anticolon	Cellular ? (T-cells)	Tissue damage ? Tissue damage ?

FIGURE 3. The classes of immunoglobulins implicated either in the pathogenesis pathophysiology of several of the most important psychosomatic diseases.

bulin-G (IgG) antibodies are directed against and form complexes with the person's own humoral antibodies belonging to the IgA, IgG, and IgM classes of normal antibodies in most but not all patients with rheumatoid arthritis. The complexes are ingested by synovial cells or deposited in blood vessels and rheumatoid nodules.

Anticolon (autoimmune) antibodies occur in the sera of patients with ulcerative colitis and regional enteritis. The antigen stimulating their production is not known. They do not seem to be the result of injury to colonic mucosa.

All of the antibodies mentioned so far also occur in the serum of healthy persons, particularly in the serum of the healthy relatives of patients with these diseases. IgE antibodies are characteristically found in non-asthmatic patients exposed to parasites (such as *Ascaris*), and to allergens (such as flour). They also occur in patients with a past history of allergic disease now in remission. Antibodies such as the IgE, antithyroid antibodies, and the rheumatoid factors, therefore, seem to play a predisposing (and etiological) role, and in some instances a pathogenetic role (the IgE antibodies in atopic disease).

The Role of the Endocrine System in Human Disease

The endocrine system is regulated through the hypothalamo-pituitary axis (HPA). The HPA is one of three major outflow systems from the brain. Environmental changes, social and psychological tasks and constraints are reflected in changes in output of some of the pituitary polypeptide hormones. These hormones either have specific regulatory actions on a gland and its products, or they have more general actions on the body. For example, human growth hormone (hGh) stimulates the growth of the body and its organs, or maintains the integrity of certain areas of the body such as the parietal cells of the stomach (46). The adrenocorticotrophic hormone (A.C.T.H.) also promotes the synthesis of epinephrine from norepinephrine, besides controlling corticosteroid production.

The pituitary polypeptides are in turn regulated by hypothalamic releasing hormones (R.H.) and factors (R.F.) and by the hormones they stimulate in target glands in a series of negative feedback loops. Some of the R.H.'s and R.F.'s are in turn regulated by putative catecholaminergic and serotonergic neurotransmitters. Some R.H.'s and R.F.'s also seem to have direct effects on the brain—the thyrotropin releasing hormone (T.R.H.) increases the turnover rate of brain norepinephrine (47) which, in turn, inhibits T.R.H. The products of target glands—the sex hormones, adrenal cortical, pancreatic and thyroid hormones—have additional effects on the brain and its functions. In disease they may disturb perception, cognition and

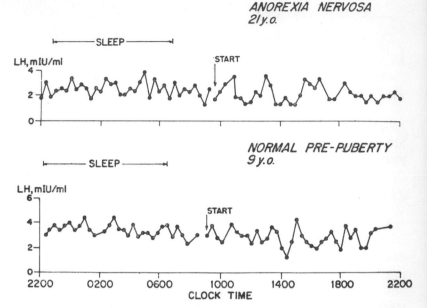

FIGURE 4. Comparison of a circadian LH secretary pattern in a 21-year-old woman with anorexia nervosa (top) and that in a normal 9-year-old prepubertal girl (bottom). (From Katz, J. L., et al. *Hormones, Behavior, and Psychopathology*, Raven Press, New York 1976)

emotion so that the patient is brought to the attention of the liaison psychiatrist.

The pituitary polypeptide hormones go through a maturational sequence (48). In primary anorexia nervosa arrests of development of this sequence occur (49) (Figure 4). After menopause, gonadotrophic hormone levels are no longer under the inhibitory influences of the female sex hormones, and are, therefore, elevated. The pituitary polypeptide hormones have a circadian rhythm. In some diseases this pattern of one hormone can either be altered, disrupted or be out of phase with the pattern of the other hormones. Altered circadian patterns are seen in Cushing's syndrome, primary anorexia nervosa and the psychoses (50). Disrupted patterns may be associated with disease (51).

Summary of Predisposing Factors

Our present knowledge of the predisposing factors to some of the major diseases is summarized in Figure 5. This information supports Alexander's contention that social and psychological factors are not by themselves predisposing: It is not the specific conflict (as a "marker" of a specific psychological sensitivity to certain life experiences) that determines the choice of the disease. Rather the specific conflict is combined with one or several physiological, immunological or biochemical predisposing factors: The "choice" of the disease is determined by a constellation of factors. No psychosomatic disease is merely "psychogenic."

The matter is even more complex—having this combination of factors does not mean that the disease will inevitably occur: The predispositions to a disease only put their owner at risk for the disease (Figure 2). In addition, the specific combinations of predisposing factors may only determine a subform of a disease. We have learned that the same mechanisms may produce different lesions—gastrinomas are characterized by peptic duodenal ulcer in some patients, and only diarrhea, steatorrhea and weight loss in others. Different mechanisms, *per contra*, may produce the same lesions (viz. gout). In fact, we have learned that the diseases under discussion are all heterogeneous—a conclusion which would account for the fact that in the past 25 to 30 years, psychosomatic investigation and theory have (often) consisted of a dialectic between proponents and opponents of the opinion that certain diseases are characterized by specific, unconscious psychological conflicts. In retrospect, this heated debate obscured the fact that the diseases under study were not uniform—different subforms of the disease exist. The likelihood, therefore, emerges that a specific conflict—in the sense that Alexander (10) used the concept—characterizes one variety of the disease but not another. In fact, this conclusion is implicit in Alexander's validating studies published in 1968 (11). The different subforms of a disease arise from the heterogeneity either of their etiologic and pathogenetic mechanisms or pathophysiology:

Disease or Syndrome	Predisposing Factors	
Anorexia Nervosa	1. Genetic ⟶	1. Turner's Syndrome
	2. Psychological	2. ? Failure of F.S.H and
	3. Social	L.H. pattern to mature.
		3. ? Increased hypothalmic
		receptor sensitivity to
		estrogens.
Bronchial Asthma	1. Genetic	1. Bronchoconstrictor
(Allergic)	2. Psychological	tendency
(Extrinsic)		2. Predisposition to form
		IgE antibodies
(Infectious)	1. Psychological	?
(Intrinsic)		
Graves' Disease	1. ? Genetic	1. Predisposition to form
	2. Psychological	L.A.T.S., L.A.T.S. protector,
		H.T.S., antithyroid antibodies
		2. ? Regulatory disturbances
		(T_3 ⟶ [T.S.H.)
		⟶ [T.R.H)

FIGURE 5. A summary of the actual or hypothesized predisposing factors in seven of the psychosomatic diseases.

1) Some patients with primary anorexia nervosa (AN) have Turner's syndrome: The chromosomal abnormalities constitute an etiological predisposing factor for primary AN (42, 52). Yet, most patients with primary AN have no chromosomal abnormalities. In some patients with primary AN psychological and social factors are antecedent causes of the disease. The termination of oral contraceptive therapy is followed by primary AN in about 5 percent of all the women taking the "pill" (53).

FIGURE 5 (*continued*)

Disease or Syndrome	Predisposing Factors	
Essential Hypertension:	1. Genetic 2. Social 3. Psychological	1. Vascular Hyperreactivity 2. High, normal, 'low Serum-Renin Activity 3. Regulatory Disturbances (Angiotensin-Aldosterone.)
Peptic Ulcer	1. ? Genetic 2. Psychological	1. Elevated serum pepsinogen levels 2. Increased parietal cell mass 3. Enlarged N. Vagus 4. Increased parietal cell sensitivity 5. Regulatory Disturbance (Gastrin-HCl)
Rheumatoid Arthritis	1. ? Genetic 2. Psychological 3. ? Social	1. ? Latent virus 2 Predisposition to form rheumatoid factors 3. Bruton-type agammaglobulinemia
Ulcerative Colitis	1. ? Genetic 2. Psychological	1. Tendency to form anti-colon antibodies

2) Allergic mechanisms play a role in only 30-50 percent of all patients with bronchial asthma. In the rest, viral infections combined with psychological factors excite asthmatic attacks.

3) A number of etiological mechanisms can predispose to gout. Several enzymatic defects may raise serum uric acid (SUA) levels by increasing purine biosynthesis or retarding purine disposition. Or the increased reabsorption of uric acid by the kidney also raises SUA. Elevated SUA levels do not inevitably lead to gout (54, 55). Furthermore, some patients with gout have normal SUA levels (54).

4) Subforms of essential hypertension (EH) also exist. Some young, male patients with "borderline" hypertension have an elevated cardiac output and pulse rate at rest (56). Their peripheral resistance is only slightly elevated, but later it increases as an adaptation to the increase in cardiac output. In other patients with EH renin levels are either high, normal or low. In many there are various additional, regulatory disturbances between angiotensin II and aldosterone production (57).

5) About 1 percent of all patients with peptic duodenal ulcer (DU) have gastrinomas (58). The remainder of patients with chronic DU can also be subdivided into different groups or subforms. Some patients with chronic DU are hypersecretors of hydrochloric acid and pepsin. In other patients the secretory status is normal (59). Others, but not all patients with DU, have an increased parietal cell mass (60). Abnormalities of the regulation of gastric acid secretion by the gastric hormone, gastrin, occur in other DU patients (61, 62). Therefore, a variety of anatomical and physiological disturbances are observed in DU.

6) The serum of most but not all patients with rheumatoid arthritis contains immunoglobulin-G-rheumatoid factors. In a minority of patients these factors cannot be recovered (63). Still other patients are predisposed to rheumatoid arthritis by virtue of the fact that they suffer from the Bruton-form of agammaglobulinemia (64).

Perhaps the most cogent example to date of the validity of the conclusion of the heterogeneity of some diseases has been provided by the work of Moos and Solomon (65, 66, 67). They studied the healthy siblings of patients with rheumatoid arthritis. The siblings were divided into two groups on the basis of whether their sera contained rheumatoid factor(s) or not. Employing the M.M.P.I., they found that the healthy siblings of patients whose sera contained rheumatoid factor(s) psychologically resembled their siblings with rheumatoid arthritis more than they did their healthy siblings whose sera contained no rheumatoid factor(s) with one exception—in contrast to their sick relatives they were functioning well in their everyday lives. In a similar vein healthy subjects with high levels of serum pepsinogen resemble psychologically patients with peptic ulcer more than they do healthy subjects with low serum levels who may occasionally also have an ulcer.

Having concluded that the etiology of psychosomatic disease is not merely psychogenic, we are still left with a major mystery that awaits clarification. We do not know how the psychological factors that play some role in the etiological variance of these diseases come about. All adult patients with the diseases mentioned are psychologically immature as evidenced by their dependency conflicts and cognitive defects. In the past these fixations or arrests in maturation or development have been ascribed to life experiences — such as losses —or to disturbances in the mother-child relationship. The data upon which these conclusions rest are retrospective. Although the early life experiences of animals do seem to have a potent effect on producing disease (68, 69, 70), there may also be other ways of conceptualizing the fact that patients are characterized by arrests of development. For instance:

1) Early life experience may alter neuronal functioning, which in turn alters the processing of subsequent experience.

2) Early experience may alter the developing chemistry of the brain to alter subsequent neuronal functioning and the processing of experience.

3) Early experience may alter bodily functioning or interfere with physiological maturation. The arrest in physiological maturation may influence personality development and may act as a predisposing factor in disease.

4) Genetic variation may alter both brain and bodily function, so as to alter the processing of experience.

Finally, some evidence is beginning to be accumulated to suggest that genetic variation and early experience may both produce the same phenotype.

FACTORS THAT INITIATE DISEASE

The factors that predispose to disease have been enumerated. They determine the "choice" of a disease. We are also able to specify the onset conditions of many diseases, but we know much less about the pathogenetic mechanisms that these conditions entrain. The factors that predispose to some forms of a disease—such as elevated levels of serum uric acid (SUA), serum pepsinogen, or a specific conflict—are not necessarily involved in its pathogenesis. They may play an insufficient role in inciting the disease. Nor does the presence of IgE or of IgG rheumatoid factors in blood invariably and respectively lead to attacks of bronchial asthma or rheumatoid arthritis: Some added factors must be present for disease onset.

The Onset Conditions of Disease

Alexander (10) specified the onset conditions of all diseases he studied. He stated, for example, that:

1) Bronchial asthma often began in adult patients when they married;

2) Graves' disease had its onset when the fear of death was reactivated by a physical accident;

3) Rheumatoid arthritis might begin when a person could no longer be of help, dominate or rule another;

4) Ulcerative colitis started in a setting in which the patient failed in a hopeless struggle for accomplishment.

In these settings the specific conflicts were reactivated and very strong feelings of sadness, fear, anger or hopelessness were engendered. Somehow these feelings were then translated by the brain into neuronal and hormonal discharge to produce the specific physiological or anatomical changes that characterize the disease.

Alexander's description of the onset conditions of these specific diseases was probably too restrictive. For instance, some child patients with bronchial asthma develop attacks mainly while away from home and their mother, and other children develop them only when with their mothers.

Alexander implied that the precipitating event activated the conflict and produced distressing (unpleasant) feelings. But he did not state that the activated conflict and the precipitating event could not be coped with. Since that time, it has become abundantly clear that adaptive-defensive failure is correlated with physiological changes and the onset of disease (71-75).

Diseases such as anorexia nervosa, bronchial asthma, peptic duodenal ulcer and ulcerative colitis may begin in social and personal contexts besides those described by Alexander (29, 76-79). To be specific, we (77) have noted that primary anorexia nervosa may begin when the patient 1) leaves home; 2) is subjected to peer pressure to lose weight; 3) is exposed to sexual temptation, or to her first sexual experience; 4) wishes vengefully to defy her parents; 5) has had her first child. But this syndrome may also begin after cessation of oral-contraceptive medication (53).

In contrast to these observations and contentions that disease begins in one or more quite particular contexts, is the broader and more generalized view of the psychosocial framework of disease onset that has been enunciated by Engel (80) and Schmale (81). Their central thesis is that personal loss and bereavement are the usual setting in which many diseases (in addition to those reviewed) are initiated. According to Engel, the psychologically predisposed person —especially if dependent—responds to loss and bereavement by perceiving and interpreting it as a threat to personal security, and by feeling helpless and hopeless, so that he gives up altogether. In effect, an adaptive psychological failure occurs. Presumably, this adaptive failure has physiological concomitants that antecede illness onset in the predisposed person.

Both Alexander and Engel assume that it is not the precipitating event *per se* that is of central importance, but rather its meaning for the person and the responses it generates. However, their different interpretations of the essential character of the precipitating "event" of process are difficult to reconcile. Alexander believed that the specific psychological conflict sensitized the patient to respond to specific life experiences. The life experience was colored and made particularly poignant by the conflict. The conflict was activated by the experience ("the repressed returned"), and was accompanied by strong feelings. He implied that the activated conflict did not disrupt other areas of the patient's psychological functioning and, therefore, his adaptation. Engel's concept is much more far-ranging: Helplessness and hopelessness color all one's attitudes, and future prospects. If a person feels helpless, he cannot cope with anything. If there is no hope, future prospects are bleak.

Engel's formulation suggests also that it is not the conflict as such that specifies the vulnerability to illness, but variations in adaptive psychological capacities.

As noted, these contradictory views are not easily reconciled on the basis of the available evidence. Engel's observations and formulations appear to be valid for some patients with certain illnesses, but not for others. They are supported by his observations on patients with ulcerative colitis, and by some of the studies on rheumatoid arthritis, peptic duodenal ulcer, and a subgroup of patients with bronchial asthma. On the other hand, Knapp and his associates (82) observed that in some patients with bronchial asthma, helplessness and hopelessness were not antecedents and correlates of the asthmatic attack, but that attacks were preceded by a biphasic cycle of excitement and anxiety followed by depression. Nor is Engel's general conclusion that illnesses begin in a non-specific setting borne out by Weisman's observations (79). Weisman has described that several different kinds of settings, in addition to bereavement, may antecede recurrences of peptic ulcer. Weisman also correlated the settings in which recurrences began with the psychological conflicts of his patients: Different settings correlated with different conflicts.

The evidence suggests that specific conflicts as described by Alexander occur in about one-half of the patients with these diseases (11). These conflicts sensitize them to rather specific life experiences that act as the initiating event for disease onset. If one studies the personal relationships of these patients, rather than their conflicts, another initiating event comes to the fore—bereavement. But bereavement is not the exclusive event. It is in some patients. In other patients there was no single conflict and no single event. In them, different conflicts are activated by different life events and experiences.

These conflicting observations and views have usually been ascribed to the unreliability of clinical observation, or to the lack of sensitivity of psychological tests, used to verify clinical psychiatric observations.

But, as I have already suggested, each of the diseases reviewed in this essay is, in all likelihood, heterogeneous in character. Therefore, the different psychiatric observations and formulations may be correct for one subgroup of the disease and not another.

The onset of certain diseases may also begin when patients consume alcohol and medications such as aspirin, indomethacin or butazolidine (in the case of peptic ulcer), or because they consume salt for which they have a preference (in the case of high blood pressure) (83). Noise, the sound of battle, exacting work under pressure, and rapid social changes are other factors that may play a role in disease onset (84).

The Role of Bereavement

Following a real bereavement morbidity and mortality are increased. The mortality among widowers 55 years old or older in the first six months after the death of their spouse was 40 percent greater than in married men who had suffered no such loss (85). The mortality of younger men and women who have recently lost a spouse is also higher than expected (86). The loss of a spouse does not necessarily lead to death, but it does increase the risk of mental illness serious enough to require hospitalization (87, 88).

Bereavement that is not coped with and that produces the "giving-up, given-up" complex has been estimated to precede many different diseases (80). Bereavement plays an important role in many, if not all, patients with psychosomatic diseases. Real or threatened loss has been cited by many authors as a factor contributing to the initiation of other diseases as well (81): cancer (89-91), tuberculosis (92), diabetes mellitus (93), and lymphomas and leukemias (94), juvenile diabetes mellitus (95) and heart failure (96). Depressive moods, the attitude of giving-up and the loss of all hope also adversely affect the outcome of surgical operations (97, 98).

The cause of a comprehensive psychobiology of disease would be furthered immeasurably were we to know the physiological mechanisms that produce an increased mortality and morbidity, and enhance the risk of surgery in hopeless, depressed and helpless patients, or those who have given up. We do know, however, that some bereaved persons may cope psychologically with their loss and when they do certain correlated physiological (hormonal) responses are minimal. When they do not cope hormone levels increase and their 24-hour rhythms may be altered.

We owe to Hofer (99-102) the elucidation of some of the physiological responses to separation. Separating young rats from their mothers has demonstrable physiological effects, the full range of which has not as yet been elucidated. Different facets of the separation experience affect different systems. The milk the mother provides maintains the infant rat's normal heart rate but it has no effect on the behavioral changes on separation.

Other animal studies have described the long-range impact of separation on behavior. Baby animals were taken away from their mothers at birth, and "artificially" reared. The results indicate that, over the long term, every major aspect of adult behavior—social, reproductive, maternal, and aggressive—was affected (103, 105, 107). In animals the experience of separation also induces profound, immediate behavioral consequences, including marked motor activity, pitiful crying, sleep disruption, that gradually merges into immobility, and very characteristic species-specific postures (103-106).

Analysis of the acute effects of separation in 14-day-old rats has revealed that the processes of governing these behavioral changes are different from those at work on the cardiac and respiratory systems (99, 100). Absence of the mother immediately induces in infant rats a progressive increase in locomotor, self-grooming, and "emotional" behavior (defecation-urination) with an onset time of 4 to 8 hours. Infusions of milk over 24 hours have no significant effect on these behavioral changes, but provisions of a nonlactating foster mother prevents them. Here, the behavioral interaction with the mother appears to be the major element, and further studies have suggested that deprivation of tactile and olfactory sensory stimulation is critical, while thermal, visual, auditory and vestibular systems are far less likely to be importantly involved. These studies begin to reveal some of the processes by which maternal separation exerts its effects on behavior in this species.

The information provided through both animal and human studies indicates that separation and bereavement usually, but not invariably, produce changes in behavior and physiological function. Not everyone is affected in the same way by bereavement. Some grieve. Others become helpless and hopeless. Some become physically, and others emotionally ill. Those who change have been sensitized to actual, threatened or imaginary loss or bereavement by prior experience with loss. They are also less capable of dealing with current losses. Those who do not change are either not threatened by separation and bereavement, or are able to cope with them by the usual process of grief and mourning. Other bereaved people find surrogates to replace the lost person who sustain them in their loss. The capacity to adapt in a way that reduces the "stresses" of bereavement allows the bereaved to "integrate" these experiences in a healthy way. The threat of bereavement may produce different behavioral and physiological consequences than the actuality of loss. The long-term effects of separating young animals from their mothers at birth are general and profound. They may differ from the acute, short-term effects of separating young animals sometime after birth. Bereavement in human beings is associated with increased morbidity and with physiological changes. The specific disease a person gets is determined by multiple predisposing factors. But we do not know how the physiological changes accompanying bereavement interact with predisposing factors. Nor do we know whether the relationship between the physiological, behavioral and psychological changes is a causal one.

The Transduction of Experience by the Brain

No matter whether we ascribe to the view that disease begins in particular contexts or in the more general context of bereavement or life change, the psychobiologist is still faced with an intellectual challenge without peer that has so far resisted the best efforts of philosophers and scientists. Specifically, we do not know how the life events that cause distressful experiences are coded and translated (or transduced) into neuronal and neurochemical events that in turn produce bodily changes in the predisposed, culminating in disease (108, 109). In the past, the mind-body problem has usually been thought of by psychosomatic theorists in linear or transactional terms.

Three Classical Models of Transduction

I believe that one of the major reasons for our failure to solve the central problem of transduction is that we have had only one hypothesis in psychobiology to guide us. This hypothesis is a linear one. It states that psychological distress is directly translated into physiological changes. A variant of this hypothesis is that physiological changes, mediated by visceral afferents, can be consciously experienced. But we do not know how impulses arriving over sympathetic or vagal afferent pathways can be perceived or acquire conscious meanings. We are faced by the insuperable problem of how nerve impulses, changes in enzyme levels, or turnover rates of transmitter substances (putative or actual) can produce ideas, thoughts, images, feelings and moods, or vice-versa!

A familiar approach to transduction—the traditional linear model employed by most psychobiologusts—is represented in Figure 6 (110). Here, the social event or situation is perceived (1) acquires

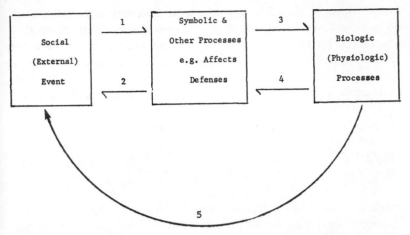

FIGURE 6. The Transactional Model (Modified from Knapp, P. H., *Psychosom. Med.* 33:363, 1971). In this model the social (external) event or stimulus produces psychologic experiences and responses (1) which may in turn modify the social transaction or event (2). The psychologic process directly causes the physiologic one (3) which may (e.g., in a delirium) modify the psychologic process (4). The processes (3) by which psychologic processes are transduced into physiologic ones are usually not specified, or they are unknown. The manifest physiologic process may influence the social one (5), either by positive or negative feedback. (For example, an asthmatic attack in a child way influence another person or a group.) (From Weiner, H., *Psychosom. Med.* 34:355, 1972).

emotional meaning and produces a physiological response. The emotional impact of the event may interact with inferred defense mechanisms that, if effective, modify and temper the physiological responses (3) which may themselves be perceived (4) or affect the social event (5)—for example, the child in an asthmatic attack may elicit a solicitous (or other) response from a parent, nurse, or a group of its peers.

A modification of this model states that correlated psychological and physiological responses appear to be so different because each is the product of the different techniques whereby we study them. The mental experience—the thought, mental image or feeling—is the *inner* aspect of the subject's response to the event as he perceives it. The neural and bodily events are the *outer,* and often measurable, aspect of his response to the event. The connection between the mental and the neural and bodily processes cannot be established by simple cross-identity. The difference between these processes (e.g., extension in space and time in the case of bodily events and non-extension in the case of mental ones) lies in the way they are presented and made accessible to us. They must, therefore, be studied by different techniques. We may legitimately study the heart rate physiologically during the solution of a difficult mathematical problem. The solution of the problem may be exquisitely correlated in time with an increase in heart rate. But we cannot assume that the task of finding the solution causes the increased heart rate. Concurrent events may not be causally related. They may, for example, be the product of some third, unmeasured or unidentified variable.

The third and classical model of transduction is based on the view that despite the coextensiveness of the psychological and physiological, the two belong to wholly unrelated realms. Although we may study the physiology and psychology of an ill person together, they really have nothing to do with each other and proceed independently. In this view, a bereavement may produce grief, but the physiological changes involved in weeping, or in rheumatoid arthritis, are independent of the experience of loss. With this model, in effect, the physiological cannot occur in any manner truly accessible to our understanding.

An External Loop Model of Transduction

We do not understand how nerve impulses can achieve psychological representation in the form of thoughts, memories and feelings. And we have no concept to help us explain how feelings bring about physiological changes in the body. Therefore, we do not understand how a situation can be perceived as threatening or frightening, and then be transduced into physiological discharge through the outflow channels of the brain. In a similar vein, the concept that a chronic unconscious conflict can produce tonic vagal discharge to increase gastric acid secretion is unproven and unprovable. Because these conceptual and empirical problems have not been solved, we do not understand the mechanisms by which changes in psychological state initiate disease.

Perhaps, the mystery of the "leap from the mind to the body" is not so deep after all, if we were to assume that the gaps between mind, brain and body do not have to be bridged directly. The gap could be narrowed a little if we could prove that the threatened or bereaved person behaves differently than he did before threat or loss. It is not the emotional states but the changes in behavior—for example, not eating, insomnia, drinking alcohol and taking medication—that become the immediate antecedents of the disease. It is, of course, true that we do not know how the mind or brain regulate actions and behavior, but we do know that drinking alcohol or taking aspirin may incite exacerbations of peptic duodenal ulcer. In fact, Weisman (79) observed that in some patients with peptic duodenal ulcer, various emotional and psychological reactions led to the drinking of alcohol. Similarly, Katz and his coworkers (111) observed that in 60 percent of their subjects attacks of gout followed situations in which predisposed patients felt that they had to prove themselves in their jobs, which led to excessive eating and use of alcohol. Patients with hypertension seem to prefer diets high in salt if given a choice. These examples suggest that, for at least some predisposed persons, the psychological responses to "threatening" situations or bereavement are mediated through changes in diet, in eating, and in drinking behavior. The examples suggest a different model of transduction than the ones traditionally used in psychosomatic medicine. In this model, the patient's actions or behavior are an "external loop." A variant of the external loop model may also provide insight into some aspects of primary anorexia nervosa. About one-third to one-half (or more) of all cases of this disease begin with amenorrhoea. Recent evidence indicates that the amenorrhoea and the disease are correlated with immature (age-inappropriate) secretory patterns of pituitary luteinizing and follicle stimulating hormone (49). It is not known, however, if these immature secretory patterns antecede the illness, or why they occur at all. In any event

External Loop Model A

Social Event ——————————————→ Perceived ——————————————→ Acquires meaning
correlated emotional
response

——————————→ Behavioral ——————————————————→ Bodily change
·change in diet,   (alcohol intake antecedes
drinking habits   duodenal·ulcer onset or
exacerbation)

External Loop Model B

·Physiological brain variation——————————→

Physiological change ——————————→ Misinterpreted ——————————→
(amenorrhoea)   as pregnancy

Induction of symbolic (conflictful) ———————————————→ Change in
meaning (oral impregnation fantasy)   behavior (dieting)

the amenorrhoea *antecedes* the remorseless dieting in some patients with anorexia nervosa. The frequently described oral impregnation fantasies, rather than being the antecedents of the illness, may be the consequences of the amenorrhoea. The amenorrhoea is misinterpreted by the patient as a pregnancy. The patient incorrectly attributes the cause of the pregnancy to conflictful fantasies of oral impregnation, which in turn leads to her not eating.

The two variants of the "external loop" model can be represented in the following manner:

Clearly Model B is not the only explanatory schema for anorexia nervosa. It might not apply, for example, to those instances where amenorrhoea is a late manifestation of an illness that begins with not eating and weight loss. One conception of this form of "primary" anorexia nervosa is that it is not initially a disturbance of eating but a failure to recognize enteroreceptive hunger signals, and the inability to discriminate these from other bodily sensations and feelings. Either the sensation of hunger or its meaning has never been learned, or the development of this failure to discriminate is associated with early experiences during the feeding of the infant. In addition, a child with true anorexia nervosa is typically found to be very compliant and well-behaved and, at the onset of puberty, does not eat because of a fear of growing fat or of growing up.

Yet there is one striking fact that this account does not consider: True anorexia nervosa occurs about ten times as frequently in girls as in boys. When it occurs in boys, it customarily precedes puberty; in girls, it follows puberty. This incidence suggests a protective role for male sex hormones or an initiating role for female hormones. During puberty (the age at which the incidence of some forms of anorexia nervosa is highest) a reorganization of hypothalamic function and the hypothalamic-pituitary axis occurs. In normal adolescence, there may also be bouts of asceticism and self-denial during which all gratification, including eating, is suppressed, followed by bouts of self-indulgence. Patients with anorexia nervosa are even more remorseless in not eating. Yet they often also gorge themselves with food and then vomit. The behavioral, psychological, and physiological events in anorexia nervosa can be seen as a by-product of the aberrant reorganization of hypothalamic function during adolescence, as manifested by tonic inhibition of eating behavior, increased motor activity, and failure of adult patterns of LH and FSH release to occur (although other pituitary hormones such as TSH and possibly hGH may be normally produced and released). The antecedents of this disturbance may be life experiences that alter hypothalamic function—specifically levels of neurotransmitter synthesis, release, reuptake or degradation. In this view, early experiences alter bodily function and the psychology of the child. The burden of the inception of the illness is placed, then, not only on conflictful fantasies but on a complex interplay of experience, physiology, and psychology in which the conflictful fantasy may in some patients be a response to, and not the cause of the amenorrhoea.

Collateral Models of Transduction

Alexander's concept that the emotional response to the precipitating event in psychosomatic diseases was transduced into physiological changes was a modification of Freud's ideas about the production of the symptoms and signs of conversion hysteria—a (sexual) conflict was converted into somatic symptoms and signs that symbolically expressed the conflict. Alexander believed that in psychosomatic diseases the emotional response to the conflict was expressed in physiological changes that produced anatomical lesions.

Alexander may still be correct in some instances, but the evidence suggests that he was not completely right in all cases. The conflict may be the psychologic response to a physical change in the body. And the onset or exacerbation of a psychosomatic disease may be brought on by the patient's ill-advised actions.

Alexander also assumed that the preceived threat brought about the conflict and its emotional response that, in turn, generated the physiological response. He never considered two possibilities: 1) that the perception of an event could be mediated by one brain system, while at the same time, *but separately*, the percept could bring about physiological changes by another system of pathways in the brain; 2) that the threatening event or situation did not have to be perceived as a whole but could be analyzed by the mind (brain) into separate components. As a result of this analysis one component acquires psychological meaning and another component results in physiological changes.

Research on sublimal perception has provided indirect evidence to support the first possibility (112, 113). A weak visual stimulus may occasion a physiological effect but may not be apperceived—a dissociation between the psychological and the physiological effects occurs. The second possibility is supported by the fact that some neurons in the visual cortex respond selectively to one aspect of a stimulus and not to another (114-120). And in the young animal, separated from its mother, different physiological systems respond to different aspects of the separation experience (99-102).

Further support is given to the idea that a single stimulus may produce different effects in the organism by different or collateral pathways in the brain. One process in which the entire transduction of input and the resulting physiologic changes are known provides clear-cut evidence for this idea. I refer to the process by which light affects the functioning of the pineal gland.

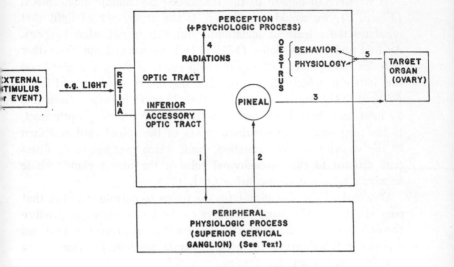

FIGURE 7. Concomitance of a physiologic process and an assumed psychologic process, presumably not causally related.

The model portrayed is based on the regulation of oestrus in the rat by melatonin whose synthesis is controlled (reduced) by light.

Light falling on the retina sets off a train of neural impulses which:

1. Pass via the inferior accessory optic tract → medial forebrain bundle → medial terminal nucleus of the accessory optic system → preganglionic fibers in the spinal cord → superior cervical ganglion.

2. From the superior cervical ganglion impulses pass to the parenchymal cells of the pineal gland to release noradrenaline which increases melatonin synthesis.

3. Melatonin is released to suppress oestrus, presumably by its action on the ovary.

4. The experience of light is presumably mediated by the classical visual pathways.

5. Presumably the decrease of oestrogens affects behavior by its impact on brain circuits, while also regulating the release of trophic pituitary hormones.

If we were to adhere to the traditional psychophysiologic model (Figure 6), we would say that it is the *experience* of light that regulates the release of melatonin. But this is not what happens. Axelrod and his associates (121, 122) have worked out the rather complex and indirect pathway from the retina to the pineal gland and the matter in which the biosynthetic machinery of the gland is influenced (123). In the mammal (Figure 7) nerve impulses stimulated by light pass through the retina to the inferior accessory optic tract, to the preganglionic sympathetic fibers of the spinal cord and then to the superior cervical ganglion, from which postganglionic fibers pass upward to the parenchymal cells of the pineal gland, whose terminals release norepinephrine (121, 122).

Obviously, light also stimulates the retina to entrain impulses that pass via the classic visual pathways to the visual cortex to produce the *experience* of light. It needs to be emphasized, however, that this experience is subserved by quite separate mechanisms from those that influence pineal functioning.

The principle illustrated by Axelrod's work is not unique to the pineal gland. When the stimulus for a behavior has been clearly identified and the behavior has been carefully analyzed, one finds that even the components of the *behavior,* although they appear to form an interrelated whole, are actually separate and distinct and, as such, require individual analysis. These separate components may be subserved by different neural pathways. One example is the contact-placing reaction produced by a light touch on the dorsum of a cat's paw. Careful analysis of this behavior discloses that the bending of hairs entrains impulses that travel by at least two routes. As illustrated in Figure 8, the early components of the biceps response (EMG) and the first phase of the placing movement are activated by the ventroposterior nucleus (VP) of the thalamus. Later components are probably activated by a complex circuit that passes through the VP, sensorimotor cortex, pyramidal tract, red nucleus, interpositus nucleus of the cerebellum, the ventrolateral-ventroanterior nucleus of the thalamus, and, once again, through the sensorimotor cortex (124, 125). What is more, these circuits are not fixed. A lesion in one circuit may cause the behavior to disappear for a

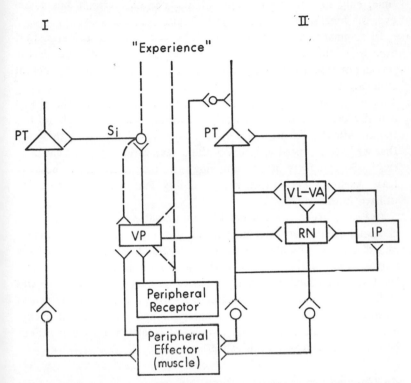

FIGURE 8. Some of the brain circuits responsible for the contact placing reaction in the cat. The two (I & II) known pathways and circuits which subserve a very simple behavior (contact placing) in the cat. The heavy lines denote known circuits, the broken lines putative ones. At each level (e.g., IP, VI-VA and PT) the information is processed differently. Note that there are at least two circuits subserving different aspects of the behavior. (After Amassian, V. E., et al., *Brain Research* 40:171-78, 1972). PT=Pyramidal tract neuron; Si=Somatosensory cortex; IP=Nucleus interpositus of cerebellum; RN=Red nucleus; VL-VA=Ventrolateral and ventroanterior nucleus RN=Red nucleus; VL-VA=Ventrolateral and ventroanterior nucleus of thalamus; VP=Ventroposterior nucleus of thalamus. (From Weiner, H., *Psychosom. Med.* 34:355, 1972).

time, only to return when, presumably, another circuit has taken over the function of the destroyed circuit.

In summary, we may conclude from the available evidence that even a simple behavior produced by a very simple stimulus is the product of separate components that are regulated by different neural circuits.

It is not yet possible to say how many instances of the model actually occur in nature. Clearly, however, Axelrod's work refutes the traditional, linear, theoretical model of mind-body interaction that we have accepted virtually without reservation and that has been the basis for efforts in psychobiology until now. Thus, at the very least, Axelrod's work raises the possibility that other models can be utilized in the future.

In essence, then, we can no longer automatically assume that psychosocial events and external stimuli alter bodily function in health and disease sole by their impact on the mind. Recent studies have suggested alternative models of the mind-body interaction by which the brain transduces experience to produce changes in behavior and bodily function. This transduction may occur via collateral neural pathways. In this situation psychological and physiological events may occur simultaneously; they may be correlated, but they cannot be considered to cause each other.

An "Internal Loop" Model of Transduction

A sixth model of transduction has been proposed by Reiser (8) (Figure 9). Under this model, the inability to cope with the threat of a perceived "stress" and the reactivation of an unconscious conflict which constitutes that person's psychological sensitivity are associated with emotional arousal and a spectrum of autonomic and hormonal responses, which in turn affect brain function and psychological responses. For example, cognitive processes (126) and a susceptibility to anxiety (127) are influenced by the infusion of hydrocortisone (128) or epinephrine; cognition may also be affected by peripheral autonomic changes (129). Glucocorticoids may affect catecholamine (130) and indoleamine (131, 132) levels in the brain

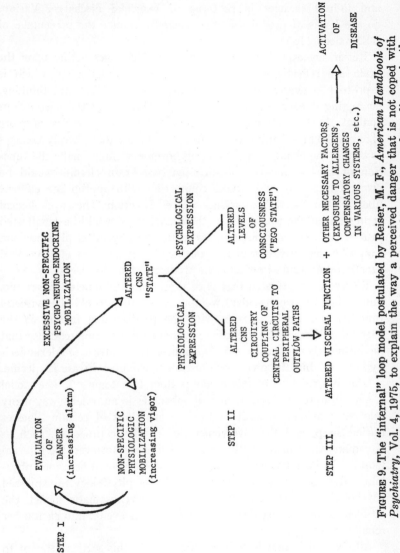

FIGURE 9. The "internal" loop model postulated by Reiser, M. F., *American Handbook of Psychiatry*, Vol. 4, 1975, to explain the way a perceived danger that is not coped with might lead to altered ego states and physiological changes to produce disease in the predisposed.

and induce changes in patterns of neuronal discharge. Various dosage levels of prednisone can markedly reduce the percentage of REM sleep (133).

Reiser suggests that these physiological changes acting upon the brain are reflected in altered psychological functioning, which is expressed in ever more primitive ways of perceiving and thinking, evaluating danger, and coping with the threat and the unconscious conflict. In Reiser's postulated cycle of events, a series of more vigorous bodily changes would next result. As these bodily changes continue, the changes in circulating hormones would make the function of the brain more plastic—inactive brain circuits would be brought into play and "make connection with appropriate efferent fibers to the viscera" to produce altered function. The psychological expression of the activation of these pathways would be manifested in altered states of consciousness while the physiological expression would be the activation of new outflow pathways that alter visceral function and would interact with predispositions to disease.

Reiser also postulated that once the outflow channels (autonomic, humoral and neuromuscular) were activated they would alter visceral function and would interact with the predisposing factors of the particular disease. The initiating psychoneuroendocrine sequence that he outlined is not specific for each illness (in contrast to Alexander's hypotheses) but the predisposition to a particular disease is specific.

The internal loop of this model is Step I in Figure 9. The model has much to recommend it, since it subsumes in an orderly way many relevant phenomena, such as the exacerbations of certain illnesses during sleep, and the involvement of rhythmic processes, such as circadian cycles in the pathogenesis of illness. However, the internal loop model does not explain how an alarm response occasions physiological mobilization, or how altered brain physiology is expressed psychologically. As with the traditional psychosomatic model, the problem of translating these two categories of events into each other remains unsolved.

All six models that have been discussed in this section attempt to bridge the gap between environmental events, mental processes, brain mechanisms, physiological mechanisms and disease. Their value is heuristic. Alternative ways of organizing data may provide us with the insights needed ultimately to develop an accurate overview that bridges the gap between mind, brain, and body in health and disease —a gap that remains a crucial factor in biology and medicine.

Role of the Brain in the Pathogenesis of Disease

Implicit in the foregoing is that social and psychological factors do play a role in the inception of disease by altering brain function— a conclusion that is borne out by experimental animal research using a variety of techniques. For example, high blood pressure can be produced experimentally in animals by a number of different methods. Conditioning procedures (134, 135), ethological techniques (70), brain stimulation (136) and section of the sinus nerve (137) or destruction of the nucleus of the solitary tract in the medulla oblongata (138, 139) can all produce high blood pressure in animals. Implicit in the result of these procedures is that the brain participates in the development of high blood pressure.

Experimental hypertension can also be produced by treating rats with desoxycorticorsterone acetate (DOCA) and salt (140, 141), by constricting the renal artery (142), or tightly wrapping the kidney. Genetic strains of hypertensive rats can be bred, of which the best known are the salt-sensitive (143) and the spontaneously hypertensive strains (144). It might seem that high blood pressure produced by this second group of procedures or by selective breeding should develop without the participation of brain mechanisms. Surprisingly enough this impression is not correct. The brain participates in different ways in the development or maintenance of every one of these forms of experimental high blood pressure (145).

In the rat the inception of DOCA-salt hypertension is associated with increased peripheral sympathetic neural discharge, and increased catecholamine turnover in the adrenal medulla (146, 147). Destruction of catecholaminergic neurons in the brainstem by instilling 6-hydroxydopamine into the ventricles of rats reduces the peripheral sympathetic discharge and prevents the development of DOCA-salt hypertension in rats (148). But once high blood pressure levels are established with DOCA-salt treatment, intraventricular installation of 6-hydroxydopamine does not lower the high blood pressure levels (148, 149). Similarly, the high blood pressure produced by constricting a renal artery of a rat can also be averted, but not cured, by pretreatment with intraventricular 6-hydroxydopamine (145).

Renal artery constriction is associated with the release of renin and, therefore, increased angiotensin II production. In addition to many different effects, angiotensin II enters the brain *via* the *area postrema* (150, 151) to produce powerful pressor effects, that are mediated by catecholaminergic neurons in the brainstem. Increased peripheral sympathetic discharge ensues (152-155) and the blood pressure rises. The effects of angiotensin II on the brainstem can be blocked by depleting the brain of catecholamines (and serotonin) with reserpine (155) or destroying catecholaminergic neurons with 6-hydroxydopamine.

Angiotensin II levels are high in the cerebrospinal fluid, at the time that the spontaneously hypertensive rat develops high blood pressure (145). [Antibodies against angiotensin II administered to such rats lower the blood pressure (156)]. Usually, spontaneously hypertensive rats developed high blood pressure when 11-12 weeks old. The injection of 6-hydroxydopamine into the lateral ventricles of rats of the spontaneously hypertensive strain, who are less than 10 weeks old, prevents the development of elevated blood pressure (148). But as soon as high blood pressure has been allowed to develop, the treatment with 6-hydroxydopamine does not lower the blood pressure (149). Once high blood pressure levels are established in these animals, treatment with parachlorphenylalanine—an inhibitor of serotonin synthesis—lowers the high blood pressure levels in this strain of rats (157).

These findings suggest that the initiation of high blood pressure in this strain of rats is mediated by noradrenergic and dopaminergic neurons in the brainstem. Serotonergic neurons in the brainstem, on the other hand, are involved in maintaining the high blood pressure levels once they are established.

These experiments indicate that the brainstem participates at some stage in the development and maintenance of every form of experimental hypertension. A more general conclusion is also warranted —the mechanisms that predispose to a disease, such as experimental hypertension, are not the same as those that initiate it. Furthermore, the factors that sustain the disease are different from those that initiate it. Should this conclusion be true, the investigator of the psychobiology of disease would have to look for different psychophysiological interactions that explain the predisposition, initiation and maintenance of a disease. But more about this point later.

The brain also participates in asthmatic attacks, despite the claims of immunobiologists that the release of the chemical mediators of allergen-IgE antibody interactions are sufficient to produce bronchoconstriction. In the immediate form of hypersensitivity and in experimental asthma in animals, bronchospasm and hyperventilation are mediated by vagal reflexes (158). First Karczewski and Widdicombe (159) showed that the intravenous injection of antigen into passively sensitized rabbits produced bronchoconstriction and hyperventilation. Cooling the cervical vagus inhibited these effects. Cutting the nerves averted them. Then Gold and his colleagues (160) demonstrated that the exposure of dogs to allergens to which they were sensitive raised airway resistance that could be blocked either by afferent or efferent vagal blockade. When the allergen was instilled into one lung only, bilateral bronchoconstriction was produced. Vagal blockade on the challenged side eliminated the bronchoconstriction on both sides. This work implies that allergens by stimulating sensory receptors in the lung increase reflex vagal activity to cause bronchoconstriction.

Anaphylactic shock is accompanied by increases in vagal afferent and efferent activity in the guinea pig. Karczewski (158) found that the afferent activity was caused by stimulation by the pulmonary stretch receptors brought about by bronchoconstriction. The afferent activity gave rise, in turn, to an increase in efferent activity, thus causing further bronchoconstriction. It is, therefore, possible that histamine or other mediators may stimulate receptors in the lung to increase vagal afferent activity.

Gold's observations imply the participation of a reflex mechanism mediated by the brainstem. Efferent vagal discharge contributes to

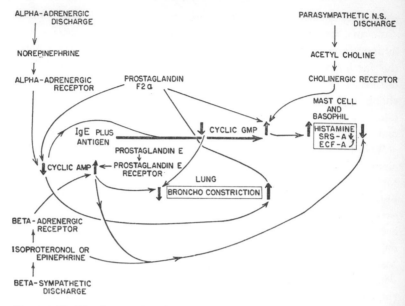

FIGURE 10. The factors involved in the regulation of bronchial patency. Bronchoconstriction is enhanced by α-adrenergic discharge, prostaglandin $F_2\alpha$, the release of the chemical mediators of anaphylaxis (on right) and parasympathetic nervous system discharge. Bronchorelaxation is produced by β-sympathetic nervous discharge prostaglandin E release. In bronchial asthma a bias towards bronchoconstriction may occur (Weiner, 1977).

bronchoconstriction, presumably after receptors in the lung are stimulated by the allergen. The results of this experiment strongly suggest that bronchoconstriction in bronchial asthma cannot only be explained by the local effect of histamine and other mediators of the antigen-antibody reaction on bronchiolar smooth muscle.

The results of research in animals also imply the participation of the brain in the pathogenesis of gastric ulcers (68, 69, 161, 162).

PATHOGENETIC MECHANISMS

Although we know a great deal about the complex pathophysiology of many diseases, we know little about their pathogenesis. Obviously, the pathogenesis of bacterial and viral diseases is well-known. Similarly, the precise pathogenetic mechanisms of the allergic form of bronchial asthmatic attacks (Figure 10) and juvenile diabetes mellitus are almost completely understood. But the same statement cannot be made for Graves' disease because we do not know how infection, an operation, the fear of dying or bereavement causes the T_3 suppression test to become abnormal, and hypermetabolism to occur. The pathogenesis of peptic duodenal ulcer is largely known but undoubtedly complex—a statement that also applies to gout, the malignancies, rheumatoid arthritis and ulcerative colitis.

No *a priori* reason exists that would incline one to the view that the pathogenetic mechanisms in any one disease are uniform. This statement is based on the fact that high blood pressure in man can occur as the result of renal artery constriction, reninomas, phaeochromocytomas, aldosterinomas, coarctation of the aorta, increased intracranial pressure, etc. Once these conditions are excluded, we are left with a large population of patients whose high blood pressure is called "essential." But the inciting causes of essential hypertension are not uniform: Some women taking the oral contraceptive pill develop the disease, but only if they have a family history of it, or are discovered to have a previously covert constriction of a renal artery. In addition, there is abundant evidence (56, 163) that early in the course of the disease, in some (young) patients with "borderline" hypertension, the cardiac output (CO) is increased, but the peripheral resistance (PR) is normal or only slightly raised (164). After a while PR in these patients rises, and CO returns to normal (165). The increased CO, which is often accompanied by an increase heart rate at rest, occurs in patients whose blood pressure fluctuates above or below 140/90 mm Hg (i.e., patients with "borderline" hypertension) but it does not occur in all young patients and may be age-dependent (166). The increased CO, but not the increased PR, is responsive to propanolol (167, 168).

These findings suggest that: 1) at the onset of some forms of essential hypertension the initial change is in CO, not PR. Only later does PR rise as a physiological adaptation to the increased CO (169); 2) the increased CO may be mediated by increased beta-adrenergic sympathetic drive on the heart, emanating from the brain; 3) different mechanisms may initiate essential hypertension in different forms of the disease.

Amongst these mechanisms may be a disturbance in the control of renin release. Until recently it was believed that the release of renin by the granular, juxtaglomerular cells in the walls of the afferent arterioles of the kidney was instigated either by a fall in renal artery pressure or by a fall in plasma volume (170, 171). But adrenergic stimulation also releases renin (172, 173) when appropriate measures are taken to avert changes in blood flow to the kidney and in pressure within the renal artery. It is now fairly clear that brain stimulation, specifically of the medulla oblongata, increases (174), and stimulation of the anterior hypothalamus (175) decreases plasma renin activity. Therefore, there are at least two different mechanisms (other than increases in PR) that have recently been shown to be capable of raising blood pressure (BP) and that are under direct CNS control.

That essential hypertension may be the end product of a variety of different predisposing and initiating mechanisms should not be surprising. Even in patients with essential hypertension, plasma renin activity (PRA) is normally distributed. The level of PRA seems to be a stable characteristic of these patients over time (57). The earlier statement that different pathogenetic mechanisms may produce the same disease is based on the evidence just reviewed.

COMMENTS ON THE PATHOPHYSIOLOGY OF DISEASE

The diseases discussed in this chapter are characterized by disturbances of regulation (109). These disturbances have been studied after disease onset. They take a variety of different forms, and they may persist after remission of the disease.

1) It has been known for a long time that some patients with peptic duodenal ulcer have persistent elevations of basal hydrochloric acid output during the day and night (59, 176). Since that time a variety of anatomical variations and regulatory disturbances have been discovered that would in part explain the persistently

high acid output: Some patients have a larger than usual parietal cell mass (177), and in others the diameter and cross sectional area of the vagus nerve is increased in size (178). Peptic duodenal ulcer can occur when extra-gastric gastrin is produced by a pancreatic or duodenal tumor (58). Gastrin production then escapes the regulatory (inhibitory) action of gastric acid. Other patients, without tumors but with peptic duodenal ulcers, have, on the average, elevated basal acid secretion but normal (compared with controls) basal serum gastrin (62) which suggests a defect in the inhibition of gastrin release that ordinarily follows acidification. Still other duodenal ulcer patients show a gastrin response to a protein meal that is more elevated and prolonged than that of control subjects, which suggests an increased sensitivity of gastrin cells to this stimulus and/or a failure of the inhibition of gastrin release by the subsequent acid secretion (63). Some duodenal ulcer patients have been reported to secrete more acid per unit of exogenous pentagastrin (the active portion of the gastrin molecule), which suggests an increased sensitivity of parietal cell receptors of gastrin in these patients (58) (Figure 11).

2) In some forms of essential hypertension the regulatory relationship between renin (SRA)—angiotensin II and aldosterone levels is disturbed (Figure 12). In the presence of low levels of SRA, aldosterone levels are unexpectedly normal (instead of low) possibly due to a heightened sensitivity of the receptor site on adrenal cortical cells to angiotensin II (179).

3) Another form of regulatory disturbance is seen in Graves' disease. The production and secretion of the two thyroid hormones (T_3 and T_4) are normally under the control of dietary iodine and protein, the iodide content of the thyroid gland, and pituitary thyrotropin that is, in turn, regulated by T_3 levels in serum and the hypothalamic thyrotropin stimulating hormone (Figure 13). In Graves' disease the control of thyroid hormone production and secretion is preempted by the continuous stimulation of the gland by at least three immunoglobulins—the L.A.T.S., the L.A.T.S. protector, and the H.T.S.—which have hormonal properties.

4) The regulation of the patency of the bronchial tree is altered

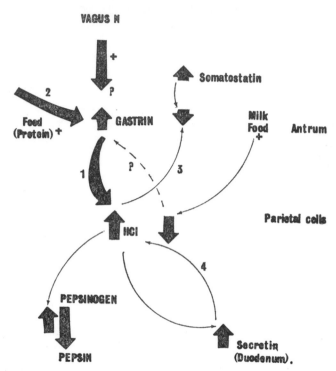

FIGURE 11. Several types of regulatory disturbances that have been described in patients with peptic duodenal ulcer: 1) In some patients administered gastrin has an excessive stimulating effect on the secretion of hydrochloric acid by gastric parietal cells; 2) in other patients a protein meal excessively stimulates gastrin and hydrochloric acid secretion; 3) in another group of patients the inhibition of gastrin secretion by hydrochloric acid is diminished. In the presence of high levels of acidity in the stomach gastrin levels remain normal, not low; 4) in some patients with gastrinoma, secretin may further stimulate hydrochloric acid secretion, rather than inhibiting the stimulating effects of gastrin on hydrochloric acid secretion.

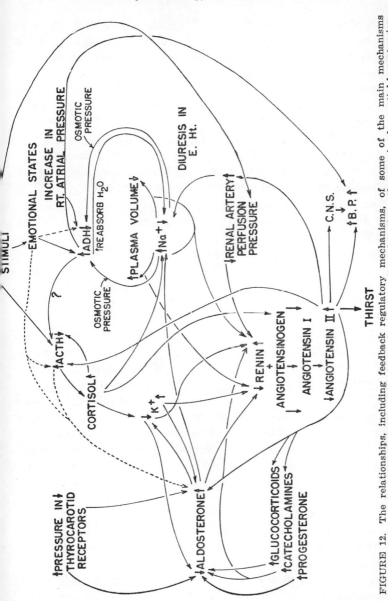

FIGURE 12. The relationships, including feedback regulatory mechanisms, of some of the main mechanisms involved in the maintenance of B.P., which have also been implicated in the pathogenesis of essential hypertension. The vertical arrows indicate increases or decreases of levels For example, an increase of angiotensin II levels in the blood is reflected in increased secretion of aldosterone and vice versa. The other arrows depict both the positive (as in the foregoing example) and negative feedback regulatory mechanisms involved in the control of B.P. Other mechanisms are not displayed.

in bronchial asthma. The alteration takes the form of a tendency to bronchoconstriction. Bronchial patency is usually maintained by a balance between beta-adrenergic sympathetic mechanisms (tending to cause dilatation), and alpha-adrenergic sympathetic and cholinergic mechanisms (producing constriction). A shift in balance of the regulatory mechanisms that are mediated by cyclic nucleotides would produce the bronchoconstrictor tendency: Specifically, augmented levels of cyclic-GMP and decreased levels of cyclic-AMP would produce this tendency (180, 181).

Without this tendency to bronchoconstriction upon which reflex mechanisms, the chemical mediators of anaphylaxis and psychological factors, play asthmatic attacks do not occur (182, 183).

5) In rheumatoid arthritis, the predisposition seems to take the form either of excessive or inadequate immunoglobulin formation. In the case of excessive formation, the immunoglobulins form complexes with other immunoglobulins (IgG-IgG, IgG-IgA, IgG-IgM complexes). Either an excess or a deficiency of immunoglobulin-G formation seems to lead to a failure of antigen-antibody clearance from the body, with the result that the complexes are deposited in blood vessels. In this example, the *relationships* between the amounts of antibody formed in response to the antigen are altered. Here, either excessive or inadequate antibody formation relative to the antigen may predispose to the illness. In either case, the tendency to form inadequate or excessive antibody seems to be genetically determined, and may entail a defect in the genetic control of antibody formation or in some other mechanism, such as the cyclic-AMP system.

6) In gout either excesses of uric acid production or a diminution of its disposition (both due to a variety of genetic variations) occur.

7) A disease such as primary anorexia nervosa is characterized by a failure of maturation of a critical regulatory mechanism. Specifically, the circadian pattern of the luteinizing hormone (L.H.) and follicle stimulating hormone (F.S.H.) fails to mature in the adult women with the disease. The failure may be either genetically (42) or experientially determined (184-186). It is not due to pituitary failure (187) but to a hypothalamic defect. This defect is most parsimoniously conceived of as an increased or persistent (from

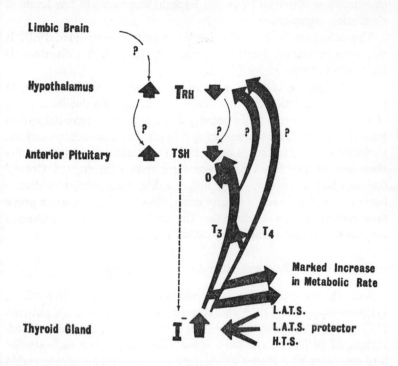

FIGURE 13. Postulated effect of the long acting thyroid stimulating hormone (L.A.T.S.), its protector, and the human thyroid stimulating hormone (H.T.S.) in producing a markedly raised level of the thyroid hormones (T₃ and T₄) in the hyperthyroidism of Graves' disease. The usual regulating, feedback system between thyrotropin (TSH) and the thyroid gland is broken. TSH levels are normal or low because of the continuous inhibition of TSH release by T₃. Additional TRH production or release is inhibited by raised T₃ and T₄ levels. But additional T₃ does not suppress but may actually increase I¹³¹ uptake, suggesting that T₃ rather than inhibiting TSII release may actually stimulate it or leave it unaffected (O) (Abnormal T₃ suppression).

childhood) sensitivity of anterior hypothalamic cells to low levels of circulating estrogens.

The defect seems to persist despite weight recovery (188-190). It may be a permanent feature of some patients with this disease as is their motor hyperactivity (189).

The persistence of these features in primary anorexia nervosa, of gastric hypersecretion in some "cured" patients with duodenal ulcer, of variations in serum renin activity in patients with essential hypertension when B.P. normalizes, of IgE levels and a bronchoconstrictor tendency in some instances of bronchial asthmatic patients in remission, and of the L.A.T.S. in some patients with treated Graves' disease who become euthyroid, suggests that these regulatory disturbances may also antecede disease onset. Should this speculation prove to be correct, we can conclude that the predisposition to some diseases consists of a disturbance in regulation (109).

FACTORS THAT SUSTAIN DISEASE

With the exception of Engel's studies (76) on ulcerative colitis, Ferguson-Rayport's (191) and Ruesch's study of thyrotoxic patients (192), and Wiener's study (193), few longitudinal, long-term observations of patients have been made. The purpose of such studies is to determine why these chronic diseases have such an unpredictable and variable history. Some cases remit unexpectedly or fluctuate inconsistently, other progress inexorably towards disability and death. We still do not know how to account for the variable course of these diseases. Psychosocial factors may play several different roles. As we have seen, childhood bronchial asthma may remit rapidly when the child is removed from his home. The onset of the accelerated ("malignant") phase of hypertensive disease has been correlated with life situations and events (as well as raised levels of serum renin) that are similar if not identical to those in and with which the illness is first detected.

The psychological responses to chronic disease and disability may help to sustain them. Some patients refuse to take prescribed medication because they do not provide relief or they cause unpleasant side effects. Chronic disease is frequently accompanied by depression and helplessness. The helpless patient refuses to participate in his treatment. The hopeless patient sees no point in it. The uncertainty about the outcome of the disease or the sudden onset of illness may be frightening to some, while others who are chronically ill become resigned or may even openly or covertly welcome their invalidism (192, 193). How these various reactions influence the course of the illness is still largely unknown. Nor do we know how each of these various psychological responses interacts with the pathophysiology of an illness or the chronic changes—whether in the joints, the bronchioles or the colon—that have already taken place.

In all retrospective studies, the more general reactions to an illness must be clearly separated from the more specific responses with which illness onset is associated, and from the specific meanings that are engendered by the disease and may play a role in sustaining it. In the future it should be fruitful to separate out those multiple variables, at the various levels of biological organization, that predispose to, initiate, and sustain illness. For instance, we now know that following the first attack of some disease changes in the function of organs persist. The disposition of form IgE antibodies and to respond with bronchoconstriction continues despite the absence of clinical asthma. Permanent changes in the colonic mucosa without clinical symptoms persist after remission from the first attack of ulcerative colitis. Persistent changes in many aspects of thyroid function may follow Graves' disease even though the patient is in clinical remission. The elevated basal secretion of pepsin and hydrochloric acid in the stomach continues during the quiescent phase of duodenal ulcer in some patients. Therefore, one may conclude that these apparently permanent changes are, in part, responsible for exacerbations of each disease. And they interact with recurring failures in psychologic adaptation to cause renewed bouts of the disease.

Secondary and permanent changes in cells, tissues and organs occur as the result of the disturbances in physiology. These changes sustain the disease. Long-standing high blood pressure predisposes to damage to arterioles and arteries. If the renal artery is damaged and narrowed, high blood pressure may be increased or sustained. Damage to cerebral arteries may impair the psychological adaptation of the hypertensive patient. The increased peripheral resistance in essential hypertension is enhanced by secondary swelling of the arteriolar wall. Spasm or narrowing by scars or spasm of the pyloric portion of the duodenum in duodenal ulcer may slow gastric emptying time and expose the duodenum and stomach to high concentrations of gastric acid. These and other secondary changes in these diseases help to sustain them and prevent remission or cure.

LIAISON PSYCHIATRY

The principles in understanding disease enumerated above may also be applied to the activities of the liaison psychiatrist who is often concerned with the impact of disease on the person. He studies how acute or chronic disease affects the person's life and his adaptation to it, to injury, surgery, the hospital, and special therapeutic techniques (194, 195).

The patient's adaptation to these situations may be impaired further by brain damage due to senility, brain disease or delirium, making it more difficult or impossible to adapt to the factors that produced the disease, and to the disease itself.

Many medical diseases are associated either with delirium, psychosis or depression. These states must be managed by a combination of psychopharmacological agents or psychotherapeutically. The medical staff needs to be taught the principles of their management.

Because of a combination of social attitudes, and of attitudes acquired during the course of medical education, the elderly, the drug addict, the hypochondriac, and the alcoholic patient are at special risk in the hospital. The liaison psychiatrist can be of help in helping to rehabilitate such patients. He can further the diagnostic skills of his colleagues in helping them to recognize the delirious, the demented, the hypochrondriacal and the hysterical patient.

CONCLUSION

To summarize the present state of our knowledge of disease: Disease is seen as a complex biological phenomenon characterized by a failure of adaptation (196, 197). Such a definition would also account for the fact that persons may have a disease and not be ill. Adaptive failure results:

1) When external events for multifarious reasons overwhelm the adaptive capacity of the organism: Many categories of events may do so.

2) When the adaptive capacity of the organism is limited genetically, physiologically or psychologically. The adaptive capacity of the organism is in part a function of age. It changes with growth, maturation and development.

3) When adaptive mechanisms overrespond to produce disease.

A great deal of evidence has been accumulated to suggest that disease begins in settings that lead to psychological adaptive failure: 1) The events may be overwhelming; 2) the events cannot be changed, or escape from them is not possible; 3) the person's psychological capacity for adaptation is impaired. Or, the person is particularly sensitive to the events. Or, the events cause conflict that may impair adaptation.

On the psychological level we are predisposed to disease by conflict, specific sensitivities to events or an impaired adaptive capacity. But the psychological predisposition does not by itself determine disease. The specific disease is additionally determined by specific predispositions that are either genetic, immunological, viral, endocrine or physiological. The predispositions take various forms: They consist of a variety of disturbances in regulation. These either limit physiological adaptation or produce excessive adaptive responses (e.g., anaphylaxis). However, a person may be psychologically and physiologically predisposed and not fall ill. The failure of psychological adaptation is usually signalled by distress that may take the form of anxiety, depression or feelings of helplessness. When adaptive failure occurs the person relinquishes hope and gives up.

We still do not know how distress is translated by the brain into physiological change in the predisposed person. Nor do we know how the changes interact with the disturbances in regulation. These disturbances may occur within cells—in self-regulatory systems—or in those systems external to the cell that regulate its functions.

We have learned nonetheless that different pathogenetic mechanisms may cause the same disease (e.g., in gout) and the same mechanisms may cause different diseases (e.g., herpes virus, gastrinomas, etc.). And we have also learned that the mechanisms that initiate a disease may not be the ones that sustain it.

Lastly, we do not know how most of the predispositions come about because our knowledge of developmental biology and psychology is rudimentary.

REFERENCES

1. MANDELBROTE, B. M. and WITTKOWER, E. D.: Emotional Factors in Graves' Disease. *Psychosom. Med.* 17:109, 1955.
2. WALLERSTEIN, R. S., HOLZMAN, P. S., VOTH, H. M., and UHR, N.: Thyroid "Hot Spots": A Psychophysiological Study. *Psychosome. Med.* 27:508, 165.
3. WEINER, H., THALER, M., REISER, M. F., and MIRSKY, I. A.: Etiology of Duodenal Ulcer. I. Relation of Specific Psychological Characteristics to Rate of Gastric Secretion (Serum Pepsinogen). *Psychosom. Med.* 19:1, 1957.
4. WEINER, H. and HART, S.: Promising Interactions Between Psychiatry and Medicine. In D. A. Hamburg and H. K. H. Brodie (Eds), *American Handbook of Psychiatry*, Volume 6. New York: Basic Books, 1975.
5. VEITH, I.: Psychiatric Thought in Chinese Medicine. *J. Hist. Med.* 10:261, 1955.
6. GRODDECK, G. W.: The Book of the It: Psychoanalytic Letters to a Friend (tr., revised: author). *Arch. Psa.* 1:174-189, 1926.
7. GARMA, A.: *Peptic Ulcer and Psychoanalysis*. Baltimore: Williams and Wilkins, 1958.
8. REISER, M. F.: Changing Theoretical Concepts in Psychosomatic Medicine. In *American Handbook of Psychiatry*, Volume 4, M. F. Reiser, ed. New York: Basic Books, 1975.
9. DUNBAR, H. F.: *Psychosomatic Diagnosis*. New York: Hoeber, 1943.
10. ALEXANDER, F.: *Psychosomatic Medicine*. New York: Norton, 1950.
11. ALEXANDER, F., FRENCH, T. M., and POLLOCK, G. H.: *Psychosomatic Specificity*. Chicago: University of Chicago Press, 1968.

12. HARBURG, E., ERFURT, J. C., HAUENSTEIN, L. S., CHAPE, C., SCHULL, W. J., and SCHORK, M. A.: Socio-ecological Stress, Suppressed Hostility, Skin Color, and Black-White Male Blood Pressure: Detroit. *Psychosom. Med.* 35:276, 1973.
13. RUESCH, J.: The Infantile Personality: The Core Problem of Psychosomatic Medicine. *Psychosom. Med.* 10:134-144, 148.
14. MCDOUGALL, J.: The Psychosoma and the Psychoanalytic Process. *Int. Rev. Psychoanal.* 1:437, 1974.
15. MARTY, P. and DE M'UZAN, M.: 'La "pensée opératoire" '. *Rev. Franc. Psychoanal.* 27: Suppl. 1345, 163.
16. NEMIAH, J. C. and SIFNEOS, P. E.: Affect and Fantasy in Patients with Psychosomatic Disorders. In O. W. Hall (Ed.), *Modern Trends in Psychosomatic Medicine-2.* London: Butterworths, 1970.
17. NEMIAH, J. C., and FREYBERGER, H., and SIFNEOS, P. E.: Alexithymia: A View of the Psychosomatic Process. In O. W. Hill (Ed.), *Modern Trends in Psychosomatic Medicine-3.* London: Butterworths, 1976.
18. SIFNEOS, P.: The Prevalence of "Alexithymic" Characteristics in Psychosomatic Patients. In H. Freyberger (Ed.), *Topics of Psychosomatic Research.* Basel: Karger, 1972.
19. COBB, S., and ROSE, R. M.: Hypertension, Peptic Ulcer and Diabetes in Air Traffic Controllers. *J.A.M.A.* 224:489, 1973.
20. DOHRENWEND, B. S., and DOHRENWEND, B. P.: *Stressful Life Events: Their Nature and Effects.* New York: John Wiley and Sons, 1974.
21. ENGEL, G. L.: A Psychological Setting of Somatic Disease: The 'Giving Up—Given Up' Complex. *Proc. Roy. Soc. Med.* 60:553, 1967.
22. KASL, S. V., GORE, S., and COBB, S.: The Experience of Losing a Job: Reported Changes in Health, Symptoms and Illness Behavior. *Psychosom. Med.* 37:106, 1975.
23. PARKES, C. M.: *Bereavement.* New York: International Universities Press, 1972.
24. RAHE, R. H.: Epidemiological Studies of Life Change and Illness. *Int. J. Psychiat. Med.* 6:133, 1975.
25. KATZ, J., GALLAGHER, T., HELLMAN, L., ACKMAN, P., ROTHWAX, Y., SACHAR, E. J., and WEINER, H.: Psychological Covariants of Hydrocortisone Secretion Rates in Women With Breast Tumors. *Psychosom Med.* 32:1-18, 1970.
26. SCHMALE, A. H.: Giving Up As a Final Common Pathway to Changes in Health. *Adv. Psychosom. Med.* 8:20, 1972.
27. KASL, S. V., COBB, S., and BROOKS, G. W.: Changes in Serum Uric Acid and Cholesterol Levels in Men Undergoing Job Loss. *J.A.M.A.* 206:1555, 1968.
28. KAPP, F. T., ROSENBAUM, M., and ROMANO, J.: Psychological Factors in Men With Peptic Ulcers. *Amer. J. Psychiat.* 103:700, 1947.

29. DE M'UZAN, M., and BONFILS, S.: Étude et classification des aspects psychosomatiques de l'ulcère gastro-duodenal en milieu hospitalier. *Rev. Franc. et Clin. Biol.* 6:46, 1961.

30. HENRY, J. P., and CASSEL J. C.: Psychosocial Factors in Essential Hypertension. Recent Epidemiologic and Animal Experimental Evidence. *Amer. J. Epidem.* 90:171, 1969.

31. STAMLER, J., STAMLER, R., and PULLMAN, T.: *The Epidemiology of Essential Hypertension.* New York: Grune and Stratton, 1967.

32. GRELLAND, R.: Thyrotoxicosis at Ulleval Hospital in the Years 1934-1944 With a Special View to Frequency of the Disease. *Acta Med. Scand.* 125:108, 1946.

33. IVERSEN, K.: *Temporary Rise in the Frequency of Thyrotoxicosis in Denmark 1941-1945.* Copenhagen: Rosenkilde and Bagger, 1948.

34. IVERSEN, K.: An Epidemic Wave of Thyrotoxicosis in Denmark During World War II. *Amer. J. Med. Sci.*, 217:121, 149.

35. SCHWEITER, P. M. J.: Calorie Supply and Basal Metabolism. *Acta Med. Scand.* 119:306, 1944.

36. MILLER, H., and BARUCH, D. W.: Psychosomatic Studies in Children. Maternal Rejection and Allergic Manifestations. *Psychosom. Med.* 10:275, 1948.

37. REES, L.: The Significance of Parental Attitudes in Childhood Asthma. *J. Psychosom. Res.* 7:181, 1963.

38. DUBO, S., MCLEAN, J. R., CHING, A. Y. T., WRIGHT, H. L., KAUFMAN, P. E., and SHELDON, J. M.: A Study of Relations Between Family Situation, Bronchial Asthma, and Personal Adjustment in Children. *J. Pediat.* 59:402, 161.

39. PINKERTON, P., and WEAVER, C. M.: CHILDHOOD ASTHMA. In O. W. Hill (Ed.), *Modern Trends in Psychosomatic Medicine-2.* New York: Appleton-Century Crofts, 1970.

40. JACKSON, D. D., and YALOM, I.: Family Research on the Problem of Ulcerative Colitis. *Arch. Gen. Psych.* 15:410, 1966.

41. HARRIS, H.: Molecular Basis of Hereditary Disease. *Brit. Med. J.* 2:135, 1968.

42. KRON, L., KATZ, J. L., GORZYNSKI, G., and WEINER, H.: Anorexia Nervosa and Gonadal Dysgenesis: Further Evidence of a Relationship. *Arch. Gen. Psych.* (in press).

43. TEMIN, H. M.: The DNA Provirus Hypothesis. *Science* 192:1075, 1976.

44. ADAMS, D. D.: Pathogenesis of the Hyperthyroidism of Graves' Disease. *Brit. Med. J.* 1:1015, 1965.

45. ADAMS, D. D.: LATS Protector, The Human Thyroid Stimulator. *New Zeal. Med. J.* 81:22, 1975.

46. ENOCHS, M. R., and JOHNSON, L. R.: Growth Hormone: A Possible Regulator of Gastrin. *Gastroenterology* 68:889, 1975.

47. KELLER, H. H., BARTHOLINI, G., and PLETSCHER, A.: Enhance-

ment of Cerebral Noradrenaline Turnover by Thyrotropin-Releasing Hormone. *Nature* 248:528, 1974.

48. BOYAR, R. M., FINKELSTEIN, J. W., ROFFWARG, H., KAPEN, S., WEITZMAN, E., and HELLMAN, L.: Synchronization of Augmented Luteinizing Hormone Secretion With Sleep During Puberty. *New Engl. J. Med.* 287:582, 1972.

49. BOYAR, R. M., KATZ, J. L., FINKELSTEIN, J. W., KAPEN, S., WEINER, H., WEITZMAN, E., and HELLMAN, L.: Anorexia Nervosa: Immaturity of the 24-hour Luteinizing Hormone Secretory Pattern. *New Engl. J. Med.* 291:861, 1974.

50. CARROLL, B. J.: Psychoendrocrine Relationships in Affective Disorders. In O. W. Hill (Ed.), *Modern Trends in Psychosomatic Medicine-3*. London: Butterworths, 1976.

51. CURTIS, G. C.: Psychosomatics and Chronobiology: Possible Implications of Neuroendocrine Rhythms. *Psychosom. Med.* 34:235, 1972.

52. LISTON, E. H., and SHERSHOW, W.: Concurrence of Anorexia Nervosa and Gonadal Dysgenesis: A Critical Review with Practical Considerations. *Arch. Gen. Psych.* 29:834, 1973.

53. FREIS, H., and NILLIUS, S. J.: Psychological Factors, Psychiatric Illness and Amenorrhea After Oral Contraceptive Treatment. *Acta Psych. Scand.* 49:653-658, 1973.

54. HEALEY, L. A.: Notes on Joint Diseases. I. Gout Is Not Hyperuricemia. *Northwest Med.* 69:105-106, 1970.

55. KATZ, J. L., and WEINER, H.: Psychosomatic Considerations in Hyperuricemia and Gout. *Psychosom. Med.* 34:165, 1972.

56. JULIUS, S., and SCHORK, M. A.: Borderline Hypertension—A Critical Review. *J. Chron. Dis.* 23:723, 1971.

57. BRUNNER, H. R., LARAGH, J. H., BAER, L., NEWTON, M. A., GOODWIN, F. T., KRAKOFF, L. R., BARD, R. H., and BUHLER, F. R.: Essential Hypertension: Renin and Aldosterone, Heart Attack and Stroke. *N. Engl. J. Med.* 286:441, 1972.

58. ISENBERG, J. I., WALSH, J. H., and GROSSMAN, M. I.: Zollinger-Ellison Syndrome. *Gastroenterology* 65: 140-165, 1973.

59. WORMSLEY, K. G., and GROSSMAN, M. I.: Maximal Histalog Test in Control Subjects and Patients with Peptic Ulcer. *Gut* 6:427-435, 1965.

60. COX, A. J.: Stomach Size and Its Relation to Chronic Peptic Ulcer. *Arch. Pathol.* 54:407-422, 1953.

61. MCGUIGAN, J. E., and TRUDEAU, W. L.: Differences in Rates of Gastrin Release in Normal Persons and Patients with Duodenal Ulcer Disease. *N. Engl. J. Med.* 288:64-66, 1973.

62. TRUDEAU, W. L., and MCGUIGAN, J. E.: Serum Gastrin Levels in Patients with Peptic Ulcer Disease. *Gastroenterology* 59:6-12, 1970.

63. KELLGREN, J. H., and BALL, J.: Clinical Significance of the Rheumatoid Serum Factor. *Brit. Med. J.* 1:523, 1959.

64. STROBER, W., GLAESE, R. M., and WALDMANN, T. A.: Immunologic

Deficiency Diseases. *Bull. Rheum. Dis.* 22:686, 1971-72.

65. Moos, R. H., and Solomon, G. F.: Psychologic Comparisons Between Women with Rheumatoid Arthritis and Their Non-Arthritic Sisters. 1. Personality Test and Interview Rating Data. *Psychosom. Med.* 27:135, 1965.

66. Moos, R. H., and Solomon, G. F.: Psychologic Comparisons Between Women with Rheumatoid Arthritis and Their Non-Arthritic Sisters. II. Content Analysis of Interviews. *Psychosom. Med.* 27:150, 1965.

67. Moos, R. H., and Solomon, G. F.: Social and Personal Factors in Rheumatoid Arthritis: Pathogenic Considerations. *Clin. Med.* 73:19, 1966.

68. Ackerman, S. H., Hofer, M. A., and Weiner, H.: Age at Maternal Separation and Gastric Erosion Susceptibility in the Rat. *Psychosom. Med.* 37:180, 1975.

69. Ader, R.: Psychosomatic Research in Animals. In O. W. Hill (Ed.), *Modern Trends in Psychosomatic Medicine-3.* London: Butterworths, 1976.

70. Henry, J. P., Meehan, J. P., and Stephens, P. M.: The Use of Psychosocial Stimuli to Induce Prolonged Systolic Hypertension in Mice. *Psychosom. Med.* 29:408, 1967.

71. Wolff, C., Friedman, S. B., Hofer, M. A., and Mason, J. W.: Relationship Between Psychological Defenses and Mean Urinary 17-Hydroxycorticosteroid Excretion Rates: I. A Predictive Study of Parents of Fatally Ill Children. *Psychosom. Med.* 26:576, 1964.

72. Hofer, M. A., Wolff, C. T., Friedman, S. B., and Mason, J. W.: A Psychoendocrine Study of Bereavement. I. 17-Hydroxycorticosteroid Excretion Rates of Parents Following Death of Their Children From Leukemia. *Psychosom. Med.* 34:481, 1972.

73. Hofer, M. A., Wolff, C. T., Friedman, S. B., and Mason, J. W.: A Psychoendocrine Study of Bereavement. II. Observations on the Process of Mourning in Relation to Adrenocortical Function. *Psychosom. Med.* 34:492, 1972.

74. Katz, J. L., Ackman, P., Rothwax, Y., Sachar, E. J. Weiner, H., Hellman, L., and Gallagher, T. F.: Psychoendocrine Aspects of Cancer of the Breast. *Psychosom. Med.* 32:1, 1970.

75. Katz, J. L., Weiner, H., Gallagher, T. F., and Hellman, L.: Stress, Distress and Ego Defenses. *Arch. Gen. Psych.* 23:131, 1970.

76. Engel, G. L.: Studies of Ulcerative Colitis. III. The Nature of the Psychologic Processes. *Amer. J. Med.* 19:231, 1955.

77. Katz, J. L., Boyar, R., Weiner, H., Gorzynski, G., Roffwarg, H., and Hellman, L.: Toward an Elucidation of the Psychoendocrinology of Anorexia Nervosa. In E. Sachar (Ed.), *Hormones, Behavior and Psychopathology.* New York: Raven Press, 1976.

78. KNAPP, P. T., and NEMETZ, S. J.: Acute Bronchial Asthma—Concomitant Depression with Excitement and Varied Antecedent Patterns in 406 Attacks. *Psychosom. Med.* 22:42, 1960.
79. WEISMAN, A.: A Study of the Psychodynamics of Duodenal Ulcer Exacerbations with Special Reference to Treatment and the Problem of Specificity. *Psychosom. Med.* 18:1-42, 1956.
80. ENGEL, G. L.: A Life Setting Conducive to Illness: The Giving-Up, Given-Up Complex. *Arch. Int. Med.* 69:293, 1968.
81. SCHMALE, A. H., JR.: Relation of Separation and Depression to Disease. I. A Report on a Hospitalized Medical Population. *Psychosom. Med.* 20:259, 1958.
82. KNAPP, P. H., MUSHATT, C., NEMETZ, J. S., CONSTANTINE, H., and FRIEDMAN, S.: The Context of Reported Asthma During Psychoanalysis. *Psychosom. Med.* 32:167, 1970.
83. SCHECHTER, P. J., HOROWITZ, D., and HENKIN, R. I.: Sodium Chloride Preference in Essential Hypertension. *J.A.M.A.* 225:1311, 1973.
84. LIPOWSKI, Z. J.: Psychosomatic Medicine: An Overview. In O. W. Hill (Ed.), *Modern Trends in Psychosomatic Medicine-3*. London: Butterworths, 1976.
85. YOUNG, M., BENJAMIN B., and WALLIS, C.: The Mortality of Widowers. *Lancet* 2:454, 1963.
86. KRAUS, A. S., and LILIENFELD, A. M.: Some Epidemiological Aspects of the High Mortality in a Young Widowed Group. *J. Chron. Dis.* 10:207, 1959.
87. ADAMSON, J. D., and SCHMALE, A. H., JR.: Object Loss, Giving Up and the Onset of Psychiatric Disease. *Psychosom. Med.* 27:557, 1965.
88. PARKES, C. M.: Recent Bereavement As A Cause of Mental Illness. *Brit. J. Psychiat.* 110:198, 1964.
89. BAHNSON, C. B.: Psychophysiological Complementarity in Malignancies: Past Work and Future Vistas. *Ann. N.Y. Acad. Sci.* 164:319, 1969.
90. KISSEN, D. M.: Psychological Factors, Personality, and Lung Cancer in Men Aged 55-64. *Brit. J. Med. Psychol.* 40:29, 1967.
91. LESHAN, L. I.: An Emotional Life History Pattern Associated with Neoplastic Disease. *Ann. N.Y. Acad. Sci.* 125:780, 1966.
92. DAY, G.: The Psychosomatic Approach to Pulmonary Tuberculosis. *Lancet* 260:1025, 1951.
93. HINKLE, L. E., and WOLF, S.: A Summary of Experimental Evidence Relating Life Stress to Diabetes Mellitus. *J. Mt. Sinai Hosp.* 19:537, 1952.
94. GREENE, W. A., JR.: Psychological Factors and Reticuloendothelial Disease. I. Preliminary Observations on a Group of Males with Lymphomas and Leukemias. *Psychosom. Med.* 16:220, 1954.
95. STEIN, S., and CHARLES, E.: Emotional Factors in Juvenile Dia-

betes Mellitus: A Study of Early Life Experiences of Adolescent Diabetics. *Amer. J. Psychiat.* 128:700, 1971.

96. PERLMAN, L. V., FERGUSON, S., BERGUM, K., ISENBERG, E. L., and HAMMARSTEN, J. F.: Precipitation of Congestive Heart Failure: Social and Emotional Factors. *Ann. Int. Med.* 75:1, 1971.

97. KIMBALL, C.: A Predictive Study of Adjustment to Cardiac Surgery. *J. Thoracic Cardiovasc. Surg.* 58:891, 1969.

98. KENNEDY, J. A., and BAKST, H.: The Influence of Emotions on the Outcome of Cardiac Surgery: A Predictive Study. *Bull. N. Y. Acad. Med.* 42:811, 1966.

99. HOFER, M. A.: Regulation of Cardiac Rate by Nutritional Factor in Young Rats. *Science* 172:1039, 1971.

100. HOFER, M. A.: Studies on How Early Maternal Separation Produces Behavioral Change in Young Rats. *Psychosom. Med.* 37:245, 1975.

101. HOFER, M. A., and WEINER, H.: The Development and Mechanisms of Cardio-respiratory Responses to Maternal Deprivation in Rat Pups. *Psychosom. Med.* 33:353, 1971.

102. HOFER, M. A., and WEINER, H.: Physiological Mechanisms for Cardiac Control by Nutritional Intake After Maternal Separation in the Young Rat. *Psychosom. Med.* 37:8, 1975.

103. KAUFMAN, I. C., and ROSENBLUM, L.: Effects of Separation from Mother on the Emotional Behavior of Infant Monkeys. *Ann. N. Y. Acad. Sci.* 159:681, 1969.

104. BRONFENBRENER, U.: Early Deprivation in Mammals: A Cross Species Analysis. In G. Newton and S. Levine (Eds.), *Early Experience and Behavior*. Springfield: Thomas, 1968.

105. HARLOW, H. F.: The Development of Affectional Patterns in Infant Monkeys. In B. M. Foss (Ed.), *Determinants of Infant Behavior*. London: Methuen, 1961.

106. HINDE, R. A., and SPENCER-BOOTH, Y.: Effects of Brief Separations from Mother on Rhesus Monkeys. *Science* 173:111, 1971.

107. MASON, W. A., DAVENPORT, R. K., JR., and MENZEL, E. W., JR.: Early Experiences and the Social Development of Rhesus Monkeys and Chimpanzees. In G. Newton and S. Levine (Eds.), *Early Experience and Behavior*. Springfield: Thomas, 1968.

108. WEINER, H.: Presidential Address: Some Comments on the Transduction of Experience by the Brain. *Psychosom. Med.* 34:355-380, 1972.

109. WEINER, H.: *The Psychobiology of Human Disease*. New York: Elsevier-North Holland, 1977.

110. KNAPP, P. H.: Revolution, Relevance and Psychomatic Medicine: Where the Light is Not. *Psychosom. Med.* 33:363, 1971.

111. KATZ, J. L., WEINER, H., GUTMAN, A., and YU, T.-F.: Hyperuricemia, Gout and the Executive Suite. *J.A.M.A.* 224:1251, 1973.

112. BLOCK, J. D., and REISER, M. F.: Discrimination and Recognition

of Weak Stimuli. I. Psychological and Physiological Relationships. *Arch. Gen. Psych.* 6:25, 1962.

113. REISER, M. F., and BLOCK, J. D.: Discrimination and Recognition of Weak Stimuli. II. A Possible Autonomic Feedback Mechanism. *Arch. Gen. Psych.* 6:37, 1962.

114. HUBEL, D. H.: Single Unit Activity in Striate Cortex of Unrestrained Cats. *J. Physiol.* (London) 147:226, 1959.

115. HUBEL, D. H.: Single Unit Activity in Lateral Geniculate Body and Optic Tract of Unrestrained Cats. *J. Physiol.* (London) 150:91, 1960.

116. HUBEL, D. H., and WIESEL, T. N.: Receptive Fields of Single Neurons in the Cat's Striate Cortex. *J. Physiol.* (London) 148:574, 1959.

117. HUBEL, D. H., and WIESEL.: Receptive Fields of Optic Nerve Fibers in the Spider Monkey. *J. Physiol.* (London) 154:572, 1960.

118. HUBEL, D. H., and WIESEL, T. N.: Receptive Fields, Binocular Interaction and Functional Architecture in the Cat's Visual Cortex. *J. Physiol.* (London) 160:106, 1962.

119. HUBEL, D. H., and WIESEL, T. N.: Responses of Monkey Geniculate Cells to Monochromic and White Spots of Light. *Physiologist* 7:162, 1964.

120. HUBEL, D. H., and WIESEL, T. N.: The Functional Architecture of the Striate Cortex. In F. D. Carlson (Ed.), *Physiological and Biochemical Aspects of Nervous Integration.* Englewood Cliffs: Prentice Hall, 1968.

121. AXELROD, J., SHEIN, H. M., and WURTMAN, R. J.: Stimulation of C^{14}-melatonin Synthesis from C^{14}-tryptophan by Noradrenaline in Rat Pineal in Organ Culture. *Proc. Nat. Acad. Sci. U.S.A.* 62:544, 1969.

122. AXELROD, J.: Noradrenaline: Fate and Control of Its Biosynthesis. *Science* 173:598, 1971.

123. MOORE, R. Y., HELLER, A., WURTMAN, R. J., and AXELROD, J.: Visual Pathway Mediating Pineal Response to Environmental Light. *Science* 155:220, 1967.

124. AMASSIAN, V. E., WEINER, H., and ROSENBLUM, M.: Neural Systems Subserving the Tactile Placing Reaction: A Model for the Study of Higher Level Control of Movement. *Brain Res.* 40:171, 1972.

125. AMASSIAN, V. E., ROSS, R., WERTENBAKER, C., and WEINER, H.: Cerebellothalamocortical Interrelations in Contact Placing and Other Movements in Cats. In T. L. Frigyesi, E. Finvik and M. D. Yahr (Eds.), *Corticothalamic Projections and Sensorimotor Activities.* New York: Raven, 1972.

126. POLLIN, W., and GOLDIN, S.: The Physiological Effects of Intravenously Administered Epinephrine and Its Metabolism in Normal and Schizophrenic Men. II. *J. Psychiat. Res.* 1:50, 1961.

127. LEVITT, E. E., PERSKY, H., BRADY, J. P., and FITZGERALD, J. A.: The Effect of Hydrocortisone Infusion in Hypnotically Induced Anxiety. *Psychosom. Med.* 25:158, 1963.
128. WEINER, S., DORMAN, D., PERSKY, H., STACK, T. W., MARTIN, J., and LEVITT, E. E.: Effects on Anxiety of Increasing the Plasma Hydrocortisone Level. *Psychosom. Med.* 25:69, 1963.
129. CALLAWAY, E., and THOMPSON, S. V.: Sympathetic Activity and Perception. *Psychosom. Med.* 15:433, 1953.
130. MAAS, J. W., and MEDNIEKS, M.: Hydrocortisone-Mediated Increase of Norepinephrine Uptake by Brain Slices. *Science* 171: 178, 1971.
131. AZMITIA, E. C., JR., and McEWEN, B. S.: Corticosterone Regulation of Tryptophan Hydroxylase in Midbrain of Rat. *Science* 166:1274, 1969.
132. GREEN, A. R., and CURZON, G.: Decrease of 5-Hydroxytryptamine in the Brain Provoked by Hydrocortisone and Its Prevention by Allopurinol. *Nature* (London) 220:1095, 1968.
133. GILLIN, J. C., JACOBS, L. S., FRAM, D. H., and SNYDER, F.: Acute Effect of a Glucocorticoid on Normal Human Sleep. *Nature* (London) 237:398, 1972.
134. BYKOV, K. M.: *The Cerebral Cortex and the Internal Organs.* Moscow, Medgiz, 1947.
135. FORSYTH, R. P.: Blood Pressure and Avoidance Conditioning. *Psychosom. Med.* 30:125, 1968.
136. FOLKOW, B., and RUBINSTEIN, E. H.: Cardiovascular Effects of Acute and Chronic Stimulations of the Hypothalamic Defence Area in the Rat. *Acta Physiol. Scand.* 68:48, 1966.
137. KEZDI, P.: *Baroreceptors adn Hypertension.* New York: Pergamon, 1967.
138. DOBA, N., and REIS, D. J.: Acute Fulminating Neurogenic Hypertension Produced by Brainstem Lesions in the Rat. *Circ. Res.* 32:584, 1973.
139. DOBA, N., and REIS, D. J.: Role of Central and Peripheral Adrenergic Mechanisms in Neurogenic Hypertension Produced by Brainstem Lesion in Rats. *Circ. Res.* 34:293, 1974.
140. GROLLMAN, A., HARRISON, T. R., and WILLIAMS, J. R., JR.: The Effect of Various Steroid Derivatives on the Blood Pressure of the Rat. *J. Pharmacol. Exp. Ther.* 69:149, 1940.
141. KNOWLTON, A. I., LOEB, E. N., STOERK, H. C., and SEEGAL, B. C.: Desoxycorticosterone Acetate. The Potentiation of its Activity by Sodium Chloride. *J. Exp. Med.* 85:187, 1947.
142. GOLDBLATT, H.: Renal Origin of Hypertension. *Physiol. Rev.* 27: 120, 1947.
143. DAHL, L. K., HEINE, M., and TASSINARI, L.: Role of Genetic Factors in Susceptibility to Experimental Hypertension Due to Chronic Excess Salt Ingestion. *Nature* (London) 194:480, 1962.

144. OKAMOTO, K., and AOKI, K.: Development of a Strain of Spontaneously Hypertensive Rats. *Jap. Circ. J.* 27:282, 1963.
145. CHALMERS, J. P.: Brain Amines and Models of Experimental Hypertension. *Circ. Res.* 36:469, 1975.
146. DECHAMPLAIN, J.: Hypertension and the Sympathetic Nervous System. In S. Snyder (Ed.), *Perspective in Neuropharmocology.* Oxford: Oxford University Press, 1972.
147. DECHAMPLAIN, J., and VAN AMERINGEN, M. R.: Role of Sympathetic Fibers and of Adrenal Medulla in the Maintenance of Cardiovascular Homeostasis in Normotensive and Hypertensive Rats. In E. Usdin and S. Synder (Eds.), *Frontiers in Catecholamine Research.* Oxford: Pergamon Press, 1973.
148. FINCH, L., HAEUSLER, G., and THOENEN, H.: Failure to Induce Experimental Hypertension in Rats After Intraventricular Injection of 6-Hydroxydopamine. *Brit. J. Pharmacol.* 44:356, 1972.
149. HAEUSLER, G., FINCH, L., and THONEN, H.: Central Adrenergic Neurons and the Initiation and Development of Experimental Hypertension. *Experientia* 28:1200, 1972.
150. JOY, M. D., and LOWE, R. D.: The Site of Cardiovascular Action of Angiotensin II in the Brain. *Clin. Sci.* 39:327, 1970.
151. LEWIS, P. J., REID, J. L., CHALMERS, J. P., and DOLLERY, C. T.: Importance of Central Catecholaminergic Neurons in the Development of Renal Hypertension. *Clin. Sci.* 45:115S, 1973.
152. FUKYAMA, K.: Central Modulation of Baroreceptor Reflex by Angiotensin. *Jap. Heart J.* 14:135, 1973.
153. GILDENBERG, P. L.: Site of angiotensin vasopressor activity in the Brainstem. *Fed. Proc.* 30:432, 1971.
154. SWEET, C. S., and BRODY, M. J.: Arterial Hypertension Elicited by Prolonged Intravertebral Infusion of Angiotensin in the Conscious Dog. *Fed. Proc.* 30:432, 1971.
155. SWEET, C. S., and BRODY, M. J.: Central Inhibition of Reflex Vasodilatation by Angiotensin and Reduced Renal Pressure. *Amer. J. Physiol.* 219:1751, 1970.
156. GANTEN, D., HUTCHINSON, J. S., HACKENTHAL, E., SCHELLING, P., ROSAS, B. P., and GENEST, J.: Intrinsic Brain Iso-Renin-Angiotensin System, (ISO-RAS) and Hypertension in Rats. Third International Meeting of the International Society of Hypertension, Milan, 1974. *Clin. Sci. Suppl.*
157. JARROT, B., MCQUEEN, A., and LOUIS, W. J.: Serotonin Levels in Vascular Tissue and the Effects of a Serotonin Synthesis Inhibitor on Blood Pressure in Rats. *Clin. Exp. Pharmacol. Physiol.* Suppl. 2:201-5, 1975.
158. KARCZEWSKI, W.: The Electrical Activity of the Vagus Nerve in Anaphylactic Shock. *Acta Allerg.* 17:334, 1962.
159. KARCZEWSKI, W., and WIDDICOMBE, J. G.: The Role of the Vagus Nerves in the Respiratory and Circulatory Reactions

to Anaphylaxis in Rabbits, *J. Physiol.* (London) 201:293, 1969.

160. GOLD, W. M., KESSLER, G. R., and YU, D. Y. C.: Role of Vagus Nerves in Experimental Asthma in Allergic Dogs. *J. Appl. Physiol.* 33:719, 1972.

161. ACKERMAN, S. H., and WEINER, H.: Peptic Ulcer Disease: Some Considerations for Psychosomatic Research. In O. W. Hill (Ed.), *Modern Trends in Psychosomatic Medicine-3.* London: Butterworths, 1976.

162. YAGER, J., and WEINER, H.: Observations in Man, Chapt. II, Peptic Ulcer. *Adv. Psychosom. Med.* 6:40, 1970.

163. ERICH, R. H., CUDDY, R. P., SMYLYAN,, H., ET AL.: Haemodynamics in Labile Hypertension. *Circulation* 24:299, 1966.

164. FOLKOW, B.: The Haemodynamic Consequences of Adaptive Structural Changes of the Resistance Vessels in Hypertension. *Clin. Sci.* 41:1, 1971.

165. FREIS, E. D.: Hemodynamics of Hypertension. *Physiol. Rev.* 40:27, 1960.

166. JULIUS, S., and CONWAY, J.: Hemodynamic Studies in Patients with Borderline Blood Pressure Elevation. *Circulation* 38:282, 1968.

167. JULIUS, S., SANNERSTEDT, R., and CONWAY, J.: Hemodynamic Effects of Propranolol in Borderline Hypertension. *Circulation* 37 (Suppl. 6) : 109, 1968.

168. ULRYCH, M., FROHLICH, E. D., DUSTAN, H. P., ET AL.: Immediate Hemodynamic Effects of Beta-Adrenergic Blockade with Propranolol in Normotensive and Hypertensive Man. *Circulation* 37:411, 1968.

169. PATTERSON, G. C., SHEPARD, J. T., and WHELAN, R. F.: Resistance to Flow in the Upper and Lower Limb Vessels in Patients with Coarctation of the Aorta. *Clin. Sci.* 16:627, 1957.

170. TOBIAN, L.: A Viewpoint Concerning the Enigma of Hypertension. *Amer. J. Med.* 52:595, 1972.

171. EIDE, I., LOYNING, E., and KIIL, F.: Evidence for Hemodynamic Autoregulation of Renin Release. *Circ. Res.* 32:237, 1973.

172. GANONG, W. F.: Effects of Sympathetic Activity and ACTH on Renin and Aldosterone Secretion. In J. Genest and E. Koiw (Eds.), *Hypertension.* Berlin: Springer-Verlag, 1972.

173. VANDONGEN, R., PEART, W. S., and BOYD, G. W.: Adrenergic Stimulation of Renin Secretion in the Isolated Perfused Rat Kidney. *Circ. Res.* 32:290, 1973.

174. PASSO, S. S., ASSAYKEEN, T. A., ORSUKA, K., ET AL.: Effect of Stimulation of the Medulla Oblongata on Renin Secretion in Dogs. *Neuroendocrinology* 7:1, 1971.

175. ZEHR, J. E., and FEIGL, E. O.: Suppression of Renin Activity by Hypothalamic Stimulation. *Circ. Res.* 32: (Supp. I, 1-17), 1973.

176. DRAGSTEDT, L. R., LULU, D. J., RILEY, W. J., and LAWSON, L. J.: Cephalic Hypersecreting Primary Gastric Ulcer Patients. *Arch. Surg.* 102, 462, 1971.

177. COX, A. J.: Stomach Size and its Relation to Chronic Peptic Ulcer. *Arch. Pathol.* 54:407, 1953.

178. GRAVÄARD, E.: A Study of the Vagus Nerves at the Lower End of the Esophagus, With Special References to Duodenal Ulcer and Acute Gastroduodenal Ulcerations. *Scand. J. Gastroenterol.* 3:327, 1968.

179. LARAGH, J. H., SEALEY, J. E., and BRUNNER, H. R.: The Control of Aldosterone Secretion in Normal and Hypertensive Man: Abnormal Renin-Aldosterone Patterns in Low Renin Hypertension. *Amer. J. Med.* 53:649, 1972.

180. KALINER, M., ORANGE, R. P., and AUSTEN, K. F.: Immunological Release of Histamine and Slow Reacting Substance of Anaphylaxis From Human Lung. IV. Enhancement by Cholinergic and Alpha Adrenergic Stimulation. *J. Exp. Med.* 136:546, 1972.

181. ORANGE, R. P., AUSTEN, W. G., and AUSTEN, K. F.: Immunological Release of Histamine and Slow Reacting Substance of Anaphylaxis from Human Lung. I. Modulation by Agents Influencing Cellular Leveles of Cyclic 3', 5'-Adenosine Monophosphate. *J. Exp. Med.* 134:136s, 1971.

182. GOLD, W. M.: Asthma. *Amer. Thoracic Soc. News* 1:12, 1976.

183. SCADDING, J. G.: Meaning of Diagnostic Terms in Broncho-Pulmonary Disease. *Brit. Med. J.* 2:1425, 1963.

184. BRUCH, H.: Anorexia Nervosa and its Differential Diagnosis. *J. Nerv. Ment. Dis.* 141:555, 1966.

185. BRUCH, H.: *Eating Disorders.* New York: Basic Books, 1973.

186. HILL, O. W.: Anorexia Nervosa. In O. W. Hill (Ed.), *Modern Trends in Psychosomatic Medicine-3.* London: Butterworths, 1976.

187. KATZ, J. L., BOYAR, R. M., HELLMAN, L., and WEINER, H.: L.H.R.H. Responsiveness in Anorexia Nervosa. *Psychosom. Med.* (in press) 1977.

188. BOYAR, R. M., KATZ, J. L., ROFFWARG, H., WEINER, H., and HELLMAN, L.: Gonadotropin Secretory Patterns in Patients with Anorexia Nervosa and Normal Body Weight. *J. Clin. Endocrinol. Metab.* (in press).

189. KATZ, J. L., BOYAR, R. M., HELLMAN, L., and WEINER, H.: Anorexia Nervosa: Degree of Weight Recovery and the Normalization of Luteinizing Hormone Patterns are not related (in preparation).

190. RUSSELL, G. E. M.: Anorexia Nervosa: Its Identity as an Illness and its Treatment. In J. H. Price (Ed.), *Modern Trends in Psychological Medicine-2*, pp. 131-164. London: Butterworths, 1970.

191. FERGUSON-RAYPORT, S. M.: The Relation of Emotional Factors

to Recurrence of Thyrotoxicosis. *Canad. Med. Ass. J.* 15:993, 1956.

192. RUESCH, J., CHRISTIANSEN, C., PATTERSON, L. C., DEWEES, S., and JACOBSON, A.: Psychological Invalidism in Thyroidectomized Patients. *Psychosom. Med.* 9:77, 1947.

193. WIENER, D. M.: Personality Characteristics of Various Disability Groups. *Genet. Psychol. Monogr.* 45:175, 1952.

194. PASNAU, R. O. (Ed.): *Consultation-Liaison Psychiatry.* New York: Grune and Stratton, 1975.

195. STRAIN, J., and GROSSMAN, S. (Eds.): *Psychological Care of the Medically Ill.* New York: Appleton-Century-Crofts, 1975.

196. HARTMANN, H.: Psychoanalysis and the Concept of Health. *Int. J. Psa.* 20:1, 1939.

197. DUBOS, R.: *Man Adapting.* New Haven: Yale University Press, 1965.

2

Central Control in Endocrine Systems

H. Keith H. Brodie, M.D.

INTRODUCTION

Research in psychiatry has been hampered by the lack of animal models of the major mental illnesses, as well as by the relative inaccessibility of the human brain for biological study. With the discovery of drugs which are effective in the treatment of schizophrenia, mania, and depression, and with an understanding that these drugs affect certain of the monoaminergic systems in the human brain, several hypotheses have been proposed identifying specific defects in adrenergic, serotonergic, and dopaminergic neurotransmission as the biologic substrate of the major psychoses. The rate of release and turnover of these monoamines is difficult to assess. A study of human endocrine systems offers the opportunity to assess turnover in certain monoaminergic pathways controlling the release of polypeptides which activate steroid hormone release.

The purpose of this chapter is to review the neurobiology of human endocrine systems, the psychiatric aspects and precipitants of endocrinopathies, and endocrine changes associated with mental illness.

NEUROBIOLOGY OF ENDOCRINE SYSTEMS

The neurobiology of endocrine systems is a five-chain system (1). Figure 1 illustrates the five components of this chain. The first com-

FIGURE 1

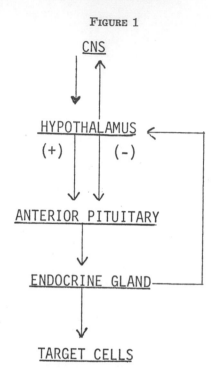

ponent is the central nervous system. Environmental stimuli are fed
in through multiple pathways to the mesencephalon which contains
dopaminergic, noradrenergic and serotonergic fibers. These fibers
enervate the limbic forebrain which in turn enervates the second component of the system, the hypothalamus.

The hypothalamus synthesizes polypeptide hormones which act
on the third system component, the pituitary gland. These hormones
are referred to as releasing factors or inhibiting factors. They are
released from nerve endings in the median eminence where they enter
capillaries of the primary plexus of the hypophysical-portal circulation which carries them through the long portal vessels of the hypo-
physical stalk into the sinusoids of the anterior lobe of the pituitary
gland. These releasing factors and inhibiting factors act on the pitui-

tary to either stimulate or diminish its release of hormones which activate the fourth system component, the endocrine glands.

Endocrine glands release steroid hormones which affect target cells in the body. In addition, the concentration of steroid hormones in the blood stream is monitored by the hypothalamus which increases or decreases pituitary activation of the endocrine gland in proportion to the amount of steroid produced. This feedback loop, as illustrated in Figure 1, is a negative feedback loop and serves as the primary control of the endocrine system.

To cause the release of four major pituitary hormones: follicle-stimulating hormone, luteinizing hormone, thyroid-stimulating hormone, and adrenocorticotropic hormone, the hypothalamus synthesizes polypeptides which stimulate the pituitary. Both inhibitory and stimulatory hypothalamic factors have been identified by bioassay for the regulation of prolactin, growth hormone, and melanocyte-stimulating hormone, all secreted by the pituitary gland. These factors are shown in Figure 1. Prolactin, growth hormone, and melanocyte-stimulating hormones do not activate endocrine glands per se, but act directly on target cells.

The control system involved in the release of cortisol from the adrenal cortex illustrates the physiology of the neuroendocrine system (Figure 2). Input to the hypothalamus from the central nervous system is mediated by neurons which are stimulated in a wide variety of stress situations, all of which seem to increase ACTH secretion from the anterior pituitary gland. Such events as acute trauma and burns, emotional stress, electroshock therapy, surgical operations, exercise, and hypoglycemia all seem to activate the hypothalamus to release corticotropin-releasing hormone (CRF). CRF activates the pituitary gland to produce adrenocorticotropic hormone, which in turn stimulates the adrenal cortex to release cortisol. Cortisol exerts a negative feedback on the pituitary gland, diminishing the release of ACTH and also a negative feedback on the hypothalamus, decreasing the release of corticotropin-releasing hormone. This hypothalamic-pituitary-adrenal axis serves to control the release of cortisol which in turn affects numerous target cells in the body.

The pituitary-thyroid axis is stimulated by cold or environmental

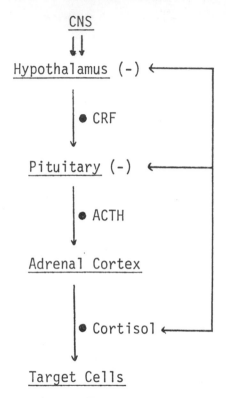

FIGURE 2

Hypothalamic—Pituitary axis controlling Cortisol
CNS: Central Nervous System
CRF: Corticotropin-releasing factor
ACTH: Adrenocorticotropic hormone

stress which activates the hypothalamus via noradrenergic neurons to secrete thyrotropic-releasing hormone. This in turn activates the pituitary gland to release thyroid-stimulating hormone (TSH) which activates the thyroid to release thyroid hormones which produce a negative feedback on the pituitary dampening the further release of TSH (Figure 3). The concentration of plasma TSH is a curvilinear function of the concentration of plasma thyroid hormone T_4. It has

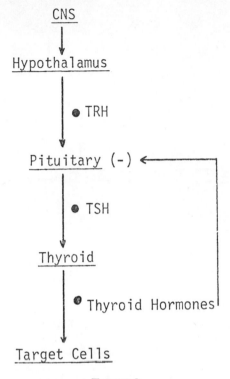

FIGURE 3

Hypothalamic—axis controlling thyroid hormones
TRH: Thyrotropin-releasing hormone
TSH: Thyrotropin-stimulating hormone

been hypothesized (2) that TSH serves as a positive feedback stimulus on the hypothalamus to increase its release of TRH at the same time TSH serves as a negative feedback on the CNS to diminish its activation of the hypothalamus to release TRH. Thus, the feedback loops in the hypothalamus-pituitary-thyroid axis, although complex, follow the general principles outlined in Figure 1.

The hypothalamus regulates the release of growth hormone from the pituitary gland. This hormone does not activate another endocrine

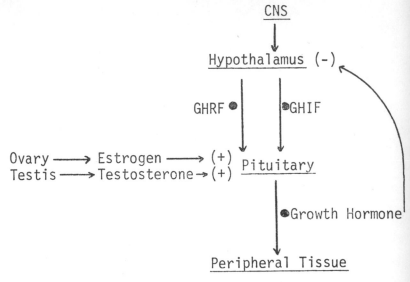

FIGURE 4

Hypothalamic—Pituitary axis controlling growth hormone
GHRF: Growth hormone releasing factor
GHIF: Growth hormone inhibiting factor

gland; rather it acts directly on peripheral tissue. Input from the CNS secondary to stress and exercise stimulates the hypothalamus to release growth hormone-releasing factor referred to as somatotropin releasing factor. This stimulus is mediated by a dopaminergic pathway. An inhibitory pathway, which is serotonergic, stimulates the release of growth hormone-inhibiting factor or somatotropin inhibiting factor from the hypothalamus. This factor diminishes the release of growth hormone from the pituitary gland and seems to be activated primarily during certain phases of the sleep cycle. Growth hormone serves as a negative feedback on the hypothalamus to diminish the release of growth hormone-releasing factor. The sex steroids, estrogen and testosterone, serve as a stimulus to the pituitary gland to release growth hormone (Figure 4).

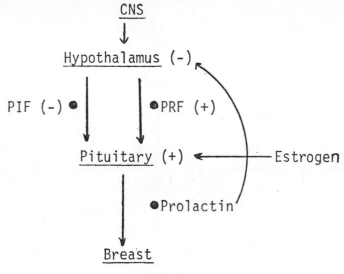

Hypothalamic—Pituitary axis controlling **prolactin**
PRF: Prolactin-releasing factor
PIF: Prolactin-inhibiting factor

The hypothalamic regulation of prolactin secretion is quite similar to the hypothalamic control of growth hormone concentrations. Specifically, suckling stimulates the breast which activates the CNS initiating a serotonergic stimulus to the hypothalamus to release prolactin-releasing factor (Figure 5). This in turn acts on the pituitary to release prolactin which in turn activates the breast. Stress as received by the CNS stimulates dopaminergic fibers to the hypothalamus to release a prolactin-inhibiting factor diminishing the release of prolactin by the pituitary. It is of note that estrogen excretions by the ovary and the placenta sensitize the pituitary to the effects of prolactin-releasing factor. It is interesting to note that Selye, many years ago, discovered that continued secretion of milk from the mammary gland after the delivery of the child depends primarily

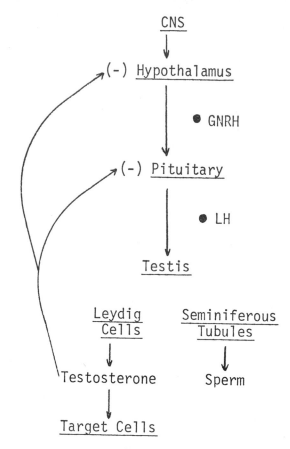

FIGURE 6

Hypothalamic—Pituitary axis controlling testosterone
GNRH: Gonadotropin-releasing factor
LH: Luteinizing hormone

upon the release of prolactin due to the mechanical stimulation of the nipple by suckling.

The pituitary-gonadotropin axis is enervated by noradrenergic fibers from the mesencephalon which stimulate the limbic forebrain bundle which in turn enervates the hypothalamus to secrete gonadotropin-releasing hormone (Figure 6). This hormone, a polypeptide, stimulates the release of follicle-stimulating hormone (FSH) and luteinizing hormone (LH), both referred to as gonadotropins. These compounds activate the testes. Luteinizing hormone stimulates the leydig cells of the testes to produce plasma testosterone. The follicle-stimulating hormone activates the seminiferous tubules to produce spermatozoa. There is a negative feedback on the hypothalamus activated by testosterone such that an increase in plasma testosterone decreases the pituitary secretion of luteinizing hormone by decreasing the secretion of gonadotropin-releasing hormone from the hypothalamus.

There is a more complicated relationship between gonadotropin-releasing hormone, LH, and the female estrogen hormones. If one reviews the sequence of events in the normal menstrual cycle, the release of LH and FSH appears to coincide with a slight peak in estrogen at the time of ovulation. A few days after this, progesterone level begins to rise, reaching a peak approximately eight days subsequent to the LH and FSH peaks just prior to ovulation. It is clear that estrogen and progesterone exert a negative effect on the hypothalamic release of gonadotropin hormone which is responsible for the hypothalamic release of LH and FSH. Thus, in the female, there is a sequential as well as a direct feedback loop which up until now has defied the development of a precise, mathematical model (Figure 7).

In summary, the endocrine control achieved by the hypothalamus originates in the central nervous system as activated by stress, suckling, exercise, and numerous other environmental stimuli. The CNS inputs to the hypothalamus through monoaminergic neurons in the mesencephalon which enervate the limbic forebrain which in turn enervates the hypothalamus (3). Hypothalamic activation of the anterior pituitary gland for the gonadotropic hormones and thyroid-

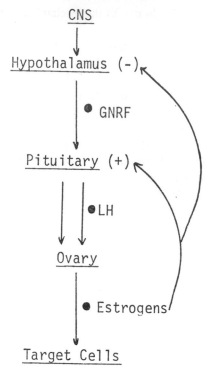

FIGURE 7

Hypothalamic—Pituitary axis controlling estrogens
LH: Luteinizing hormone
GNRF: Gonadotropin-releasing factor

stimulating hormone is mediated through catecholaminergic, primarily noradrenergic neurons which stimulate the hypothalamus to secrete releasing factors. These stimulate the anterior pituitary to secrete FSH, LH, and TSH. These compounds activate specific endocrine glands to produce a steroid hormone. Suprahypothalamic regulation of CRF release involves excitatory and inhibitory pathways, the latter mediated by adrenergic neurons. The release of prolactin, growth hormone, and melanocyte-stimulating hormone by the anterior pituitary is controlled by the hypothalamus through the release of inhibitory as well as releasing factors. For prolactin and growth hormone, dopaminergic and serotonergic fibers from the CNS to the hypothalamus are responsible for the release of inhibiting and releasing factors controlling excretion of these polypeptides. Specifically, serotonergic fibers activate the release of prolactin-releasing factor and somatotropin-inhibiting factor; dopaminergic fibers activate the release of prolactin-inhibiting factor and somatotropin-releasing factor. These factors in turn act on the anterior pituitary to either stimulate or decrease the release of prolactin and growth hormone.

The relationship between the monoaminergic pathways regulating the hypothalamus which regulate the pituitary secretion of hormones, some activating endocrine glands and others acting directly on other organs, is depicted in Figure 8.

There are three major monoaminergic pathways regulating hypothalamic function. Noradrenergic pathways are responsible for the release of gonadotropin-releasing factor and thyrotropin-releasing factor. Dopaminergic pathways are responsible for the release of prolactin inhibiting factor and somatotropin releasing factor. These four factors may be affected in depression if this illness is related to a decrease in catecholaminergic activity in human brain. In the treatment of schizophrenia, the administration of dopamine blockers diminishes the activation of the hypothalamus to release prolactin inhibiting factor thus increasing prolactin. Dopamine blockers also diminish somatotropin releasing factor with a subsequent decrease in the release of growth hormone. Serotonergic fibers are responsible for the stimulation of prolactin-releasing factor and somatotropin inhibiting factor. These pathways will be described in greater detail in the section of this chapter devoted to the topic of endocrinopathies associated with psychiatric illness.

PSYCHIATRIC ASPECTS AND PRECIPITANTS OF ENDOCRINOPATHIES

The psychiatric aspects and precipitants of endocrinopathies involve the very close relationship between the mesencephalon, the

FIGURE 8

Neuro-Endocrine Systems

Monoaminergic Pathway Regulating Hypophysiotropic Function	Hypothalamic Secretion	Pituitary Secretion	Endocrine Gland Secretion
Serotonin	Prolactin releasing factor	Prolactin	
Dopamine	Prolactin inhibiting factor		
Dopamine	Somatotropin releasing factor	Growth hormone	
Serotonin	Somatotropin inhibiting factor		
?	Melanocyte-stimulating hormone releasing factor	Melanocyte stimulating hormone	
?	Melanocyte-stimulating hormone inhibiting factor		
Norepinephrine	Gonadotropin releasing factor	Luteinizing hormone	Testosterone & Estrogen
		Follicle stimulating hormone	
Norepinephrine	Thyrotropin releasing factor	Thyroid stimulating hormone	Thyroxine
?	Corticotropin releasing hormone	Adrenocorticotropic hormone	Cortisol

limbic forebrain, and the hypothalamus which results in direct input to the pituitary gland and to the control of several endocrine glands. Thus, it is to be expected that environmental stress and psychological factors influence to no small degree the secretion of endocrine hormones. An increase or decrease in the concentration of these hormones may effect the brain producing abnormalities of mood, cognition or orientation.

Hypopituitarism is caused by postpartum necrosis of the anterior pituitary gland, a condition known as Sheehan's syndrome, or by tumors such as chromophobe adenoma or crainopharyngioma or by cranial injuries and infections. This syndrome is most pronounced in its effect on the thyroid gland and on the adrenals. It is associated with a severe and retarded depression, apathy, lethargy, memory impairment for recent events and in severe cases with delusions and signs of a mild organic brain sydrome.

There are two principal syndromes associated with an increase in cortisol levels—One is Cushing's syndrome caused by adrenal hyperplasia, or tumors of the adrenal or pituitary glands. This syndrome is primarily associated with depression. In Whybrow's excellent review of the literature on psychiatric changes accompanying Cushing's syndrome (4), he notes in four studies involving 54 patients that over a third of the patients exhibited depression while only slightly over 3 percent showed euphoria. Sixteen percent of the patients studied evidenced disturbed cognition and slightly under 10 percent showed symptoms of psychosis. The depressions in these patients seemed equally divided between agitated and retarded with patients showing marked emotional lability, impotence, and hypersensitivity to environmental stimuli. Psychoses associated with Cushing's syndrome are usually paranoid in nature involving auditory hallucinations. Koran and Hamburg (5) indicate that 15-25 percent of patients with Cushing's syndrome evidenced psychotic symptoms.

The other population of patients with increased cortisol levels is the group to whom this hormone is being administered in the treatment of some disease. It is of note that these patients exhibit a much greater degree of euphoria, very few becoming depressed according to Whybrow's review of 36 cases published in the literature of which 50 percent became euphoric on steroid administration and only 3 percent depressed. A third of these subjects showed disturbed cognition and 14 percent developed psychoses.

Thus, in summary, the principal psychiatric manifestation of an increased cortisol level is an affective disturbance: Of those patients with Cushing's disease, over a third become depressed whereas half of those patients given exogenous cortisol become euphoric.

Addison's disease is associated with a decrease in cortisol production from the adrenal gland and results primarily from disturbed hypothalamic, pituitary or adrenal gland pathology. Patients with Addison's disease are extremely irritable, show predominately a depressive mood with psychomotor retardation and great apathy and weakness. The majority of patients with Addison's disease have these mental changes as well as a mild degree of organic brain syndrome with a prominent memory defect. Psychoses in Addisonian patients are rare (4).

Whereas the treatment of choice for the psychiatric sequelae associated with Cushing's disease or the administration of exogenous steriods is surgical intervention to remove the hormone producing tumor or a decrease in the exogenously administered steroids, the treatment of the mental symptoms associated with Addison's disease is the administration of cortisone.

Hyperthyroidism (Graves' disease) produces mild to moderate emotional and cognitive disturbances in almost all patients with this syndrome resulting from excessive amounts of thyroid hormones. Hyperthyroid patients are anxious, tense, irritable, hyperexcitable and emotionally labile. They frequently show depression without psychomotor retardation, they have impairment of recent memory and are easily distractible. Chances of psychosis developing in a hyperthyroid patient are low; however, if psychosis appears it may resemble schizophrenia or manic depressive psychosis. Prior to the advent of anti-thyroid drugs, the development of thyroid storm was associated with an acute brain syndrome progressing to coma (5).

Hypothyroidism occurs in association with Hashimoto's thyroiditis, pituitary failure to produce TSH, iodine deficiency, the administration of radioactive iodine to control hyperthyroidism, or subsequent to a subtotal thyroidectomy. Koran and Hamburg (5) note that mental changes are always associated with hypothyroidism. In infants, hypothyroidism results in the development of cretinism, a syndrome associated with sluggishness, somnolence and lack of interest in food. The untreated infant shows evidence of retarded bone age, delayed eruption of teeth, dwarfed stature and severe mental retardation. Cretinism is usually due to a maternal deficiency of iodine.

In the adult, hypothyroidism produces psychomotor retardation, slowness in comprehension, drowsiness, and impairment of recent memory and decreased initiative. The mood is labile and can vary from depression to excitability and mania. If untreated, hypothyroidism can lead to the development of myxedema madness which is associated with the clouding of consciousness, delirium, stupor, organic brain syndrome and ultimately coma. Suspiciousness and auditory hallucinations are common.

The psychiatric sequelae associated with excess thyroid hormones are treated with antithyroid drugs; the hypothyroid patient is treated with thyroid replacement.

It is of note that there are no distinctive psychiatric disturbances associated with an excess of decrease in growth hormone concentrations. Patients with acromegaly, the syndrome associated with an increased growth hormone secretion by the pituitary, have been noted to have some alterations of personality consisting mainly of a lack of initiative and spontaneity. However, Smith et al. (6) in their excellent review conclude that no specific psychiatric abnormality is associated with this disease.

Hypoparathyroidism has been associated with an organic brain syndrome (4). This decrease in parathyroid secretion results in a diminution in the circulating available calcium and may result from surgical trauma to the parathyroid gland in the course of a thyroid resection. Hypoparathyroidism is associated with deliruim, dementia and, in over 50 percent of the cases reviewed by Whybrow (4), a disturbed cognition resulting in impaired intellectual functioning.

Hyperparathyroidism was found by Whybrow (4) to be associated in over 40 percent of the cases studied with depression. This syndrome is associated with an increase in parathormone and an increased serum calcium level. Cognition is also impaired in hyper-parathyroidism and Petersen (7) has demonstrated a curvilinear relationship between the impairment of cognition and the increase in serum calcium concentrations in his subjects.

Changes in sex hormones play a major role in the development of psychiatric symptoms. Koran and Hamburg (5) note a definite increase in the number of women who commit suicide and acts of violence during the four days before menstruation and during the days of menstrual bleeding as compared to the rest of the 28 day menstrual cycle. They claim that 20 percent of women regularly experience moderate to severe psychic mood changes during the course of the menstrual cycle, which is usually characterized by a period of irritability, anxiety, and depression in the few days before the menstrual period at a time of rapid decline in both serum estrogen and progesterone levels. Thus, it may be the sharp decline in levels of these steroids which is responsible for the mental changes associated with this time of the menstrual cycle. Anticipatory guidance is recommended for these women in order to help them cope during periods of increased emotional vulnerability. Benzodiazapine may be helpful for a woman who has severe and recurrent episodes of anxiety during this time. Further, if premenstrual water retention is a problem, periodic utilization of a diuretic may prove beneficial. For patients with severe dysmenorrhea, an effective analgesic should be considered.

Psychiatric symptoms seen in association with rapidly decreasing steroid levels in the female occur also during the postpartum period. Koran (5) notes that women in their reproductive years have a four- to five-fold increased risk of mental illness during their first three months postpartum. Two-thirds of those patients developing postpartum syndromes will become symptomatic within the first 10 days after delivery. During the first postpartum week, estrogen and progesterone levels decrease to approximately 1 percent of their antepartum values. In addition, there is a rapid increase in the secretion of prolactin during this period. Thus, the brain is exposed to a rapidly fluctuating endocrine climate which may relate to the development of a postpartum psychiatric disorder. Postpartum disorders are associated with suspiciousness, insomnia, restlessness, irritability, marked depression and in severe form may be associated with hallucinations of voices telling the patient to kill her child. It is of interest that Freedman et al. (8) note up to 40 percent of normal women report emotional or cognitive dysfunction in the early postpartum period, with psychosis occurring in approximately 0.2 percent of the women studied. Treatment of the disorder should emphasize anticipatory guidance in prenatal care, the use of minor tranquilizers and sedatives if the symptoms are mild, and the use of major tranquilizers should a frank psychosis develop.

The involutional period is associated with a decrease in estrogens and testosterone which in turn relates to an increase in pituitary secretion of luteinizing hormone and follicle stimulating hormone. It is unclear which is related to the symptoms of depression and paranoia seen in the involutional period of the life cycle. No doubt psychological factors related to the loss of reproductive capacity and the experience of having seen one's finest day relate to the onset of these involutional syndromes. It is of note that estrogen replacement therapy seems to reverse the loss of sexual interest, as well as decreasing anxiety, irritability and depression associated with menopause. The dose administered should be small, approximately 0.5 miligrams of diethylstilbestrol daily over 20 days repeated after a drug holiday of one week's duration.

In the male, Klinefelter's syndrome, a genetic disorder associated with hypogonadism, results in an absence of the normal increase in testosterone secretion at puberty (9). This results in impotence, a diminished IQ, and an increased incidence of a variety of psychotic states. The character structure of patients with Klinefelter's syndrome includes schizoid withdrawal and antisocial psychopathy. Testosterone replacement therapy in the adult appears to be of little value but, according to Sachar (9), it may be of value in the child or adolescent.

It is of note that diabetes mellitus, a disease affecting approximately 2 percent of our population, is associated with mental symptoms which become especially prominent in severe untreated diabetic acidosis (9). This syndrome is associated with confusion, obtundation, somnolence, and eventually coma (10). Kety et al. (11) have shown that cerebral oxygen consumption in this state is substantially reduced and that in all likelihood the mental symptoms are not a result of insulin deficiency per se but rather related to the presence of blood borne ketones which act like ether anesthetics on CNS. It should be noted that emotional stress has been identified as triggering diabetes mellitus through an alteration in the rates of secretion of ACTH, growth hormone, and adrenal steroids, all of which alter insulin secretion affecting glucose metabolism.

Hypoglycemia (9) is associated with numerous mental symptoms, including anxiety, anger, violence, apathy, confusion, psychomotor agitation or retardation, depression, delusions, hallucinations, and fugue states. This syndrome in which blood glucose levels are less than 50 milligrams per milliliter is associated with insulin secreting tumors as well as exogenous insulin overdose in diabetic patients. It is also associated with a prediabetic state and other disorders of carbohydrate metabolism. There is evidence to suggest that stress may induce a reactive hypoglycemia which can produce many of these symptoms. The treatment of hypoglycemia should be directed at the underlying organic cause. For essential reactive hypoglycemia a low carbohydrate diet rich in protein and fat is often beneficial. Psychotherapy has been reported to be curative in one study (12).

ENDOCRINE CHANGES IN ASSOCIATION WITH THE MAJOR PSYCHIATRIC SYNDROMES

Perhaps the best studied syndrome associated with an endocrinopathy is periodic catatonia. In this syndrome, the periodic psychoses are related to a significant rise in the plasma concentration of protein bound iodine as demonstrated by Gjessing in 1964 (13).

A study of the schizophrenias has to date unearthed no significant relationship between the onset or course of these psychoses and any abnormality of the endocrine systems. However, it should be noted that compounds used in the treatment of schizophrenia, the butyrophenones and phenothiazines, produce a dopaminergic blockage which in turn diminishes the secretion of prolactin inhibiting factor, thus resulting in an increase in serum prolactin levels. Thus, the measurement of prolactin in schizophrenic patients being treated by pheno-thiazines or butyrophenones may be a good index of whether or not enough medication is being given to achieve dopaminergic blockage (14).

Unlike schizophrenia, depression is associated with marked endo-crine changes. Sachar (15) has noted a marked elevation in cortisol levels in depressed patients which he relates to diminished hypothala-mic catecholaminergic activity. Specifically, the release of cortico-tropin releasing factor is inhibited by catecholaminergic neurons. If depression is associated with a catecholamine deficit as hypothesized by Bunney and Davis (16) and Schildkraut (17), one would expect an increase in CRF release due to the absence of inhibition from catecholaminergic fibers. The increased CRF produces an increase in ACTH and a subsequent elevation of cortisol levels. Further, as noted above, noradrenergic fibers are responsible for the release of gonadotropic releasing factor which in turn stimulates secretion of luteinizing hormone. If depression is associated with a diminution in catecholaminergic activity, then it should also be associated with a decrease in luteinizing hormone. This has been elegantly demonstrated by Sachar (15) and his group who have shown that postmenopausal unipolar depressed women have a lower mean plasma LH concentra-tion compared to age matched normals.

Recent work from Goodwin's laboratory (18) at the NIMH in-dicates that prolactin suppression which is produced by an increase in the prolactin inhibiting factor secondary to the administration of L-DOPA differentiates between unipolar and bipolar depressed patients. He notes a decrease in serum prolactin levels after a 500 milligram oral dose of Levodopa. Goodwin noted that the eight bipolar patients studied showed a statistically significant drop in serum prolactin which was greater than that noted in unipolar de-pressed patients. This difference was significant during the three hours of the study. This exciting finding may allow us to phar-macologically dissect depressed patients into a unipolar and bipolar group. Because of the efficacy of Lithium in the treatment of bipolar patients, the prolactin suppression test may be a good indicator of Lithium response and clearly warrants further study.

Because the releasing factor responsible for the stimulation of growth hormone secretion in the pituitary is controlled by dopaminergic neurones, Sachar hypothesized that depressed patients, due to a catecholaminergic deficit, might secrete less growth hormone in response to insulin induced hypoglycemia (19). He has shown the failure of depressed patients to secrete growth hormone in response to insulin induced hypoglycemia and hypothesized that this is related to a depletion of CNS catecholamines. Thus it is of note that all of the endocrine changes associated with depression can be explained by the catecholamine hypothesis of affective disease.

Another psychiatric syndrome associated with endocrinopathy is anorexia nervosa. In this illness, serum LH levels are below normal (20) and may relate to the amenorrhea seen in this patient population. Further, serum T-3 levels are noted to be below normal (21) in patients with anorexia nervosa. Because both LH and T-3 are secreted by hypothalamic pituitary systems which are activated by noradrenergic neurons, it is possible to relate anorexia nervosa to a decrease in norepinephrine activity in the hypothalamus. This finding has important therapeutic implications.

Summary

In reviewing the neurobiology of human endocrine systems, we have noted that the central nervous system receives information from the environment and stimulates the mesencephalon and limbic system which transmit through monoaminergic fibers impulses to the hypothalamus which result in the release of hormones from the pituitary and other endocrine glands. The concentrations of these hormones are controlled through negative feedback loops, and shifts in hormonal concentration may be responsible for changes in human mood, cognition, and orientation. Several psychiatric illnesses are associated with changes in endocrine status. These may be explained on the basis of a common CNS defect in monoaminergic transmission which may indicate a possible mode of therapeutic intervention. Drugs utilized in the treatment of schizophrenia may be responsible for prolactin release which might serve as an important indicator of dopaminergic blockage and possibly of therapeutic efficacy.

No doubt future work in this field will provide us with more meaningful utilization of endocrine function as a determinant of distinct subgroups of depressed or schizophrenic patients, for an assessment of the peripheral endocrine status of these patients serves as a window on the monoaminergic systems of the CNS allowing us an opportunity to measure their activity. An assessment of the activities of these systems may allow us to diagnose and to treat the mentally ill with greater precision. For the monoaminergic balances seen in the limbic system are clearly important in the development of schizophrenia or the affective psychoses and they are easily studied through an assessment of endocrine function.

REFERENCES

1. REICHLIN, S.: Neuroendocrinology. Chapter 12 in R. H. Williams (Ed.), *Textbook of Endocrinology*. Philadelpia: W. B. Saunders Co., 1974, pp. 774-826.
2. *Ibid*, p. 794.
3. SACHAR, E. J.: A neuroendocrine strategy in the psychobiological study of depressive illness. Chapter 8 in J. Mendels (Ed.), *The Psychobiology of Depression*. New York: Spectrum Publications, Inc., 1975, pp. 123-132.
4. WHYBROW, P. C. and HURWITZ, T.: Psychological disturbances associated with endocrine disease and hormone therapy. In E. J. Sachar (Ed.), *Hormones, Behavior, and Psychopathology*. New York: Raven Press, 1976, p. 125-143.
5. KORAN, L. M. and HAMBURG, D. A.: Psychophysiological endocrine disorders. Chapter 26.9 in A. M. Freedman, H. I. Kaplan, and B. J. Sadock (Eds.), *Comprehensive Textbook of Psychiatry, II*. Baltimore: Williams and Wilkins Co., 1975, pp. 1673-1684.
6. SMITH, C. K., BARISH, J., CORREA, J., and WILLIAMS, R. H.: Psychiatric disturbance in endocrinologic disease. *Psychosomatic Medicine*, Vol. 34, pp. 69-86, 1972.
7. PETERSEN, P.: Psychiatric disorders in primary hyperparathyroidism. *J. Clin. Endocrinol. Metab.*, 28:1491, 1968.
8. FREEDMAN, A. M., KAPLAN, H. I. and SADOCK, B. J.: *Modern Synopsis of Comprehensive Psychiatry, II*. Pg. 523, 1976.
9. SACHAR, E. J.: Psychiatric disturbances associated with endocrine disorders. Chapter 12 in M. F. Reiser (Ed.), *American Handbook of Psychiatry, IV*. New York: Basic Books, Inc., 1975, pp. 299-312.
10. WILLIAMS, R. H. and PORTE, D.: The pancreas. Chapter 9 in R. H. Williams (Ed.), *Textbook of Endocrinology*. Philadelphia: W. B. Saunders, Co., 1974, pp. 502-626.

11. KETY, S. S., POLIS, B. D., NADLER, C. S., ET AL.: The blood flow and oxygen consumption of the human brain in diabetic acidosis and coma. *J. Clin. Invest.*, 27:500-510, 1948.
12. MARKS, C. and ROSE F. C.: *Hypoglycemia.* Oxford: Blackwell, 1965.
13. GJESSING, L.: Studies of periodic catatonia: I: Blood levels of PBI and urinary excretion of VMA in relation to clinical course. *J. Psychiat. Res.*, 2:123, 1964.
14. CROW, T. J., DEAKIN, J. F. W., JOHNSTONE, E. C. and LONGDEN, A.: Dopamine and schizophrenia. *The Lancet* (ii), pp. 563-566, 1976.
15. SACHAR, E. J.: A neuroendocrine strategy in the psychobiological study of depressive illness. Chapter 8 in J. Mendels (Ed.), *The Psychobiology of Depression.* New York: Spectrum Publications, Inc., 1975, p. 129.
16. BUNNEY, W. E., JR. and DAVIS, J. M.: Norepinephrine in depressive reactions: A review. *Arch. Gen. Psychiat.*, 13:483-494, 1965.
17. SCHILDKRAUT, J. J.: The catecholamine hypothesis of affective disorders: A review of supporting evidence. *Amer. J. Psychiat.*, 122:509-522, 1965.
18. GOLD, P. W., GOODWIN, F. K., WEHR, T., REBAR, R., and SACK, R.: Growth hormone and prolactin response to levodopa in affective illness. *The Lancet* (ii), pp. 1308-1309, 1976.
19. SACHAR, E. J., FINKELSTEIN, J. and HELLMAN, L.: Growth hormone responses in depressive illness: Response to insulin tolerance test. *Arch. Gen. Psychiat.*, 24:263-269, 1971.
20. KATZ, J. L.: Psychoendocrine considerations in anorexia nervosa. Chapter 7 in E. J. Sachar (Ed.), *Topics in Psychoendocrinology.* New York: Grune and Stratton, 1975, pp. 121-133.
21. CROXSON, M. S. and IBBERTSON, H. K.: Low serum triiodothyronine (T_3) and hypothyroidism in anorexia nervosa. *J. Clin. Endocrinol. Metab.*, 44:167-174, 1977.

3

Recent Advances in Psychophysiology: Potential Relevance to Liaison Psychiatry

Robert L. Roessler, M.D.

This chapter is concerned with the integration of results from the experimental laboratory with clinical problems. Each of the following specific questions will be addressed: 1) What is the effect of modifying stimulus characteristics upon physiological responses? 2) What is the relationship between relatively stable characteristics of humans (traits) and physiological responses? 3) What is the effect of fluctuating states upon physiological responses? 4) Most importantly, what is the effect of the interactions of all of the foregoing classes of variables? In addition, the current status of biofeedback research and its clinical applications will be discussed.

Let us turn first to a review of some well established effects of modifying stimuli upon the physiological responses of normal persons. Experimental psychophysiology has been concerned to a considerable degree with the study of the physiological responses to change in the intensity of simple light, sound, temperature, pain and tactile stimuli. These experiments have shown that: 1) There are a variety of relationships between stimulus intensity and response magnitude.

95

Depending upon the modality of the stimulation and the response variable, the response may be linear, curvilinear or all-or-none (1, 2). 2) If the stimulus does not change, habituation occurs, i.e., the degree of response to successive stimuli decreases progressively (3). 3) "Signal stimuli," those which require some behavioral response, evoke responses which do not habituate, or do so at a different rate than those not requiring a response (4). 4) When the pattern of response variables is examined in relationship to the nature of stimulation, there is so-called "stimulus specificity" (5). The pattern among physiological responses elicited by light differs from that elicited by sound, for example. 5) The temporal context of a stimulus influences the degree of response (6). One important pattern produced by relatively simple changes, such as decreasing the frequency of stimulus occurrence, results in an "orienting" response characterized by cephalic vasodilation associated with peripheral vasoconstriction. This pattern contrasts with that evoked by very intense stimuli, particularly painful ones; such stimulation results in a "defensive" response, characterized by generalized vasoconstriction. Orienting and defensive responses were first defined by the Russian physiologist Sokolov in the early 1960s and have since been confirmed by investigators throughout the world (3, 4, 9). It is clear that even relatively minor changes in stimulus configuration can produce changes in the pattern of physiological response. Moreover, the nature of the defensive response suggests a possible relationship to the pattern elicited by noxious stimuli, a possibility certainly relevant to our clinical concerns. (I will return to this possibility later in the context of discussing the effects of the individual differences.) 6) The time required for recovery is in general a function of the magnitude of response (7).

What are the implications of the foregoing facts of liaison psychiatry? The most important implication is that there is no such phenomenon as generalized activation. Neither the sympathetic nor parasympathetic divisions of the autonomic nervous system discharge as a whole nor does any other system, including the central nervous system and the endocrine system (8). Both simple and complex stimuli elicit stimulus-specific patterns of response; i.e., there are as many patterns of physiological response as there are stimuli and patterns of stimuli. The human organism has a repertoire of physiological and behavioral responses that facilitate exquisite adaptation to the most subtle changes in environment. We should therefore abandon such terms as "activation" and "stress" because of the simplistic notions of physiological and behavioral organization which they imply. Instead, we should study very carefully the changes in pattern produced by systematically modifying stimulus configurations.

One way of systematically modifying stimulus configuration is the use of motion pictures. Relaxing, humorous and sexually arousing motion pictures induce differing patterns of response from those intended to provoke anxiety (10, 11, 12). Similarly, recollection of events evoking different emotions have been reported to be associated with different patterns of response in facial muscles (13).

These results have obvious clinical relevance, suggesting that the degree of response in some physiological measures and the pattern among them might be employed as indirect, quantified measures of the intensity and type of stimuli impinging upon a person at a given time. However, the implied isomorphism between stimulus and response is far too simple, as clinicians would be the first to suspect. Variables other than stimulus variables also critically affect response magnitude and patterning.

For a more complete understanding of response patterning, it is necessary to examine the effects of individual differences. While many individual differences—age, sex, intelligence and race—affect physiological responses, we are most concerned in liaison psychiatry with individual differences related to psychiatric diagnosis and to personality. Psychophysiological research in both these areas has been active. In reviewing this research I will focus upon the same response variables discussed earlier in relation to stimulus effects: response magnitude, habituation and the orienting and defensive responses.

Among psychiatric patients in general, those showing the greater magnitude of response to orienting stimuli have a better prognosis than those who respond with lesser magnitude. Those with the better prognosis also habituate more rapidly (14). When anxious patients are compared with healthy controls on rate of habituation to orienting stimuli, the rate of habituation is more rapid in healthy subjects than in anxious patients; within the patient group, the most anxious patients habituate least rapidly. Agitated depressed patients habituate even more slowly, and retarded depressives show so little response that habituation cannot be measured. Conversion hysterics do not habituate at all (15). Among schizophrenic patients, approximately half do not respond to orienting stimuli. Those who do respond habituate very little as compared with healthy subjects (16). Psychopaths also show a lesser degree of response to orienting stimuli than do healthy subjects and show lesser habituation as well (17).

The foregoing summary of research on the physiological response to simple stimuli among psychiatric patients supports the following generalization. The more severe the degree of psychopathology, the lesser the degree of physiological response and the slower the rate of habituation. Expressed positively, the adaptive physiological response, as defined by the responses of persons free of psychopathology, is a large initial response followed by rapid diminution of response to subsequent identical stimuli. The adaptive utility of this pattern might be expressed as follows: when a stimulus evokes an orienting response, the psychologically healthy person is strongly alerted for potential action. However, when the stimulus is subsequently assessed as one not requiring action, presentations of the same stimulus thereafter are assessed progressively more rapidly as not requiring action until they evoke no physiological response whatever. In psychopathology this capacity to discriminate is impaired and the degree of impairment is greater in persons with more severe pathology.

The relationship of personality variables to patterns of physiological response has also been the focus of extensive research. Neuroticism, anxiety, ego strength, defensiveness, repression-sensitization, locus of control, field dependence, extroversion, and impulsivity are the traits which have been most studied. They have been so extensively studied, in fact, that it will be helpful to examine first the

TABLE 1

Intercorrelations Among Personality Variables
(*N = 135, †N = 42, ‡N = 30)

	Ego Strength	Neuroticism	Trait Anxiety	Repression	Extroversion	Impulsivity	Field Dependence	External Control
Ego Strength*	1.00							
Neuroticism*	−.72	1.00						
Trait Anxiety*	−.76	.88	1.00					
Repression*	−.75	.87	.91	1.00				
Extroversion*	.00	.00	.00	.50	1.00			
Impulsivity†	−.47	.33	.50	.33	.64	1.00		
Field Dependence‡	−.36	.41	.34	—	.28	—	1.00	
External locus of control‡	−.29	.46	—	—	.00	.05	.05	1.00

relationships among them to assist in organizing, interpreting and generalizing the results of innumerable individual studies.

With the exception of field dependence, the usual measures of personality variables in experimental psychophysiological research have been scores on self-report personality inventories. Factor analysis of the items in such inventories typically yield two primary factors, neuroticism and extroversion. If these self-report dimensions are valid and if our clinical theories are correct, high neuroticism should be related to high trait anxiety, to high defensiveness, to low ego strength, to field dependence, to high repression, and to external locus of control. Similarly, impulsivity should be positively correlated with extroversion and negatively with ego strength. Table 1 summarizes the empirical relationships of these variables among the subjects in a number of experiments. As one can see, the predicted theoretical relationships do in fact exist. We can therefore summarize the principal relationships between personality and physiological measures under two groups of studies: those relating to ego strength or neuroticism and those related to extroversion.

The greater the degree of ego strength, the greater the degree of physiological response to standardized stimuli (10). This generalization is illustrated specifically by the mean skin conductance response of high and low ego strength subjects shown in Figure 1. Note that the high ego strength subjects respond more than do the low ego strength subjects to each of the three conditions: a humorous film, a bland travelogue film and rest. Note also that the response of the high ego strength group is much more variable under all three conditions and that habituation occurs during the bland film and during rest but not during the humorous film. (The rise at the end of the bland film was apparently a response to finale background music.) The low ego strength subjects also failed to discriminate among different stimulus conditions as much as did the high ego strength subjects. This was illustrated by subtracting the temporally corresponding values during the bland film from those during the humorous film. These difference scores are shown in the upper right in the figure. Note that these skin conductance difference scores are lower in the low ego strength group, indicating that they failed to

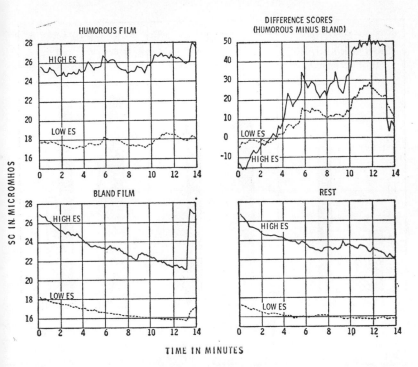

FIGURE 1. Mean skin conductance responses of a group of high ego strength subjects and a group of low ego strength subjects during a humorous film, during a bland film, and during rest.

discriminate as much physiologically between a relaxing film and a humorous one as did the high ego strength subjects. Parallel results were obtained in an experiment in which the physiological response to a noxious film, a bland film, and rest were compared (10). Low ego strength (high neurotic subjects) are less, not more, physiologically responsive than are subjects high in ego strength and this lesser responsiveness is not specific to the character of stimulation insofar as the skin conductance variable is concerned. (This lack of stimulus specificity in skin conductance should not be construed as an exception to my previous comments regarding stimulus specificity; other

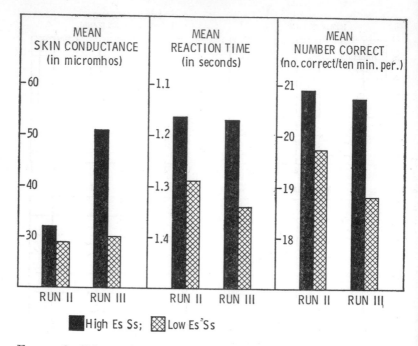

FIGURE 2. Skin conductance and performance data during a shock avoidance vigilance task following sleep (run II) and following sleep deprivation (run III).

physiological variables in these experiments did differ with the character of the stimuli.)

The subjects in the foregoing experiments were not required to respond behaviorally. What are the differences between high and low ego strength subjects when a response is required? Figure 2 shows the skin conductance responses of high and low ego strength groups when they were required to detect a signal of impending electric shock and abort that shock by pressing an appropriate button. This data is derived from an experiment in which the subjects first practiced on the task (run I), then under a baseline acclimated condition (run II) and finally after 24 hours of sleep deprivation (18). Note again the differences between the two groups in skin conductance levels. Note also that the skin conductance level of the high ego strength group rose under the sleep deprivation condition while that of the low ego strength group did not change significantly. In this experiment there were also measures of performance. As you see, the high ego strength group maintained the rapidity of their reaction time and the number of correct reponses following sleep deprivation, while the performance of the low ego strength group deteriorated. Under signal conditions, then, the degree of physiological response is also greater in high ego strength subjects, just as it is in response to simple non-signal stimuli. This greater physiological responsivity is, in turn, associated with better performance.

The degree of habituation under signal conditions was examined in a similar experiment in which the subjects performed on the same vigilance task (10). High ego strength subjects under these conditions *increased* in their level of skin conductance over time while low ego strength subjects decreased. This is a direction of difference opposite to that under non-signal conditions, where the habituation of low ego strength subjects was less than that of high ego strength subjects. We can now add to the generalizations listed after discussing the adaptive physiological response to non-signal stimuli. The adaptive physiological response to signal stimuli is a strong response continued as long as a behavioral response is required; failure to respond strongly and to continue to respond is associated with a decrement in performance.

There is also evidence that the trait of extroversion is related to the magnitude of physiological responses and to their patterning (e.g., 19, 20). There is evidence, too, of a relationship between impulsivity, a component of extroversion, and psychophysiological responses and a relationship between impulsivity and simple behavioral responses as well (21). Time does not permit detailing these results but they can be summarized by stating that they parallel approximately those discussed earlier in relation to psychopathy. To the extent that the parallel is only approximate, they reflect an interaction of extroversion with ego strength. The physiological patterns associated with a combination of low ego strength and high extroversion ("neurotic psychopath") differ from the patterns associated with high ego strength and high extroversion, for example (22). The physiological correlates of the interaction among these personality variables are not yet fully understood. Further research in this area is necessary.

Another individual difference of great clinical importance is individual response (IR) specificity. IR specificity is the tendency for a given person to respond most on the same physiological variable, regardless of the nature of the stimulus (23). Some persons respond most strongly with a rise in blood pressure to all stimuli, for example. In the history of psychosomatic medicine, this phenomenon is related to the crucial question of why one person develops hypertension and another person develops a peptic ulcer in circumstances which appear to be very similar. I recall being asked this question during my American Board orals 25 years ago. My answer then was that it was not known. Sadly, the answer is still largely unknown; we have learned very little about individual response specificity in 25 years. There is more evidence of a familial incidence of some types of individual response specificity, such as blood pressure responding, but it is not clear which variables contribute to this familial incidence. There is a great need for intensive longitudinal research on IR specificity to clarify the etiology of psychophysiological disorders. In addition, IR specificity complicates the interpretation of the results of experiments focused upon individual differences in patterns of physiological response. Further, in all experiments focused upon the relationship between stimuli and physiological responses, a sufficiently large number of subjects must be used to offset the fact that some persons will be IR specific, i.e., will respond maximally on a given variable regardless of the nature of stimulation.

Now let us turn to a consideration of the effect of states upon physiological responding. While it is clear that we must take many states into account clinically, I will emphasize two to illustrate the importance of states generally. Earlier, I presented evidence of the effects of fatigue induced by sleep deprivation upon physiological responsivity and its differential effect upon high and low ego strength subjects. I will now underscore the importance of the inter-action of state with trait by directing your attention again to Figure 2. If fatigue had not been taken into account there would have been no apparent personality effect, i.e., if both fatigued and non-fatigued physiological and performance levels were averaged. The clinical importance of these interaction effects is also illustrated by the vicious circle with which we are so often concerned in liaison psychiatry. Psychopathology, particularly depression and anxiety, affect the efficiency of sleep and reduced sleep efficiency in turn leads to further fatigue. The further fatigue in turn leads to further deviation in patterns of physiological and behavioral responses.

Another state variable of great importance in determining the pattern of physiological responses is that of attention or involve-ment (24). If subjects are not involved sufficiently to follow instruc-tions, for example, their physiological and behavioral responses will of course be different than if they do attend to instructions. Expressed differently, if subjects' attention is directed inward rather than outward, their physiological and behavioral responses will reflect this direction of attention. The differing physiological pat-terns associated with attention outward versus attention inward have been the subject of intensive basic research. Lacey has labeled the physiological pattern associated with attention outward as "frac-tionation of response" (25). In a number of experiments he and others demonstrated repeatedly that when attention is directed inward, as during a mental arithmetic task ("environmental rejec-tion," in Lacey's terms) both the heart rate and skin conductance increase. On the other hand, when subjects' attention is directed outward, as it is when they have received a warning signal to per-form on a reaction time task ("taking in," in Lacey's terms), heart rate decelerates and skin conductance increases. Moreover, the degree of heart rate deceleration is strongly related to a behavioral measure, the rapidity of reaction time. There is some evidence that the physiological differences between attention directed inward and attention directed outward parallel those distinguishing the orienting and defensive patterns described earlier; the physiological pattern associated with the orienting response is similar to attention outward and the defensive response pattern is similar to attention inward (9).

The mechanisms underlying these differing physiological patterns have been the focus of considerable research and debate. The phenomenon itself is one of the hard facts in psychophysiology, however. It has also been shown to have direct clinical relevance. The pattern of phobic patients' physiological responses to phobic stimuli is cardiac acceleration associated with increased skin conductance (a defensive or attention inward response); their responses to neutral and ambiguous stimuli are characterized by cardiac deceleration paired with an increase in skin conductance, an attention outward response (25, 26, 27). There is evidence, in other, words, that the defensive response may be related to state anxiety induced by phobic stimuli.

Spence and his collaborators used this experimentally derived information to study another issue of clinical interest. They played a tape recording of a simulated psychoanalytic interview to a sample of trained therapists, therapists in training, and inexperienced undergraduates (28). All three groups were instructed to focus upon direct and indirect references to the termination of treatment. When such references were present, heart rate was lower than during control passages when such cues were absent. In addition, there was a positive correlation between the degree of heart rate deceleration and the amount of clinical experience. Even more intriguing, cardiac deceleration occurred in response to termination cues that were not recalled later as well as to those that were recalled. In other words, there was a suggestion that this physiological pattern might be associated with unconscious or preconscious perception.

To illustrate the importance of states I have reviewed the physiological patterns associated with only two: fatigue and attention. It is obvious that these two states may interact; all of us have personally experienced attention inward when fatigued and we have also observed this interaction in our patients. It is equally obvious that other states may be and frequently are coincident with fatigue and attention-inward states such as anxiety and depression. States rarely occur in "pure culture." This fact has thus far been largely ignored in experimental research on the psychophysiology of affective states, an area of critical importance to psychiatry. The most important conclusion to be derived from this review of states is that we must find ways to identify and quantify all of the states present at a given moment. A related conclusion is that, since these combinations of affects often fluctuate very rapidly as a result of rapid change in stimuli, we must find ways of quantifying them very rapidly. Self-report measures, which have sometimes been used, do not fill the need because their nature makes them applicable only to relatively long periods and because they may not be accurate because of the operation of defenses.

Recently, some success has been achieved by using experienced clinicians to rate fear, anger, and depression every twenty seconds during videotaped psychotherapeutic interviews. These ratings were in turn related to distinctive spectral characteristics of the patient's voice for each affect. Epochs of conflict in affect also differed from pure affect in their voice spectrum characteristics (29). Clinical rating of videotaped spontaneous emotion may be a means of accurately identifying and quantifying affect states and their mixtures.

Throughout this discussion I have emphasized the importance of the interaction of three classes of variables—stimuli, traits and states—in determining physiological response patterns. Some experiments quantifying all three and their interactions have been conducted. Paradoxically, these experiments were motivated in part by the results of research which has been cited frequently as evidence that physiological variables are unrelated to affective states. I refer to the research of Stanley Schachter (30). In one experiment, for example, he showed that the affect elicited by an injection of epinephrine differed as a function of how the subjects interpreted the situational context. Because there was no concurrent physiological recording, however, it is impossible to conclude from the data of this experiment whether physiological patterns did or did not differ with the subjects' interpretation.

Subsequent experiments focused upon the effect of interpretation of situations—upon so-called "cognitive assessment"—have included concurrent physiological recording, however. In a series of experiments, Lazarus has shown that the degree of physiological response to noxious stimulation was reduced by instructions intended to evoke the use of defenses. Moreover, the degree of physiological response was in turn related to the personality of the subjects: intellectualization was a more effective defense for persons with obsessive personalities than were other defenses (31). Monat has recently carried this research a step further, showing that cognitive assessment interacted with coping strategies and that both of these variables were in turn related to the degree of change in physiological variables and in self-report measures of state (32). The results of this research need to be verified independently and extended to patient samples.

In summary, patterns of physiological responses are the product of extremely complex interactions among and within three classes of variables: stimulus variables, individual difference variables and state variables. Despite this great complexity, there is already clear evidence that persons differing in personality and psychiatric diagnosis process environmental information differently and that these differences is thus far limited to simple behaviors such as reaction there is also evidence of differences in overt behavior associated with these physiological differences. The evidence of behavioral differences are thus far limited to simple behaviors such as reaction time; there is a clear need to relate physiological patterns to more complex interpersonal behavior. There is also evidence that physiological patterns can be modified by manipulating attention and by the operation of ego defenses; the success of such manipulations is in turn related to personality. An area of research which has recently been neglected is research on the psychophysiology of affects. Experiments designed to identify and quantify mixtures of affects and their rapid change may clarify the physiology of affect and affect change. Such information might then be useful in treatment.

Experimental psychophysiology has already spawned a procedure which has been very widely employed to treat many of the symptoms with which we deal in liaison psychiatry. During the 1975 meeting of the College, Cancro observed that psychiatry, more than most medical specialties, suffers from fads (33). The fad to which I am referring here is known to almost everyone, professional and layman alike—so-called "biofeedback." No overview of the clinical relevance of psychophysiological research would be complete without a critique of the therapeutic applications of biofeedback techniques.

Biofeedback is one form of operant conditioning. In classical Pavlovian conditioning, a stimulus which has not previously been effective in evoking a physiological response is paired in close temporal relationship with a stimulus effective in evoking the response. In operant conditioning, rather than pairing stimulus with stimulus, information concerning one aspect of the response is provided to the organism and this feedback augments the response. For example, if the objective is the achievement of ability to decrease and increase heart rate, a red light might appear following those R-R intervals which are longer than a criterion, an orange light might appear for intervals equal to the criterion and a green light for those shorter than the criterion. After a variable number of exposures to such bio-feedback, many persons show heart rate slowing associated with a red light and heart rate acceleration associated with a green light.

The foregoing procedure and variations on it have been used to demonstrate voluntary control over innumerable "involuntary" physiological variables including heart rate, systolic and diastolic blood pressure, dominant rhythm of the electroencephalogram, skin temperature, gastric acidity, peripheral and central blood flow, muscle potentials and many others, including penile tumescence! Claims have been made for the effective treatment of hypertension, cardiac arrhythmias, headache and epilepsy. In addition to the amelioration of specific physiologic dysfunctions, reports have also appeared claiming more general changes such as reduction in anxiety levels and enhanced creativity.

It is perhaps understandable that biofeedback techniques have been applied so widely. The procedures are relatively simple, inexpensive, and time-saving and appear to be applicable to a wide range of psychophysiologic disorders. In addition, the method can be utilized by persons trained at the technician level. Even more appealing, they can also be employed in self-treatment. In short, if the more extravagant claims were to be accepted at face value, there would be no need for our continuing concern with symptoms in psychiatry and, many think, no need for psychiatrists!

In my opinion, the evidence that the biofeedback effect is a real one is convincing. Increases and decreases in physiological levels have been demonstrated repeatedly in carefully controlled experiments in both man and lower species. However, such experiments have also demonstrated the influence of a number of additional variables which affect crucially the treatment potential of biofeedback.

First, the magnitude of the biofeedback effect is typically a small one. Heart rate decreases resulting from biofeedback average 3-5 beats per minute and blood pressure changes average 8-10 Hg., for example (34). Changes of this magnitude are appreciably less than those which have been achieved by pharmocotherapy and other treatment modalities. The amount of biofeedback-induced change is also related to the variability in the resting physiological level. In general, the more variable the resting level, the greater the magnitude of the biofeedback effect. In other words, the more a patient's heart rate changes spontaneously, the more it changes with biofeedback. A related fact, relevant to the treatment of the physiological correlates of anxiety, is that those persons whose ego strength is highest are best able to modify their level of heart rate (35). In other words, those least in need of treatment show the greatest physiological change with biofeedback!

The magnitude of the biofeedback effect is also affected by a myriad of additional variables including those mentioned earlier— age, the characteristics of the experimental environment, the expectations of the patients, sex, ambient experimental environment (e.g., temperature), and even the recording site. Many of the experiments which have reported favorable treatment outcomes failed to control for the effects of such variables. For example, electromyographic biofeedback has been reported to be an effective general relaxation technique. However, it has been shown that biofeedback-induced frontalis muscle relaxation does not generalize to forearm and lower leg musculature. In addition, there was no evidence of a reduction in subjective measures of tension (36).

The weight of the research evidence indicates that the biofeedback effect is a highly specific one, relating only to the specific variable and specific site. Perhaps the most dramatic example of this highly specific effect is the research demonstrating the effects of biofeedback on the firing of single motor neurons (37). Generalized relaxation effects as a result of biofeedback from a single physiological variable are therefore not likely.

One of the most serious deficiencies of the studies which report favorable results of biofeedback treatment is the lack of follow-up, frequently even short-term follow-up. A related problem is that, when follow-up has occurred, it has often been limited to self-reports, and quite probably, to biased sampling—those patients returning for follow-up or those submitting follow-up reports are likely to be those who have experienced favorable outcomes.

Finally, the most serious deficiency of biofeedback treatment is that it is symptomatic treatment. While no physician would quarrel with the use of symptomatic treatment when etiologic treatment is not available, every physician would fault the implicit (and sometimes explicit) assumption in many biofeedback studies that the etiology of the physiological dysfunction is unimportant.

I think it is clear from this overview of the present status of biofeedback applications to treatment that they are, at best, of very limited value. This is not to say, however, that biofeedback may not be a useful technique in increasing our understanding of psychophysiologic disorders. The very high degree of specificity of the feedback effect mentioned earlier may help to illuminate some of the basic issues in psychophysiological research about which I spoke earlier. Bernard Engel, for example, has utilized this high degree of specificity in the feedback effect to elucidate some of the basic physiologic mechanisms of heart rate control(38). The most responsible investigators conducting biofeedback research emphasize this potential and are appropriately cautious about treatment applications.

In summary, experimental psychophysiology has recently focused increasingly upon basic questions which are relevant to our clinical concerns. The ways in which stimulus, trait and state variables interact in producing physiological patterning are becoming increasingly clear and show promise of becoming even clearer. Biofeedback research will likely assist in achieving greater understanding of physiological patterns but present evidence suggests that it will have minimal potential as a treatment procedure.

REFERENCES

1. ROESSLER, R., ALEXANDER, A., and GREENFIELD, N.: Ego Strength and Physiological Responsivity. I. The Relationship of the Barron ES Scale to Skin Resistance, Finger Blood Volume, Heart Rate and Muscle Potential Responses to Sound. *Archives of General Psychiatry*, 8:142, 1963.
2. ROESSLER, R., BURCH, N., and CHILDERS, H.: Personality and Arousal Correlates of Specific Galvanic Skin Responses. *Psychophysiology*, 3:115, 1966.
3. SOKOLOV, E. N.: Higher Nervous Functions: The Orienting Reflex. *Ann. Rev. Physiology*, 25:545, 1963.
4. STERN, J. A.: Physiological Response Measures During Classical Conditioning. In: N. Greenfield, and R. Sternbach (Eds.), *Handbook of Psychophysiology*. New York: Holt, Rinehart & Winston, Inc., 1972.
5. LACEY, J. I.: Psychophysiological Approaches to the Evaluation of Psychotherapeutic Process and Outcome. In: E. A. Rubenstein and M. B. Parloff (Eds.), *Research in Psychotherapy*. Washington: National Publishing Company, 1959.
6. GRAHAM, F. K.: The More or Less Startling Effects of Weak Prestimulation. *Psychophysiology*, 12:238, 1975.
7. GREENFIELD, N., ALEXANDER, A., and ROESSLER, R.: Ego Strength and Physiological Responsivity. II. The Relationship of the Barron ES Scale to the Temporal and Recovery Characteristics of Skin Resistance, Finger Blood Volume, Heart Rate, and Muscle Potential Responses to Sound. *Archives of General Psychiatry*, 9:129, 1963.
8. WOLF, S.: Emotions and the Autonomic Nervous System. *Arch. Intern. Med.*, 126:1024, 1970.
9. GRAHAM, F. K. and CLIFTON, R. K.: Heart-Rate Change as a Component of the Orienting Response. *Psychological Bulletin*, 65:305, 1966.
10. ROESSLER, R.: Personality, Psychophysiology, and Performance. *Psychophysiology*, 10:315, 1973.
11. LAZARUS, R. S. and AVERILL, J. R.: Emotion and Cognition: With Special Reference to Anxiety. In: C. D. Spielberger (Ed.), *Anxiety, Current Trends in Theory and Research. Vol. II.* New York: Academic Press, 1972.
12. ZUCKERMAN, M.: Physiological Measures of Sexual Arousal in the Human. In: N. Greenfield and R. Sternbach (Eds.), *Hand-*

book of Psychophysiology. New York: Holt, Rinehart & Winston, Inc., 1972.

13. SCHWARTZ, G. E., FAIR, P. L., SALT, P., MANDEL, M. R., and KLERMAN, G. L.: Facial Muscle Patterning to Affective Imagery in Depressed and Nondepressed Patients. *Science*, 192: 489, 1976.

14. STERN, J. A., SURPHLIS, W., and KOFF, E.: Electrodermal Responsiveness Related to Psychiatric Diagnosis and Prognosis. *Psychophysiology*, 2:51, 1965.

15. LADER, M.: The Psychophysiology of Anxious and Depressed Patients. In: D. C. Fowles (Ed.), *Clinical Applications of Psychophysiology*. New York: Columbia University Press, 1975.

16. VENABLES, P. H.: A Psychophysiological Approach to Research in Schizophrenia. In: D. C. Fowles (Ed.), *Clinical Applications of Psychophysiology*. New York: Columbia University Press, 1975.

17. HARE, R. D.: Psychophysiological Studies of Psychopathy. In: D. C. Fowles (Ed.), *Clinical Applications of Psychophysiology*. New York: Columbia University Press, 1975.

18. STRAUSBAUGH, L. J. and ROESSLER, R.: Ego Strength, Skin Conductance, Sleep Deprivation, and Performance. *Perceptual and Motor Skills*, 31:671, 1970.

19. GALE, A.: The Psychophysiology of Individual Differences: Studies of Extroversion and the EEG. In: P. Kline (Ed.), *New Approaches in Psychophysiological Measurement*. London: Wiley, 1973.

20. HORNE, J. A. and OSTBERG, O.: Time of Day Effects on Extroversion and Salivation. *Biological Psychology*, 3:301, 1975.

21. BARRATT, E. S.: Perceptual-Motor Performance Related to Impulsiveness and Anxiety. *Perceptual and Motor Skills*, 25:485, 1967.

22. LYKKEN, D. T.: Neuropsychology and Psychophysiology in Personality Research. In: E. Borgotta and N. Lambert (Eds.), *Handbook of Personality Theory and Research*. Chicago: Rand McNally, 1968.

23. ROESSLER, R. and ENGEL, B. T.: The Current Status of the Concepts of Physiological Response Specificity and Activation. *Int'l J. Psychiatry in Medicine*, 5:359, 1974.

24. SINGER, M. T.: Presidential address—engagement-involvement: a central phenomenon in psychophysiological research. *Psychosomatic Medicine*, 36:2, 1974.

25. LACEY, J. I.: Somatic Response Patterning and Stress: Some Revisions of Activation Theory. In: M. H. Appley and R. Trumbull (Eds.), *Psychological Stress*. New York: Appleton-Century-Crofts, 1967.

26. KLORMAN, R., WIESENFELD, A., and AUSTIN, M. L.: Autonomic Re-

sponses to Affective Visual Stimuli. *Psychophysiology*, 12:553, 1975.

27. HARE, R. D. and BLEVINGS, G.: Defensive Responses to Phobic Stimuli. *Biological Psychology*, 3:1, 1975.

28. SPENCE, D. P., LUGO, M., and YOUDIN, R.: Cardiac Correlates of Cognitive Processing. *Psychosomatic Medicine*, 36:420, 1974.

29. ROESSLER, R. and LESTER, J. W.: Voice Predicts Affect in Psychotherapy. *Journal of Nervous and Mental Diseases*, 163:166, 1976.

30. SCHACHTER, S.: The Assumption of Identity and Peripheralist-Centralist Controversies in Motivation and Emotion. In: M. Arnold (Ed.), *Feelings and Emotions*. New York: Academic Press, 1970.

31. LAZARUS, R. S.: The Self-Regulation of Emotion. In: L. Levi (Ed.), *Emotions, Their Parameters and Measurement*. New York: Raven Press, Publishers, 1975.

32. MONAT, A.: Temporal Uncertainty, Anticipation Time, and Cognitive Coping Under Threat. *Journal of Human Stress*, 2:32, 1976.

33. CANCRO, R.: Genetic Considerations in the Etiology and Prevention of Schizophrenia. In: G. Usdin (Ed.), *Schizophrenia: Biological and Psychological Perspectives*. New York: Brunner/Mazel, 1975.

34. FEY, S. G. and LINDHOLM, E.: Systolic Blood Pressure and Heart Rate Changes During Three Sessions Involving Biofeedback or No Biofeedback. *Psychophysiology*, 12:513, 1975.

35. STEPHENS, J. H., HARRIS, A. H., BRADY, J. V., and SHAFFER, J. W.: Psychological and Physiological Variables Associated with Large Magnitude Voluntary Heart Rate Changes. *Psychophysiology*, 12:381, 1975.

36. ALEXANDER, A. B.: An Experimental Test of Assumptions Relating to the Use of Electromyographic Biofeedback as a General Relaxation Training Technique. *Psychophysiology*, 12:656, 1975.

37. BASMAJIAN, J. V.: Electromyography Comes of Age. *Science*, 173:740, 1972.

38. ENGEL, B. T.: Operant Conditioning of Cardiac Function: A Status Report. *Psychophysiology*, 9:161, 1972.

4

The Development of
Liaison Programs

Maurice H. Greenhill, M.D.

The liaison program in the field of liaison psychiatry refers to
the organizational structure within which the delivery of mental
health services to the medically and surgically ill takes place. Clinical
care is its primary purpose, and its principal correlates are education and research. Education has its special characteristics within
the liaison program since it includes the teaching of psychiatric
methods, psychosocial influences, and clinical comprehensiveness in
health and disease to non-psychiatric personnel as well as to psychiatric trainees and members of the psychiatric profession. To these
facets of education might be added, as of more recent date, the
teaching of the psychiatric implications in critical care medicine and
in bioethics. Psychosomatic research uses the liaison program; indeed,
in some centers the liaison program exists for the principal purpose
of providing clinical subjects and a site for training in research for
psychosomatic fellows.

THE IDIOSYNCRATIC FEATURES OF THE LIAISON
PSYCHIATRY FIELD

In the direct relationship of psychiatry to medicine there are
unique characteristics which have been well identified (1-4). They

115

will help to explain the directions taken by liaison programs over their 40-year history and the models of liaison systems which evolved. A number of obstacles have been encountered by every planner of liaison services, and each one has met the particular set of obstacles with a design which to him gave a promise of working.

Among the idiosyncratic features of the relationship of psychiatry to medicine is the circumstance that liaison psychiatry is practiced on sites which belong to other clinical departments, where affiliations are attempted with professionals who are little motivated to affiliate. The liaison psychiatrist comes face to face with deep resistance. He has to deal with differing value systems. At the same time he may be the stepchild of his own department. He is often poorly supported financially by his own department and usually not at all by the department to which he gives his service. The thrust of his work indicates that he wants to humanize the care of the sick, be their advocate, and correct their helplessness. He is sensitive to the injustices to which the sick are subject. Teaching in the face of opposing values and pressing to change attitudes, he is a determined proselytizer. He cannot rely upon the substance and methods of his discipline without resorting to strategy to effect acceptance and produce results. Expectations of his performance by other medical disciplines are not enthusiastic. Those patients whom he desires to help do not ask for his help and may be unmotivated for it. Whether or not a liaison program can be launched or maintained may be dependent upon the interest and support of one man, such as the chairman of the department of medicine. Hospital administration usually has lukewarm interest in such programs, except to protect the legal and financial rights of the institution.

The status of the liaison psychiatrist within psychiatry seems to rank behind the general clinical psychiatrist, the psychoanalyst, the child psychiatrist, the social psychiatrist and the subspecialist in schizophrenia and borderline disorders. One wonders whether the liaison psychiatrist is some form of 20th century medical masochist, half-deluded and saintly at the same time. Yet he has persisted in his mission to guide medicine into less selectively perceived pathways while shaping the designs and objectives of his programs around the obstacles and idiosyncrasies of the work.

HISTORY OF THE DEVELOPMENT OF PROGRAMS

The clinical discipline within medicine which deals with the interrelationship of all possible parameters and systems in the disease process and their clinical application has been called by a variety of terms such as liaison psychiatry, consultative-liaison psychiatry, psychosomatic medicine, comprehensive medicine, and integrative medicine. Lipowski (5) has attempted to define the meaning of these terms and what they represent when he states that "Psychosomatic medicine as a scientific discipline attempts to collect a body of facts and build a unified theory about the interrelationships between man's psychological and biological attributes and functions on the one hand, and his physical and social environment on the other." He defines consultation-liaison psychiatry as "the area of clinical psychiatry that encompasses clinical, teaching, and research activities of psychiatrists and allied mental health professionals in the nonpsychiatric divisions of a general hospital." He goes on to note, "The designation 'consultation-liaison' reflects two interrelated roles of the consultants. 'Consultation' refers to the provision of expert diagnostic opinion and advice on management regarding a patient's mental state and behavior at the request of another health professional. 'Liaison' connotes a linking of groups for the purpose of effective collaboration."

Beigler and his co-workers (6) more succinctly call attention to two major categories of liaison psychiatry: "(1) the consultation-type functions and (2) the specifically 'liaison' functions. The former comprise the services usually rendered by a psychiatrist summoned as a consultant; the latter constitute . . . functions of the psychiatrist as he works over an extended period of time on the various nonpsychiatric divisions of a general hospital." Some programs refer to themselves as a consultative-liaison services, others as liaison services, while both are fulfilling the same functions. These functions are dedicated to the delivery of mental health care to the medically ill.

In essence, liaison psychiatry has come to be the name of choice as most disciplines of medicine work through clinical alliances to make possible the inclusion of psychosocial variables in the health and disease considerations of man. The initiative for establishing this bridge has come largely from psychiatry, hence the expression "liaison psychiatry" rather than "liaison medicine."

The history of psychosomatic medicine and conceptual developments within liaison psychiatry in terms of theoretical models and research development has been well surveyed (7-12), but the history of the development of liaison programs has only been touched upon lightly in previous communications (3, 10, 12).

Liaison psychiatry was an outgrowth of the psychosomatic movement, which was started in Germany and Austria in the second and third decades of this century and reached its greatest momentum in the United States between 1930 and 1950. Many theoretical, research, and clinical studies of the interrelationship of the emotions and bodily functions were conducted under the incentive of psychoanalytic investigators, physiologists, and clinical psychiatrists. Methods of applying the new concepts and vehicles of administration soon developed concurrently. In 1929 Henry (13) published a remarkable paper in the American Journal of Psychiatry with the title "Some Modern Aspects of Psychiatry in General Hospital Practice." This was the first exposition of the consultation model of service, and it enunciated many of the classical obstacles and their solutions.

In 1933, a great catalytic force set in motion the true development of liaison programs. The Medical Sciences Division of the Rockefeller Foundation (14), under the leadership of Alan Gregg, decided to place major emphasis on the development of psychiatry by establishing funding for full-time teachers of psychiatry in selected American medical schools and by establishing departments of psychiatry or extensions of departments within certain university hospitals. Grants were given for these purposes to Harvard (Massachusetts General Hospital) (1934), University of Colorado (1934), University of Chicago (1935), Tulane University (1936), Wash-

ington University in St. Louis (1938), and Duke University (1940).*
Alan Gregg's foresight, and that of his associate, Robert Lambert, set
the course of psychiatry for a generation and put psychiatry squarely
in the general hospital on course for impact with the rest of medicine.

The growth and influence of these departments developed at
different rates but all eventually made striking contributions to
psychiatry, medicine, and psychosomatic medicine. The first two to
exert influence in liaison psychiatry were the University of Colorado
Medical Center and the Harvard's Massachusetts General Hospital.
In September, 1934 the Psychiatric Liaison Department of the
Colorado General and Psychopathic Hospitals was established, a
development made possible through the efforts of Dr. Franklin G.
Ebaugh, Chairman of the Colorado Department, whose contributions in psychiatry, as we know, were extensive. In a paper entitled
"The Psychiatric Liaison Department of the University of Colorado
Medical School and Hospitals," Billings (15) gives credit to Ebaugh
for influencing Alan Gregg to establish pilot psychiatric projects
in university hospitals.

In the Colorado Psychiatric Liaison Department, Billings was
assisted by Commonwealth Fellows from the Psychopathic Hospital
and later by U.S. Public Health Service physicians. "The department
purposely had no hospital beds assigned to it and no specific niche
in the outpatient clinic. Patients were examined, treated, and utilized
as the focus for teaching and research wherever they might be bedded
—whether in a pediatric, surgical or medical ward." Billings states
that the liaison department was organized around three aims:

1. To sensitize the physicians and students to the opportunities
   offered them by every patient, no matter what complaint or
   ailment was present, for the utilization of a common sense

---

* The size of these grants is interesting in terms of comparisons
with current grants in an inflationary period: Colorado—$10,000 per
year for 5 years, 1934-1938; Massachusetts General Hospital—$80,000,
1934 (to establish and maintain a department), $78,000 per year,
1935-1940; Tulane University—$12,000 per year for 2 years, 1936-
1938; Duke University—$25,000 per year for 7 years, 1940-1947 (to
establish and maintain a department).

psychiatric approach for the betterment of the patient's condition, and for the making that patient better fitted to handle his problem—somatic or personality-determined or both.

2. To establish psychobiology as an integral working part of the professional thinking of physicians and students of all branches of medicine.

3. To instill in the minds of physicians and students the need the patient-public has for tangible and practical conceptions of personality and sociological functioning. This was to be not so much in the sense of "prevention" of mental disorders per se, but rather in the sense of preventing false thinking, misconceptions, misunderstanding, folk-lore and taboos which made it difficult for the patient to accept help or to allow the physician to be of help (15, p. 30).

These goals, according to McKegney in 1975 (1), remain after 40 years the most common current model of consultative-liaison teaching.

The second influential liaison program was that of the Department of Psychiatry at the Massachusetts General Hospital. This department was established under the direction of Stanley Cobb (16). Cobb had enormous prestige with leaders in the other medical disciplines in Boston, and his quiet confidence in the importance of the neuro-sciences, including psychiatry, radiated to his faculty and trainees. His principal associates were Jacob Finesinger and Erich Lindeman. He advocated inclusion of psychoanalytic investigation and teaching and had on his staff such psychoanalysts as Felix and Helene Deutsch and Hans Sachs.

This department had a 12-bed inpatient unit devoted to the care of patients with neuroses and medical problems with psychiatric involvement, a large outpatient section, and a consultation service. Emphasis was placed on the consultation process, methods of alliance with other clinical departments, and research in psychosomatic medicine. During the first decade of its existence the following contributors to liaison psychiatry served as residents or Rockefeller Fellows there: Ruesch, Sargent, Rosenbaum, Greenhill, Saslow, Bandler, Nemiah, Miller, Shands, and Weisman.

As liaison departments, Colorado and the Massachusetts General Hospital were essentially consultation services, and were the first to begin explorations into the borderland of psychiatry with medicine. Further progress in opening up this borderland took place at Mount Sinai Hospital in New York City. In 1946, M. Ralph Kaufman began the organization of a psychiatric department there, and his skill as a creative innovator and administrator was applied principally to adapting the theories and methods of psychiatry to the general hospital. In 1948 he and Margolin predicted that the relationship of psychiatry to the general hospital could neither be static nor uniform.

> The organization of the psychiatric service in a general hospital at any given time depends on the level of sophistication with respect to psychology. *Therefore, no blueprint of an organization can be regarded as universally applicable* (author's italics). However, inasmuch as it is generally held that the psychosomatic point of view is not uniformly practiced, the following organization is designed for a general hospital with minimal existing psychiatric facilities. As will later be seen, its structure will be sufficiently dynamic and flexible as to permit revision, in terms of shifts of emphasis and foci of activity as the level of psychological indoctrination changes (17, p. 611).

These predictions have been borne out and have been considered in the organization of many liaison services. What has been especially relevant is the principle *"no blueprint of an organization can be regarded as universally applicable."* There is no one ideal liaison program; each is shaped to fit the potentials of the institution and its liaison psychiatrists.

Kaufman and Margolin (17) spelled out their objectives for a liaison program in a general hospital.

> The administrative set-up must be built around the professional needs of the institution. The *primary* needs are always:
>
> 1. Psychiatric services: i.e., diagnoses and treatment of the hospital population, both outpatient and inpatient.

2. Teaching, which involves two aspects—one, the further training of the psychiatric staff, and two, the indoctrination and teaching of every member of the hospital staff from administration through chiefs to house staff.

3. Research (p. 612).

The emphasis of the Mount Sinai Department was to give clinical psychiatric service to the general hospital population connected with other medical disciplines and not to a customary psychiatric population from the community. This was done by a process of infiltrating psychiatrists throughout the traditional services of the hospital. Each service in the hospital had a senior psychiatrist attached as a member of its attending staff. There were also other inpatient liaison psychiatrists who did consultations; liaison psychiatrists in the various outpatient clinics in other departments; and a 22-bed "psychosomatic ward."

The Mount Sinai liaison program has remained unique in the history of the field by virtue of its ability to "saturate" the general hospital with liaison psychiatrists. This capability was related to its location and position in New York City situated as it was in the middle of a large census tract of psychiatrists in Manhattan who were eager to act as voluntary attending men. A massive program was successfully operated at relatively low cost. It thus set a model for the consultation-liaison service in community hospitals with one or no full-time psychiatrist but an appreciable number of voluntary attending psychiatrists. This, after all, may have been the most valuable contribution of the Mount Sinai experience.

In 1962, Bernstein and Kaufman (18) reported on the status of the liaison program at Mount Sinai, 16 years after its origin. The emphasis had changed from "indoctrination and infiltration" to having the psychiatrist be "functionally and operationally a member of the medical team." A feature of the assignment was that the psychiatrist "is free to see any patient who is admitted to the medical service whether there is an official request or not." The design had become more of a liaison model, which was by that time in effect in other centers.

The classic liaison model reached its fruition at the University of Rochester (19-22). It was started by Engel and Romano in 1946 and has been under the leadership of Engel continuously for 30 years (Schmale is now co-director). It has had the full support of the Department of Psychiatry and of the Department of Medicine. It has been one of the principal teaching arms of psychiatric under-graduate teaching at Rochester, and has trained a large number of psychosomatic fellows (109 between 1946-77), 60 percent of whom became full-time medical educators. The idiosyncratic features of limited psychiatric status and lukewarm interest from internal medicine have not been major obstacles, although vicissitudes in these areas have occurred in some instances in connection with resistance of internists and with prestige factors. In the course of time, the Rochester Liaison Service, because of its contributions and its international reputation, has reached a firm status of its own.

From the beginning, the organizational objective of the Rochester service has been to be a part of the medical service, and to be considered by the Department of Medicine as one of its subspecialties. Its operational strategy seems to have been to merge with medicine. The medium for the implementation of the psychosomatic approach in the clinical departments other than Psychiatry has been the Medical Psychiatric Liaison group. This group through the years has consisted of five to 10 full-time senior staff and 6 to 9 fellows in training. The senior staff has remained constant to the extent that five of the present 10 are full professors. All senior staff are Board qualified or Board certified in both medicine and psychiatry and are active in departmental administrative meetings in both the Depart-ment of Medicine and the Department of Psychiatry. Like leaders in several other liaison programs, the majority of the staff first had training in internal medicine and then qualified for psychiatry out-side of traditional psychiatric residency programs, usually on psycho-somatic fellowships or through psychoanalytic training. Although they eschew both psychiatry and medicine, the primary identification appears to be with medicine. This largely reflects Engel's opinion that the role model for the student who will learn skill in both psychology and somatic aspects of illness must first of all be an internist (20). We will return to this point later.

Although the offices of the liaison group are in the Department of Psychiatry, practically all of the work is done on the medical service. The principal emphasis of the liaison program is an educational one—to train internists to consider psychological factors in the diagnosis and treatment of their patients, and to train future teachers of internists. An intensive effort is made in a curriculum for medical students with the same goal in mind. A less concentrated and brief program for psychiatric residents is held. Teaching exercises on the medical units include rounds with internists and liaison staff or fellows, assignments to clinical locations, assignments to medical patients, supervision, continued case conferences, and preceptorships. The tightness of the liaison arrangement whereby the liaison worker acts as a resource person in both psychiatry and medicine and serves as the role model of the internist who can integrate psychosocial factors into his clinical considerations by performance is the hallmark of the Rochester liaison program. This seems to be a physician's program for physicians: It displays firm adherence to the medical model over 30 years, with other disciplines involved but of secondary importance. Likewise, the training of internists appears to be unstructured, and is apparently done through rounds, conferences, and personal contacts. In the several reports in the literature from the Rochester group much is written concerning the graduate and undergraduates programs, but little directly regarding the specifics of training non-psychiatric personnel on service. Nor have consultation aspects of the work been reported. Evaluation studies on the results of the program seem to be limited to opinions of directors and assessment comments by medical students.

A liaison program whose principal aim was the training of the medical house officer was the Duke program (23). This was initiated by the author in 1947 and was in existence until 1952 when he left Duke to join Finesinger at the University of Maryland. In those years the group consisted of the director, five psychosomatic fellows, three psychosomatic liaison nurses, a psychiatric social worker, two medical social workers, and a variable number of clinical psychologists.

The organizational plan for the program was a close liaison with the Department of Medicine. This was strongly supported by the Chairman of the Department of Medicine, Eugene Stead, who gave the liaison group *carte blanche* in clinical work and teaching on his floors and in the medical clinic. He regularly attended psychosomatic conferences on inpatients and continued case conferences on outpatients and insisted on the attendance of his house officers. The goal here was to make the psychiatrist a role model, and the professor of medicine a role model of the internist who accepts the psychiatrist and can collaborate with him.

The group worked entirely on two medical floors and in the medical clinic, where they were considered a part of the health team, everpresent to share the work. They did formal and informal consultations on patients, held consultations with medical and nursing staffs, and supervised house staff and nurses. Multidiscipline interrelationships were an object of study. Questions constantly considered were: What can the internist do and what can he not do with psychosocial variables? What should he be taught? How can the psychiatrist best teach it? How can the internist relate to the psychiatrist and the psychiatrist to him in an optimal fashion? What is the best design of clinical service to reach most patients within the medical dimension?

Over 100 medical house officers were in the liaison program from 1947-1952. A carefully devised evaluation study was carried out on 47 of them who served between 1947-1949. The results and some methods of teaching non-psychiatric physicians were reported in *Psychosomatic Medicine* in 1950 by Greenhill and Kilgore (23) and will be referred to again later.

At the Johns Hopkins Hospital, Eugene Meyer (24-26) developed and operated a productive liaison program between 1945 and 1960, which carefully investigated and reported upon the consultation process and the countertransference problems of liaison psychiatrists. He had the help of a small group of co-workers and had the interest of Adolf Meyer, Whitehorn, Lidz, and Fleck. The later two (27) strongly stated the objectives of liaison psychiatry in 1950,

> During the period of hospitalization on the medical wards there is little intent and little opportunity to take over and treat the patient primarily by psychotherapy. Such efforts are made after discharge or upon transfer to the psychiatric service. The principal objective is to aid, modify, and amplify the treatment regimen by utilizing or altering the patient's personality traits and his attitudes toward his surrounding and his illness. The attention to the personality problems may be the critical factor in making medical treatment possible or effective (p. 104).

In 1948 Saslow (28) made the first of several reports on a program at Washington University in St. Louis where the principal site of liaison work was in a medical clinic especially organized for the purpose. Medical "D" clinic served for several years in the education of medical students, medical interns, and psychiatric residents. Saslow referred to this as "an experiment with comprehensive medicine," which he considered to be "medicine geared mainly to the restoration or achievement of sustained optimal functioning of the patient as an organism rather than mainly to the diagnosis and treatment of a specific disturbance in such functioning, i.e., an illness."

During the long and illustrious course of psychosomatic medicine at the University of Cincinnati, a variety of approaches to patient care and teaching were tried, first under Romano, and then, for more than two decades, under Maurice Levine. These included a busy and effective consultation service, special liaison services, principally for research purposes, continued education courses for practicing physicians, and a psychosomatic ward. No one liaison model emerged here. Great weight was given to the hospital psychosomatic conference as a liaison tool.

By 1960 consultation-liaison programs were underway or in formation in the majority of teaching hospitals. The one at Yale had consultation as its emphasis and never jelled into a structured liaison design. The interest in the Department of Psychiatry in the interfaces between psychiatry and other systems had its effect on trainees who in the next generation carried forth a strong liaison interest (McKegney, Kimball). Kornfeld developed an effective consultation service at Columbia with strong liaison interests in select critical care issues. At Downstate School of Medicine in New York, Reichsman established an active liaison program on the model at Rochester, where he had worked.

The consultation-liaison programs at the Albert Einstein College of Medicine in New York deserve special mention because three models exist here simultaneously, and because they demonstrate the difficulties in maintaining liaison services and in getting durable results in liaison teaching. The clinical facilities at Einstein are multiple, but reference here will be limited to three general hospitals, Jacobi Hospital (City administration), Montefiore Hospital (voluntary), and the Hospital of the Albert Einstein College of Medicine (a university hospital under lease to Montefiore Hospital).

Since the founding of the Department of Psychiatry in 1954-55, Jacobi Hospital has been the principal clinical teaching site. With Milton Rosenbaum as Chairman, the department has had a strong psychosomatic interest, attested to by the fact that from its full-time faculty came three presidents of the American Psychosomatic Society and two editors-in-chief of the journal *Psychosomatic Medicine*. The main thrust of liaison teaching at Jacobi was in undergraduate education (Weiner directed teaching in the pre-clinical courses), in consultation service of three months during the second year of psychiatry residency, and in psychosomatic conferences with a medical service led on alternate weeks by Rosenbaum and Reiser for many years. The department was never able to launch a true liaison program, partly because of the power system in which clinical services were controlled by house staff, but also because psychoanalytic teaching took precedence over an organizational goal. At present Jacobi Hospital still has a resident's consultation service with which it has made an effort to place residents for brief periods on specific units in a liaison arrangements. A small active pediatric liaison plan has been in effect for many years.

When Reiser and Weiner moved to Montefiore Hospital, a well structured division of liaison psychiatry was established, based on a biological psychiatry and medical model. A strong consultation service, an active research program, an educational program for liaison fellows, and liaison connections with two medical units, the hemodialysis center, and the ambulatory clinic are in effect. This program and its obstacles are presented in the book by Strain and Grossman (29) *Psychological Care of the Medically Ill.* The biological psychiatry emphasis at Montefiore through the years is expressed at the delivery level by the liaison program.

The third program at Einstein is the one at the University Hospital. Although administratively operated by Montefiore Hospital, it has its independent Department of Psychiatry. By necessity it is organized much in the fashion of the Mount Sinai Hospital department under Kaufman in the 1940's and 1950's, namely with one full-time psychiatrist director (M. Greenhill) and many voluntary attending persons. The clinical responsibility for patients resides with the faculty. There is an active psychiatric consultation service done exclusively by attending psychiatrists. Because of the characteristics of clinical need at the hospital with its emphasis on critical care medicine, a different model of liaison service developed, namely, a critical care model, which proved to be more effective in this instance than the traditional liaison program.

What is to be noted particularly in this trio of liaison programs is that although medical students, interns, and residents connected with Einstein have experience in one or more of these programs, although the Department of Psychiatry is recognized as strong and effective, and although a large and influential group of liaison teachers and internationally recognized role models have been at work, patient care has been little influenced over 20 years. The attending staff at Einstein Hospital who were trained at Einstein, were no more induced to use psychiatry, according to statistics on consultation and clinical management (30), than those who were trained elsewhere.

PSYCHOSOMATIC UNITS

In the history of the development of liaison programs psychosomatic units or psychosomatic wards figured briefly. The attempt to explore the possibility of treating patients with psychosomatic disorders in a psychiatric setting was a reasonable one. It seemed to make sense to have a unit wherein both medical and psychiatric procedures could be carried out by a combination of psychiatric and medical staffs. Such units were under the supervision of psychiatry on its home ground with internists and medical residents assigned to it. At the same time one or more psychosomatic fellows trained there and psychiatric residents rotated through the unit. Patients were admitted from medical and surgical floors and were taken for treatment or study only. Nursing staffs were psychiatric, medical, or a combination of both. The other disciplines associated with a psychiatric unit were present. All of the psychiatric therapies were available, and in the era in which psychosomatic units were most active, psychotherapy was the principal therapeutic modality.

These units are to be distinguished from psychiatric units in general hospitals. With the high incidence of reported psychiatric disorder within the general hospital population (15.0% - 72.5%) (9), it would be expected that psychiatric units would devote their efforts to the care of such general hospital patients. This has never been the case. Psychiatric units admit the occasional case in this category, but their selection process usually emphasizes the admission of characteristic psychiatric disorders, such as depression, schizophrenia, borderline states, severe neurotic reactions, and psychiatric diagnostic problems. Departments of psychiatry tend to subscribe to such an admission policy because the pressure from the community to take this type of sick person is great, there is a belief that admission of medically ill patients will contaminate the therapeutic milieu of the customary psychiatric unit, and psychiatric nurses find it difficult to take care of medical patients and psychiatric patients at the same time. The paradox of all this is that psychiatry itself has developed another obstacle to liaison psychiatry through its aim of treating psychiatric patients in units in general hospitals, thereby cutting off available beds for the psychiatric treatment of certain medically ill patients who need it in a psychiatric setting. This also tends to increase the resistance of non-psychiatrist physicians, who, no matter how much they may criticize psychiatry, feel supported when there is a "backup" area for their patients who may become disturbed.

The only psychosomatic wards established, as far as the author can determine, were at the University of Cincinnati, Mount Sinai Hospital in New York, Montefiore Hospital in New York, and the University of Maryland in Baltimore. The Cincinnati and Mount Sinai wards were put into operation at about the same time in the middle of the 1940's.

In 1961 Kaplan and Curtis (31) described the Cincinnati unit,

> The patients on this 12-bed unit are men and women with physiologic disorders of various types. Ordinarily, they are not acutely ill, but usually they have experienced illness over a moderately long period. Most of the conditions observed are classified diagnostically within the psycho-physiologic autonomic and visceral category, e.g., hypertension, peptic ulcer, neurodermatitis, diabetes, asthma, ulcerative colitis and the like. . . . The average hospital stay is approximately two months, with a range of several weeks to a year. During this time patients are studied comprehensively in terms of their psychophysiological states. The patients are in both individual and group psychotherapy and the small size of the unit affords an opportunity for very close observation of individual behavior and of the group interaction (p. 359).

This description generally fits the other psychosomatic wards. The University of Cincinnati unit is still in existence and has been used in many research studies on a variety of clinical states, but an evaluation of the unit has never been reported (32). At present it emphasizes psychopharmacology and biofeedback.

The 22-bed unit at Mount Sinai was called a "psychiatric ward" although the types of cases selected for admission were similar to those at Cincinnati. For example, Kaufman reported in 1953 (33) on the diagnoses of cases on the unit on a given day and they included ulcerative colitis (4), essential hypertension (1), anorexia nervosa (1), diabetes mellitus (1), duodenal ulcer (2), gastric ulcer (1), hyperthyroidism (1), post-gastrostomy (1), coccygodynia (1), rheumatoid arthritis (1), fugue state (1), psychosis with somatic delusions

(1), psychoneurosis, conversion, cardiac symptoms (1), manic-depressive, depressed, hypochondriasis (1). He stated

> This was an unselected group in the sense that it represented the patients on a ward of the psychiatry service on a given day. One has but to read the list of primary diagnoses to realize how far psychiatry and medicine have advanced in the utilization of basic psychiatric concepts in the practice of medicine. Here we see patients whose primary illnesses do not fall into the well known psychiatric syndromes. Actually it is only rarely that a patient with a schizophrenic or a manic-depressive psychosis finds his way to the psychiatric service. This is because the basic philosophy, as a psychiatric unit in a general hospital, is to be primarily of service to the population of such a general hospital (pp. 371-372).

Such a philosophy had not held up as far as the 951 psychiatric units in general hospitals in the United States in 1974 were concerned, including Mount Sinai.

The psychosomatic ward at the University of Maryland was operated in 1953-55 by the author with the help of Arthur Schmale before he went to Rochester. It was a 19-bed unit in the Psychiatric Institute connected with an active medical unit in the main hospital. The population was comparable to those at Cincinnati and Mount Sinai. The therapeutic milieu and its influence on the course of medical disorders were particularly studied with special reference to ward crises. Also investigated were the effects of modification of daily regime on medical patients, the limits of medical responsibility for psychiatrists, and the influence of family interventions. It had largely a social psychiatry and interpersonal approach and was meant to be a model unit for the teaching of house staff and psychiatric residents.

The Montefiore psychosomatic unit of 22 beds was started in the late 1950's and disbanded in 1966. Its population was a general medical one in which certain patients with "psychosomatic disorders" were studied psychoanalytically. As with the unit at Maryland, no evaluation studies have been reported.

Although psychosomatic units are a logical extension of general hospital psychiatry, they have, for the most part, not survived, probably because 1) liaison psychiatrists tend not to work continuously with chronic patients in their psychiatrist-internist roles, 2) there is a lack of financial support from psychiatry, medicine, and hospital administration, 3) long-term hospitalization implicit to the careful multi-dimensional study of medically ill patients is not possible in contemporary health care economic systems, and 4) most of those which existed had as their aim the intensive psychoanalytic study of the medical patient after the design of the Chicago Institute of Psychoanalysis and others, and this approach has not survived.

It would seem sensible to reconsider the question of the advisability of specific settings for the careful study of medical patients, particularly from the viewpoint of clinical investigation. It seems naive to expect that the intricate problems of giving adequate care to the seriously ill in the face of psychiatric complications can be achieved in the brief contact, "patchwork" manner in which it is now delivered.

LIAISON CONSULTATION

At the core of liaison work is the dynamic contact between the liaison psychiatrist and the key figures in the clinical field: patients, families, physicians, nurses, social workers, administrators, psychologists, and others. The interaction at this point of contact is called liaison consultation and the principal participant is the liaison psychiatrist whose task it is to serve as the resource expert on psychological and social variables in disease. The substantive knowledge, methods, and techniques of psychiatry are brought to bear on the task. The liaison psychiatrist is expected to have additional knowledge concerning the characteristics of forces at the interfaces of psychiatry and the other medical disciplines. The points of dynamic contact are variable so that the consultations may be with the patient alone, with the patient and consultee, with the patient and nurse, with the patient and all key persons in his clinical field, with the consultee alone, with the family alone, or with other combinations. This fluidity of consultative endeavor is one of the principal skills of the liaison psychiatrist. He is adept at changing role models and is familiar with systems and boundaries of systems.

This concept brings into view an aspect of the liaison program which has been labeled "the informal consultation." Traditionally this phrase refers to any exchange about the patient between the patient's physicians and a psychiatrist other than for a consultation through administrative channels. Such informal consultations occur not only between primary, secondary, and tertiary physicians and the liaison psychiatrist, but even more frequently between nurses, social workers, and a variety of ancillary personnel and the psychiatrist. I daresay that the mass of the work of liaison programs is done through the informal consultation, and in particular in such consultations between the psychiatrist and those members of the staff who are not physicians.

Schwab (34) has referred to three approaches to consultation work: 1) the patient-oriented approach, 2) the consultee-oriented approach, and 3) the situation-oriented approach. To these a fourth might be added: The professional-oriented approach. In this approach psychiatrists consult with physicians regarding patients whom the latter does not want seen or whom it may not be necessary to see, may advise them on the psychological management of patients without interviewing everyone, and may conduct psychotherapy supervision as a learning experience for the medical trainee or practicing physician without meeting the patient. Nurses and social workers subscribe to this approach frequently, and in addition, some patients are electively not seen in staff conferences held in their behalf. There are no studies as yet to evaluate the frequency of the professional-centered consultation.

The types of consultative approach and the models of psychiatric consultation crystallized during the evolution of liaison psychiatry and help us to understand designs of programs and changes in programs. The patient-oriented approach is the traditional psychiatric consultation. Much has been written on how to do a psychiatric consultation in terms of the patient-oriented approach (18, 28, 33, 34, 35, 36, 37, 158). There is general agreement on the method:

preparation for the consultation, the setting for the examination, the approach to the patient, the interview, the consultant-patient relationship, the written report, and transactions with the consultee.

As liaison psychiatry developed and wider methods of application occurred, other consultation approaches evolved, which did not change the character of the classic psychiatric consultation, but placed emphasis on one aspect or another of that consultation. In 1959 Schiff and Pilot (38) introduced the idea of the consultee-oriented approach.

> It is based on a point of view which is primarily consultee-oriented rather than patient-oriented, and attempts to examine carefully the manner in which the consultation is requested and the background of each situation. The assumption is made that every psychiatric consultation, if not every consultation, stems from the referring physician's concerns, of which the most cogent are frequently not explicitly stated (p. 357).

This contribution alerted the psychiatrist to the referring physician's transactions in the clinical process and was therefore of value.

The third approach to consultation, the situation-oriented, was described by Greenberg in 1960 (39).

> At times, the interaction of members of the clinical staff may produce an atmosphere in which certain aspects of the patient's historical behavior produce anxiety in one or more staff members, or in which covert symptoms become manifest, . . . A situation-oriented approach is suggested to meet with the conditions found in some research settings, as well as with the conditions in a general hospital. This approach takes into account the interpersonal transactions of all the people involved in the direct care of the patient (p. 691).

We have here a transposition of the concepts and methods of Stanton and Schwartz (40) in the psychiatric hospital setting, and Greenberg acknowledges this. Such a point of view had already begun in some liaison programs in the 1950's, but Greenberg was the first to report it in connection with the consultation process. It constituted the recognition of milieu therapy and group process in the social structure of the liaison program, an approach which has steadily grown.

The fourth approach, described above, is the professional-centered approach. In the optimal situation all of these approaches are used simultaneously or as indicated.

Theoretical models of consultation are described in the literature. In concept they are not so very different from the approaches to consultation except that they seem to include unified theories on the background and meaning of the consultation and how the process is worked through. There are to date three consultation models described in the literature: 1) the operational group model, 2) the communications model, and 3) the therapeutic consultation model. Added to these is a fourth, the crisis-orientation model, which is briefly presented here.

The operational group model was described by Meyer and Mendelson in 1961 (26). It is essentially a social process model suggested by the hypotheses of Caudill (41) in his observations of a psychiatric hospital. Meyer and Mendelson write, "From the social-psychological standpoint, the 'operational group' is a way of designating the fact that the subculture of a medical ward has its own working necessities and that patients, even though they are all 'sick,' have various ways of fitting or not fitting into this subculture." The operational group consists of four people, the patient, the internist, the consulting psychiatrist and the nurse. By the systematic collection of data from the transactions of these four people, the identification of the problem and its solution are forthcoming. Meyer and Mendelson state, "The story of the natural history of the consultation process has a beginning, a middle, and an end, which we shall present as the request for consultation, the psychiatrist's redefinition of the patient situation, and the psychiatrist and the operational group." Schwab (34) interprets the concept in saying, "The request for psychiatric consultation reflects a crisis within the group, usually a disruption of trust and communication between the patient and the 'caring-for' people. The entrance of the psychiatrist redefines the operational group, thus reducing anxiety and establishing trust and communication. The interactions between the patient and staff then become therapeutic." This appears to be one form of crisis intervention in the medical-social structure setting.

The communication model was described by Sandt and Leifer (42) in 1964. It represents once more the application of a social science theoretical model to medicine, in this instance, communications theory. The authors do not go beyond analyzing the communication (language) factors in the request for psychiatric consultation by decoding latent reasons for the request. Brosin (43) in 1968 carried the communication concept beyond the request onto the consultation process by suggesting that the consultant and consultee carry on a message system throughout the duration of the case. The successful encoding and decoding of messages determine the outcome of the specific liaison arrangement between consultee and consultant.

Weisman and Hackett's (36) therapeutic consultation model has as its objective the formulation and implementation of a management program for patients with psychological problems. They have written, "There are four phases to the work of therapeutic consultation: Rapid evaluation, with special attention to the personal factors and the reason for consultation; psychodynamic formulation of the major conflict, predominant emotional patterns, ego functions, and object relationships; rational planning of a therapeutic intervention, based on the formulation; and active implementation by the psychiatrist himself." The theoretical approach is "patient-oriented, rather than disease-oriented" in that it attempts to provide psychiatric management by focusing upon crisis, conflict, and reality testing in the patient's brief hospitalization.

The crisis-oriented consultation model may seem to be a modification of Weisman and Hackett's Therapeutic Model, but is distinguishable as a separate model because the method of intervention by the psychiatrist is different. Instead of being patient-oriented, the emphasis is on crisis-orientation. The consultation is not static at the point in time when it is requested. With the therapeutic model (36) the consultant considers the major crisis at the time of request, rapidly evaluates it, makes a psychodynamic formulation of it, noting "emotional patterns, ego functions, and object relations," and arranges a program of therapy based on that psychodynamic formulation. It is envisioned as being "streamlined, brief, and with limited aims." It has a psychoanalytic orientation around a point of conflict, which is searched for as quickly as possible. On the other hand the crisis-oriented model has more of a behavioral therapy emphasis (44). It considers psychosocial factors as emotional stressors that produce exacerbations of symptoms and behavioral reactions in the sick person which are presented by him in some form as a crisis. The exacerbation which brought him to the hospital and his course in the hospital may be marked by a series of crises and he may be influenced in the social setting of the medical unit by crises within the staff or by those of other patients. In the consultation, the liaison psychiatrist identifies the event-dysfunction sequences (45), and the patient's communication defenses which attempt to shield him from disclosures to the staff. The consultant also screens for staff involvement in the relevant crisis and for the sources of crisis in the milieu. Thus a pattern of behavioral and somatic reactions to emotional stress is noted and communicated to the staff. Physicians and nurses learn to ferret out correlations between stressful events and symptoms more easily than receiving psychodynamic formulations, no matter how simple. They often begin to do this themselves. What is also important is that the identification of the crisis alone may be enough for both patient and the physicians or nurses to move toward its remission. This is a rapid time-limited method useful and practical in the brief duration of hospitalization as it is today. More extensive work with the patient can be done by the psychiatrist after discharge. As for the internist he is encouraged to continue the crisis-orientation in the ambulatory care of the patient. This is not crisis intervention so much as crisis identification and acknowledgment of crises to the patient, measures which are to be recommended in clinical management.

Identification and acknowledgment of crisis as part of the rubric of the healing art were pointed out by the author (46) in 1958:

Above and beyond all things, the human being needs awareness and tolerance on the part of others for his vicissitudes in interpersonal adaptation. Such tolerance is conveyed through the medium of communication which feeds back recognition and acknowledgment of this need within appropriate limits. Such is the essence of the affection which is required for man's true realization of himself. The sharing of the recognition of this need, the communication of the sensitivity to it, and the demonstration of mutual respect for it are the translation of the language of affection within the professional limits conducive to successful psychotherapy (p. 41).

Today, I would add that such caring and such concern are the essence of humanistic clinical intervention.

The crisis-orientation model suggests a method of application of George Engel's research approach to the "psychosomatic interface," as he calls it. In 1967 (47) he wrote:

For the time being I believe the most useful access to the psychosomatic interface is through discovery of simultaneity or sequence of psychic and somatic phenomena, inadequate as that may be. And the most pressing task is to study with the greatest care and in the finest detail the characteristics of the psychic process occurring in such time periods of simultaneity or sequence (p. 8).

Having reviewed the psychiatric consultation in the liaison program and having considered the approaches and models which have developed over the past 40 years, let us now take a look at how these mental health services are delivered to those patients who are medically and surgically ill. There are several categories of such patients who require mental health services, but there are a limited number of studies (11, 18, 48, 49) on frequency. The most recent by Kligerman and McKegney (48) lists diagnoses and their incidence in a large series of consultations in a teaching hospital:

1. Acute and Chronic Brain Syndromes 31.0%
2. Depressive Reactions 57.4%
3. Conversion Reactions 11.5%
4. (Other) Neurotic Reactions 32.2%
5. "Classical" Psychosomatic Disease 8.8%

When one considers Schmale's figures on depression and separation reactions in medical patients (49), one sees that the incidence of depression ranges from 57.4-69.0 percent.

This is, however, only a portion of those needing help. These are the ones on whom consultations had been requested. There are others. Kligerman and McKegney (48) report that between 39 percent and 45.8 percent of the patients on the Yale-New Haven Hospital Medical Service were moderately or severely emotionally disturbed. Lipowski (9) cites the prevalance of psychiatric morbidity in "medical" populations in nine studies as ranging between 15 percent and 72.5 percent, depending on the study.

In contrast, the frequency of psychiatric consultations requested is low. Kligerman and McKegney (48) reported that only 2.94 percent of all patients at Yale-New Haven Hospital have such consultations. At the same center Duff and Hollingshead (50) reported there were consultations requested on only 6 percent of 161 identified psychiatric problems on a medical-surgical unit. From eight other studies (9) over several years, the frequency ranged from 4-13 percent with an average of 9 percent. At the Einstein Hospital, with a high critical care census, only 3 percent of admissions have a psychiatric consultation (30). There, of the first 100 preterminal and terminal cases with cancer admitted in 1976, only six had psychiatric consultations requested. Out of 100 cancer cases referred by physicians there for liaison consultation, 76 percent came as a result of primary referral by nursing, social service, and families through putting pressure on the physician. Of the 24 patients referred directly by physicians, 23 had acute brain syndromes, and one a depression.

The natural questions which arise are: Does this represent a striking lack of interest and strong resistance on the part of physicians, even where there are active educational programs? Does it mean that there is so much of the professional-oriented approach, the informal consultation, and so many educational exercises that more patients are receiving mental health services than we think? Or that through the liaison system itself there is enough "know-how" on the part of non-psychiatric personnel that the mental health needs of patients are being met? Or are there forces at work which eventuate in the emotional needs, the "felt needs," and even the psychopathology being grossly neglected, no matter how great the zeal and efforts of liaison people? There are no evaluation studies, but the answer is probably some of each. I am of the opinion that after 40 years and two generations of effort by liaison psychiatrists, physicians as a class do little about emotional care.

What happens to the vast majority of medical and surgical patients who receive little emotional care? In addition to the brain syndromes, the neurotic reactions, the depressions, and the psychosomatic disorders, there are a variety of emotional states that patients experience in reacting to their illnesses and to the hospital environment. Some of these are appropriate coping mechanisms, others are overdetermined and are anxiety reactions, hostility states, regressive phenomenon, and management problems (51). They originate as, or become, interpersonal problems, and result in crises which should require appropriate recognition. What happens is usually a matter of chance depending on the location of the patient in the hospital. If there is a liaison service attached to his medical floor his emotional problem may be discovered by virtue of a liaison psychiatrist on rounds, a consultation request, the awareness of one or more nurses, or a sensitive therapeutic milieu in which an aide may start a message about his needs moving up through the hierarchy of professional channels. On the other hand, if he is on a surgical floor, or in a hospital with a consultation service only or with no liaison arrangement at all, he will have little structure for rescue. Often his only chance for help may be through nursing.

NON-MEDICAL DEVELOPMENTS AND LIAISON PROGRAMS

There are two developments in liaison work which are not solely related to medicine, but which are deeply significant. One is the introduction of the social model into the concepts and procedures of liaison medicine and the other is the expanding role of disciplines other than medicine as the supporting structure for the emotional care of patients.

The development of liaison programs has moved from the sophisticated medical model of Colorado, the Massachusetts General Hospital, Rochester, Hopkins, Montefiore Hospital, and Cincinnati to a recognition that the social environment—i.e., the many disciplines, the structure of hospitals, the health care system—has a powerful role. Lidz, Fleck, Grolnick, Brodsky, Bergen, Enelow and Myers, Greenhill, Berblinger, Fitzpatrick, Miller, Schulman, Meissner, Karasu, Hertzman and many others have contributed to the literature on this influence. There is no longer a way to deny a social model in liaison psychiatry. In 1977 every liaison program is involved in it whether it is acknowledged or not. The reality of the general hospital as a community, subject to all the social transactional forces of the geographic community, and of the liaison psychiatrist as a community psychiatrist, until recently never admitted, makes it a useless exercise to compare the medical model with the social model.

The very existence of liaison programs and their strategies depends on group process. The triad of the patient-physician-consultant is an undeniable group, subject to process. The social structure of the hospital, the presence of systems in the delivery of health services, the transactions between medical disciplines, consumerism, advocacy, peer review, administrative process, social value systems, economics, and many other forces are indigenous to the hospital culture. This concept extends the boundaries of liaison psychiatry to include social-group factors in the operational design of programs and in the process of the liaison between psychiatry and medicine.

For that reason the flux of social forces around the hospital patient, such as those just cited, must be considered. Physicians seem to have little awareness of these forces, but nurses, social workers, and skilled modern hospital administrators know of their presence and often seek to work with them.

One example of a social group factor in patient care is the relative anonymity of the hospital patient. Physicians and nurses may make decisions and do procedures on medical and surgical patients without knowing much about them as people. The patients are there in the midst of a medical environment enmeshed in systems and social processes. No one may elicit "the story" that each patient has. That story is composed of the particular combination of vital facts and emotional stresses which provides the psychosocial data of the clinical condition. Medical and nursing personnel may have but a superficial acquaintance with patients; in many charts "family history, non-contributory" is written. Liaison programs have done little to change the anonymity of medical patients. They have tried in a segmental way by creating "islands of excellence," but in truth, the mass of patients are excluded. Another example of social effect is that strategies upon which liaison programs are organized are often dependent upon negotiating social forces. One such negotiation aimed at reducing the anonymity of the patient was the attempt at the Einstein Hospital to get physicians to allow nurses to write their observational and process notes on the same part of the chart used by physicians for their progress notes. The negotiation succeeded, but it was only a beginning in modifying anonymity.

THE ROLES OF OTHER PROFESSIONAL DISCIPLINES IN LIAISON PROGRAMS

If it is true that the physician cannot, for one reason or another, reach all of the concerns of his patients, and that liaison psychiatrists are too few in number to meet the psychiatric problems of the medically ill, let alone deal with their emotional needs, who is to do it? The triage of patients for the primary physician, the tertiary physician, and the psychiatrist is a continual issue but in the end concerns only a fraction of patients. Who else is there to deal with the remainder of those with psychiatric morbidity or suffering emotional pain? Should it be nurses, social workers, clinical psychologists, paraprofessional counselors, a multidisciplinary team, or who?

When all is said and done, across the expanse of suffering and concern, the nurse deals with the emotional care of the patient more than anyone else. As a matter of proximity alone, it falls to the nurse either to be exposed to the crises of patients or to be confronted by them through default, because there may be no one else. But besides that, the nurturance aspects of nursing itself fortifies in some an attitude of caring and concern which they brought with them in their choice of profession. McKegney (1) has written, "The psychosocial data from the individual medical-surgical nurse are narrow in perspective." I presume this is true of untutored young nurses, when it comes to observing and reporting such data. But their actions in meeting psychosocial crisis in the patient are frequently correct. There is a growing army of medical-surgical nurses who are knowledgeable and sophisticated. They are trained by highly intelligent nurse-clinician teachers. The nursing profession has an impressive literature on liaison work and their bibliographies on interviewing technique, for example, rival those of psychiatry in size, and may be more applicable to the medical patient. The minimization of the value of nursing by liaison psychiatry has been difficult to understand.

As for nursing itself, there are two ways in which it became involved in liaison programs, one through in-service training, the other through the development of the concept of the psychiatric liaison nurse. Inservice training, either in seminars, courses and workshops or through attendance at ward rounds, liaison conferences, interdiscipline conferences, T-groups, or individual supervision by psychiatrists or liaison nurses has become standard procedure in most programs that place credence in the role of modern nursing. On the other hand, it is the only way for the inclusion of planned psychosocial nursing care by medical-surgical nurses in those institutions which do not have a psychiatric liaison nurse nor an emotional care clinician.

The development of the concept of the psychiatric liaison nurse has been underway for almost 30 years. In 1948, three nurses were added to the liaison staff at Duke, one trained as a mental health public health consultant and two medical-surgical nurses, one of whom was a Fellow in Psychosomatic Nursing. The nurse consultant, Florence Burnett, explored and developed methods of teaching psychological care to medical-surgical nurses which are still in use. The Nursing Fellow, Virginia Crenshaw, developed applications of interviewing technique to nursing communication and utilized for the first time *nursing crisis vignettes* in teaching psychological nursing, which are now commonplace in nursing education.

In 1949, Bernstein, Small, and Reich (63) described the role of nursing in the Psychosomatic Unit at Mount Sinai Hospital, particularly the nature of the nurse-patient relationship. In 1951, Burnett, Sites, and Greenhill (64) published "Learning the Mental Health Approach Through the Chronic Medical Patient," and in 1956 Greenhill (65) published a paper on interviewing for medical-surgical nurses. Between 1963 and 1976, twenty-two influential articles on interviewing in the medical setting have appeared in the nursing literature (66-87). During the same period 10 publications (64, 88-96) have appeared on liaison nursing, seven of which were related to the functions of the psychiatric liaison nurse.

Barton and Kelso (95) in 1971 called attention to the following functions: The liaison nurse 1) provides perspective from the viewpoint of the nursing profession, 2) gathers information about patients for the diagnostic process, 3) is involved in the milieu in prevention of crisis and intervention in crisis, 4) provides specialized nursing care otherwise unavailable, 5) coordinates available resources by improving communication, 6) provides an educational experience for the members of the liaison team in the transactional field of the patient (nursing care), and 7) participates in research into aspects of nursing care. In 1973 Kimball (97) cited the report of Pranulis on the role of the psychiatric liaison nurse (PLN) at Yale, which include not only participation in diagnostic evaluations, staff sensitivity training, problem solving regarding gaps in patient-staff communication, and a brief psychotherapeutic approach, but also acting as a triage person for referral of the patient to the most appropriate liaison team member.

An example of the activity of a psychiatric liaison nurse can be given from the work of Goodman at the Einstein Hospital, where such nursing participation started in 1967 (98). Referrals from the nursing service alone to the PLN were 233 in 1970. These were cases which had not been referred for psychiatric consultation and included depressions, anxiety states, nursing management problems with demanding or manipulative patients, reactions of patients to dying, family adjustments to illness, nursing staff reaction to patient, nursing management of hyperactivity and inappropriate behavior, and organic mental syndrome. In addition in that year, the PLN held 54 nursing staff conferences, 259 interdisciplinary conferences, and collaborated on 50 cases with liaison psychiatrists. Here also the PLN has a large "on the line" educational function together with the liaison psychiatrists in demonstrating and teaching psychological care much as the liaison psychiatrist does with non-psychiatrist physicians. Her objective is to teach crisis identification, emotional support, management of the hospital unit milieu, and care of the critically ill by engagement, support, and indicated confrontation.

Inasmuch as nurses as a class are within the environment of the sick continuously, their role is large, but social work and clinical psychology are exploring their positions in the triage system. From the beginning of liaison programs, physicians have often been more comfortable in referring the psychosocial aspects of patient care to medical social workers. Such help has been valuable in terms of planning for aftercare, but sometimes could not do as much as required for active hospital clinical management. In a liaison team, the social worker contributes much as a community organization specialist for the benefit of continuity of care. An attempt was made by Shochet (99) to train and utilize paraprofessionals as mental health counselors on medical-surgical units for case finding and triage. Somewhat the same plan is in use at the Einstein Hospital where "emotional care workers" have been trained for particularized functions with cancer and dialysis patients (30).

Liaison programs appear to have needs for extended service as their development proceeds.

EDUCATION AND TRAINING

Dyrud (100) has written, "Teaching is sharing to the best of our ability." This is particularly relevant in liaison psychiatry wherein occurs so much sharing of psychiatric knowledge with other disciplines in the face of reluctant acceptance or resistance to learning. To teach the physician to include psychosocial variables in patient care and then to deal with them himself or to teach him to permit a psychiatrist to participate has proven to be a special and challenging task for the psychiatric educator. What the liaison psychiatrist is opting for is an improvement in clinical science through education for the benefit of the somatically ill patient.

In the strict sense, clinical science indicates that the professional deals with multiple variables simultaneously, sorting and weighing them through a moving process toward equilibrium or dissolution for the patient. In dealing with variables, one changes their priority from time to time to attain one's clinical goals. Ideally one should not become fixed on one set of variables or on one theoretical model. What seems to be a fact in medicine is that the physician fixes upon one set of of variables, according to his specialty. But no matter what his specialty, his theoretical model is always the somatic process, and very seldom does he consider it essential to include psychological and social variables within his purview. In fact most physicians seem to have a sort of "receptive aphasia" for such variables. This therefore makes them incomplete clinicians, and the liaison psychiatrist has taken upon himself the task of making them whole again. It is a strange distortion which permits medical scientists to insist on strict controls in the laboratory or double blind studies in clinical research while at the same time they leave almost completely uncontrolled so many variables in clinical science.

Engel (21) seems to make the same point when he writes on the education of the physician for clinical observation.

> In the final analysis it is the physician's effectiveness and accuracy as an observing instrument that determine the range and reliability of the data ultimately available to him for judgments and for processing by other technology. Clearly then, an essential task for medical education is to develop the physician as the most effective and reliable observing instrument possible (p. 159).

From the time that Billings established a liaison department at Colorado with the objective "to sensitize the physicians and students to the opportunities offered them by every patient" and ever since Kaufman and Margolin spelled out as one of the goals of a liaison program in a general hospital "teaching, which involves two aspects—one, the further training of the psychiatric staff, and two, the indoctrination and teaching of every member of the hospital staff from administration through chiefs to house-staff," education has been a primary function of liaison programs. In fact, when one studies these programs and communicates with their leaders the teaching aspect often seems to be the primary purpose. From the tenor of Billings and Kaufman and Margolin's educational objectives to the spirit of the writing and plans of other teachers of liaison psychiatry, the sense of mission, crusading zeal, and messianic vision is clear. The mission of liaison psychiatry, the thrust, has been to proselytize.

Descriptions of liaison teaching programs are scattered throughout the literature in psychiatry and in internal medicine, but it is surprising to discover that between 1950-1975 there were only four articles on teaching in *Psychosomatic Medicine* (23, 24, 101, 102), the journal of the American Psychosomatic Society. In those 25 years there were, in addition, two presidential addresses (103, 104) in the society on teaching which were printed in the journal. There is obviously more interest in that society in psychosomatic medicine than in liaison psychiatry (only four articles on organization of liaison programs in 25 years as well (27, 105-107)). This oversight may be largely responsible for the paucity of evaluation studies in the field. The gap has been partly filled by the *International Journal of Psychiatry in Medicine*.

Regarding the development of the educational process, programs have been surveyed in varying degrees by the author through communications with liaison directors and through the literature in connection with the following institutions: Rochester (20), Downstate Medical School (109), Peter Bent Brigham Hospital (110), Mount Auburn Hospital (Cambridge, Mass.) (4), Cushing Veterans' Administration Hospital (29, 101), Vermont (2), Duke (23), Einstein (3 programs) (30, 111), Chicago (112), and the Massachusetts General Hospital (16). Let us concentrate on these liaison programs where the most intensive teaching has been done. The pedagogical aim is to utilize the liaison psychiatrist through consultations and management of liaison relationships, to modify attitudes of other physicians in the acceptance of him as a role model, and to teach other physicians to expand their awareness to learn methods and techniques to do emotional care themselves.

The logistics of the teaching situation have special characteristics. A small number of liaison teachers (one to 10), with a small number of liaison fellows (one to 6) or none at all, have taken on the task of teaching medical students, psychiatric residents, interns, residents and fellows in other departments, nursing students, staff, and nurse clinicians, and a variety of ancillary personnel, whose multidisciplinary collaboration is needed. The strategies evolved to allow teachers to do an effective job in these impossible proportions depend on the needs of the institution and the interests and personality of the liaison leader. On the whole, the attempted strategies are: 1) to concentrate the teaching area in a limited geographic area, i.e., one or more medical units in the department of medicine, 2) to establish a demonstration model or "island of excellence" in one hospital unit or subspecialty, 3) to attempt to reach the learner while he is yet a medical student, 4) to enlarge the population of available liaison workers by concentrating on graduate training (fellowships), and 5) to utilize the services of available fellows to do the principal work of teaching house officers in other departments by peer effect. As a matter of fact, in many programs the task is so disproportionate that the patient may lose out as a focus of interest, so great must be the strategy of educating caretakers. For the senior liaison psychiatrist, this educational pressure, some research, and much clinical administration involving psychiatry, medicine, and hospital administration occupy much of his time. Furthermore, in some programs, because of these logistic problems, as well as for other reasons, the training of psychiatric residents in liaison psychiatry becomes a less important consideration.

Reichsman (109) has cited the teaching objectives of a psychosomatic program, as he calls it, as: 1) the learning of skills and of methods of observation, 2) the acquisition of information concerning mind-body relationships in health and in the pathogenesis, course, and treatment of a wide variety of diseases, 3) development of the capacity for clinical reasoning, 4) modification in attitudes and behavior toward a humanistic-scientific approach, and 5) presentation of a liaison teacher who has the image of both an internist and a psychiatrist. These objectives follow closely those of his teacher, Engel at Rochester.

On the other hand, the following are a more comprehensive group of teaching objectives which were derived from the survey of several other centers, and which are applicable, in degrees of intensity, to the education of medical students, residents, and fellows: 1) to teach those psychiatric methods and techniques which are relevant to the physically ill, including the collection and assessment of raw psychosocial data through interviewing technique, and instruction in supportive therapy, limited-goal, brief psychotherapy, and crisis intervention; 2) to present a body of substantive psychiatric knowledge the content of which is relevant to medical and surgical disorders. This would include a) delirium and dementia, b) depression, grief and separation reactions, c) psychoneurotic equivalencies in somatic disease, i.e., anxiety attacks, conversion reactions, d) emotional stress-sensitive medical disorders, i.e., peptic ulcer, asthma, etc., e) psychological reactions to illness, to interpersonal stress, and to terminal states, and f) addictive reactions and borderline states; 3) to teach the administration of psychopharmacological agents to the physically ill; 4) to present the influence of social science, with the effect of social stresses and patterns on the exacerbation and course of medical and surgical disorders; 5) to change the attitudes of the learner regarding psychological processes, the image of the psychiatrist, scientific dogma, the quest for certainty, and the counter-values of other teachers; 6) to influence the learner's methods of communication, verbal and written, to include recognition of psychosocial phenomena and willingness to engage the patient on emotional topics; 7) to interest the learner in the problems of chronicity; 8) to give the learner experiential involvement in the physician-patient relationship in medicine through continued case supervision, brief or extended; 9) to free the learner's humanitarian potential by a combination of points of concentration on interviewing technique, group process, physician-patient relationship, and modification of attitudes.

The organizational design for implementing the teaching objectives has been fairly standardized from program to program. It includes seminars on interviewing and substantive material, patient rounds, supervision, consultations, informal contacts, clinical case work, and patient-centered teaching conferences. Ward rounds, teaching conferences, and other clinical conferences are attended in the host department. Students and staff in that department are encouraged by the liaison group to attend the liaison psychiatric meetings.

The above teaching objectives are generic and can be utilized in varying degrees dependent upon the level of the learner. In the graduate training program, there are three ingredients which acquire special significance. For the liaison fellow, who is immediately put into the role of a teacher, and is receiving training for liaison leadership, particular skill in interviewing, relationships, and group process is mandatory for the teaching and administrative requirements. His teacher will emphasize those ingredients automatically. Add to that instruction in teaching methods, administration and managerial skills, advanced consultation, and evaluation and research, and a thorouogh graduate educational program for a liaison psychiatrist has been achieved.

I would like to call attention to the similarities that exist between such a program for liaison fellows and the curriculum in the Fellowship Program in Social and Community Psychiatry in the Albert Einstein College of Medicine (113). The content of the curriculum is designed to provide basic competence in eight main core areas: group process and group therapy, family process and family therapy, crisis intervention, systems theory, administration and organizational development, consultation, epidemiology, research and evaluation. Contemporary health care systems will not much longer countenance the isolation of a medical model or a social model. True liaison psychiatry is comprised of both.

ROLE MODELS IN TEACHING PSYCHOMATIC MEDICINE

We now come to the consideration of role models in the acceptance by physicians of the psychological and social influences in health and disease. In 1967, Engel wrote (20):

.... of critical importance for the establishment of the program and its subsequent growth was, I believe, the fact that I and those who joined me in the early days were fully qualified as internists. This enabled us to establish ourselves as peers on the medical service and gradually to overcome the misconception that we were alien poachers on their domain. . . . When such programs are staffed only or predominately by psychiatrists, they never really become anything other than psychiatric consultation services. As a result students and house officers never have as a model a physician who combines in his own personal skill both the psychological and somatic aspects of illness. And without such a model the student has no alternative but to believe that it takes two specialists to deal with psychosomatic issues (p. 84).

Kaufman (33) had written another point of view in 1953:

A psychiatrist is a catalyst, an integrator. He has a great deal to contribute to medicine, but his contribution must be made primarily as a psychiatrist. The writer has no patience with the type of psychiatrist who tries to smuggle himself into medicine under false colors and who feels that it behooves him to demonstrate to the surgeon or to the internist that after all he, too, is a top internist or surgeon. . . . The psychiatrist is a psychiatrist, just as the surgeon is a surgeon; and it is only as a psychiatrist, standing firmly based on his own discipline, that he can eventually demonstrates the value of his orientation in the understanding and treatment of patients (p. 373).

Engel and Kaufman are obviously prototypes of two opposing points of view. In the absence of evaluation studies in liaison psychiatry and particularly on this point, no one can claim one is right and the other wrong, for apparently both types of role model serve the purpose. If a careful evaluation study were to be done on this issue, it might be found that the dominant factors were concurrent parallel effects. In other words, one such concurrent factor might be that both Engel and Kaufman had qualities of leadership, not that one identified with being an internist and another a psychiatrist. Another concurrent factor might be that physicians resisted both liaison men and their programs, not because one was less of an internist and the other less of a psychiatrist, but for many other reasons.

The stand taken by liaison psychiatrists concerning role models appears to be influenced by their own predominant identifications. As a teacher of many years the author knows that many liaison fellows are searching for their place of identity in medicine; most of them find it, on one side of the fence or on the other, but always retaining that "liaison touch."

I think we are historically beyond the image of the internist as the role model. The role model is a proven expert clinician in any field, including psychiatry, whose enthusiasm for clinical science is contagious, and who can demonstrate that psychosocial data and interpersonal processes are powerful factors in medicine. The internist role model may be less well prepared to deal with the exigencies of social and behavioral pressures on medicine today than the psychiatrist or the professor of community medicine.

RESISTANCE

The consideration of role models has been promulgated for many years as one method of reducing resistance to liaison programs. But resistance against psychological medicine is complicated, puzzling, and stubborn. It has been discussed thoroughly through the years and many methods have been attempted to combat it. Conciliation, concession, internist identification, use of somatic language, joint rank, emphasis on physiology and biochemistry, and attitudes denoting validity of psychiatric approach are among methods which have been used by liaison psychiatrists. Early exposure of the medical student with reinforcement at later stages in his career is another. Continuing education courses for graduate physicians is still another. Causes advanced for resistance include the crowded nature of medical training, assimilation by the student of the negative attitudes toward psychiatry and psychological medicine demonstrated by the principal teachers in other fields, and anxiety related to unconscious forces within physicians and students. Other possible reasons for resistance will be discussed later under new developments in liaison programs.

Another surprising feature in the development of liaison psychiatry is the paucity of structured programs for house officers. The educational focus has been mainly on the teaching of medical students and liaison fellows in well devised curricula, but house officers have been, by and large, taught indirectly and irregularly. Engel (20) has reported in the Rochester experience, "No systematic teaching of house staff has been carried out. Many may have contact." The teaching conference for medical housestaff may be held once a week or once a month, and attendance is usually irregular, unless the professor of medicine attends also.

There are many position papers in the literature regarding teaching in psychosomatic medicine with some references to teaching housestaff, including ones by Romano (114, 115), Engel (20), Rosenbaum (116, 117), Balint (118, 119), Bibring (51), Whitehorn (120), Schmale (49), Lipowski (11), and McKegney (1, 2). They write about the need to teach interns and residents, but it is surprising that only a handful of reports exist on structured curricula for house officers in non-psychiatric departments. Apparently the only major one has been that conducted by the author at Duke in 1947-52. During that period a serious effort was made to train over 100 interns and residents in the Department of Medicine. A description and evaluation of the results of training 47 of these appeared in *Psychosomatic Medicine* in 1950. Other programs were reported by Fox (110), Kligerman (101), Reichsman (109), and Strain and Grossman (29). These last four programs had one or more of the following teaching components: 1) a small number of house officers, 2) a scheduled teaching conference, and 3) assigned or voluntary continued case supervision. Strain and Grossman (29) used what they call a "medical Ombudsman" from the department of medicine to aid in the teaching of medical residents. They state, "We hoped that by working with their housestaff in this unique way (as ombudsmen), the Chief of Medicine and his assistant director would become aware of issues ordinarily kept hidden by the system—the problems posed by the increase in patient admissions, the private patient-staff conflict, the anxiety and sense of abandonment felt by the housestaff, and the lack of attention given to the psychological perspective of the developing physician."

There may be no reason for the gap in training for psychological medicine between the medical student and the practicing physician other than resistance on the part of clinical departments and their trainees. They seem to allow only sporadic instruction on a more or less voluntary basis and merely tolerate the proximity of liaison psychiatrists and fellows. No wonder Whitehorn (121) reported that the psychological sensitivity of medical students was highest in the first year, declined during the remainder of medical school, then dropped precipitously during postgraduate training only to incline again after several years in practice.

What is the particular amnesia in liaison programs which permits this? If liaison psychiatrists aim to inculcate in housestaffs sensitivity to the emotional needs of medical patients, why do they make such a lukewarm effort about it? Are they more interested in selective teaching and research, and not as much in patient care, or do they back-off and feel it is overwhelming and useless to cope with the combined resistance of all elements of the department of medicine?

In the Duke study (23), it was possible to deal with the resistance and maintain a structured teaching program for house officers in medicine for five years. Besides having the authoritative backing of the chief of medicine, the resisters were typed and strategic "clinical" means of working with each one were developed.

Another factor which has not been thoroughly engaged by liaison psychiatry is the resistance within the department of psychiatry. Lipsitt (4) and McKegney (2) have written thoughtful appraisals. about the resistance and obstacles to the "psychosomatic approach." Most psychiatrists prefer to work with the intricacies of interpersonal relations and intrapsychic forces, specific symptom groups, and psychotherapy. They are apt to be strongly individualistic or societally oriented. How to collaborate more with their colleagues on the borderland of medicine should be seriously considered, particularly in light of social changes occuring within the health care system.

EVALUATION OF RESULTS IN LIAISON PROGRAMS

The paucity of evaluation studies in liaison psychiatry has been pointed out in this presentation. This is rather surprising when one considers the research emphasis in psychosomatic medicine throughout its existence, particularly in laboratory investigation. That these investigators who neglected to apply their skills in scientific methods in this direction would be joined by research workers from other disciplines in the field, such as by clinical psychologists and social scientists, who are more familiar with evaluation methods, is doubly surprising.

Lipowski (10) comes to grips with this situation in an article in *Psychosomatic Medicine*:

> A matter of concern is the apparent cleavage between the laboratory researcher in psychosomatics and the consultant-clinician. This is reflected in the relative dearth of clinical reports in this journal, as well as in the programs of the society's meetings. Such lack of communication is deplorable. Research, theory development, and clinical activity are integral components of psychosomatic medicine. Free flow of communication among those engaged in each of these areas is necessary for the further development of the field as a whole. Clinicians, even if they are not engaged in research, may make observation which are not to be dismissed as anecdotal material. Even a single observation may provide a seminal idea to be formulated as a testable hypothesis (p. 416).

Although this was written in 1968, it is still applicable. It seems as if there has been an inappropriate emphasis upon laboratory method, conceptualizing, and an undue fascination with developmental physiology on the part of those leaders who were internists and physiologists and came to psychiatry principally by virtue of psychoanalytic training. Their contribution to the field could have been larger if they had encouraged assessment of results in clinical and teaching aspects of liaison psychiatry.

Let us look at what evaluation studies do exist. In 1952, Southard (122) offered a helpful discussion. . . .

> an activity may be evaluated on a basis of one or more levels or types of measurement based on different value systems. At the first level, evaluation is an estimate which an individual or group places on an activity or service—what it means to the

recipients according to their own value system. At the second level, evaluation is the appraised worth; that is, a value placed on an activity or service after a reasonable examination and after appraisers have compared it with other services. It is presumed that these appraisers have had experience in their respective fields. The third level is that of scientific measurement—an expression of value measured against accepted standardized procedures. . . . (p. 17).

French (122) has set forth the *essential steps in evaluation*:

(1) Identification of the goals to be sought or measured, (2) Analysis of the problems with which the activity must cope, (3) Description and standardization of the activity, (4) Measurement of the degree of change that takes place, (5) Determination as to whether the change observed is the result of the activity or due to some other cause, and (6) Some indication of the durability of the effects (p. 21).

Evaluation regarding liaison programs can involve a legion of activities and areas but the principal ones to survey for assessment studies are those related to the cardinal areas of organization, consultation, education and patient care.

1) *Organization*—no evaluation studies exist at Level Three (scientific measurement) in connection with the efficacy of the different models of liaison programs. At Level One (the value that an individual involved in the model places on the result) there are a number of reports. For example, the Rochester group has published several papers (20, 22) describing their program in which they claim that it is effective and has produced a large number of liaison teachers. No group of outside appraisers has evaluated any of the programs and reported upon them. Grant-giving organizations have appraised specific programs from reports by those programs and through site visits, but these are not made public.

2) *Consultation*—no studies exist comparing the relative effectiveness of approaches to consultation and theoretical models of consultation. Data, all too scarce, exist on diagnostic categories and who does consultations, but this has to be distinguished from evalua-

tion, which reports upon results of an activity. There is no question that there has been a paucity of data observed and recorded, and until there is a disciplined approach to the collection of relevant data, evaluation in the field will be weak. An example of useful data collection which probably led to an unreported organizational result or modification is the study by Bernstein and Kaufman (18) on types of consultation done at Mount Sinai Hospital. We have noted the useful evaluation study by Kligerman and McKegney (48) in which they cite the percentage of diagnostic categories seen in consultation, and give evidence upon the limitations of this sample.

3) *Education*—several evaluation studies have been done on education and training. Most of these have been by the simplest method of scientific evaluation i.e., statistical reporting on and categorization of assessment questionnaires for students (123). An example of appraisal by an expert (Level Two) is the article by Stratas (124). Studies on the methodology of teaching psychological medicine are limited in number. One that deserves to be critically evaluated is by Rosenbaum, Jacobs, and Mann (117) on teaching this subject by a preceptorship method to junior medical students. It is loose in design and seems to view the data collected by personal appraisals (starts at Level Three and concludes by Level One).

In 1966 Mendel (125) published what is considered to be a classic in evaluating the status of psychiatric consultation education. A questionnaire survey was conducted of 202 psychiatric training centers. He found that 25 percent of all training centers had no consultation training or liaison programs, and that in 53 percent of consultative training programs there was no follow-up study on consultations. He also discovered that in only 30 percent of these centers was the trainee formally evaluated as to what he had learned.

In 1976, Schubert and McKegney (126) partially repeated the study by polling 92 medical schools to find that 8 percent have no training programs in liaison psychiatry. When one notes Mendel's findings regarding medical schools in 1966 (7 percent had no liaison training programs), the findings are comparable. Schubert and McKegney comment: "Psychiatric residency programs devote approximately 10 percent of their time to CL training (consultation-liaison), a slight increase over ten years ago." Mendel had reported 7 percent. They comment further: "One can only assume that there has been a comparable increase in other institutions offering psychiatric residencies" and "Program directors reported an approximately 90 percent 'favorable' reaction to such training by all trainees." Such assumptions and approximations are another example of the looseness of evaluation and research in the liaison field. What does seem to emerge is the fact that there has been little change in consultation training in ten years.

The principal studies on the evaluation of results in training non-psychiatric personnel are those by Greenhill and Kilgore (23), (house officers), and by Burnett and Greenhill (96) (nurses). Trainees were evaluated by a battery of methods and techniques including trainee questionnaires, teacher questionnaire, evaluation of teaching, consensual validation by teachers, evaluations by supervisors, typing of resistance to learning, and assessment of record writing. They found 40 percent of interns and residents in medicine cannot learn to use psychiatric techniques and methods effectively after involvement in a liaison program. They also learned that medical and public health nurses have a more open, less resistant attitude toward learning methods and techniques of emotional care of patients, but 40 percent cannot learn these effectively after an intensive inservice training course with a supervised practicum.

4) *Patient care*—there are practically no studies in existence on the results of patient care after participation of consultation-liaison psychiatrists. Do they improve, not improve, get worse? How many die and when do they die? Does psychiatric contact reduce recidivism in hospital admissions? What happens to patients touched by liaison programs as far as aftercare is concerned? Which professional discipline helps the patient the most with his psychosocial problems? There are myriads of these unanswered questions awaiting study. (How do we know where we are?) Schwab and his co-workers (127) made a careful scientific study of "Medical Inpatients Reactions to Psychiatric Consultations" as an example of what is wanting, but there is little else.

THE COST OF LIAISON PROGRAMS

It is common knowledge that liaison programs are not well supported financially. Departments of psychiatry within schools of medicine assign only a small fraction of their budgets to these endeavors, usually the salary of the director of a liaison division. This liaison leader may or may not be able to devote all of his time to liaison work. In other instances part-time salaries will be paid to liaison teachers from undergraduate teaching grants because of their role in teaching pyschiatry to medical students on medical clerkships. Otherwise liaison programs depend upon their success in obtaining grants for research projects or for the training of liaison fellows.

Examples show that the departments meant to benefit most by liaison programs, such as the department of medicine, almost never contribute to their support. At Rochester (108) with its 30-year collaboration with medicine, the budget of the liaison service in 1976 had as its source of revenue: Medicine—10 percent, Psychiatry—15 percent, Medical School—5 percent, Research and Training Grants—65 percent. At Downstate Medical Center in 1975 (109), the Department of Medicine provided one salary for a liaison fellow from the budget for its residents. I have been unable to find other examples where medicine or any other department contribute, although there may be some. There are departments of psychiatry within teaching hospitals which contribute nothing to the support of liaison services.

It is also known that psychiatrists are poorly compensated for performing psychiatric consultations. The lack of interest of patients receiving consultations which they may have accepted as a matter of "doctor's orders," their lack of motivation for psychological aid, the negative attitudes of their families toward psychiatry, the idea of stigma in the face of sometimes inadequate referral preparation by the physician, and the almost complete abnegation by third party carriers of the significance of psychiatric consultation accounts for the failures of reimbursement. Consultants spend at least double the time ordinarily given in a psychotherapy session and may receive half of the fee or none at all. At the Einstein Hospital in 1976 (30), the rate of collection for psychiatric consultations was 40 percent and those involved were experienced consultants, all in private practice and with the rank of Clinical Assistant Professor and above.

In 1972 McKegney (2) considered the cost of maintaining psychiatrists attached to the medical service for liaison duties,

> The amount of time necessary for a staff psychiatrist to perform an adequate liaison role on one non-psychiatric inpatient unit seems to approximate 10 hours per week. At the currently hourly rate for psychotherapy this primary teaching service would cost at least $15,000 to $20,000 per year per inpatient unit, if it were not for either academic pressures forcing the voluntary contribution of clinical faculty time, or the lower salaries paid full-time faculty (p. 202).

Guggenheim (128) carries these problems further in questions relating to financial reimbursement, fiscal planning and fiscal disbursements.

> Adversely influencing the available pool of those doing consultation psychiatry are the relatively low collection rates. With Blue Shield and other third-party groups frequently paying unrealistically low fee schedules, and with the decreasing NIMH training and teaching grants, the cadre of practitioners and clinical full-time members to take on financially unrewarding consultations is diminishing. Can new national health legislation be influenced to benefit consultation psychiatry? Should hospital administrations be urged to put the cost of consultation psychiatry on to the per diem rate charged for all patients? The fiscal planning of consultation work offers the challenge of developing an optimum and a minimum cost-benefit figure in consultation psychiatry. Guidelines need to be established in setting up the disbursal of a given mental health budget for a general hospital as well as for the relative evaluation of the effectiveness of different models of consultation activity (p. 178).

The problem could not have been stated more succinctly.

RECENT DEVELOPMENTS IN LIAISON PROGRAMS

Since 1965 powerful forces within medicine and society have exerted a serious effect upon liaison psychiatry and are gradually reshaping it. By 1977 these forces have gained such momentum that liaison programs have developed new models and revised strategies. It is a different world and the older models are insufficient and anti-quated. Their leaders, comfortably settled into views of the 1950's, have responded slowly.

We know that developments within medicine have markedly changed clinical medicine. Advances in technology, genetics, immunology, pathophysiology, clinical biochemistry, chemotherapy, nuclear medicine, and computer biophysics have served to modify patterns of disease and their course. These have led to a different dimension of diagnostic and therapeutic approaches, viz. cardiac surgery, peritoneal dialysis and hemodialysis, organ transplantation, computerized axial tomography, pulmonary therapy, cardiopulmonary resuscitation, organ prosthesis, immunotherapy, advanced chemotherapy, and others. The delivery of such services has changed the organizational structure of the general hospital through the establishment of special areas called critical care units. Thus there are now in existence one or more of the following units: intensive care unit (I.C.U.), intermediate intensive care unit (I.I.C.U.), recovery room-acute care unit, cardiac care unit (C.C.U.), pulmonary care unit (P.C.U.), burn unit, adult hemodialysis unit, pediatric hemodialysis unit, and others. The procedures associated with these critical care areas require teams of professionals with highly specialized functions. This has altered the traditional physician-patient relationship and has modified the power structure of clinical disciplines. The anesthesiologist, cardiac surgeon, thoracic surgeon, cardiologist, nephrologist, oncologist, pulmonary therapist, neonatologist, and nurse clinician have increased their influence within the hospital social structure relative to that of the general internist, general surgeon, and obstetrician. Their word sometimes carries as much weight in medical councils as that of the chief of medicine, a circumstance which has implications for liaison psychiatry.

Life saving and life sustaining procedures are the bases of critical care medicine. Resuscitation, terminal states, and death and dying become commonplace features and these stages extend beyond the critical care units on to the medical and surgical floors. The teaching general hospital is now a total critical care facility of graduated intensities.

Critical care medicine may be defined as that part of medicine which deals with issues that are critical in the balance between life and death. It utilizes techniques which cope with ultra-acute medical and surgical conditions in urgent, radical, and complex maneuvers often dependent upon technocracy and upon teams of professionals. These techniques may induce new issues which may become the critical ones.

The emergence of new issues has become the *bête noire* of medicine and has created new classes of iatrogenic diseases and disorders. The very weight of iatrogenic medicine is having serious implications for the profession in terms of the division of its labors, bioethical considerations, attitudes of the public toward it, and the confrontation with uncertainty.

What are some of the implications of critical care medicine for liaison programs? They are: 1) an increased incidence of psychiatric syndromes in the general hospital, 2) the emergence of new psychiatric disorders as a reflection of critical care medicine and iatrogenic inducement, 3) the transformation of the liaison psychiatrist to a biological psychiatrist, 4) new opportunities for the psychiatrist to study and treat psychological mechanisms and altered behavior in degrees and forms never witnessed heretofore, 5) the establishment of psychiatric adjunctive support systems for physicians and nurses, and 6) a developing role for the psychiatrist as the primary care physician. Each of these will be discussed briefly.

1) *The increased incidence of psychiatric syndromes in the general hospital*

Kiely (129) has discussed with thoroughness the prevalence and nature of psychiatric syndromes in critical care units.

> Among the less heralded of these has been the sharpened focus of attention on altered states of consciousness, emotional reactions, and behavioral patterns of the critically ill. Physicians and nurses are called on to appraise and evaluate cognitive clarity, feelings and behavior of patients (p. 2759).

He lists as acute critical care syndromes acute fear, sustained tension, anxiety, agitated depression, acute schizophreniform stress reaction, and acute delirium. McKegney (130) called attention to "The intensive care unit syndrome" and Kornfeld (131) has carefully elaborated on it. They refer to the effects upon the patient of the intensive unit environment. Both acute and chronic brain syndromes have increased in incidence throughout the hospital as a result of life-sustaining efforts. For example, the incidence of brain syndrome in our hospital is not infrequently 3.0-5.0 percent of the total hospital census (30).

2) *The emergence of new psychiatric disorders*

Blachly (132) called attention to a new type of delirium in the I.C.U. developing after open heart surgery. He called it "catastrophic reaction." It appears to be different from the acute delirium and acute schizophreniform stress reaction reported by Kiely (129). It develops three to five days after surgery and those I have seen gave the impression of a "state of suspended animation" which is not like catatonia. Greenhill and Frater (133) reported on a type of mild brain damage which they found in 80 percent of patients one to four years after cardiac surgery. A condition called "dementia dialytica" has been described in patients under prolonged hemodialysis (134). Unusual clinical patterns including hypomania, brief catatonic-like episodes, depressiveness, and sociopathic incidents have been seen during the vicissitudes of uremia in end stage renal disease while on dialysis. An apathetic state which makes for a difficult differential diagnosis between depression, cachexia, and toxemia is not infrequently seen in patients undergoing chemotherapy for cancer.

3) *The transformation of the liaison psychiatrist to a biological psychiatrist*

Highly integrated neural functions underly the cognitive progress and the disturbance of these in critical states reveals signs that require considerations of sensory deprivation, sensory over-load, and disturbances of systems involving neurotransmitters and biogenic amines. Profound life threatening psychobiological signs call for neuropharmacological intervention to correct imbalances in subcortical systems. The psychiatrist in this instance has to be more of a neuroscientist than an internist.

4) *New opportunities to study psychological mechanisms and altered behavior*

High levels of anxiety related to sustained life and death issues, unusual body-image distortions, possession of another's vital organ, exposure to a heart-lung machine, living exsanguination on the dialysis machine, consciousness of artificial organs, and other such states have never been experienced before in the history of man. Tolerance for protracted suffering on hemodialysis is a new condition. Denial of colossal proportions in the certainty of mutilation and at the edge of death is a common occurrence. Feelings of hopelessness and helplessness beyond that described by Schmale and Engel (135) can be elicited. The adaptation to slow dissolution in cancer demands study. The veritable absence of primary psychiatric states and the remissiveness of neuroses in the life-death borderland to me are striking. In eleven years I have never found a schizophrenic in an I.C.U.

5) *The establishment of psychiatric adjunctive support systems*

Deep involvement in life threatening conditions, heroic measures, sustaining life to new extents, therapeutic failure, and death of patients have left physicians and nurses with personal emotional loads which heretofore were either not encountered or avoidable. Much is now uncertain and ambiguous as far as rationale, course of illness, and outcome. By making the practice of medicine more acute, critical care medicine has succeeded in making it more chronic. Physicians and nurses are now left face-to-face with chronicity to a greater extent than before. They now must face the patient and family while life is being prolonged or the patient is alive with chronic residuals when he otherwise would be dead. Physicians are more often compelled to interrelate and engage with the patient. They can feel inadequate, impotent, guilty over having brought about an iatrogenic disorder, and they may be aggrieved over the loss of patients.

In this critical care system physicians and nurses need emotional support. This has been pointed out with respect to nurses in the I.C.U. and in dialysis units (136-141), but the need of physicians has been little recognized (142, 143). Liaison services can set up support systems for them.

Gerald Caplan (144) has defined support systems as "continuing social aggregates (namely, continuing interactions with another individual, a network, a group, or an organization) that provide individuals with opportunities for feedback about themselves and for validation of their expectations about others, which may offset deficiencies in these communications within the larger community context." In the liaison service at the Einstein Hospital (30) there has evolved an organizational plan which permits professionals to consult with liaison psychiatrists individually or in groups when they are emotionally stressed by critical care events. Through this means, they obtain feedback about themselves and their associated disciplines in relationship to critical patients and death.

For example, nurses on a specific unit can, when stressed, call what is referred to as a "PRN conference." This is a meeting of staff nurses, nurse clinicians, social workers, housestaff and attending man (occasionally, but with growing frequency) to discuss the impending death of a patient, occurrence of death, and failure of communication between nurses and physicians on a critical care case. I.C.U. nurses often call for a conference on a patient who is sustained in the unit over a week and active interrelationships with the patient have to be faced. Physicians are encouraged to bring more critical cases to grand rounds and teaching conferences. The number of informal consultations to discuss the physician's feelings have increased. The liaison staff has had an increased number of nurses and physicians come to them for personal counseling and to discuss ethical problems involving themselves. Sometimes it appears that critical care medicine has opened up the physician and nurse to such changes in professional values that the liaison psychiatrist is almost a spiritual advisor in the hospital environment.

All of this is a trend, but it is taking place. In our hospital, it has become a necessary component of the liaison program. Perhaps this is another way of reaching liaison objectives.

6) *The developing role of the psychiatrist as the primary care physician*

The necessity of employing a team of professionals in the clinical process of the critical care patient has radically changed the pattern of care, particularly as it affects the doctor-patient relationship. It is as if there has been a reversal of positions. Whereas before the physician had several patients, who could be viewed as a class group, now the patient has several therapists. For an open heart surgical procedure, the patient has 18 professionals on his team, irrespective of staff I.C.U. nurses. Comparable situations exist in the C.C.U., on dialysis units, and in other critical care areas. Often the clinical care is so detailed, complicated and mechanistic that the physician has little time to give to the patient as a person. The physician in most such situations has become a master technician, who orchestrates and integrates the technocracy in the life-death borderland. He is left little time for appropriate aftercare.

As a result the nature of the physician-patient relationship is different. The doctor is viewed as a seldom-seen "master-mind" who stands like Osiris with decision making powers over life and death or as a rare scientific savior. It is only in the aftercare situation that the patient reverts to an expressed need for the traditional doctor-patient relationship, although he reaches for it silently in the critical experience.

In the busyness of their technocratic world, the cardiologists, nephrologists, chemotherapists, cardiac and pulmonary surgeons, and others, have even less time and inclination to meet the learning goals of liaison psychiatrists than heretofore. In addition, the work of the caretakers in these critical areas is so specialized that coordination with other facets of medicine necessary to the patient's welfare may be underemphasized. The patient may be left emotionally isolated, unless he becomes uncontrollably delirious or a serious management problem.

When the liaison psychiatrist is called in for consultation in such instances, he often finds that the case is virtually turned over to him. Not infrequently he is called in by the I.C.U. nurses to coordinate the over-all care, particularly if physicians from more than one specialty are involved. In the aftercare of critical care patients who survive, the patient and family turn to him for rescue from anonymity or to coordinate incompletely defined care.

The position in which the psychiatrist finds himself in most critical care cases is as an unscheduled member of the team, whose advice is usually accepted because of the need for biological psychiatric treatment. At the same time there is an unstated attitude of relief on the part of the rest of the team who need the adjunctive emotional support of the psychiatrist. What happens in effect is that the liaison psychiatrist takes over the doctor-patient relationship function of the principal caretaker in a complex group situation.

There is still another position for the psychiatrist that emerges out of this design. The critical care physician and his team are so specialized that not infrequently they abdicate their over-all responsibility and the psychiatrist is left as the primary care physician.

Draper and Smits (145) have written, "Primary care physicians, too often viewed as low level generalists, are more appropriately thought of as specialists whose work demands special skills. These physicians function as managers, advocates, educators, and counselors for their patients while also serving as coordinators of other professionals involved in primary care." Fink and Oken (146) have added to the definition of primary care that it involves "longitudinal responsibility" and that it serves an "integrationist function." In calling attention to the role of psychiatry as a primary care speciality they state, "While other health care providers may be involved, the primary physician retains a coordinating, if not ochestrating, role. This specifically includes management of the social and psychological, as well as physical, aspects of care."

The primary care position of psychiatry is one of the recent developments emerging in contemporary health systems. The psychiatrist may find himself as a primary care physician in the following situations: 1) as the holistic integrator of medical care in the critical care case, 2) as the principal overseer of comprehensive medical and psychiatric care in community mental health centers, 3) as the protector of the patient where in ambulatory psychiatric care (as in private practice) the psychiatrist advocates and pursues primary care goals when patients have weak connections with community physicians, and 4) as a liaison teacher model in the training of primary care physicians. Within the hospital with critical care cases, the function of the liaison psychiatrist in being an integrationist or a primary care physician is a far cry from what is found in the traditional liaison model where the psychiatrist puts himself into the role of "the sidekick" of the internist.

The forces of critical care medicine demand modification of the liaison system. Most liaison programs have made some attempt to meet these demands by answering consultations from the critical care services or in some centers assigning a liaison team to one or more specific areas, usually the intensive care unit, the cardiac care unit, or the dialysis area. But in the main, whether or not liaison psychiatrists are attached to such units largely depends upon the special interests of the psychiatrists. In a few centers there is great interest, and significant research and descriptive studies have come from such workers as Kiely (129), Kornfeld (147), McKegney (130), Abram (136), Weisman and Hackett (148), Kimball (149), Kemph (150), Cramond (138, 139), Korsch (137), and many others. Another example of special interest is the work on death and dying by Kübler-Ross (151), Weisman (152), Pearson (153), and Levy (154). Little information exists on the place of these special teams in the overall reports of liaison programs. A few of the accounts of these programs describe efforts to sustain nurses and staff (136-141). Strain and Grossman (29) report a "liaison modular unit consisting of a psychiatrist and a social worker was created to care for ambulatory renal dialysis and transplant patients." They also refer to "the liaison model of coronary heart disease," but they give no account of how and where liaison work with cardiac patients was done. Schmale (108) indicates that at Rochester the pulmonary intensive care unit has a liaison psychiatrist connected with it because that psychiatrist has a special interest. He also reports what he calls "a primary care tract." Trainees in a primary care program are being rotated through the Rochester Liaison Program from affiliated hospitals on the initiative of a former liaison fellow. In general it appears that the inclusion of critical care areas is spotty in most liaison programs.

At the Hospital of the Albert Einstein College of Medicine there has developed what is called the Critical Care Model of Liaison Psychiatry (30). This was established both as a need and as a strategy. In a system in which there is one full-time psychiatrist, 15 active attending psychiatrists, and a close working relationship with a continuously trained department of nursing, it was more feasible to withdraw the group from the conventional liaison arrangement with medical units, and place members at strategic action points. All of the liaison arrangements are with critical care areas and psychiatrists have structured arrangements in oncology, I.C.U., C.C.U., the recovery room, a terminal care unit, adult hemodialysis, and pediatric hemodialysis. The organization for the care of cancer patients is called psychiatric oncology and has active liaison with ambulatory radiotherapy, gynecological oncology, and chemotherapy. Finely honed relationships have been developed with the directors of those services.

Consultations on other services go on as usual, but the growth in referrals comes mainly from the critical care situations in all parts of the hospital. Because of the special clinical characteristics of patients in the department of rehabilitation and because many critical care patients are assigned to that department for intermediate or chronic care, that department is included in the model. A concentrated effort is made there, and it is welcomed.

The liaison arrangements with these divisions of the hospital provide psychiatric adjunctive support in a continuous useful way. In turn the place of the liaison psychiatrist is well accepted as a member of the group, who assents to guide the psychiatric aspects of the case and steps in to integrate when necessary. Limited goals and expectations are set for the physicians, and a guiding working relationship is attempted without effort to teach. It is a pleasure for the liaison psychiatrists to feel wanted and to be taken seriously.

The image that is conveyed is that of a modern psychobiologist, who is a neuroscientist, psychopharmacologist, and a psychiatrist, with a behavioral science emphasis. Colleagues may not realize it, but there is a depth of understanding of interpersonal relations sought after in their reception of support which a psychoanalytic orientation supplies.

COMMUNITY AND SOCIETAL DETERMINANTS

The second major change in medicine in addition to the critical care effect has come from forces in the community and in society. The cost of health care is one of the major issues of the 1970's and economists have made the health care system conform to an industrial concept. The ferments caused by social medicine, ghetto medicine, and civil rights advocates resulted in governmental participation through medicare and medicaid. At that point government had a stake in medicine, and utilization review and peer review followed. The third-party carrier became a powerful participant in medicine as well through administrating governmental programs and meeting costs of care through insurance plans.

The medical social structure was cracked by the economic power from outside placed in the hands of the industrialized administrative bureaucracy (29). Once the social power of physicians was reduced, the public followed with malpractice suits, consumerism, and patient advocacy. Physicians are finally being aroused to social consciousness.

What bearing does this have on liaison programs? The power structure within the hospital has shifted. The administrator and lay boards have greater power backed as they are by Blue Cross reimbursement rates, hospital council edicts, governmental support, and utilization review. The economic and industrial emphasis takes precedence over medical and surgical systems and academic freedom. Admissions are controlled and hospitalization shortened. The length of stay averages 7-8 days and patients are discharged as soon as possible. Liaison programs have too little time to work with hospitalized patients and are beginning to shift the site of clinical work to the outpatient department (111). Rotation of house officers is accelerated, handicapping the liaison psychiatrist in his teaching (111). Economy is such an issue in clinical care in terms of cost to patient and hospital that the trend is to more emphasis on acute medicine rather than less.

Protracted care of chronic medical disorders has been the ideal clinical situation for the teaching of psychosomatic medicine and for liaison arrangements. The tendency now is to keep many patients in the community rather than in the hospital, except for brief contact or for heroic measures. The classic psychosomatic disorder either stays home or has radical surgical and medical intervention.

Not only has the social force of the community been a determinant for change, but the agent for those forces, the hospital administrator, has become a powerful influence in the changing character of medicine. He keeps in touch with attorneys, monitors malpractice possibilities, controls with the budget, is the intermediator with third parties, negotiates on salaries and equipment, and is more comfortable in the group process than the physician. Informed consent, patient advocacy, legal liability, keeping the hospital filled and in some financial ways influencing the triage of patients for admission is part of his vigilant administrative attitude.

Where the administration has been reasonable, the effect has been salutary in terms of accountability and eliminating reduplication of resources but its industrialized goals can easily take precedence over its health care and academic responsibilities. For example, the Montefiore Hospital administrator phased out the psychiatric inpatient unit and the psychiatric staff at the university hospital at Einstein (which he had leased from the university) over the protestations of psychiatry and some other departments in order to replace 23 psychiatric beds with 60 medical ones. At the same time by this stroke he virtually eliminated the liaison program—which, however, came back under a different form.

Strain (29) writes:

> In contrast to the consulting psychiatrist, who appears in response to a request for his services, the liaison psychiatrist must persuade *the hospital administration* (author's italics) and the heads of various departments of the importance of his services

—of the importance of caring not only for the patient, but about the patient. This time-consuming and difficult task requires a measure of political expertise. . . . Regardless of whether the hospital moves to an industrial bureaucracy or remains an advisory bureaucracy, only the hospital administration can ensure adequate psychological care for its patients (p. 185).

Clearly the hospital administrator has replaced the chief of medicine, and the physician is being compelled to face the social issues in medicine. These changes are bound to have an influence on the further development of liaison programs.

THE EMERGENCE OF BIOETHICS

Critical care demands critical decision-making and finance brings accountability. It was inevitable that life and death decision-making, selection of patients for limited life-saving resources and procedures, professional anxiety in the face of so much life-threatening medicine, and a more aggressive participation of patients and families in decision-making would bring forth ethical considerations which heretofore were not required of the medical profession or of the individual physician. At the same time a public sensitized to health care practices related to cost of care began to ask for an accounting of medical and hospital practices and for legal measures to justify such practices. Ethical factors crystallized from this approach as well. For the most part, judging by the growing literature on medical ethics in medical journals and the deliberations within medical societies, physicians themselves have taken considerable initiative in grappling with ethical perspectives in medicine. Committees on human experimentation are in action in several centers, hospital bioethics committees have made a start, and courses in ethical perspectives are being held in a few medical schools.

As an example, a Committee on Bioethics was established at the Einstein Hospital in 1975 under the chairmanship of the writer. It consists of chiefs of all critical care services, and representatives from administration, nursing, social service, and the paraprofessional group. The Associate Dean for Education, the Chairman of the

Department of Community Medicine, a social psychologist, and a philosopher-in-residence serve as consultants. Cases and situations with ethical implications are brought to the committee by its members or other hospital staff. The Committee does not make decisions or set policy. It may pass recommendations to the Medical Council. Its main purposes are to serve as a forum for the diffusion of responsibility in decision-making, to sensitize hospital staff to patient care ethical issues, and to identify ethical problems for correction by medicine, nursing, and administration.

The relevance of this brief report on the emergence of bioethics in health care practice lies in its relationship to liaison psychiatry. In the current ethical concerns of physicians and in their councils, they are demonstrating attitude change toward human values and the felt needs of patients which previously were antithetical to their image of the physician. Topics related to patient advocacy, doctor-patient communication, psychological components of the right-to-die and living will request, family emotional reactions to triage, the physician's anxiety regarding which patients are expendable, and the nature of litigious patients, among others, are sensitizing physicians in directions long sought by liaison psychiatrists. It appears that, from another and unexpected vantage point, the resistance of physicians to the psychosocial components of disease is being reduced, and perhaps to a degree not envisioned before. New liaison programs should be designed with the bioethics approach, and as a strategy the integral functions of patient care rather than the physician himself should be the target.

THE INTEGRAL FUNCTIONS OF PATIENT CARE

The integral functions of patient care are inhospitalization, ambulatory care, diagnostic evaluation, the management of acute and chronic disease processes, critical care, therapy, psychological care, extended care, aftercare, health maintenance, administration, economics, and bioethics. A system of mental health delivery for the general hospital which focuses upon these functions more than upon departmental liaison or a conventional medical approach alone appears to be on the horizon. Before discussing that system, a review of the models of liaison programs in general may through contrast clarify the concept of what can be called the integral model of psychological care for the medically ill. The existing models of liaison programs are the following:

The Consultation Model—patients are referred to the psychiatrist for evaluation and possible treatment, and/or for recommended emotional care by the consultee and/or caretaker staff. This is basic to all models.

The Liaison Model—psychiatrists and other mental health workers are assigned by a liaison division of the department of psychiatry to selected hospital units (usually in the department of medicine) to consult, case find, and teach. This design is sometimes referred to as the consultation-liaison model. It often relies on "islands of excellence" or model demonstration. This design has been the one of choice in many training centers, with the implication in some that ultimately liaison arrangements would cover the entire hospital. Such has never truly been achieved.

The Milieu Model—this is an extension of the liaison model in which emphasis is placed upon the group aspects of patient care, group process, staff reactions and interactions, interpersonal theory and the methods of Stanton and Schwartz. Several centers combine the liaison and the milieu models.

The Critical Care Model—the assignment of mental health personnel is to critical care units rather than to clinical departments. The goal is patient care with the psychiatrist as a participating member of the unit team, in which he often becomes the unnamed leader. Teaching combines behavioral, biological psychiatry, and psychoanalytic theoretical models. The Einstein Hospital and the Massachusetts General Hospital utilize this model. It was developed in this decade as a result of changes within clinical medicine.

The Biological Psychiatry Model—a more exacting example of the critical care model with strict emphasis upon neuroscience and psychopharmacology in which the psychiatrist stands on his security as a peer scientist. He does the psychological care through recommendation, management with psychotropic drugs, and assignment of patients to diagnosis-centered treatment units, i.e., dysphoria clinic, pain center, psychopharmacology clinic, hypochondriasis clinic, and affective states center. This has been partly tested at Montefiore Hospital and is in early process at Columbia.

The Integral Model—the aforementioned models of liaison programs depend in the main upon consultation with patients and staff and upon working relationships with physicians. A system based in addition upon the inclusion of psychological care as an integral component of patient care provides for the availability of the psychiatrist to function openly at the point of administrative and clinical need. This model is emerging as a result of social pressure upon medicine, and relies more upon hospital governance than upon triage by physicians. It is developing at the Einstein Hospital and at Montefiore Hospital as part of the changing concept of the liaison program and will be further discussed in that context.

The Changing Concept of the Liaison Program

The principal obstacle to the delivery of mental health services to medical and surgical patients is the resistance of their physicians. There has been ample proof that they use psychiatric consultations sparingly and give low priority to emotional care in their overall clinical management. The job in reaching the physician and in securing psychological care for patients has been an uphill job for the liaison psychiatrist. His mission began with enthusiasm and hope 40 years ago. He gave unselfishly of himself always with the expectation that there were strategies to be discovered by which he would attain his goal of a more caring humanistic medicine to protect the sick or a more scientific clinical medicine which would include psychosocial factors as variables. He expected that he and his disciples could make converts out of burdened physicians trained in the Virchow tradition. He has persisted with that hope, but, as scientific as he has been in his alliance with departments of medicine and in his independent laboratory research into psychological-physiological-biological interrelationships, he has neglected to do appropriate evaluation of his efforts. What scanty evaluation does exist demonstrates, as we have seen, that only a small proportion of physically ill patients receive the psychiatric consultation they need. There are no valid evaluation studies on the results of consultation. We have seen that 40 percent of house officers and nurses cannot learn to do emotional care (23). In spite of the desire and need to train physicians, their education in emotional care has been unstructured and haphazard during the critical years of internship and the residency. And now with the changing patterns of patient care when hospitals are becoming acute critical care institutions there is less opportunity of fulfilling the objectives with the methods envisioned.

Have we gained much in the last 40 years through the development of liaison programs? I think we have. Internists and surgeons are friendlier and view us as colleagues (although not to be taken too seriously on the general wards). We have somehow more access to general hospital patients but have not been able to consolidate our gains there because of absence of continuity of care. And we have been given the opportunity to explore and test out various models of organization. We have also learned much about the nature of psychological reactions to illness, emotional stressors and their effects, clinical management, the use of psychotropic drugs in somatic disorders, and the influence of social factors, both from the family and from the hospital staff. The overall results, however, show that we have failed in the delivery of mental health services to the hospital and community sick because our liaison programs reached too few patients and physicians.

There are three causes for this poor result: logistics, the resistance of physicians, including psychiatrists, and the defensive character of patients who get hospitalized. First of all, we attempted to do too much with too few hands. Large liaison programs, like the one at Rochester, with 10 psychiatrists and nine fellows, are rare. As far as is known none of the 109 fellows trained have developed services as large. But even this is too small a service to attain the goals attempted. One cannot meet the mental health needs of a large general hospital and educate the physicians with so small a number of emissaries. In most teaching centers a liaison staff of six to eight seems to be average, and most hospitals have less. The numerical design should be carefully reevaluated in each center. On logistics also, the awesome attempt to change clinical science has been attempted with little financial support.

Regarding the resistance of physicians, there are more profound causes than those thus far cited in this presentation. As John Whitehorn (120) wisely wrote in 1963:

> Perhaps the greatest benefit of a liberal education is to escape the tyranny of first impressions and of naive preconceptions—to learn to suspend judgment and actions, not indefinitely and vaguely, but long enough and sturdily enough for the orderly review of evidence and the weighing of probabilities and values. . . . It is humanly difficult to weigh alternatives unless one can cultivate some *tolerance of uncertainty* (author's italics) (p. 121).

His hope was that when students had more opportunity in "scientific questing" as part of their educational program there would be "less of the phobic aversion for the uncertainties of the human being." Physicians have been erroneously taught to be secure only with the certainty of the fact that science is absolute, which it is not, and the "tolerance of uncertainty" which is required in the multivariable subject of human behavior is anathema to them.

Another profound cause of resistance may be psychoerinysm, a term which I have used in previous publications (155, 156), derived from the Erinys in Greek mythology who were the embodiments of the avenging powers of nature. It refers to a "resistive and retaliative force within society against those movements which attempt to ameliorate mental and emotional suffering, in the process of which the psychopathological nature of man may be exposed. Psychoerinysm, at its most basic level, emanates from within psychopathology itself, from a deep awareness in man of the forces of dissolution." So stubborn is the obstacle put up by medicine against psychiatric care for its patients that it must stem from a source even more complicated than mere phobic aversion.

A third source of resistance lies within the patient. Beyond stigma, which is in itself a problem, the average person, as we know, fears psychiatry and self-revealment for his own sake and as an unconscious participant in the mass psychoerinysm. But in addition it may be—and I have long wondered about this—that the persons who have histopathological and pathophysiological responses to stress, particularly the recidivists, are a special breed who are super-defensive. I am here implying that they are psychologically defensive as a component of over-all reaction to injury, for even at the level of basic pathological processes, the totality of the organism should be accepted. And so we find patients with chronic and recurrent medical and surgical disorders largely unmotivated for psychological intervention, demonstrating marked communication defensiveness in being interviewed, avoiding or abandoning psychiatric aftercare, and having on record a poor reputation for paying psychiatric consultation fees.

Such patients participate with the physician in resistance to liaison psychiatry. Even in the face of suffering and in the environment of death many somatically ill patients enter into the medical situation with a strange enthusiasm and satisfied resignation, comfortable in communicative exchanges with the physician in somatic terminology. They seem loath to have a psychiatrist interfere. The epidemiology of this population demands much study, particularly the recidivism and the hard-core somatic families with a high incidence of multiple disorders and hospital admission rates.

In their own way, it may be that the class of patients treated by internists and surgeons discourage the physician from seeking psychological intervention and discovering psychological awareness. It may be that we as liaison psychiatrists have not been aware of an *unholy alliance* between physician and patient which keeps their somatic pact inviolate.

Departments of psychiatry and general psychiatrists are especially kept out. I believe that it is not always a matter of psychiatrists feeling uncomfortable in the medical situation and with the medical model, but more that they do not find medical patients very interesting psychiatrically. They seem psychopathologically superficial and their psychological aberrations are searched-for rather than presented. Besides psychiatrists in the main do not like to work with unmotivated patients. The extensive psychoanalytic investigations of the 1940's and 1950's revealed the deep and fascinating agenda behind the resistances of psychosomatic patients. But this class succeeded in discouraging this type of investigation as well.

This leads to an inevitable conclusion. Perhaps one of the principal aims of liaison programs—the conversion of physicians—has been premature. We have grasped a problem, but we do not have sufficient information to make much headway with it. I would suggest that we leave the doctor alone until we have that information, that we stop proselytizing, that we desist in our attempts to reform him.

The physician is an earnest and overworked professional carrying the load of sick and dependent human beings, and making crucial decisions, often in the face of fatigue. He needs our expertise but seems to fear it or drifts with our liaison programs half-heartedly. The identification of his resistance to psychosocial variables is not a criticism, but should be viewed as fact. The doctor has certain expectations of the liaison psychiatrist and we should listen to them, for our expertise has much to offer him.

Until we have the knowledge, let us not expect of the physician that he can be part psychiatrist. That is not working. The emotional care of patients does not and will not reside in his hands, but in the hands of nurses as well. Efforts to give them the major responsibility in emotional care has been enthusiastically received by them, for they are doing it anyway. The task of educating the physician in psychological medicine need not be abandoned. But it is slow work, about which there is still much to be learned. It will take a long time, and the sick patient should not have to wait. In the meantime let us design programs in which psychiatry is more direct and decisive in the care of the sick and dying. Social forces have now given us that opportunity and the timing is right to grasp it.

The emergence of critical care medicine to change the patterns of patient care, the effects of social accountability upon the flow of patient care and its financing, and the recalcitrance of physicians to act upon the reality of a psychological and humanistic medicine are serving to reduce the influence and control of the individual physician in decision-making. Slowly he appears to be relinquishing some power to medical councils, peer review, hospital administration, and governmental persuasion. As a result, an integral model of patient care takes form. It is in a developing state at the Einstein and Montefiore Hospitals.

In the integral model psychiatry is considered to be essential to the generic operation of patient care and to the functions of the hospital. It places psychiatry into position and status similar to that of clinical pathology, anatomical pathology, radiology, medicine, and nursing. It gives psychiatry appropriate open access to patient care in order to evaluate and to treat where indicated. The psychiatrist has the freedom to see any patient who needs his care and enters into staff relationships around any situation in which the staff needs his assistance. Other staff members in addition to the primary and tertiary physician, such as nurses, psychologists, and social workers, can ask for a psychiatric consultation. Such procedures reduce the responsibilities of the physician only to the extent that it takes from him the complete right to initiate formal emotional care. The key step in the free consultation procedure is that the physician is contacted by the psychiatrist before the consultation is done. If the physician resists in the face of the need for the consultation, it may become a matter for clinical and administrative review.

Additional functions of such a psychiatric service within the matrix of the hospital include integration with critical care units, memberships on critical care committees, chairmanships of the standing medical council committees on bioethics, on emotional care, and on thanatology, and membership on relevant other committees, such as pharmacology, nursing, social service, utilization review, and admissions.

There are certain clinical categories in which most psychosocial oversights occur. These are suicidal risk, homicidal risk, psychiatric states in medical and surgical patients at the time of request for hospital admission, selection of open heart surgery, dialysis, and transplant patients, repeated hospital admissions, drug and alcohol abuse, doubt concerning surgery, repeated surgery, hard core medical families, and cancer patients. In these instances, the psychiatric service is administratively mandated to do consultations, with or without the consent of the physician, the expenses to be borne by the per diem cost, as are many other basic hospital services. Not only do the psychiatrists participate in other consultations and planned therapeutic care as they have always done, but if properly organized, mandatory high risk evaluation and care are not an impossible task for them. We are doing a good part of it already in our developing integral model program at the Einstein Hospital (30); with financial support from administration and the department of psychiatry we could do it all.

A unique opportunity now exists for departments of psychiatry to take decisive leadership in this direction through negotiation with medical councils and hospital administration. Strain (29) has stated this succinctly: "Unless the liaison psychiatrist is given the authority and trappings to disseminate the knowledge and experience necessary to affect patient care, unless he is recognized within the hospital hierarchy as an ambassador with portfolio, he will remain a doctor-chaser, an ear-clutcher, a patient-chaser, pleading to be heard."

We return to an old and unfinished theme. What should be the image and the role of the general hospital psychiatrist in his work of bringing mental health services to the sick? In 1977 it should not be that of the internist, setting what is now an unreachable standard, psychiatrist and internist all rolled into one. I personally doubt that such a role model can "fill the bill." Today the psychiatrist needs much experience and skill in group process to lead and participate in administrative, bioethical, and social councils, to cope with community pressures and economic factors, to possess wide administrative skills, and to emphasize his belief in the strengths of psychiatry. In the critical areas he has to know more neuroscience than internal medicine. Throughout the clinical milieu and its demands he must demonstrate that his primary identification is with psychiatry, with its rich content to be applied at multiple psychological, biosocial, and medical end points. It is worth repeating what Kaufman (33) wrote long ago: "A psychiatrist is a psychiatrist, just as a surgeon is a surgeon; and it is only as a psychiatrist, standing firmly based on his own discipline, that he can eventually demonstrate the value of his orientation in the understanding and treatment of patients."

West (157) has often been quoted for the following statement: "The psychiatrist of tomorrow will be much more of a neuroscientist than he is today: he will at the same time perforce become more of a social and behavioral scientist as well." Tomorrow is today as far as general hospital psychiatry is concerned, and in the scattered and frenetic searches of psychiatry for its place in the sun, it may well be that the model of the general hospital psychiatrist will prevail.

REFERENCES

1. MCKEGNEY, F. P.: The Teaching of Psychosomatic Medicine: Consultation-liaison Psychiatry. *Amer. Hankbook of Psych.*, 4:910, 1975.
2. MCKEGNEY, F. P.: Consultation-liaison Teaching of Psychosomatic Medicine: Opportunities and Obstacles. *J. Nerv. and Mental Dis.*, 154:3, 198-205, 1972.
3. KRAKOWSKI, A. J.: Consultation-liaison Psychiatry: A Psychosomatic Service in the General Hospital. *Int'l. J. Psych. in Med.*, 6:283-292, 1975.
4. LIPSITT, D. R.: Some Problems in the Teaching of Psychosomatic Medicine. *Int'l. J. Psych. in Med.* 6: 317-329, 1975.
5. LIPOWSKI, Z. J.: Psychosomatic Medicine in a Changing Society: Some Current Trends in Theory and Research. *Compreh. Psych.*, 14:3, 203-215, 1973.
6. BEIGLER, J. S., et al.: Report on Liaison Psychiatry at Michael Reese Hospital. 1950-1958. *AMA Arch. of Neur. & Psych.*, 81:733-746, 1959.
7. KIMBALL, C. P.: Conceptual Developments in Psychosomatic Medicine 1939-1969. *Annals of Int. Med.*, 73:307-316, 1970.
8. LIPOWSKI, Z. J.: Review of Consultation Psychiatry and Psychosomatic Medicine. *Psychosom. Med.*, 29:3, 153-171, 1967.
9. LIPOWSKI, Z. J.: Review of Consultation Psychiatry and Psychosomatic Medicine II. Clinical Aspects. *Psychosom. Med.*, 29:3, 201-224, 1967.
10. LIPOWSKI, Z. J.: Review of Consultation Psychiatry and Psychosomatic Medicine III. Theoretical Issues. *Psychosom. Med.*, 30:4, 395-422, 1968.
11. LIPOWSKI, Z. J.: Consultation-liaison Psychiatry: An Overview. *Amer. J. Psych.*, 131, 6, 623-629, 1974.

12. WITTKOWER, E. D., et al.: A Global Survey of Psychosomatic Medicine. *Int'l J. Psych.*, 7:499-516, 1969.
13. HENRY, G. W.: Some Modern Aspects of Psychiatry in General Hospital Practice. *Amer. J. Psych.* 86:481-499, 1929.
14. ROCKEFELLER FOUNDATION: Information furnished by Rockefeller Foundation, Health Sciences Division and Central Reference Service, 1976. Courtesy Edith King.
15. BILLINGS, E. G.: The Psychiatric Liaison Department of the University of Colorado Medical School and Hospital. *Amer. J. Psych.* 122:28-33, 1966.
16. COBB, S. and FINESINGER, J.: Psychiatric Unit at the Massachusetts General Hospital, Monthly Bulletin. *Massachusetts Society Ment. Hyg.*, 15, Sept.-Oct., 1936.
17. KAUFMAN, M. R. and MARGOLIN, S. G.: Theory and Practice of Psychosomatic Medicine in a General Hospital. *Med. Clinics of N. Amer.*, 611-616, May 1948.
18. BERNSTEIN, S. and KAUFMAN, M. R.: The Psychiatrist in a General Hospital: His Functional Relationship to the Non-Psychiatric Services. *J. of Mt. Sinai Hosp., N. Y.*, 29:385-394, 1962.
19. ENGEL, G. L., et al.: A Graduate and Undergraduate Teaching Program on the Psychological Aspects of Medicine. *J. of Med. Ed.*, 32:859-871, 1957.
20. ENGEL, G. L.: Medical Education and the Psychosomatic Approach: A Report on the Rochester Experience 1946-1966. *J. Psychosom. Res.*, 11:77-85, 1967.
21. ENGEL, G. L.: The Education of the Physician for Clinical Observation. The Role of the Psychosomatic (Liaison) Teacher. *J. of Nerv. & Ment. Dis.*, Vol. 154, No. 3, 159-164, 1972.
22. SCHMALE, A. H., et al.: An Established Program of Graduate Education in Psychosomatic Medicine. *Adv. Psychosom. Med.*, IV:4-13, 1964.
23. GREENHILL, M. H. and KILGORE, S. R.: Principles of Methodology in Teaching the Psychiatric Approach to Medical House Officers. *Psychosom. Med.*, 12:38-48, 1950.
24. MENDELSON, M. and MEYER, E.: Countertransference Problems of the Liaison Psychiatrist. *Psychosom. Med.*, 23:2, 115-122, 1961.
25. MEYER, E. and MENDELSON, M.: The Psychiatric Consultation in Postgraduate Medical Teaching. *J. Nerv. & Ment. Dis.*, 130:78, 1960.
26. MEYER, E. and MENDELSON M.: Psychiatric Consultations with Patients on Medical and Surgical Wards: Patterns and Processes. *Psychiatry*, 24, 197-220, 1961.
27. LIDZ, T. and FLECK, S.: Integration of Medical and Psychiatric Methods and Objectives on a Medical Service. *Psychosom. Med.*, 12:103, 1950.

184   *Psychiatric Medicine*

28. SASLOW, G.: An Experiment with Comprehensive Medicine. *Psychosom. Med.*, 10, 167-175, 1948.
29. STRAIN, J. and GROSSMAN, S.: *Psychological Care of the Medically Ill: A Primer in Liaison Psychiatry.* New York: Appleton-Century-Crofts, 1975.
30. GREENHILL, M. H.: Annual Report on the Department of Psychiatry, Hospital of the Albert Einstein College of Medicine, Office of the Administrator, 1975, 1976.
31. KAPLAN, S. M. and CURTIS, G. C.: Reactions of Medical Patients to Discharge or Threat of Discharge From a Psychosomatic Unit of a General Hospital. *Postgrad. Med.*, 29:358-364, 1961.
32. ROSS, W. D. and LEVINE, M.: Training in Psychomatic Medicine. *Adv. Psychosom. Med.*, 4:14-22, 1964.
33. KAUFMAN, M. R.: The Role of the Psychiatrist in a General Hospital. *Psychiatric Quarterly*, 27:367-381, 1953.
34. SCHWAB, J. J.: *Handbook of Psychiatric Consultation.* New York: Appleton-Crofts, 1968.
35. CUSHING, J. G. N.: The Role of the Psychiatrist as Consultant. *Amer. J. Psych.*, 106:861-864, 1950.
36. WEISMAN, A. D. and HACKETT, H. T:. The Organization and Function of a Psychiatric Consultation Service, *Int. Rec. Med.*, 173:306-311, 1960.
37. MENDEL, W. M. and SOLOMON, P.: *The Psychiatric Consultation.* New York: Grune & Stratton, 1968.
38. SCHIFF, S. K. and PILOT, M. L.: An Approach to Psychiatric Consultation in the General Hospital. *Arch. Gen. Psych.*, 1:349-357, 1959.
39. GREENBERG, I. M.: Approaches to Psychiatric Consultation in a Research Hospital Setting. *Arch. Gen. Psych.*, 3:691-697, 1960.
40. STANTON, A. H. and SCHWARTZ, M. S.: *The Mental Hospital: A Study of Institutional Participation in Psychiatric Illness and Treatment.* New York: Basic Books, Inc., 1954.
41. CAUDILL, W.: Effects of Social & Cultural Systems in Reactions to Stress. *Social Science Research Bulletin*, 14, 1958.
42. SANDT, J. J. and LEIFER, R.: Psychiatric Consultation. *Compr. Psychiat.* 5:409, 1964.
43. BROSIN, H.: Communication Systems of the Consultation Process. In W. Mendel and P. Solomon (Eds.), *The Psychiatric Consultation.* New York: Grune & Stratton, 1968.
44. RAHE, R. H., MCKEAN, J. D. and ARTHUR, R. J.: A Longitudinal Study of Life-Change and Illness Patterns. *J. Psychosomatic Res.*, 10:355-366, 1967.
45. SASLOW, G.: Course for U.S. Army Physicians, Office of the Surgeon General, U.S.A., 1948-51.
46. GREENHILL, M. H.: The Focal Communication Concept. *Amer. J. Psychotherapy*, Vol. XII, No. 1, 30-41, 1958.
47. ENGEL, G. L.: The Concept of Psychosomatic Disorder. *J. of Psychosom. Res.*, 11:3-9, 1967.

48. KLIGERMAN, M. J. and McKEGNEY, F. P.: Patterns of Psychiatric Consultation in Two General Hospitals. *Psych. in Med.*, 2:126, 1971.
49. SCHMALE, A. H.: Relationship of Separation and Depression to Disease. *Psychosom. Med.*, 20:259-277, 1958.
50. DUFF, R. R. and HOLLINGSHEAD, A. B.: *Sickness and Society.* New York: Harper & Row, 1968.
51. BIBRING, G. L.: Psychiatry and Medical Practice in a General Hospital. *The New Eng. J. Med.*, 254:366-372, 1956.
52. FLECK, S.: Unified Health Service and Family Focused Primary Care. *Int'l. J. Psych. in Med.*, 6:4, 501-516, 1975.
53. GROLNICK, L.: A Family Perspective of Psychosomatic Factors in Illness: A Review of the Literature. *Family Process*, Vol. 11, No. 4, 457-486, Dec. 1972.
54. BRODSKY, C. M.: A Social View of the Psychiatric Consultation. The Medical View and the Social View. *Psychosomatics*, 8:61-68, 1967.
55. BERGEN, B. J.: Psychosomatic Knowledge and the Role of the Physician: A Sociological View. *Int'l. J. Psych. in Med.*, Vol. 5, No. 4, 431-442, 1974.
56. ENELOW, A. J. and MYERS, V. H.: Postgraduate Psychiatric Education: The Ethnography of a Failure. *Amer. J. Psych.*, 125:5, 627-331, 1968.
57. GREENHILL, M. H., FITZPATRICK, W. N. and BERBLINGER, K. W.: Recent Developments in Teaching of Comprehensive Medicine. *N. C. Med. J.*, Vol. 11, No. 11, 615-619, 1950.
58. MILLER, W. B.: Psychiatric Consultation: Part 1. A General Systems Approach. *Psych. in Med.*, Vol. 4, No. 2, 135-145, Spring 1973.
59. MILLER, W. B.: Psychiatric Consultation: Part II. Conceptual and Pragmatic Issues of Formulation. *Psych. in Med.*, Vol. 4, No. 3, 251-271, 1973.
60. SCHULMAN, B. M.: Group Process: An Adjunct in Liaison Consultation Psychiatry. *Int'l. J. Psych. in Med.*, 6:4, 484-499, 1975.
61. MEISSNER, W. W.: Family Dynamics and Psychosomatic Processes. *Fam. Proc.*, 5:142-161, 1966.
62. KARASU, T. B. and HERTZMAN, M.: Notes on a Contextual Approach to Medical Ward Consultation: The Importance of Social System Mythology. *Int'l. J. Psych. in Med.*, 5:1, 41-49, 1974.
63. BERNSTEIN, S. S., SMALL, S. M. and REICH, M. J.: A Psychosomatic Unit in a General Hospital. *Amer. J. Nursing*, Vol. 49, No. 8, Aug. 1949.
64. BURNETT, F. M., SITES, P., GREENHILL, M. H.: Learning the Mental Health Approach Through the Chronic Medical Patient. *Pub. Health Nursing*, June 1951.

65. GREENHILL, M. H.: Interviewing with a Purpose. *Amer. J. Nursing*, 6:1259-1262, 1956.
66. DYE, M. C.: Clarifying Patient's Communications. *Amer. J. of Nursing*, 63:56-59, August 1963.
67. DUMAS, R. C.: Psychological Preparation for Surgery. *Amer. J. of Nursing*, 63:52-55, 1965.
68. GREGG, D.: Reassurance, in J. K. Skipper and R. C. Leonard (Eds.), *Social Interaction and Patient Care*. Philadelphia: J. B. Lippincott Co., 1965.
69. GOLDIN, P. and RUSSELL, B.: Therapeutic Communication. *Amer. J. of Nursing*, 69:1928-1930, September 1969.
70. BERMOSK, L. S.: Interviewing: A Key to Therapeutic Communication in Nursing Practice. *Nursing Clin. of North America*, Vol. 1, No. 2, 205-214, June 1966.
71. BERMOSK, L. S.: Interviewing in Nursing: A Key to Effective Supervisor-Staff Relationships. *Supervisor Nurse*, 46-56, March 1973.
72. COULTER, P. P. and BROWER, M. J.: Parallel Experience: An Interview Technique. *Amer. J. of Nursing*, 69:1028-1030, May 1969.
73. DAVIS, A. J.: The Skills of Communication. *Amer. J. of Nursing*. 63:66-70, January 1963.
74. DUGAN, A. B.: Nursing Autonomy: Key to Quality Nurturance. *J. of Nursing Admin.*, July-August, 1971.
75. DUMAS R. G., ANDERSON, B. J. and LEONARD, R. C.: The Importance of the Expressive Function in Preoperative Preparation, in J. K. Skipper and R. C. Leonard (Eds.), *Social Interaction and Patient Care*. Philadelphia: J. B. Lippincott, Co., 1965.
76. ELDER, R. G.: What is the Patient Saying? In J. K. Skipper and R. C. Leonard, *Social Interaction and Patient Care*. Philadelphia: J. B. Lippincott, Co., 1965.
77. GOZZI, E. K., MORRIS, M. J. and KORSCH, B. M.: Gaps in Doctor-Patient Communication—Implications for Nursing Practice. *Amer. J. of Nursing*, 69:529-533, March 1969.
78. HAGGERTY, V. C.: Listening: An Experiment in Nursing. *Nursing Forum*, X, No. 4, 382-391, 1971.
79. HAYS, S. E. and ANDERSON, H. C.: Are Nurses Meeting Patient's Needs? *Amer. J. of Nursing*, 63:96-99, December 1963.
80. HAYS, J. S.: Analysis of Nurse-Patient Communications. *Nursing Outlook*, 32-35, September 1966.
81. HEUSINKVELD, K. B.: Cues to Communication with the Terminal Cancer Patient. *Nursing Forum*, XI, No. 1, 104-113, 1972.
82. MADORE, C. E. and DEUTSCH, Y. B.: Talking with Parents. *Amer. J. of Nursing*, 62:108-111, November 1962.
83. MEADOW, L. and GASS, G. Z.: Problems of the Novice Interviewer. *Amer. J. of Nursing*, 63:97-99, February 1963.

84. PEITCHINIC, J. A.: Therapeutic Effectiveness of Counseling by Nursing Personnel. *Nursing Research*, Vol. 21, No. 2, 138-148, March-April, 1972.
85. SKIPPER, J. K. and LEONARD, R. C.: The Importance of Communication. In *Social Interaction in Patient Care*. Philadelphia: J. B. Lippincott Co., 1965, 51-60.
86. TARASUK, M. B., RHYMES, J. P. and LEONARD, R. C.: An Experimental Test of the Importance of Communication Skills for Effective Nursing. In J. K. Skipper and R. C. Leonard (Eds.), *Social Interaction and Patient Care*. Philadelphia: J. B. Lippincott, 1965, 110-119.
87. TRYON, P. S. and LEONARD, R. C.: Giving the Patient an Active Role. In J. K. Skipper and R. C. Leonard (Eds.), *Social Interaction and Patient Care*. Philadelphia: J. B. Lippincott Co., 1965, 120-127.
88. BURSTEN, B.: The Psychiatric Consultant and the Nurse. *Nurs. Forum*, 2:7-23, 1963.
89. JOHNSON, B. S.: Psychiatric Nurse Consultant in a General Hospital. *Nurs. Outlook*, 11:728-29, 1963.
90. ROBINSON, L.: Liaison Psychiatric Nursing. *Perspect. Psychiat. Care*, 6:87-91, 1968.
91. PETERSEN, S.: The Psychiatric Nurse Specialist in a General Hospital. *Nurs. Outlook*, 17:56-68, 1969.
92. JACKSON, H. A.: The Psychiatric Nurse as a Mental Health Consultant in a General Hospital. *Nur. Clinics of N. Am.*, 4:527-40, 1969.
93. HOLSTEIN, S. and SCHWAB, J.: A Coordinated Consultation Program for Nurses & Psychiatrists. *J.A.M.A.*, 194:103-105, 1965.
94. PEPLAU, H. E.: Psychiatric Nursing Skills and the General Hospital Patient. *Nurs. Forum*, 3:29-37, 1964.
95. BARTON, B. and KELSO, M. T.: The Nurse as a Psychiatric Consultation Team Member. *Psychiatry in Medicine*, 2:108-115, 1971.
96. BURNETT, F. M. and GREENHILL, M. H.: Some Problems in the Evaluation of an Inservice Training Program in Mental Health. *Amer. J. of Public Health*, 44:12, 1954.
97. KIMBALL, C. P. (Ed.): A Report of the First Workshops in Liaison Psychiatry & Medicine. *Psychosom. Med.*, 35:176, 1973.
98. GOODMAN, J.: Annual Reports on Psychiatric Liaison Nursing, Hospital of the Albert Einstein College of Medicine (unpublished) 1967-73.
99. SHOCHET, B.: The Role of the Mental Health Counselor in the Psychiatric Liaison Service of the General Hospital. *Int'l. J. Psych. in Med.*, 5:1, 1-16, 1974.
100. DYRUD, J. E.: Remarks delivered at the 56th Annual Board of Trustees' Dinner for the Faculty, Jan. 7, 1976. *The University of Chicago Record*, Vol. X, No. 2, April 3, 1976.

101. KLIGERMAN, S.: A Program of Teaching a Psychodynamic Orientation to Resident Physicians in Medicine. *Psychosomatic Med.* 14:277-283, 1952.
102. STUNKARD, A.: A New Method in Medical Education. *Psychosom. Med.*, 22, 5, 400-406, 1960.
103. HOLMES, T. H.: Some Observations on Medical Education. *Psychomatic Medicine*, 31, 3, 269-273, 1969.
104. ROSENBAUM, M.: A Critique of Teaching Psychosomatic Medicine. *Psychosom. Med.*, 21:4, 332-340, 1959.
105. WILLARD, H. N., and SEIXAS, F. A.: Preventive Rehabilitation. *Psychosomatic Med.*, 21, 3, 235-246, 1959.
106. SCHOTTSTAEDT, W. W., PINSKY, R., MACKLER, D. and WOLF, S.: Prestige and Social Interaction on a Metabolic Ward. *Psychosomatic Medicine*, 21, 2, 131-141, 1959.
107. HAWKINS, O. R.: The Gap Between the Psychiatrist and Other Physicians. *Psychosom. Med.*, 24, 1, 94-102, 1962.
108. SCHMALE, A. H.: Personal Communication, University of Rochester, 1976.
109. REICHSMAN, F.: Teaching Psychosomatic Medicine to Medical Students, Residents and Postgraduate Fellows. *Int'l. J. Psych. in Med.*, 6:307-316, 1975.
110. FOX, H. M.: Teaching Integrated Medicine—Report of a Five Year Experiment at Peter Bent Brigham Hospital. *J. Med. Educ.* 26:421-429, 1951.
111. STRAIN, J.: Personal Communication, Montefiore Hospital, 1976.
112. HIENE, RALPH W. (Ed.): *The Student Physician as Psychotherapist.* Chicago: The University of Chicago Press, 1962.
113. PECK, H. B.: Proposed Revisions in Advanced Training in Hospital & Community-Based Psychiatry. Bronx Psychiatric Center, Bronx, N.Y., 1976, (unpublished).
114. ROMANO, J.: The Elimination of the Internship—An Act of Regression. *Amer. J. Psych.*, 126:1565-1576, 1970.
115. ROMANO, J.: The Teaching of Psychiatry to Medical Students: Past, Present and Future. *Am. J. Psychiatry*, 126:8, 1115-1126, Feb. 1970.
116. ROSENBAUM, M.: News of the Society: A Critique of Teaching Psychosomatic Medicine. *Psychosom. Med.*, 21:4, 332-339, 1959.
117. ROSENBAUM, M., JACOBS, T. J. and MANN, D.: Studies in Teaching Psychological Medicine by Means of a Preceptorship Method. *Comprehensive Psych.*, 9:4, 283-292, 1968.
118. BALINT, M.: Medicine and Psychosomatic Medicine—New Possibilities in Training and Practice. *Comprehensive Psychiatry*, Vol. 9, No. 4, 1968, 267-274.
119. BALINT, M., BALL, D. H. and HARE, M. L.: Training Medical Students in Patient-Centered Medicine. *Comprehensive Psych.* 10:4, 249-258, 1969.
120. WHITEHORN, J. C.: Education for Uncertainty. *Perspect. Biol. Med.*, 7:118, 1963.

121. WHITEHORN, J. C.: Discussion Remarks, Annual Meeting American Psychiatric Association, 1954. Also personal communication, 1954.

122. Evaluation in Mental Health: A Review of the Problem of Evaluating Mental Health Activities. Report of the subcommittee on Evaluation of Mental Health Activities, Community Services Committee, National Advisory Mental Health Council, M. H. Greenhill (Chairman). U.S. Dept. of HEW. Health Service Publication: 413, 1955.

123. TUCHER, G. J. and REINHARDT, R. F.: Psychiatric Attitudes of Young Physicians: Implications for Teaching. *Amer. J. Psych.* 124:7, 146-151, 1968.

124. STRATAS, N. E.: Training of Non-Psychiatric Physicians. *Amer. J. Psych.*, 125:1110, 1969.

125. MENDEL, W. M.: Psychiatric Consultation Education—1966. *Amer. J. Psych.* 123:2, 1966.

126. SCHUBERT, D. S. P. and McKEGNEY, F. P.: Psychiatric Consultation Education—1976. *Arch. Gen. Psych.*, 33:1271-1273, 1976.

127. SCHWAB, J. J., CLEMMONS, R. S., VALDER, B. S. and RAVLERSON, J. D.: Medical Inpatients' Reactions to Psychiatric Consultations. *J. Nerv. & Ment. Dis.*, 215-222, 1966.

128. GUGGENHEIM, F. G.: A Report of the First Workshop in Liaison Psychiatry and Medicine. Kimball, C. P. (Ed.). *Psychosom. Med.*, 35:2, 176, 1973.

129. KIELY, W. F.: Psychiatric Syndromes in Critically Ill Patients. *J.A.M.A.*, 235:25, 2759-2761, 1976.

130. McKEGNEY, F. P.: The Intensive Care Syndrome. *Conn. Med.*, 30:633-636, 1966.

131. KORNFELD, D. S.: Psychiatric View of the Intensive Care Unit. *Brit. Med. J.*, 1:108-110, 1959.

132. BLACHLY, P. H. and STARR, A.: Post Cardiotomy Delirium. *Amer. J. Psychiatry*, 121:371-375, 1964.

133. GREENHILL, M. H. and FRATER, R. M. B.: Family Interrelationships Following Cardiac Surgery. *Arch. Found. Thanatology*, 6:1, 1976.

134. RASKIN, N. H. and FISHMAN, R. A.: Neurological Disorders in Renal Failure. *New Eng. J. Med.*, 294, 204-210, January 22, 1976.

135. SCHMALE, A. H. and ENGEL, G. L.: One Giving Up-Given Up Complex illustrated on film. *Arch. Gen. Psych.* 17:135-145, 1967.

136. ABRAM, H. S.: Psychological Aspects of Intensive Care Units. *Med. Annals of D.C.*, 43:59-62, 1974.

137. KORSCH, B. M., et al.: Experiences with Children and Their Families During Extended Hemodialysis and Kidney Transplant. *Ped. Clinics of N.A.*, Vol. 18, No. 2, 1971.

138. CRAMOND, W. A., KNIGHT, P. R., and LAWRENCE, J. R.: The Psychiatric Contribution to a Renal Unit Undertaking Chronic Hemodialysis & Renal Homotransplantation. *Brit. J. Psych.*, 113:1201-1212, 1967.

139. CRAMOND, W. A., et al.: Psychological Aspects of the Management of Chronic Renal Failure. *Brit. J. Med.*, 1:539, 1968.

140. VREELAND, R. and ELLIS, G. L.: Stresses on the Nurse in an Intensive Care Unit. *J.A.M.A.*, 208:332-336, 1969.

141. HAY, D. and OKEN, D.: The Psychological Stresses of Intensive Care Nursing. *Psychosom. Med.*, 34, 109-118, 1972.

142. NADELSON, T.: The Emotional Reactions of Medical Staff: A Focus of Psychiatric Consultation. *Psych. Med.*, 2:240-246, 1971.

143. JONES, R. G. and WEISZ, A. E.: Psychiatric Liaison with a Cancer Research Center. *Comprehensive Psychiatry*, Vol. 11, No. 4, 336-345, July 1970.

144. CAPLAN, G. and KILLILEA, M. (Ed.): *Support Systems and Mutual Help—Multidisciplinary Exploration.* New York: Grune & Stratton, 1976.

145. DRAPER, P. and SMITS, H. L.: The Primary Care Practitioner-Specialist or Jack-of-all Trades. *New Eng. J. Med.*, 293:903-907, 1975.

146. FINK, P. H. and OKEN, D.: The Role of Psychiatry as a Primary Care Specialty. *Arch. Gen. Psych.*, 33:998-1003, 1976.

147. KORNFELD, D. S., et al.: Psychiatric Complications of Open Heart Surgery. *New Eng. J. Med.*, Vol. 273, No. 6, Aug. 5, 1965, 287-292.

148. WEISMAN, A. D. and HACKETT, T. P.: Predilection to Death: Death and Dying as a Psychiatric Problem. *Psychosom. Med.*, 23, 3, 232-256, 1961.

149. KIMBALL, C. P.: A Predictive Study of Adjustment to Cardiac Surgery. *J. Thorac. Surg.*, 58:891-896, 1969.

150. KEMPH, J. P.: Renal Failure, Artificial Kidney & Kidney Transplant. *Amer. J. Psych.*, 122:1270, 1966.

151. KÜBLER-ROSS, E.: *On Death and Denying.* New York: The Macmillan Co., 1969.

152. WEISMAN, A. D.: *On Death and Dying: A Psychiatric Study of Terminality.* New York: Behavioral Publications, Inc., 1972.

153. PEARSON, L. (Ed.): *Death and Dying: Current Issues in the Treatment of the Dying Person.* Cleveland: The Press of Case Western Reserve University, 1969.

154. LEVY, N. B.: *Living or Dying: Adaptation to Hemodialysis.* Springfield, Illinois: Charles C Thomas, 1974.

155. GREENHILL, M. H.: Fifty Years of American Psychiatry—Directions in Clinical Psychiatry. *Research Communications in Psychology, Psychiatry and Behavior*, Vol. 1, No. 2, 341-345, 1976.

156. GREENHILL, M. H.: The Self-Destruction of Psychiatry. *Research Communications in Psychology, Psychiatry and Behavior*, Vol. 1, No. 2, 347-354, 1976.
157. WEST, L. J.: The Future of Psychiatric Education. *Amer. J. Psych.* 130:5, 521-528, 1973.
158. RIPLEY, H. S.: Psychiatric Consultation Service in a Medical Inpatient Department. *Amer. J. Med. Sciences*, 199:2, 261-268, 1940.

Part II

THE PSYCHIATRIST AND PHYSICAL DISEASE

5

The Challenge of Newer Research Findings for Psychosomatic Theories

Morton F. Reiser, M.D.

INTRODUCTION

What is the relationship of mind to brain, brain to body and both to illness? The question is as old as the species. The answer will probably be as complex.

This chapter deals with the question as it stands after 1940. World War II gave psychiatry a great deal of impetus and success, and thus interest, money, and time to explore the etiology and pathogenesis of the mind/body/illness relationship. Splitting the early research into two overlapping periods (1940-1960) (1955-1972), I will discuss the theoretical bases, empirical studies, and evolving understanding derived from both.

The concluding section of the chapter admits that between the problem's complexity and the incompleteness of our knowledge, there

---

* This chapter is adapted from Chapter 21, "Changing Theoretical Concepts in Psychosomatic Medicine," from *American Handbook of Psychiatry*, Volume 4, second edition, revised and expanded, Silvano Arieti, Editor-in-Chief; Morton F. Reiser, Editor, Copyright 1975 by Basic Books, Inc., Publishers, New York.

is no satisfactory general theory that parsimoniously explains the relationship of psychological factors to physical changes both in health and disease. However, the knowledge we have thus far does suggest a scheme for future research efforts. The latter part of this chapter will discuss a framework for further study.

PART I: 1940 - 1960

In the 1940's and 50's, research followed two paths. One combined medical and psychological investigations of people who were ill. The other examined not only patients, but also healthy individuals tested in the laboratory.

The work on medical patients was geared to identifying and elucidating the role of conflict and arousal on the onset, progress, exacerbation and remission of physical illness. It was the study of phenomena which had been universally observed: Psychological factors can have a major effect on physical illness. It was verified, however, with careful studies by internists and psychiatrists (1-13). They demonstrated unquestionably that many physical ailments first manifested themselves during periods of psychosocial crisis. These studies also confirmed that psychological factors affect the course of disease: Not only did complications occur in conjunction with psychological stress, but disease processes often accelerated during sustained psychosocial turmoil and went into remission during periods of relative psychological tranquility. Further, it was shown that by attending to and treating psychological distress, the physician could ameliorate symptoms, affect the course of illness, and even, at times, favorably influence pharmacologic effects of drugs. (Although converse effects were also observed, clinicians were understandably hesitant to test them (14, 15).) Unfortunately these studies have only limited implications for understanding the underlying mechanisms at work.

In the second area of study, patients and, later, healthy individuals were examined in the psychophysiologic laboratory. The ultimate goal of such studies was to produce measurable functional changes in target organs and systems of healthy subjects that mimicked patterns of specific disease states. These included gastric hyperacidity and hypermotility, elevated blood pressure, tachycardia, changes in measures of external respiratory dynamics, etc.

The basic experimental design consisted of physiologic functions being repeatedly measured both during relaxed states and during periods of manipulated emotional states (anger, anxiety, etc.). Every tissue and organ of the body innervated by the autonomic nervous system and accessible for observation, intubation, or electronic recording was studied.

On the positive side, in reaction to a wide variety of stimulation, all tissues and organs exhibited reactions to diverse experimental manipulations. *But,* none demonstrated such reactions with the degree of regularity, predictability, and experimental control which would definitively support hypotheses of etiology or pathogenesis. To this day, even with advanced technology and methodology, serious problems of control, instrumentation, data reduction, statistical evaluation and interpretation persist (16, 17, 18, 19).

Such logistics are not the only problems in psychosomatic research. At this point of the review, it is appropriate to consider some of the dilemmas which consistently confuse and frustrate theory construction and evaluation.

Said simply, the science of the mind and the science of the body are two different realms. They use different language, constructs, concepts, tools and techniques, all at different levels of complexity and abstraction (20). Thus, a psychological and physiological observation of the same patient in the same state will produce two different sets of data and formulations. In effect, our research is essentially dealing with covariance data from two different realms which can be shown to occur at frequencies beyond chance. Such findings say little about causality. Thus, the finding that the development of a lesion, such as a duodenal ulcer, occurs contemporaneously with a specific kind of dysphoric mood could be accounted for via four models (see Figure 1).

1) There is no relationship. The duodenum is a vulnerable organ and would break down under any stress.

I   NO RELATIONSHIP

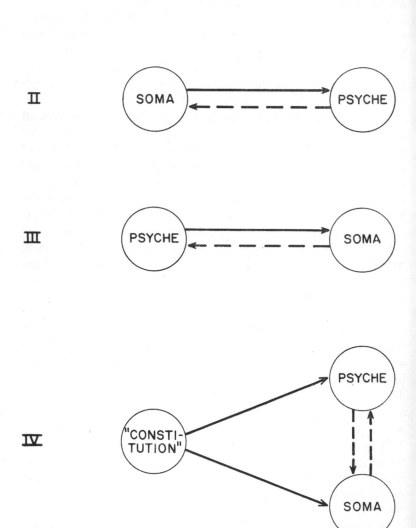

FIGURE 1

2) The lesion precipitated the altered psychological state (somatopsychic sequence).

3) The dysphoric state is pathogenic and if sustained would lead to a peptic ulceration (psychosomatic sequence). (Both the somatopsychic and the psychosomatic sequence allow for reciprocal feedback reactions and escalating cycles.)

4) The fourth model is predicated on the view that the covarying psychological and physiological components are interactive expressions of a central organismic trait (constitution) which in turn reflects both genetic and early perinatal, neonatal and childhood experiential influences (somato-psycho-somatic model).

Another matter that complicates data interpretation in psychosomatic research and leads to confusion about cause and effect in pathology is that there are at least three phases in the natural history of a disease: 1) pre-illness, 2) onset, and 3) course of the established illness. In most instances, these stages are discrete, distinct and albeit independent in respect to underlying mechanisms.

For psychosomatic research, the pre-illness phase raises questions about predisposing (constitutional) factors—genetic and experiential factors that "program" the organism to have a capacity for a specific disease. Onset involves the forces and mechanisms which actually precipitate the illness. These forces are usually operative for only a short period and are probably different and distinct from factors which influence predisposition. The third phase is the course of disease—remission, exacerbation, acceleration, etc. Following the establishment of disease, a third set of factors come into play. For psychosomatic research, these factors have special significance. As the individual becomes aware of the illness and its ramifications, this awareness becomes part of the self-image, acquires symbolic significance, and is incorporated into ongoing conflicts and psychological life. It is misleading and incorrect to assume that mechanisms involved in precipitation of illness and in influencing the course of the illness are identical to each other or to those involved in determining predisposition to the illness.

With these considerations in mind, we turn to the major theoretical issue of the years between 1940 and 1960: *specificity*. Do specific psychological attitudes or reactions bring about specific changes in organs and systems? Are there specific psychological phenomena which are necessary and/or sufficient to produce a specific disease state?

The early research was predicated on that notion. Observations at that time appeared to support the fact that certain aspects of personality and psychological life would contribute to the development of disease processes and thus produce a specific, predictable disease entity. General clinical experience and psychological profiles gleaned from interviews and projective tests supported such a model. Patients with certain diseases, for example duodenal ulcer, shared many personality traits with each other, more so than with a general patient population or with patients with other diseases. As Engel (2) described, a clinician, knowing only the diagnosis of ulcerative colitis, can give a fairly accurate personality sketch of an individual. On the other hand, however, the description of a personality constellation will not predict a diagnosis of the correct illness or even the event of any illness.

The question arose, "Do patients share their psychological traits because they are a reaction to the physical ailment?," thus making the psychological manifestations reactive. Such questions are unanswerable in retrospective research. In fact, although they may have been important to early researchers seeking a linear cause and effect model, the importance of the answer wanes in light of recent theories to be discussed later.

Nonetheless, researchers of that time dedicated themselves to finding causal relationships and elucidating the significance of specificity. Dunbar (21) proposed a personality profile which, though detailed, had little clinical or theoretical utility. Later, Wolff and his collaborators (5, 22) hypothesized that stress diseases were part of the human physiological response to stress: "Forces or individuals that jeopardize the life or love of a human being . . . which interfere with the realization of his aspirations and needs or block the exercise of his potential (are) reacted to by mobilization of an individual's defenses" (22). Their effect and costs to the individual depended on his weakness or strength and the integrity of the participating structures. Thus Wolff and his collaborators saw physical reactions as adaptive, protective, defensive and a function of personality, past experience and the stimuli. They conceptualized patterns of defensive responses in terms of specific bodily functions and systems, e.g., eating or ejection-riddance.

Their research methods utilized easily observable personality features, derived from conscious layers of the patient's personalities and life experiences. They also carried out simultaneous psychological testing and physiological observation. Although all this laboratory-based research may sound removed from psychoanalytic theories (discussed below), in fact, both sets of formulations have compatible, if not shared, central themes. They differ, of course, in the level of personality function stressed, the amount of inference and abstraction, and the complexity of scope and focus. Nonetheless, similarities to Alexander's thinking (see below) can be discerned from Wolff's statement on "protective patterns of defense involving eating: the stomach and the duodenum":

> One of the earliest aggressive patterns to manifest itself in the infant is that associated with hunger and eating. In later life, this pattern may reassert itself in certain individuals when they feel threatened; at such times of danger, feelings of anger and deprivation of longing for emotional support or of need for being "cared for" may be repressed by the equally insistent assertion that the individual is strong, independent, capable of doing alone or standing 'on his own feet' either through actual deprivation of emotional support or an unwillingness to accept it. This feeling state shows itself in the stomach as one of readiness for eating, hypersalivation may also occur. The gastric hyperfunction associated with these feelings is manifested by increased blood flow, motility and acid secretion. Under such circumstances the mucous membrane was found to be unusually fragile. The hyperdynamic state of the stomach was found to be associated with symptoms, namely heartburn and localized epigastric pain relieved by food and soda whether or not ulceration was present." (22)

Grace (6) and Graham (23), Wolff's students, later formulated a "specificity of attitude" hypothesis: Everyone with the same disease would have the same attitude toward the life event which precipitated or exacerbated the disease. Different attitudes fostered different diseases. Attitude was defined as:

"1. How a person perceives his own position in a situation—what he feels is happening to him, and 2. What action, if any, he wishes to take" (23). According to Graham, the attitude thought to bring about duodenal ulcer was "felt deprived of what was due him and wanted to get even (didn't get what he should, what was owed or promised, and wanted to get back at, get revenge, do to him what he did to me)" (24). The ramifications of each attitude were then tested in a number of techniques, including, physical measurements during hypnotically induced states, and "post-diction" by blind raters who would match recorded interviews with specific disease states.

In 1932, Franz Alexander and his associates began their psycho-analytic studies of patients with chronic organic ailments that seemed to be precipitated or worsened by emotional conflict. Alexander differentiated between what he called "visceral neurosis" (the primary interest of psychosomatic medicine) and conversion hysteria defined by Freud (25, 26). In some ways the concept of conversion hysteria set the stage for the search for specificity. That is, as conversion hysteria was seen as a symbolic resolution of conflict, the "visceral neuroses" were seen as the concomitants of unresolved conflict. Alexander theorized that the appropriate physiological changes would occur due to the chronic affect (suppressed or repressed) associated with unresolved conflict (27). The central feature was that pathogenic physiological changes were seen as concomitants of mature adult emotions, conceptualized via Cannon's concept of fight-flight physiology: sympatho-adrenal and parasympathetic activation. Thus, essential hypertension was viewed as the result of the physical aspects of rage (sympatho-adrenal activation and blood pressure elevation) repressed and suppressed over time. Alexander and his colleagues studied seven diseases: bronchial asthma, rheumatoid arthritis, ulcerative colitis, essential hypertension, peptic ulcer, neurodermatitis, and thyrotoxicosis, and formulated seven categories of unresolved conflict—one for each. Thus, duodenal ulcer was formulated as increased gastric secretion as a result of the wish to fulfill unmet oral needs (28):

> The central dynamic feature in duodenal peptic ulcers is the frustration of dependent desires originally oral in character. The craving to be fed appears later as a wish to be loved, to be given support, money, and advice. This fixation on early dependent situations of infancy comes in conflict with the adult ego and results in hurt pride, since the infantile craving must be repressed. Oral receptiveness when frustrated often changes into oral aggressiveness, and this also becomes repressed because of guilt feelings it provokes. Both oral dependent and oral aggressive impulses may then be frustrated by internal factors—shame and guilt.
>
> The most common defense against both oral dependent and oral acquisitive impulses is overcompensation. The latently dependent or acquisitive person overtly appears as an independent, hard-working individual who likes responsibility and taking care of others. He responds to challenges with increased activity and ambition, works hard and assumes greater and greater responsibilities. This in turn increases his secret longing to lean on others. To be loved, to be helped is associated from the beginning of life with the wish to be fed. When this help-seeking attiture is denied its normal expression in a give-and-take relationship with others, a *psychological regression* takes place to the original form of a wish to ingest food. *This regressive desire seems to be specifically correlated with increased gastric secretion* (Italics mine).
>
> Not all patients suffering from duodenal ulcer overcompensate for their dependent desires with an outward show of 'go-getting' activity. Many of them are overtly dependent, demanding, or disgruntled persons. In such individuals, the dependent tendencies are frustrated not by internal repudiation, but by external circumstances. But even in these overtly demanding patients, a definite conflict about dependent cravings can be discovered. The crucial psychological finding in all ulcer patients is the frustration (external or internal) of passive, dependent, and love-demanding desires that cannot be gratified in normal relationships.
>
> Onset of illness occurs when the intensity of the patient's un-

satisfied dependent cravings increases either because of external deprivation or because the patient defends against his cravings by assuming increased responsibilities. The external deprivation often consists in the loss of a person upon whom the patient has been dependent, in leaving home, or in losing money or a position that had given the patient a sense of security. The increased responsibility may take the form of marriage or the birth of a child or the assumption of a more responsible job (29).

Each psychodynamic constellation also had a specific "onset situation" or precipitating period which triggered old conflicts. Thirdly, Alexander posited an "X Factor" or constitutional vulnerability of specific tissue, organ, or system. This linear formulation held that all three conditions had to be present, i.e., each was a necessary but not sufficient condition. For example, despite the psychodynamic and constitutional prerequisites, disease would not occur without the onset situation.

In light of current knowledge and concepts, these early specificity hypotheses of both Wolff and Alexander seem parochial. Although the theories were ambitious and detailed, they were limited to seeing the person and the illness mainly in terms of intrapsychic functioning, and peripheral autonomic effector mechanisms and end-organ systems. Among other things, they neglected serious consideration of non-specific mechanisms as well as a whole range of important factors ranging from the cultural and developmental to the cellular and molecular.

Other psychoanalytic researchers at the time (such as Grinker, Deutsch, and Schur) emphasized somewhat different issues in their theoretical formulations. They postulated that the visceral neuroses involved not only psychological regression, but also a physiological regression, in which the patient's patho-physiological functioning was reminiscent of the unstable, unmodulated primitive physiological patterns of infancy. Their developmental theories acknowledged many influences on this pathological physiological regression. Among them were genetic and early experiential factors, randomly programmed or conditioned by chance, and reinforced by maternal and familial relationships during the early years of life. Margolin (30) and Szasz

(31) also followed this line of reasoning and Szasz coined the phrase "regressive innervation."

These formulations, which were also of the multiple factor type, differ from Alexander's in two important ways. First, instead of being strictly linear, geared to direct cause and effect, they are more transactional and incorporate diverse influences. Secondly, the physiological component of their theories stresses infancy and early childhood physiology and development, rather than the physiological responses of mature adults.

Grinker (32) further elaborated on early physical/psychological development. He postulated a series of changes and differentiations starting with the unity of mind and body at birth, and ending with complex integration and differentiation of adulthood. He thus conceptualized psychosomatic illnesses and psychoses as representing extreme stages of breakdown of that system, ending in the overwhelming primitive panic state, comparable to neonatal total response.

Schur (33, 34) similarly addressed constitutional development. He suggested two congruent psychosomatic developmental themes, especially in response to danger: 1) In the somatic realm, there is a progressively refined system response to danger—from the infant's total response to the adult's complex, specific finely modulated response; and 2) in the psychological realm, there is the progression from primary process to secondary process thinking and the development of discrete mature ego functions. He saw stress-related regressive alterations in ego state as precipitating primitive regressive physiology which would in turn lead to disease. Schur emphasized that the ego reacts to danger in two ways: evaluation and response. He saw psychosomatic illness as the result of the ego defenses failing under stress, and thus leading to reactivation of unconscious conflict. He postulated that as the individual responds progressively more grossly or primitively to danger (evaluation), "resomatization" occurs and infantile somatic responses are reactivated (response), resulting in disease.

Besides the physiological return to primitive functioning, Deutsch was also impressed by the use of primitive body language (symbolism) in psychosomatic patients (35). In his scheme, constitutional factors, plus pregenital conversion, early conditioning and genetics, predetermine the organ and system which will malfunction.

It is interesting that some psychoanalytically based researchers, such as Sperling (36-39) and Garma (40) following Groddeck (41) have conceptualized psychosomatic visceral disorders as representing symbolic conversion reactions. Although their clinical data are familiar and repeatable for psychoanalytic clinicians working with medical patients, the theoretical model does not fit easily into the mainstream of current psychosomatic research nor is it testable by empirical means. As pointed out earlier, such retrospective historical studies confound attempts to establish cause and effect. It seems likely that the symbolic psychological content arises as a reaction to the knowledge of illness and its incorporation into the self image. In retrospective studies, given the methods now available, it is not possible to establish symbolic process as arising prior to the illness and hence implicate it in etiology.

I have taken the time to review this early research not only because it gives a sense of a highly productive period that stimulated an exciting and important epoch of psychophysiological research, but also because many of the ideas, especially the epigenetic models of Grinker, Deutsch, and Schur, are surprisingly compatible with many recent biological findings. The work of this early period produced a rich and important foundation of data and observations, even if some of the conclusions can in retrospect be seen as off-target. Most of the early clinical observations have become part of our general medical knowledge. Alexander's clinical observations have proven to be verifiable and valuable as psychological findings and contributions to theory (42-45).

In terms of actual theory which explains mind/body/disease, these theories have not held up under sophisticated research technology. They cannot be summarily dismissed, however; their information, observations and perspective will continue to have at least partial value (29, 24), and will have to be considered in later formulations.

PART II: 1955 - 1972

The biological and neurobiological breakthroughs that have occurred since the mid-1950's changed the focus of psychosomatic research. Whereas early researchers sought discrete intrapsychic causes for specific disease entities, these newer developments in neurobiology made such narrowness of focus untenable. Advances in technology, electronics, the computer sciences, etc., permitted new insights and investigations into previously unexplored biological processes. As the results came in, the complexity and subtlety of the interacting factors and mechanisms obviated the early linear theories. Early researchers had relatively little information regarding: (a) the role and mechanisms of the central nervous system (which, of course, mediates the individual's cognitive, emotional, and physical responses); (b) the role of cellular and molecular processes; (c) the role of genetics; (d) the interaction of developmental, experiential, and genetic factors—not to mention broader interpersonal, social, and cultural influences—in determining "constitutional" factors.

Once such factors were taken into account, the simple classification of psychosomatic illness itself was challenged. It became clear that the mind and body could not be dealt with as separate entities. Recent researchers have widened their views to account for the confluence of biological, psychological and social factors in health and disease. This section will review some of that research, especially that which has influenced our thinking about the complex interrelationship of the mind, brain, and body and has thus set the stage for future explorations.

Longitudinal Predictive Studies of Persons at Risk

Given that a certain group of people have a biological predisposition for a disease, why does only a portion of that group actually get the disease? Longitudinal studies of "populations at risk" were designed to examine what predisposing physical, psychological and psychosocial factors affect pathology. In the best known of these studies, Mirsky and his co-workers studied peptic duodenal ulcer (42). Their work refined Alexander's concept of a physical vulnerability. Mirsky formulated that the necessary but not sufficient physical component (hypersecretion of pepsinogen) (42, 46, 47) plays a central role in personality development by influencing the mother-infant relationship and thus also contributes to determining the type of social-conflict situations that may become pathogenic in adulthood. Empirical data from studies by Weiner, Thaler, Reiser and Mirsky supported this formulation. Independently studying psychological data, they ferreted out core conflict issues (Alexander) and predicted who, of a large number of individuals with high pepsinogen levels, would actually develop ulcers under the psychosocial stress of basic military training (42, 43). Although these studies lend credence to Alexander's clinical observations and clinical formulations, they do not actually address the question of physiological mechanisms involved in precipitation of the ulcer and do not bear directly on his central psychosomatic hypotheses. Alexander's clinical formulations on thyrotoxicosis were also partially supported by Dongier and Wittkower (44) and by Wallerstein et al. (45), who showed a relationship between the psychological traits described by Alexander in patients with thyrotoxicosis and the increased incorporation of I (131) by the thyroid gland of euthyroid individuals. Again, the relationship of this physiological property to disease is not known. Weiner (48) suggests that these same psychological traits may be associated with pathological conditions of both increased and decreased secretory function of the thyroid gland, i.e., with propensity to thyroid disorder of either type.

Interestingly, Alexander tried to incorporate the results of the rapidly advancing research data into his theories. Shortly before his death he wrote:

> These three variables—inherited or early acquired organ or system vulnerability, psychological patterns of conflict and defense formed in early life, and the precipitating life situations— are not necessarily independent factors. It is possible that constitution at least partially determines both the organ vulnerability and the characteristic psychological patterns. At present little is known about the interdependence of these two variables. There is strong indication, however, that the correlation between

constitution and characteristic psychiatric patterns is not a simple one. Constitution alone without certain emotional experiences of early life, particularly the early mother-child relation, may not produce a consistent pattern (29).

Once the biological sine qua non is identified, many longitudinal studies of patients at risk become possible and pertinent (49, 50). It is possible to study those at risk for gout (hyperuricemia) (51) and rheumatoid arthritis (immune proteins) over extended periods. Long-range prospective studies have obvious ramifications for coronary artery disease, with its many predisposing variables (obesity, cigarette smoking, hyperlipidemia, exercise, hypertension, etc.) (52).

The real question for psychosomatic theory is how to fit a concept like Friedman's and Rosenman's (53, 54) Type A personality into a disease model. Does Type A personality lead to a more stressful life and thus help induce coronary arteriosclerosis? Or is it the counterpart of a specific constitution which is physically vulnerable to coronary artery disease (Figure 1, Model IV)?

Mortality and Morbidity of Bereavement

The importance of psychosocial stress on health—indeed the ability to sustain life—is highlighted by studies on the mortality and morbidity of bereavement. In the late 1960's, Rees and Lutkins (55) studied a small community in Wales for one year. Two groups of approximately 900 each were matched for age, sex and marital status. The individuals in the experimental group, however, had each recently lost a close relative. During the year of bereavement, the rate of death for the bereaved sample was seven times that of the controls. Moreover, the rate of death was twice as high if the relative had died outside the home (including in the hospital). Parkes, Benjamin and Fitzgerald (52), studying widowers in Britain, arrived at similar results; they found that coronary artery disease accounted for the majority of deaths in the first six months of bereavement. When Bennet (56) studied victims of the 1968 Bristol flood, he found that within a year of the flood, 50 percent more people whose homes had been flooded died than those whose homes were not. These studies make it apparent that bereavement and loss and their related affective states have a profound influence on health and even life itself.

Engel and Schmale (57, 58, 59), who had earlier studied the relation of object loss and separation to the onset of illness, labeled the gamut of emotions involved as "helplessness" and "hopelessness" associated with attitudes of "giving up" and "given up" (60). Engel suggests that this state may be the body's "other" biological reaction to danger (other than fight or flight); he calls it "conservation withdrawal" (57). Thus, he postulates that the body's metabolic changes would be anabolic instead of fight or flight's catabolic mechanisms, the basis of earlier psychosomatic theories. Engel's "conversation withdrawal" implies a nonspecific, overall effect which would make the body more vulnerable to pathogenic factors of any type.

Psychoneuroendocrinology

Psychoneuroendocrinology provides a major link between clinical and basic research. It has added to our ever increasing awareness of the role of non-specific mechanisms in pathogenesis and also given us some insights into the possible relationship of these non-specific reactions to mechanisms that may be more directly involved in specificity. This field of study has also provided our first inklings into the complex, intricate, and still unexplained CNS mechanisms which mediate between our higher mental processes, and the basic body processes that maintain tissue integrity and system function. It has also generated what little knowledge we have of the highly sophisticated system which links the limbic forebrain to the autonomic nervous system (and thus to peripheral tissues) and to the pituitary and through it to the entire endocrine system which extends the influence of central nervous system processes throughout the body via the action of hormones (61, 62, 63). These findings obviously have important implications for psychosomatic theory.

Studies on experimental animals have shown that alterations in endocrine function due to psychosocial stress not only alter the animal's resistance to pathogenic organisms, but also affect the viability and growth rate of implanted tumor viruses (64, 65). This lowered resistance probably comes from CNS mechanism's affecting the body's immunological reactions, such as tissue sensitivity to histamine, and levels of circulating antibodies (66, 67). In this way, hormones, alone and in combination, probably affect not just "stress" and hormone-dependent diseases, but also infectious and neoplastic disorders.

A second area of importance involves the balancing effect of the ego defenses on the level of activation of stress hormone systems (sympatho-adrenal system and the pituitary-adrenal system). Sachar et al. (68) first examined this delicate balance (reciprocity between effectiveness of ego defense and level of endocrine activation) in patients with acute schizophrenic excitement. Others have verified the relationship in acute and chronic conditions as well. These findings increase our knowledge which will eventually help understand how intrapsychic phenomenon may be interposed between psychosocial vectors and alterations in body physiology. Effective ego defenses may protect against sudden endocrine activation; or increased endocrine activity may come into play when ego defenses are inadequate or failing. Of clinical interest, the adrenal steroids affect not only peripheral tissue metabolism, but also, more subtly, CNS functioning (69, 70).

A third area of interest is the study of biological rhythms as reflected in brain function and consciousness. Early theorists had been intrigued with the possible pathogenic importance of transiently or intermittently altered states of mental function. For example, in "Studies on Hysteria" Breuer and Freud (25) wrote of a hypothetical "hypnoidal" state as a biologic substrate for symptom formation. In the 1950's, Schur put forth the role of "altered ego state" (partially altered states of consciousness) in developing pathology (33, 34). And, it has indeed been found that, like the autonomic nervous system, the endocrine system seems to follow regular rhythms—not only the circadian diurnal rhythm, but also seasonal rhythms, the menstrual cycle in women, and some ultradian rhythms such as the 90-minute REM sleep cycle. Under the best of circumstances, these rhythms are synchronized or working in a complementary fashion. Researchers are beginning to develop data suggesting, however, the importance of desynchronization for psychopathology and pathophysiology [see for example Curtis (71), Kripke (72), and Sachar et al. (73)]. In addition, the autonomic nervous system functions differently in different stages of sleep (62, 74). This has special implications for diseases with nocturnal variations, such as nocturnal angina. It also appears that the body works on a continuing ultradian 90-minute cycle throughout the entire day, which may relate not only to homostatic physiological patterns, but also to levels of consciousness and behavior (72, 75).

Studies on these psycho-neuroendocrine phenomena provide an interesting common area for combined psychiatric and physiological research. Individuals can be simultaneously and intensively monitored both psychologically, especially psychoanalytically, and physiologically (neuroendocrine function) during periods of intense life stress. In light of new findings on these mechanisms and cycles, new studies of older established findings would be useful in theory development (76).

Another area of recent neuroendocrine research of interest for psychosomatic medicine involves recent findings on catecholamines. Researchers Henry, Axelrod and their associates (77) have found markedly increased levels of biosynthetic enzymes involved in epinephrine and norepinephrine metabolism and biosynthesis and increased adrenal weight in response to psychosocial stress in mice. This same stress wil produce hypertension and renal pathology in experimental animals. Adrenal cortical hormones also influence the enzymes which synthesize and metabolize CNS catecholamines (61). If the psychoneuroendocrine stress response is part of the CNS regulation of biogenic amine metabolism, it may help explain at least in part aspects of those major clinical affective disorders which involve disturbances in biogenic amine transmitter systems of brain (78).

Autonomic Conditioning

We are becoming increasingly aware of the potential role that instrumental conditioning of autonomic responses may play in the development of illness. Early specificity theorists recognized the possible role of classical conditioning of visceral changes and some used it to explain predisposition to illness, but this would limit the possibilities to those changes that can be evoked by "unconditioned stimuli" such as shock, loud noise, etc. However, the demonstration by DiCara and Miller (79, 80) that the autonomic nervous system can be instrumentally conditioned means that any change in the viscera's functional repertoire can be shaped or augmented by instrumental learning, thus greatly augmenting the possible pathogenic significance of conditioning for affecting predisposition to disease. This work also demonstrates the existence of functional afferent pathways to the brain from autonomically innervated structures. Study of the feedback mechanism to the brain from the viscera by way of the autonomic nervous system could help clarify many important issues regarding the role of both the central and autonomic nervous systems in the integration of psychological and biological functioning.

Developmental Psychophysiology

Developmental psychophysiology addresses the role of early experiences in the establishment of "constitution." Studies of laboratory animals have given insights into the role of early experimental manipulation on later adult psychological and biological development. Levine et al. watched the effects of early "handling" on psychological and biological responses to stress (81). Similarly there have been studies on the long-term effects of sex hormones administered at critical developmental periods (82, 83). Looking at the issues of disease susceptibility, Ader and Friedman (64, 84, 85) developed some very convincing data on the results of various infantile manipulations (e.g., crowding vs. solitary conditions) on later susceptibility and resistance—not only to stress-producing stimuli but also to viral and infectious agents as well.

Using rats, Hofer (86) and Reiser studied the maturation of physiological mechanisms regulating heart rate and rhythm. Besides demonstrating asynchronomy of development of sympathetic and vagal systems, they also identified possibly critical developmental stages. These stages could prove to be precursors of adult pathological responses (87).

Developmental psychophysiology has great potential for addressing questions about the relative role of heredity and environment on constitution. Longitudinal studies using manipulations of specially bred animals could determine not only the roles of genetic predisposition to illness and environment, but also the mechanisms involved in effects of pharmacologic agents. One of the archetypical psychosomatic studies was that of Henry et al. (77) mentioned earlier. They looked at the interactions and relationship between and among psychosocial stress, endocrine and metabolic enzyme systems, early developmental experience and organ pathology in an experimental disease model system of hypertension in mice. These studies address the full scope and complexity of the issues.

In summary, psychosomatic research has developed from early case descriptions and clinical experiments searching for specific psychological factors which produced clearly defined disease patterns, to a field of research which attempts to approach society/mind/brain/body/disease questions via their many interrelated components, from the social and cultural, to the psychological and biological, including cellular and molecular levels.

PART III: STATE OF THE ART

To formulate a psychosomatic theory, we must see man as existing in a "bio-psycho-social" field (see Figure 2). With intracellular processes at one end and a panoply of social, cultural, and even historical influences at the other, this open transactional system allows constant bi-directional flow of information and energy. The brain is the key organ; it influences and serves both mental and physical functions negotiated via the central and autonomic nervous system and neuroendocrine system. Besides mediating the individual's relationship with his social environment by supporting mental functions, the brain also somehow "transduces" (88) nonphysical, immaterial, e.g., symbolic, aspects of that environment, into physical-physiological impulses which in turn may initiate phys-

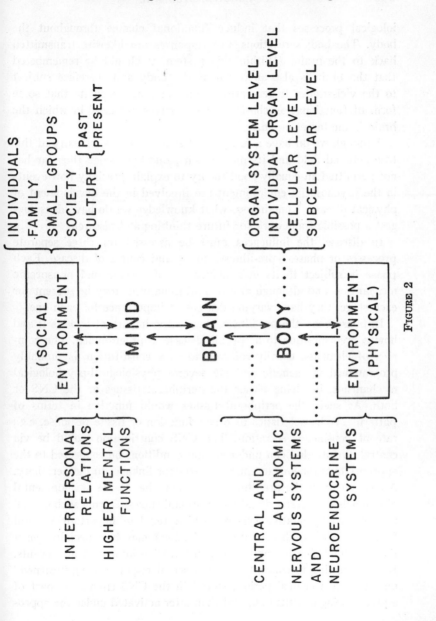

FIGURE 2

iological processes that induce functional change throughout the body. The body's reactions and responses are likewise transmitted back to the brain. (Within this system, it should be remembered that the brain is also an organ of the body and therefore subject to the vicissitudes it generates. Thus, one can speculate that some form of functional psychosis may be "stress diseases" in which the brain is the target organ.)

Although we do have a fairly good sense of the complexity of this transactional field and its mechanisms, our knowledge thus far has not permitted an equally good theory to explain precisely how events in the psychosocial environment are involved in the development of physical disease. Nonetheless, what knowledge we do have does suggest a possible framework for future thinking and research.

In disease, the influences must be assessed for three separate processes or phases—pre-illness, onset, and course of disease. Each phase is subject to its own admixture of specific and nonspecific mechanisms and although any or all mechanisms may be present for each stage, they have varying degrees of importance for each one.

In phase one—the pre-illness phase—the important issue is if and how a predisposition to a specific disease is programmed. The complex of elements, usually referred to as a constitution, is probably programmed via genetic and via several physiological-psychological mechanisms, involving either the peripheral tissues or the CNS or both. As such, the peripheral tissues would function in terms of patterns or characteristics of organ function or tissue response, e.g., rate of pepsinogen secretion. The CNS contribution would be via central circuits that can under certain conditions be connected to the appropriate autonomic or endocrine effector linkages to the periphery. A component of the pre-illness phase may be, as the developmental physiologists suggest, critical maturational stages. During such crucial periods neurovegetative systems which regulate important visceral functions (such as heart rate and rhythm) may be especially sensitive or vulnerable to conditioning by outside influences and events. It is interesting to conceptualize a visceral response being "learned" during such a critical period, stored in the CNS circuits as part of a predisposing constitution, and then later activated under the appropriate life conditions. The validity of such a construct is underlined given early childhood shaping and reinforcement. In Mirsky's formulations (42, 46) on duodenal ulcers, he posits that a genic constitutional predisposition (e.g. gastric hypersecretion), expressed in behavior (need to be nurtured and nourished), will influence the caregiver's response to the baby or child. These responses will in turn modify the child's behavior (e.g. frustration or intensification) which will in turn be responded to, etc. In this way, a core conflict specifically and inextricably linked to the constitutional predisposition is created. Meanwhile, this vulnerability is the source of reactive or protective ego defenses which develop around it. The quality, nature and imperfection of such a defensive matrix in turn determine the kind of psychosocial stress situations which would overwhelm it and thus activate conflict. Although the data only allow speculation about the relative contributions of genetic predisposition and early life experiences, it is likely that pathology develops via such an epigenetic interrelated pattern of biological, psychological and social vulnerabilities.

The onset of illness is precipitated by a different set of factors, often set in motion by the psychosocial environment. For theory formulation, the question is how psychosocial stress is related to the activation of physical illness. One important issue is the role of non-specific factors, especially the psychoneuroendocrine system stress response and its effect on immune mechanisms, bio-enzymes, etc. (see Part II of this chapter). Again, in each individual, the stress that will overwhelm his/her defense matrix and precipitate illness will be related to his/her core conflict, individual history and personality organization. Faltering defenses can affect adrenal cortical and other endocrine activity to make the individual less resistant to infection— an infection to which he/she would normally have been immune. This nonspecific reaction is common in all medical practice. In addition, there is a small group of individuals in whom the disease "agent" is not external (pathogenic organisms), but internal—a predisposition previously latent or inactive. The question is, how do the nonspecific changes related to psychoneuroendocrine stress activate that disease process? Or, how do the changes effected by the endocrine response

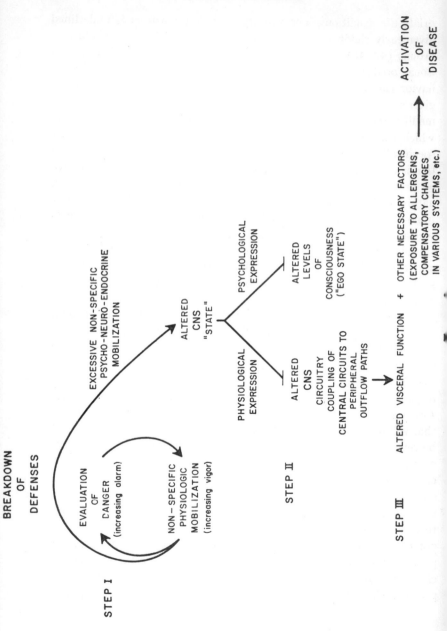

permit or release the expression of the previously inactive but potentially pathologic function? Recent findings suggest a number of answers. It has been found that as a result of psychosocial stress, neurovegetative and endocrine changes occur which affect higher mental processes, such as cognition (89, 90), and therefore may affect perception and evaluation of danger signals and levels of anxiety (69, 70). It is possible that sustained psychological conflict and the concomitant weakened defenses could bring about the following self-reinforcing cycle: As psychological processes which evaluate danger regress and become more primitive and symbolic, the physiological responses become more intense as danger signals are evaluated with increased alarm (Figure 3, Step I). In addition, one could speculate that the brain's resultant exposure to vigorous and continuous changes in circulating hormones could activate preprogrammed pathogenic CNS circuits which would connect, via appropriate efferent fibers, to the viscera and alter visceral functioning (Figure 3, Step II).

As I have written previously (91, 92), these altered CNS conditions might be manifested psychologically as subtly altered states of consciousness (25, 33, 34). Clinical observations and studies of patients with different levels of consciousness and different levels of free anxiety support such a notion. For example, 1) the REM sleep cycle is known to be associated with less well regulated and more primitive patterns of autonomic function; 2) some episodes of serious illness (myocardial infarction, status asthmaticus, hemorrhage from duodenal ulcer) are precipitated or exacerbated in sleep; and 3) the ultradian 90-minute rhythm (REM cycle) may continue through the 24-hour period and be manifest in behavior (e.g., increased eating behavior) during waking hours (75).

Finally, for the precipitation of a particular disease state, the altered visceral function produced in Step 2 (as outlined above) would have to combine with factors essential to the particular disease (e.g., exposure to allergens, pathogens, compensator and secondary changes in the same and other systems). Of course, these would be different for each disease.

In summary, the precipitation of disease primarily involves a series of nonspecific psychoneuroendocrine changes that may be permissive of illness in everyone. For a small number of persons such changes may be manifested by internal changes—e.g., specifically pre-programmed patterns of visceral innervation, which had been defined by combinations of early experience and genetic endowment which are pathogenic for disease.

In the third phase of disease, the course of the disease, both specific and nonspecific mechanisms may operate, both separately and in combination, and differently than in the onset phase. As the disease progresses and organ reserve decreases, the importance of specific factors varies. The role of nonspecific changes may increase, as the body becomes less able to deal with the disruptive effects of nonspecific stress responses. At the same time, as the individual incorporates and elaborates the disease into his self image, it becomes part of his ongoing mental life and not only becomes associated with the original conflict but also creates new areas of conflict as well (93). Thus, more conditioning and feedback may occur between emotional events and the viscera. The idiosyncratic symbolic meanings and issues associated with the disease become increasingly apparent in current life and conflicts. Thus, as the psychoanalytic or psychotherapeutic patient speaks increasingly of these meanings, signs and symptoms, it may appear (inaccurately) that the disease originated as a symbolic conversion reaction. As I have tried to illustrate here, it's not that simple.

Although much of this speculation on the mechanisms in "psychosomatic" illnesses is sheer guesswork, I have tried to reconcile older accepted theories with the newer biological findings and perhaps suggest areas for future research. Undoubtedly, the answers on the relationship of mind/body/illness will be derived from the understanding of the brain as it controls and integrates the biological, psychological and social environment.

REFERENCES

1. WEISS, E. and ENGLISH, O. S.: *Psychosomatic Medicine*. Philadelphia: W. B. Saunders Co., 1957.

2. ENGEL, G. L.: Studies of Ulcerative Colitis. *American Journal of Medicine*, 16, 1954, pp. 416-433.
3. FERRIS, E. B., REISER, M. F., STEAD, W. M., and BRUST, A. A.: Clinical and Physiological Observations of Interrelated Mechanisms in Arterial Hypertension. *Transactions, Association of American Physicians*, 61, 1948, pp. 97-107.
4. WOLF, S. and SHEPARD, E. M.: An Appraisal of Factors that Evoke and Modify the Hypertensive Reaction Pattern. In H. Wolff, S. Wolf, Jr. and C. Hare (Eds.), *Life Stress and Bodily Disease*. Baltimore: The Williams & Wilkins Co., 1950.
5. WOLFF, H. G.: Life Stress and Bodily Disease—A Formulation. In H. Wolff, S. Wolf, Jr. and C. Hare (Eds.), *Life Stress and Bodily Disease*. Baltimore: The Williams & Wilkins Co., 1950.
6. GRACE, W. J.: Life Situations, Emotions and Chronic Ulcerative Colitis. In H. Wolff, S. Wolf, Jr. and C. Hare (Eds.), *Life Stress and Bodily Disease*. Baltimore: The Williams & Wilkins Co., 1950.
7. MIRSKY, I. A., FUTTERMAN, P., KAPLAN S., and BROH-KAHN, R. H.: Blood Plasma Pepsinogen I, The Source Properties, and Assay of the Proteolytic Activity of Plasma at Acid Reactions. *J. Lab. & Clin. Med.*, 40, 1952, p. 17.
8. ENGEL, G. L. and ROMANO, J.: Studies of Syncope; Biologic Interpretation of Vasodepressor Syncope. *Psychosom. Med.*, 29, 1947, p. 228.
9. LEVINE, M.: *Psychotherapy in Medical Practice*. New York: Macmillan, 1942.
10. ROSENBAUM, M.: Psychosomatic Aspects of Patients with Peptic Ulcer. In Eric D. Wittkower and R. A. Cleghorn (Eds.), *Recent Developments in Psychosomatic Medicine*. Philadelphia: J. B. Lippincott Co., 194.
11. SASLOW, G., GRESSEL, G., SHOBE, F., DuBois, P., and SCHROEDER, H.: The Possible Etiological Relevance of Personality Factors in Arterial Hypertension. In H. Wolff, S. Wolf, Jr. and C. Hare (Eds.), *Life Stress and Bodily Disease*. Baltimore: The Williams & Wilkins Co., 1950.
12. LIDZ, T., and WHITEHORN, J.: Life Situations, Emotions and Graves Disease. In H. Wolff, S. Wolf, Jr. and C. Hare (Eds.), *Life Stress and Bodily Disease*. Baltimore: The Williams & Wilkins Co., 1950.
13. BINGER, C. A. L., ACKERMAN, N. W., COHN, A. F., SCHOEDER, H. A., and STEELE, J. H.: Personality in Arterial Hypertension. *Psychosomatic Medicine Monographs*, New York: Hoeber, 1945.
14. REISER, M. F.: Models and Techniques in Psychosomatic Research. *Comprehensive Psychiatry*, 9, 1968.
15. SHAPIRO, A.: Influence of Emotional Variables in the Evaluation of Hypotensive Agents. *Psychosom. Med.*, 17, 1955, p. 291.

16. GRINKER, R. SR.: *Psychosomatic Research.* New York: Norton, 1953.
17. REISER, M. F.: Research Findings on the Influence of Counter-transference Attitudes on the Course of Patients with Hypertension in Medical Treatment, Round Table on Hypertension, Mid-Winter Meeting; American Psychoanalytic Association, New York: December (1952). Abstracted in Report of Round Table. *J. Amer. Psychoanal. Assoc.,* 1, 1953, p. 562.
18. STEIN, M.: The What, How, and Why of Psychosomatic Medicine. In D. Offer and D. X. Freedman (Eds.), *Modern Psychiatry and Clinical Research.* New York: Basic Books, Inc., 1971.
19. WEINER, H., THAYER, M., HEISER, M. F., and MIRSKY, I. A.: Etiology of Duodenal Ulcer I. *Psychosom. Med.,* 19, 1957, pp. 1-10.
20. VON BERTALANFFY, L.: The Mind-Body Problem. *Psychosom. Med.,* 26, 1964, pp. 29-45.
21. DUNBAR, H. F.: *Psychosomatic Diagnosis.* New York: Hoeber, 1943.
22. WOLF, S. and WOLFF, H. G.: *Human Gastric Function.* Oxford University Press. Second Edition, 1947.
23. GRAHAM, D. T., KABLER, J. D., and GRAHAM, F. K.: Physiological Response to the Suggestion of Attitudes Specific for Hives and Hypertension. *Psychosom. Med.,* 24, 1962, p. 159.
24. GRAHAM, D. T., LUNDY, R. M., BENJAMIN, L. S., KABLER, J. D., LEWIS, W. C., KUNISH, N. O., and GRAHAM, F. K.: Specific Attitudes in Initial Interviews with Patients Having Different "Psychosomatic" Diseases. *Psychosom. Med.,* 24, 1962, pp. 257-266.
25. BREUER, J. and FREUD, S.: Studies on Hysteria. In J. Strachey (Ed.), *Standard Edition.* London: Hogarth Press, 1955.
26. FREUD, S.: The Psychoanalytic View of Psychogenic Visual Disturbance. In J. Strachey (Ed.), *Standard Edition,* 11, 1957, pp. 209-218.
27. ALEXANDER, F.: Fundamental Concepts of Psychosomatic Research: Psychogenesis, Conversion, Specificity. *Psychosomatic Medicine,* 5, 1943, pp. 205-210.
28. ALEXANDER, F.: *Psychosomatic Medicine.* New York: W. W. Norton & Co., Inc., 1950, pp. 104-106.
29. ALEXANDER, F., FRENCH, T. M., and POLLOCK, G. H.: *Psychosomatic Specificity.* Chicago: The University of Chicago Press, 1968.
30. MARGOLIN, S. G.: Genetic and Dynamic Psychophysiological Determinants of Pathophysiological Processes. In F. Deutsch (Ed.), *The Psychosomatic Concept in Psychoanalysis.* New York: International Universities Press, 1953.
31. SZASZ T. S.: Psychoanalysis and the Autonomic Nervous System. *Psychoanalytic Review,* 39, 1952, p. 115.
32. GRINKER, R. SR.: Psychoanalytic Theory and Psychosomatic Research. In J. Marmoston and E. Stainbrook (Eds.), *Psycho-*

analysis and the Human Situation. New York: Vantage Press, 1964.

33. SCHUR, M.: Comments on the Metapsychology of Somatization. *Psa. Study Ch.*, 10, 1955, pp. 119-164.

34. SCHUR, M.: The Ego in Anxiety. In R. M. Loewenstein (Ed.), *Drives, Affects, Behavior.* New York: International Universities Press, 1953, pp. 67-103.

35. DEUTSCH, F.: *The Psychosomatic Concept in Psychoanalysis.* New York: International Universities Press, Inc., 1953, pp. 158-161.

36. SPERLING, M.: A Further Contribution to the Psychoanalytic Study of Migraine and Psychogenic Headaches. *Int. J. Psycho-Anal.*, 45, 1964, pp. 549-557.

37. SPERLING, M.: A Psychoanalytic Study of Bronchial Asthma in Children. In H. I. Schneer (Ed.), *The Asthmatic Child.* New York: Hoeber, 1963, pp. 138-165.

38. SPERLING, M.: Psychoanalytic Study of Ulcerative Colitis in Children. *Psychoanalytic Quarterly*, 15, 1946, pp. 302-329.

39. SPERLING, M.: The Psycho-analytic Treatment of Ulcerative Colitis, *Int. J. Psycho-Anal.*, 38, 1957, pp. 341-349.

40. GARMA, A.: *Peptic Ulcer and Psychoanalysis.* Baltimore: The Williams & Wilkins Co., 1958.

41. GRODDECK, G. W.: The Book of the It: Psychoanalytic Letters to a Friend. (Tr; revised: author), *Arch. Psa.*, 1, 1926, pp. 174-189.

42. MIRSKY, I. A., KAPLAN, S., and BROH-KAHN, R. H.: Pepsinogen Excretion (Uropepsin) as an Index of the Influence of Various Life Situations on Gastric Secretion. In H. Wolff, S. Wolf, Jr. and C. Hare (Eds.), *Life Stress and Bodily Disease.* Baltimore: The Williams & Wilkins Co., 1950.

43. WEINER, S., DORMAN, D., PERSKY, H., STACK, T. W., MARTIN, J., and LEVITT, E. E.: Effects on Anxiety of Increasing the Plasma by Hydrocortisive Level. *Psychosomatic Medicine*, 25, 1963, pp. 69-77.

44. DONGIER, M., WITTKOWER, E. D., STEPHENS-NEWSHAM, L., and HOFFMAN, M. M.: Psychophysiological Studies in Thyroid Function. *Psychosomatic Medicine*, 18, 1956, 310.

45. WALLERSTEIN, R. S., HOLZMAN, P. S., VOTH, H. M., and UHR, N.: Thyroid "Hot Spots": A Psychophysiological Study. *Psychosom. Med.*, 27, 1965, p. 508.

46. MIRSKY, I. A.: Physiologic, Psychologic, and Social Determinants in Etiology of Duodenal Ulcer. *Am. J. Digest. Dis.*, 3, 1958, p. 285.

47. MIRSKY, I. A., FUTTERMAN, P., and KAPLAN, S.: Blood Plasma Pepsinogen II; the Activity of the Plasma from "Normal" Subjects, Patients with Duodenal Ulcer, and Patients with Pernicious Anemia. *J. Lab. and Clin. Med.*, 40, 1952, p. 188.

48. WEINER, H.: Presidential Address: Some Comments on the

Transduction of Experience by the Brain; Implications for Our Understanding of the Relationship of Mind to Body. *Psychosom. Med.*, 34, 1972, pp. 355-375.

49. PILOT, M. L., PRELINGER, E., SCHAFER, R., SELIGSON, D., SPIRO, H., CHAPPLE, E., FRIEDHOFF, A., LAYMAN, W., and STARK, L.: Use of a Twin Pool in Developing Interdisciplinary Research (Abstract). *Psychosom. Med.*, 23, 1961, p. 443.

50. PILOT, M. L., RUBIN, J., SCHAFER, R., and SPIRO, H.: Duodenal Ulcer in One of Identical Twins. *Psychosom. Med.*, 5, 1963, pp. 285-290.

51. KATZ, J. L. and WEINER, H.: Psychosomatic Considerations in Hyperuricemia and Gout. *Psychosom. Med.*, 34, 1972, pp. 165-179.

52. PARKES, C. M., BENJAMIN, B., and FITZGERALD, R. G.: Broken Heart: A Statistical Study of Increased Mortality among Widowers. *British Medical Journal*, 1, 1969, pp. 740-743.

53. FRIEDMAN, M., ROSENMAN, R. H., STRAUS, R., WUMR, M.. and KOSITCHEK, E.: The Relationship of Behavior Pattern "A" to the State of Coronary Vasculature. *American Journal of Medicine*, 44, 1968, pp. 525-537.

54. ROSENMAN, R. H., FRIEDMAN, M., STRAUS, R., WUMR, M., KOSIT-CHEK, E., HAHN, W., and WETHERESSEN, M. T.: A Predictive Study of Coronary Heart Disease. *J.A.M.A.*, 189, 1964, p. 15.

55. REES, W. D. and LUTKINS, S. G.: Mortality of Bereavement. *British Medical Journal*, 4, 1967, pp. 13-16.

56. BENNET, G.: Bristol Floods 1968; Controlled Survey of Effects on Health of Local Community Disaster. *British Medical Journal*, 3, 1970, pp. 454-458.

57. ENGEL, G. L.: Studies of Ulcerative Colitis III; The Nature of the Psychologic Processes. *American Journal of Medicine*, 19, 1955, p. 231.

58. SCHMALE, A. H.: A Relationship of Separation and Depression to Disease. *Psychosom. Med.*, 20, 1958, p. 259.

59. SCHMALE, A. J. and ENGEL, G. L.: The "Giving Up" Complex Illustrated on Film. *Archives of General Psychiatry*, 17, 1967, p. 135.

60. ENGEL, G. L.: A Psychological Setting of Somatic Disease: The "Giving Up—Given Up" Complex. *Proc. Roy. Soc. Med.*, 60, 1967, p. 553.

61. WEINER, H.: Autonomic Psychophysiology: Peripheral Autonomic Mechanisms and Their Central Control. In Arieti, S. (Ed.), *American Handbook of Psychiatry*, Vol. IV. New York: Basic Books, 1975, Chapter 22.

62. HOFER, M.: The Principles of Autonomic Function in the Life of Man and Animals. In Arieti, S. (Ed.), *American Handbook of Psychiatry*, Vol. IV. New York: Basic Books, 1975, Chapter 23.

63. MASON, J. W.: Clinical Psychophysiology: Psychoendocrine Mechanisms. In Arieti S. (Ed.), *American Handbook of Psychiatry*, Vol. IV. New York: Basic Books, 1975, Chapter 24.

64. ADER, R.: The Influences of Psychological Factors on Disease Susceptibility in Animals. In M. L. Conalty (Ed.), *Husbandry of Laboratory Animals*. London: Academic Press, 1967, pp. 219-238.

65. LABARBA, R. G.: Experiential and Environmental Factors in Cancer; A Review of Research with Animals. *Psychosomatic Medicine*, 32, 1970, pp. 259-274.

66. PRZYBYLSKI, A.: Effect of Stimulation and Coagulation of the Midbrain Reticular Formation on the Bronchial Musculature; A Modification of Histamine Susceptibility. *Journal of Neuro-Visceral Relations*, 31, 1969, p. 171.

67. STEIN, M., SCHIAVI, R. C., and LUPARELLO, T. J.: The Hypothalamus and Immune Process. *Annals of the New York Academy of Science*, 164, 1969, p. 464.

68. SACHAR, E. J., MASON, J., KOLMER, H. S., and ARTISS, K. L.: Psychoendocrine Aspects of Acute Schizophrenic Reactions. *Psychosomatic Medicine*, 25, 1963, pp. 510-537.

69. WEINER, H. and REISER, M. F.: Methodological Issues in Psychosomatic Research on Cardiovascular Problems; Retrospect and Prospect. *Excerpta Medica International Congress*. Series No. 150, 1966.

70. LEVITT, E. E., PERSKY, H., BRODY, J. P., and FITZGERALD, J. A.: The Effect of Hydrocortisone Infusion in Hypnotically Induced Anxiety. *Psychosomatic Medicine*, 25, 1963, 158-161.

71. CURTIS, G. C.: Psychosomatics and Chronobiology: Possible Implications of Neuroendocrine Rhythms. *Psychosom. Med.*, 34, 1972, pp. 235-250.

72. KRIPKE, D. F.: An Ultradian Biologic Rhythm Associated with Perceptual Deprivation and REM Sleep. *Psychosom. Med.*, 34, 1972, pp. 221-233.

73. SACHAR, E. J., HELLMAN, L., ROFFWARG, H. P., HALPERN, F. S., FUKUSHIMA, D. K., and GALLAGHER, T. F.: Disrupted 24-Hour Patterns of Cortisol Secretion in Psychotic Depression. *Archives of General Psychiatry*, 28, 1973, pp. 19-24.

74. WILLIAMS, R. L. and KARACAN, I.: Sleep Disorders and Disordered Sleep. In S. Arieti (Ed.), *American Handbook of Psychiatry*, Vol. IV. New York: Basic Books, 1975, Chapter 35.

75. FRIEDMAN, S. and FISHER, C.: On the Presence of a Rhythmic, Diurnal, Oral Instinctual Drive Cycle in Man: A Preliminary Report. *Journal of the American Psychoanalytic Association*, 15, 1967, pp. 317-343.

76. KNAPP, P. H., MUSHATT, C., NEMETZ, J. S., CONSTANTINE, H., and FRIEDMAN, S.: The Context of Reported Asthma during Psychoanalysis. *Psychosomatic Medicine*, 32, 1970, p. 167.

77. HENRY, J. P., STEVENS, P. M., AXELROD, J., and MUELLER, R. A.: Effect of Psychosocial Stimulation on the Enzymes Involved in the Biosynthesis and Metabolism of Noradrenaline and Adrenaline. *Psychosomatic Medicine*, 33, 1971, p. 227.

78. MAAS, J. W.: Adrenocortical Steroid Hormones, Electrolytes, and the Disposition of the Catecholamines with Particular Reference to Depressive States. *J. Psychiat. Res.*, 9, 1972, pp. 227-241.

79. DICARA, L.: Learning of Cardiovascular Response: A Review and a Description of Physiological and Biochemical Consequences. *Trans. N. Y. Acad. Sci.*, 1971, pp. 411-422.

80. MILLER, N.: Learning of Visceral and Glandular Responses. *Science*, 163, 1967, pp. 439-445.

81. LEVINE, S. and DENENBERG, V. H.: Early Stimulation; Effects and Mechanisms; Stimulation in Early Infancy. In A. Ambrose (Ed.), *Simulation in Early Infancy*. Proceedings of the Study Group on the Functions of Stimulation in Early Post-Natal Development, London, 1967. New York: Academic Press, 1969, pp. 3-72.

82. MULLINS, R. F. and LEVINE S.: Hormonal Determinants during Infancy of Adult Sexual Behavior in the Rat. *Physiology and Behavior*, 3, 1968, pp. 333-338.

83. HARRIS, G. W. and LEVINE, S.: Sexual Differentiation of the Brain and Its Experimental Control. *Journal of Physiology*, 181, 1965, pp. 379-400.

84. ADER, R. and PLAUT, S. M.: Effects of Prenatal Maternal Handling and Differential Housing in Offspring Emotionality, Plasma Corticosterone Levels and Susceptibility to Gastric Erosions. *Psychosomatic Medicine*, 30, 1968, p. 277.

85. FRIEDMAN, S., GLASGOW, L. B., and ADER, R.: Psychosocial Factors Modifying Host Resistance to Experimental Infections. *Ann. N. Y. Acad. Sci.*, 164, 1969, p. 381.

86. HOFER, M. A. and REISER, M. F.: The Development of Cardiac Rate Regulation in Preweaning Rats. *Psychosomatic Medicine*, 31, 1969, pp. 372-388.

87. CORSON, S. A., CORSON, E. O., KIRILCUK, V., KIRILCUK, J., KNOPP, W. and ARNOLD, L. E.: Differential Effects of Amphetamines on Clinically Relevant Dog Models of Hyperkinesis and Stereotypy: Relevance to Huntington's Disease. *Centennial Symposium on Huntington's Chorea*. Raven Press, 1972.

88. WEINER, H.: The Specificity Hypothesis Revisited. *Psychosomatic Medicine*, 32, 1970, p. 543.

89. CALLAWAY, E. and THOMPSON, S. V.: Sympathetic Activity and Perception. *Psychosomatic Medicine*, 15, 1953, pp. 433-455.

90. POLLIN, W. and GOLDIN, S.: The Physiological and Psychological Effects of Intravenously Administered Epinephrine and Its Metabolism in Normal and Schizophrenic Men II. *J. Psychiat. Res.*, 1, 1961, pp. 50-67.

91. REISER, M. F.: Reflections on Interpretation of Psychophysiologic Experiments. *Psychosomatic Medicine*, 23, 1961.
92. REISER, M. F.: Toward an Integrated Psychoanalytic-Physiological Theory of Psychosomatic Disorders. In R. M. Lowenstein, M. Newman, M. Schur, et al. (Eds.), *Psychoanalysis—A General Psychology*. New York: International Universities Press, 1966.
93. HARTMANN, H.: *Ego Psychology and the Problem of Adaptation.* New York: International Universities Press, 1958.

6

The Psychology of Intensive Care: Problems and Their Management

Thomas P. Hackett, M.D. and Ned H. Cassem, M.D.

Since much of what we have come to regard as liaison psychiatry in this decade grew out of the psychiatric syndromes found in intensive care units, a consideration of these disorders seems a reasonable way to approach our topic.

Intensive care is a relatively new term for an ancient idea. The principle of constantly attending the critically ill or the dying began with the death watch. In the last three decades, the personal vigilance of the death watch slowly began to be replaced by mechanical devices. The intravenous drip, continuous suction, and the oxygen tent are the precursors of an awesome array of life support and monitoring systems.

With this machinery has come a new cadre of medical caretakers: physicians who are specially trained to treat certain categories of

From the Department of Psychiatry, Massachusetts General Hospital. Supported by contract PHS-43-67-1443, and I RO1 HE12781-01 of the National Institute of Health, Public Health Service, United States Department of Health, Education, and Welfare.

patients such as those with burns or cardiac or pulmonary conditions, and nurses with similar training. Their orientation for the most part is surgical. As a consequence, they are likely to be action-oriented, reflexly quick, and independent of mind. Unfortunately, they are apt to be impatient of the individual who is slow to heal, of the patient whose pain persists too long, and of those who complain or whine. These professionals are superbly equipped for the fray, but their fortitude is inclined to wear thin over the long haul. This produces a variety of problems for both patients and staff. As the literature of intensive care expands, it has come to include a variety of studies on how the caretaker responds to being the provider of intensive care (1, 2). Hospital authorities, particularly nursing administrators, have been alarmed at the rapid turnover of personnel in these units. It would seem that neither the lot of the patient nor of his caretaker is a happy one. However, that intensive care installations are valuable is without question. They save the lives of the old, the young and the middle aged at a rate that more than justifies their existence.

RECOVERY ROOMS

The surgical recovery room is probably the first hospital environment to come under the heading of an intensive care area. Although not originally recognized as such, nor designated by this term, recovery rooms possess both critically ill patients and specially trained nursing and medical personnel, as well as life sustaining apparatus and instruments for monitoring vital signs. Psychiatrists did not become especially interested in these units until after the second world war when intrathoracic surgery, particularly open heart procedures, began to be done in numbers. The most frequently found psychiatric disturbance in the recovery room was post operative delirium. The incidence of this depended in large part upon the type of surgery performed. It was usually said to be in the neighborhood of from 0.1 percent to 3 percent (3).

Since criteria for recognition vary widely, the true incidence of post operative delirium is impossible to obtain. The hallmark of delirium is clouding of consciousness in varying degrees from a mild cognitive impairment to severe disorientation, agitation, and perceptual distortion. Delirium is of great concern to surgeons because it complicates the post operative course, ups physical morbidity, is thought to contribute to mortality, and greatly disturbs the family and nurses. Certain operations had a higher rate of delirium than others. For example, neurosurgical procedures involving the brain were said to have a 14 percent to 17 percent incidence of delirium and bilateral cataract extractions (in which both eyes were patched) carried a 90 percent to 95 percent incidence of post operative delirium (4). It was only after psychiatrists examined the individual patients that personal variables were found to influence the likelihood of post operative delirium independently of the type of surgery done.

Increasing age predisposes the individual to the risk of post operative delirium, as does a previous history of post operative delirium (rather than a past history of functional psychosis). Alcoholism, drug addiction, or a history of head injury or chronic brain syndrome adds to the likelihood of post operative delirium. So does a limited command of English in American hospitals (5).

Although no definitive studies have been reported, it was thought that the atmosphere of the recovery room was also important in the genesis of post operative delirium. Thus, areas that were flooded with artificial light and contained no portal to the outside were prone to produce more delirium. It has been said that certain surgeons were deliriogenic. Generally, this meant that they maintained the patient under anesthesia for an unusually long time. Either that, or they gave little or no explanation of the procedure to the patient and rarely saw him either pre or post operatively. It is interesting that the personality of the surgeon has never been seriously studied as a variable to account for the presence or absence of post operative morbid events.

As more psychiatrists took interest in the surgical experience, more subtle indicators came to be described by which one would identify a subject at risk for delirium or depression post operatively. For example, patients with extremely low anxiety who exhibited marked denial of illness when faced with major surgical procedures had a high incidence of post operative distress (6). The same was said for those with extremely high anxiety which could not be effectively relieved by reassurance (5). Abram and Gill noted a 50 percent incidence of medical complications among patients with pre operative emotional illnesses (7).

The presence of overt depression during the pre operative period was found to correlate with the incidence of mortality and morbidity post operatively. Kimball and his co-workers found that those who denied anxiety and were depressed had an increase in short term post operative complications and long term post operative mortality (8). An impressive study was presented by Tufo and Ostfeld in the 1970 meeting of the American Psychosomatic Society in which they described a hundred patients they had interviewed prior to open heart surgery (9). Of these, twelve whom they found to be clinically depressed all died in the post operative or early convalescent phase.

A list of factors described in a study by Morse and Litin point to the following as being more prominent in patients who became delirious following surgery (10):

1. Alcoholism
2. Depression
3. Family history of psychosis
4. Organic brain syndrome
5. Pre operative insomnia
6. History of prior post operative psychosis
7. Retirement adjustment problems
8. Functional G.I. disturbances

The good surgical risk would be characterized by the following points (11):

1. Intellectually intact
2. Past history of coping well with stress
3. A low to moderate level of pre-operative anxiety
4. An acknowledgement of the risks of surgery
5. Confidence in a favorable outcome
6. History of previously good adjustments to illness
7. A strong motivation for good health
8. Realistic expectations
9. Freedom from depression

Pre operative evidence of central nervous system impairment is another factor of predictive value. Kilpatrick found that patients with a fatal outcome following cardiac surgery had a significant pre operative impairment in concentration and abstract thinking that was suggestive of a mild organic brain disturbance. Using the results of psychological tests, the authors were able to discriminate between survivors and nonsurvivors with greater than 90 percent accuracy (12). With this as background to the study of special units, we would like now to describe some of our own work with coronary care patients and use it as a model for the study of acute intensive care facilities in general.

CORONARY CARE UNITS (CCU)

The work to be described next in this presentation was done entirely in coronary care units. None of the patients was post operative; all had sustained an acute myocardial infarction. In some respects the population and the setting are not typical of the usual ICU where surgical patients are in the majority. However, we believe there are enough similarities (being critically ill and requiring bedrest, being monitored, witnessing cardiac arrest, having I.V.'s in place, and requiring hourly vital signs) to use the CCU experience as being typical of hospitalization in intensive care settings generally.

Our initial investigation was conducted in 1958 (13). It came about as a result of observing the first monitor pacemakers to be used on patients at our hospital. The fact that patients could hear each heartbeat as an electronic "bleep," see their ECG on an oscilloscope, and be exposed to frequent false alarms caused us to predict that an unusually high incidence of panic reactions, delirium, and paranoid decompensations would be found in this population. To demonstrate this, we interviewed and followed every patient admitted to the intensive care area who required a monitor pacemaker. The interviews, with the patient's consent, were taped. We introduced ourselves as physicians interested in how patients reacted to being monitored and asked for their help in answering a few questions. None refused. Depending upon the gravity of the patient's condition, early interviews lasted from 10 minutes to half an hour. Questions were issued in the format of a standard medical history so that few even suspected we were psychiatrists; the interview was designed to be as non-stressful as we could make it. In the course of a year, 19 cases had been collected. There were 14 males and 5 females with an age range from 46 to 82, a mean of 66, and a medium of 68. They remained in the unit an average of 3.8 days and none died.

Although 26 percent of the sample were confused and intermittently delirious as we had predicted, only one of the 19 was frightened and spontaneously complained that being monitored made him nervous. The rest denied the presence of fear, apprehension, or depression in relation both to the pacemaker and to their heart trouble. In other words, only a single patient behaved the way we predicted the lot of them would. We had not realized how commonplace and apparently effective the defense of denial can be.

For the purpose of this study, we define "denial" as the conscious or unconscious repudiation of all or a portion of the total available meaning of an illness in order to allay anxiety and to minimize emotional distress (14). The 18 patients we described as using denial by no means presented this defense in identical ways. Some rationalized their fears, others avoided talking or thinking of their health, while the remainder concentrated upon minor worries, such as hemorrhoids, in an attempt to exclude the more serious condition from consciousness. Despite the variety of methods employed to deny, two distinct patterns emerged, distinguished by the degree of rigidity with which the patient maintained this defense. The term Major Denial is used to describe those patients who stated unequivocally and unremittingly that they experienced no anxiety as a result of their illness or during their time on the monitor pacemaker. Twelve major deniers (63 percent) were found in this sample. The term Partial Denial applies to those patients who initially denied being frightened by their illness or the machinery of survival, but who eventually admitted concern. Six patients (32 percent) comprised the partial denier group. One patient could not deny anxiety with any degree of satisfaction and was openly fearful.

There were other characteristics particular to each group. The major denier demonstrated a lifelong pattern of minimizing danger and of under-reacting to threatening situations. He rarely consulted physicians for even the most serious illnesses and was staunchly fatalistic. He maintained a persistent indifference to his fate, denied experiencing the fear of dying, and disclaimed ever having been afraid. Not infrequently he used clichés to renounce danger. The following examples are typical of the major deniers' responses. We had asked a 52-year-old longshoreman why the prospect of another cardiac arrest did not bother him. He said, "Why worry? If the marker's got your name on it, you've got to buy it." Another, disclaiming any concern about being attached to a cardiac monitor, said, "Some people would be scared (by the machine), but not me. I'm called the 'iron man'." A third, when asked how he could have gone through four days in the unit, including witnessing a fatal cardiac arrest, without having a thought or care for death answered, "My middle name is Lucky."

The following is a representative account from the case history of a major denier:

> A 63-year-old Jewish salesman entered the hospital in shock for an acute myocardial infarction. After recovering consciousness, he maintained an air of friendly indifference to his disease. He was most cooperative in following orders and was well liked by his physicians, but at no time did he express the least concern about his future. When questioned specifically, he disclaimed any fear of the consequences of cardiac trouble because he was certain his heart was far better than the doctors let on. He also told us it was not his custom to worry, never had been. His wife corroborated his story. He reminisced about a World War I experience in which his vessel had been torpedoed and he found himself alone floating on a piece of flotsam in the South Atlantic. Asked if that worried him he replied, "Why should it? After all, I was in one of the main shipping lanes and was bound to be picked up." Shipping lanes, of course, are a hundred miles wide and offer no safety from storms and other hazards of the sea.

The partial denier often gave the same initial impression as his major counterpart. He might begin by disclaiming all fear, but its presence was revealed in subsequent statements. For example, one patient began by saying, "I wasn't afraid because if I'm gonna go, why panic?" This was followed by, "You've got to be alarmed a little, but why go all to pieces?" A major denier would not have acknowledged the presence of alarm. Typical of the partial denier is the following account:

> An Irish matriarch of 74 was admitted for an episode of asystole which was followed by a myocardial infarction. When asked about the monitor pacemaker, she at first thought it was, "indeed a gorgeous piece of furniture, like a console television." In speaking of her cardiac illness in general, she emphatically denied any fear. However, as the interview progressed and she remembered waking in the night and peering at the luminous tracing of the ECG, she remarked, "Oh, I'd watch it flickerin' down and flarin' up, wonderin' withir it was pointin' the way to heaven or hell for these old bones and it made me cold and shivery." Thus she gave us a vivid description of fear without exactly putting a name on it.

The one individual who feared the machine was a 56-year-old Jewish laborer who was surprised to have come down with a coronary since his health was so good. Once attached to the monitor cardiac pacemaker he became openly fearful and anxious. He said he could not bear to hear and watch the machine recording "every breath, every beat of my heart." Even though he realized it was there to help him he would have traded the safety it offered for being rid of it. He experienced obvious relief when the machine was removed.

In summary, what we learned in this study was that most people tend to deny the fear of death from acute myocardial infarction and that they succeed, or at least they appear to succeed, to a greater than lesser degree. Even the four patients who required painful external pacing to maintain their heartbeat did not evidence more anxiety than the others, nor did they become noticeably more anxious. We learned that the machinery of intensive care, the instruments that had occasioned the investigation, were perceived by the patient in a manner quite different from our own. This was a valuable personal lesson—namely, that it was foolish to expect the patient to feel and behave the way you imagined you would in his position.

The second investigation was started in 1967 and continues through the present (15). In it our task was to investigate systematically the experience of receiving intensive care in a coronary care unit. Intensive care, per se, had been seriously indicted by a number of investigators as being partly responsible for the high psychiatric morbidity common to these units. We reasoned that if this were so, then some aspects of intensive care must be more responsible than others for the so-called "intensive care syndrome." We divided the experience up into components such as: 1. Reactions to the unit itself (size, wall color, quality of light, etc.); 2. Reactions to being monitored; 3. Predominant affects of patients; 4. Reactions to witnessing cardiac arrest; 5. Reaction to being given the Last Rites; 6. Effect of surviving cardiac arrest; 7. Predominant defense mechanisms.

Fifty patients, ranging in age from 37 to 74 (mean of 58), comprised our sample. All were admitted to the unit with the diagnosis of proven or suspected myocardial infarction. Thirty-five were males, and 15 were females. Their average time in the coronary care unit was 4.8 days. Four died during the study. Patients were selected in a random fashion. The only criterion for inclusion was the ability to speak English. Thirty-seven were general hospital patients confined to a four-bed intensive care unit, while the other 13 occupied private rooms on an acute cardiac floor. The four-bed unit was a cramped, essentially windowless place, as cheerless and drab as a room in a tenement. Beds were separated by heavy, retractable, ceiling-to-floor curtains. There was no soundproofing. Sexes were mixed. The chief difference between the ward and private accommodations was privacy.

In the four-bed ward, monitors were placed on a wall shelf above and behind the patient's bed. This made it difficult for the patient to observe his own oscilloscope, but easy to see his neighbor's. In the private rooms, the monitor was on a bedside cart with the cathode screen usually visible. Constant intravenous therapy was carried out on all patients, and most had indwelling urethral catheters. Vital signs were taken hourly or more often, invariably awakening each patient.

Findings*

1. The Setting

Not one of the 48 patients questioned spontaneously complained about the atmosphere of the unit. Upon being asked specifically, eight agreed that the quarters were small or depressing or both. Six of the eight were lifelong claustrophobes. We could elicit no suggestions for improving the design of the unit, and most patients preferred to have no television or music. Despite the frequency of positive responses, most patients were glad to leave the unit when their time came. We believe the absence of complaints stemmed more from the reluctance to complain than from genuine contentment. Furthermore, when the nursing care is excellent, patients are not apt to criticize their surroundings even when encouraged to do so.

2. Cardiac Monitor

Twenty-six of the 50 patients questioned were reassured by the bedside presence of the monitor. Eighteen were neutral to its presence, and six disliked it. There was a trend indicating that women respond more positively than men do to the monitor's sound (three found it comforting) and 11 considered it annoying. Fourteen wanted to watch their own electrocardiographic tracings and made an effort to do so even though it meant twisting about uncomfortably to look over their shoulders. Three objected to seeing their oscilloscope patterns, and the remainder were neutral to it. Sixteen patients enjoyed watching the monitor of others; this group included five patients who did not want to observe their own. Nearly without exception they interpreted their neighbor's tracings as being worse

---

* Portions of the material in the following section have been adapted from "The Coronary Care Unit. An Appraisal of Its Pscyhological Hazards" by T. P. Hackett, N. H. Cassem and H. A. Wishnie, *New England Journal of Medicine*, 279:1365-1370, 1968.

than their own. Men were far more interested than women in watching the oscilloscope.

There was no apparent correlation between the patient's knowledge of the monitor's purpose and his reponse to its sight, sound, or presence.

The alarm accidentally sounded for 19 patients. The fact that only five of them admitted being frightened may be the result of previous explanations by the nurses of the monitor's function and anticipation of the possibility of false alarm.

It is easy to see that most of these patients interpreted the monitoring experience in a favorable fashion. They regarded it as an instrument that would save their life, not as a grim symbol of impending death or disability.

3. *Mood and Behavior*

Judgments of the predominant mood for each of the 50 patients were made from comments in the hospital chart, nursing notes, observations by relatives, impressions of the investigator, and subjective reports from the patient himself. At least two corroborating sources were required to confirm each investigator's observation. There was no disagreement between these sources. Anxiety was judged to be present when the patient complained of being anxious or when he appeared nervous, sweaty, fidgety, restless or constantly asked for reassurance or sedation. Depression was judged to be present either when the patient appeared despondent and was seen to cry or if he admitted to sadness or discouragement during the interview. Forty of the 50 patients were judged anxious. Eight were agitated, and 11 expressed anger; hostility, however, was seldom directed against individuals, but rather at fate, God, or circumstances. Twenty-nine admitted being depressed or exhibited behavior consistent with depression. The depression was a reaction to coronary disease and was judged to range from mild to moderate in intensity. Although the fact may be incidental, all four of the patients who died during our study were rated as depressed.

In another study of psychiatric consultations in a coronary care unit we found that the three most common reasons for referral were anxiety, depression, and the management of disruptive behavior (16). The focus of anxiety was impending death or death's heralds: pain, breathlessness, weakness, and new complications. Depression followed the injuries to self-esteem caused by the heart attack. Most management problems stemmed either from excessive denial of illness which resulted in inappropriate behavior or from hostile-dependent conflicts with the staff. Consultation requests for each problem followed different time distributions, with an early peak for anxiety on days 1 and 2, a later peak for depression on days 3 and 4, and a bimodal distribution for management referrals.

4. *Witnessing Cardiac Arrest*

Eleven of the 50 witnessed a fatal cardiac arrest. Seven of these denied fear either during or after the arrest. Only three admitted fear. These data were not collected on the eleventh patient. The initial response to watching the arrest was irritability and annoyance at the patient affected. This was rapidly followed by astonishment at the efficiency of the arrest team. All who witnessed the event described the activity with remarkable clarity. Sounds and imagination must have been involved because most accounts came through as if the bed curtain had not been drawn. For example, one patient "knew the doctor was massaging the heart." Another "knew they were opening the chest." In neither case was a thoracotomy performed, and the bed curtains were pulled shut in both.

One patient was reassured by the arrest drill because the victim was an elderly woman. He mused that if they did that much for her, they would go all out for him because he was so much younger. When asked if he worried more about himself after seeing the arrest, he replied, "Oh, no, she was an old lady." Although empathy for the victim was expressed by all eleven, none identified with the patient affected.

One unobtrusive measure to indicate that witnessing cardiac arrest may not be as benign an experience as some patients describe had to do with room preference for readmission. We asked each patient whether he would prefer private or ward accommodations should he return to the hospital. All ward patients, with the exception of those who had witnessed an arrest, picked the four-bed ward as a choice. Those who had viewed the arrest preferred a solitary room.

5. *Survival of Cardiac Arrest*

Nine of the 50 had cardiac arrest. Three died without recovering consciousness, and six survived (one, however, for only 13 days). Only two could remember anything about the event. A male patient vaguely recalled being thumped on the chest and hearing doctors' voices. The second, a woman, was unsure whether what she reported really happened or took place in a dream. "A funny experience . . . a hand down my throat squeezing my heart I felt it was happening . . . but I don't know if it happened in a dream." Two patients had nightmares immediately after the arrest. A woman dreamed of smothering in a fire, and a man of being caught trying to smoke cigarettes. The fire dreams have also been reported by Druss and Kornfeld (17). Two others had nightmares only after they returned home. One blamed sleeping medication for her bad dreams because they stopped when her bedtime barbiturate was discontinued. The other patient complained of "troubled dreams" that stopped once she returned to work.

Traumatic neuroses with chronic anxiety and emotional invalidism have not developed in the three patients who were alive at the six-month follow-up interval. Two have returned to work, whereas the third remains inactive because of physical disability. One of the two who died after leaving the hospital had signs of chronic anxiety and overdependency on his wife; the other man was emotionally stable until his death. None of the six considered themselves unique as a result of having survived a period of heart stoppage. Two regarded their arrests as the equivalent of dying, but did not elaborate on this even when urged to do so by the investigator.

In a recent report by Dobson et al. (18), 20 patients who had survived cardiac arrest by at least six months were interviewed.

Although anxiety was commonly experienced immediately after the arrest and shortly after return home, 15 patients overcame it and only five showed pronounced disturbance in mood. In these five, failure to rehabilitate properly was due to premorbid personality factors and persisting physical disability, neither of which was associated with the cardiac arrest itself.

6. *Being Given Last Rites* (19)

Thirty patients, 22 men and eight women ranging from 30 to 74, were interviewed shortly after receiving this sacrament. There was no difference in mortality between this group and a comparison population who had not been given Last Rites. Twenty-three admitted anxiety directly or were rated as anxious by the investigator. Sixteen expressed thoughts referable to death or dying. At least four said they were sure they were going to die on the way to the emergency ward. Twenty-six of the 30 patients responded positively to Last Rites. Thirteen did not qualify their favorable responses while 13 admitted to experiencing anxiety or expressed some criticism of the procedure but remained firm in their endorsement of it. Positive responders saw the procedure as something important and reassuring. For those who were ambivalently positive, the experience clearly had frightening aspects. The response of four patients was primarily anxious or negative.

The most threatening aspect of these rites had to do with the way they were presented. When the priest was calm and emphasized the routine nature of the sacrament, that it was administered to everyone with heart trouble, little protest occurred. Referring to it as the sacrament of the sick rather than Last Rites was also helpful.

Women patients seemed to respond more positively than men, private patients more so than ward patients. Those whose religion was important in premorbid life were the best responders.

The following is a humorous example of how the Last Rites shouldn't be administered, but how the patient managed to save the day, nonetheless.

A 72-year-old boiler room worker, admitted with his first myocardial infarction, said, "The priest came in and told me 'I came in a rush,' he says, 'they just called me up and told me . . . they got you in here, so I come in to anoint you.' 'Whaddya mean,' I says, 'anoint me? Anoint me for what?' He says, 'For death.' He said, 'We can't be too careful . . . because anybody with a heart attack can shuffle out in no time.' You know? . . . I laughed. We joked about it for a few minutes. He told me, 'Well, it's just a matter of form, we've got to anoint everybody with a heart condition . . . they're liable to die right away.' So he went through all the formalities and I bid him good-bye." The patient's wife said he was, "frightened when they anointed him," but the patient denied this. Both thought, however, that the priest's presentation could have been improved. Even so, they stressed that being anointed was the most important thing. Said the patient, "Everybody seriously sick should be anointed."

7. Defense Mechanisms

Twenty of the 50 were major deniers; 26 were partial deniers while four were labeled minimal deniers. The latter were not exactly fearful. They may not have complained of anxiety but would admit to it on being asked and presented no consistent criteria for the effective presence of denial. When they attempted it, they failed to make denial work.

Denial is apt to be more evident when the alternative is to acknowledge fear. For example, 28 of 45 patients admitted they had thought of death during confinement in the unit; however, only 11 of 42 admitted experiencing fear during that time. Consequently, it appears that thoughts of dying do not necessarily produce an admission of fear in these patients.

Statistical analysis of our data demonstrated no significant relation between denial and the patient's mood. Anxiety, depression, hostility and agitation were equally dispersed among the deniers. Neither age nor sex correlated significantly with the patient's use of denial. However, there was a definite trend for deniers to respond positively to the cardiac monitor. None of the minimal deniers found monitoring reassuring.

Although the numbers are small, it is noteworthy that an inverse relation exists between denial and mortality. Not one major denier died during the study; two of the four deaths were in minimal deniers. The minimal deniers, representing eight percent of the total sample, contributed 50 percent of the mortality. Computation of the probability of this outcome by Fisher's exact test gave a value of .028.

Since the foregoing observations were made primarily on a blue collar population, the reader might ask if they would hold true for those in higher socioeconomic positions. This question is especially relevant in the light of previous work and because most practitioners believe that a marked difference exists in the way illness is accepted by the affluent as against the lower middle class (20). Subsequent work with a group of 50 white collar patients of comparable age, sex and severity of illness revealed fewer differences in their responses to M.I. than would be expected. There were far more similarities than differences in the manner patients of different socioeconomic backgrounds responded to acute coronary disease. The incidence and type of psychiatric morbidity were roughly the same in both groups as was their use of denial (21).

It would seem from our observations that the ability of a patient to effectively deny emotional stress of an acute, life threatening illness might directly influence his survival. Although we have insufficient data at the present time to demonstrate this, it is our conviction that the effective denial of stress is directly related to survival. Phrased in another away, we believe that anxiety, worry, fear, depression, and anger all work against the patient's recovery. Consequently, our program of treatment in the CCU is aimed at reducing these unpleasant affects.

TREATMENT

1. *Medication*

Unless contraindicated, all patients were placed on daytime tranquilizers and a hypnotic at the hour of sleep. Since it is often difficult to detect anxiety in a population where denial is the principle defense, the routine use of a tranquilizer given on a regular rather than p.r.n. basis is recommended. Chlordiazepoxide was found to be superior to amobarbitol in a randomized, double blind study carried out by our group. Its superiority was based on a significantly lower incidence of undesirable side effects and an apparent freedom from deleterious interaction with warfarin-like substances. The dose ranged from 5 to 25 mgms. three or four times a day. Diazepam is equally effective in doses ranging from 6 to 40 mgms. per day.

In dealing with patients who occupy a bed in a surgical ICU, the dosage range of the two agents would be considerably smaller. However, when the patient is delirious and unmanageable we have used both diazepam and chlordiazepoxide effectively in the upper dose range. If these are ineffective we then employ haloperidol, an excellent drug with few reported cardiovascular side effects.

Night-time sedation was usually provided by chloralhydrate or Dalmane.

2. *Clarification*

The main purpose of clarification was to dispel the many misconceptions about heart disease. Explanations were given whenever we suspected doubt and these were supplemented by drawings in three out of four cases. It became our practice to ask each patient whether he had any personal belief or fear about his illness. We encouraged him to express it no matter how absurd it might appear. In order to abet such disclosures we gave an example of a common though largely unrecognized fear pertaining to the heart—the fear of death during sleep. A number of individuals believed that the likelihood of death in cardiac disease increases during sleep. One such patient was convinced that the reason behind the frequent taking of vital signs was because the nurses were trying to stave off death by making sure he couldn't fall asleep. Along with uncovering hidden fears, the greatest difficulty we had in terms of using clarification was in finding out what and how much the patient knew and wanted to know.

3. *Visiting*

We make it a point to learn who among the patient's family or friends are the most important for his well-being. We then encourage these persons to visit the patient prior to surgery and to be on call during the post operative period. The same holds true for those in the coronary care unit. We also make it a habit to visit the patient for short visits in the surgical ICU during the first three or four days after surgery—perhaps three times a day for 2-5 minutes each.

4. *Environmental Manipulation*

The presence of radio or television, newspapers, or publications that give the patient a strong link to his life outside the hospital are important to maintain morale. Sometimes providing the patient with a telephone, which some may construe as a source of stress, may, in fact, supply more peace of mind than worry. One executive became agitated and confused on his third day in the unit. He constantly requested a telephone for conducting business. As his mental state declined, his wish was granted out of desperation. After a morning of making and receiving calls, he was functioning normally and his spirits were excellent. Granting commode privileges or allowing a patient to sit up in a lounge chair has not infrequently undercut a nascent depression.

5. *Encouragement and Bolstering Optimism*

The patient's capacity for optimism in the face of peril is capitalized upon. This does not mean that the seriousness of his condition is minimized but rather that the extent and strength of his assets, physical and psychological, are accentuated. He is given a truthful account of his illness along with as much encouragement and hope as is realistically consistent with his condition. Optimism is bolstered and denial is supported. The patient is told not to worry because he is in the best facility that medicine can offer.

As a rule, the patient spontaneously looked upon the instruments and rituals of survival such as the cardiac monitor, close medical attention, and hourly checks of vital signs as a powerful phalanx against the threat to his life. When a patient failed to regard them as such, he was encouraged to do so by nurses. For example, the monitor was described as a "mechanical guardian angel," a machine that makes it almost impossible to die while attached. Kennedy and Bakst reported that ability to block out fear of possible complications improved the prognosis of the patients undergoing cardiac surgery (22). We supported the suppression of stressful anticipation in the same way. Just as a patient can project his fear by attributing it to others ("My wife was much more worried than I was."), so, too, he can be encouraged to let the staff do his worrying for him. The positive response of patients who received Last Rites in the emergency ward offers a similar parallel.

6. *Anticipation of Reactions*

Anticipating the severity of a forthcoming pain can often reduce its severity. The same is true of emotions. If a patient is told that he is likely to feel depressed and picture himself as a permanent invalid around his third day in the coronary care unit, he is apt to be less alarmed when despondency sets in as predicted. If he has been assured this is a normal, transient reaction for coronary patients, the anguish of depression may be reduced. Even predicting the response to small issues, such as anger at having to use the bedpan, or weakness upon the first attempt to ambulate, is helpful.

Pre operative cardiac patients are told they may be confused when first in the ICU; their sense of time will be difficult to re-establish. They may find it difficult to trust people and may question motives. Suspiciousness and paranoia may result. In other words, a paranoid delirium is described. If it actually occurs, we remind the patient that we predicted it and told him at the time it would be his mind playing tricks on him and not reality. We believe this may lower the incidence of delirium following surgery.

7. *Confrontation*

This was a particularly valuable technique when patients displayed inappropriate behavior. For example, some male patients made sexual gestures in the form of seductive talk or telling obscene jokes to nurses as a kind of masculine protest against their dependency. We've advised nurses on occasion to confront such a patient with the question: "Do you realize that almost everything you say has to do with sex?" Most patients were startled at first and some denied it. Very few were upset by the confrontation, which was made tactfully and in a friendly way. It almost invariably curbed or stopped the sexual talk. The same technique can be applied to patients who are caught in a hostile-dependent conflict. These are individuals who are demanding, overly critical, and unappreciative of the nursing staff. Sometimes a gentle confrontation by the patient's physician or the charge nurse makes a difference.

8. *Hypnosis*

Hypnosis is a safe and effective method for reducing tension and anxiety in good hypnotic subjects. It should be used far more often. As it finds more acceptance in medical circles and physicians gain familiarity with its use and limitations, it is bound to gain popularity.

RESPIRATORY INTENSIVE CARE UNITS (RICU)

The first respiratory intensive care units in the authors' experience were those wards designated as iron lung facilities for use in the polio epidemics in the 1940's and 1950's. These, like other intensive care facilities, offered special caretakers, life sustaining equipment ("iron lungs"), and certain monitoring devices.

One of the main difficulties in caring for the individual in a RICU is communication. These individuals are either stuporous or, if perfectly alert, generally have an endotracheal tube for an airway. Consequently, their ability to verbally communicate is absent or impaired. It is important to realize that this has a profound effect on the mood of the interviewer. Within a minute or two, the examiner gets frustrated and then angry, an affect that is well perceived by the patient despite efforts to conceal it. When this tendency is recognized by the interviewer, he is in a better position to control it. One of the authors has considered a number of mechanisms to reduce his frustration and has found a method which has been helpful although cumbersome. Rather than speak in words to the vocally impaired, it has been his custom to write his questions on paper. Thus, he communicates the same way and at the same rate as does the patient. An alternative to this is to learn lip reading—a difficult task at best—further complicated by the patient's inability to form words for the silent whisper. At one time, we entertained the possibility of teaching the sign language of the Plains Indians. While this language is particularly expressive, it demands the use of both hands and the body as well; it is altogether impractical for the RICU. Word charts and the use of eye blinks for yes and no are workable alternatives.

Another factor to consider in the RICU as well as in other intensive care facilities and one which cannot be emphasized too strongly is that in order to be at ease in the interview, one must be familiar with the machinery of intensive care. You should know how to turn off the ECG alarm when it sounds in response to a movement artifact. The recognition of arrythmia is important. One must know how to cap the endotracheal tube in order to allow the patient to vocalize. Similarly, the psychiatrist should know the various types of respirators, how they work, and how they may malfunction. Otheriwse he should have a technician or nurse nearby to help in case difficulties arise.

Depression is by far the most common problem in the RICU and it plagues the staff as well as the patient. The average stay in a respiratory unit is 18 days or longer; often it will extend to months. In viewing the same walls, the same faces, with recovery being very slow at best, the tedium adds to the depression. It can seldom be helped by psychotherapy because the reality factors loom so large. Nonetheless, an attempt must be made to support the patient through frequent visits by both the psychiatrist and the general physician. Family resources should be mustered to provide as much social system support as is possible. Similarly, the clergy should be mobilized and family friends as well. This effort may be augmented by the use of antidepressants, either tricyclics or the MAO inhibitors as needed. The tricyclic antidepressants, because of their anticholingeric effect, are apt to dry the mucous membranes uncomfortably and might have to be discontinued, but this is not as common a complaint as might be expected in the RICU. Stimulants such as the amphetamines or methylphenidate can also be used to help activate the patient once the process of weaning from the respirator has been completed.

Depression must be dealt with in the staff. When their patients fail to thrive, or stop trying to improve, or die, despite their efforts, the nurses and physicians become disheartened. An effort then must be made to bolster morale by having case discussions. In these group meetings, various factors can be drawn out to explain why the patient behaves the way he does. The major issue is usually staff anger and self blame. When perspective is restored, proper patient care is once again assured. It is important in these meetings to avoid personal issues between individuals, lest the group process take on a life of its own as in group therapy. When this begins to happen, the attendance drops off.

Anxiety is not a great problem in the respiratory unit except as it pertains to weaning. However, if anxiety occurs, the patient should be talked to by a psychiatrist to determine its source. Usually, simple reassurance is enough to stem it; if not, a tranquilizer can be used.

Weaning the patient from the respirator is the activity most fraught with distress in the unit. Most individuals who require breathing assistance desire more than anything else to escape from respirator dependency. However, when the moment of truth comes, they are terrified to attempt to draw breath on their own. A panic response results, and in the typical James-Lange tradition, over-breathing evokes heightened fear which leads to apnea and the weaning process becomes a nightmare. One of the best ways to treat this is by prevention. Begin by explaining that the weaning process entails anxiety. Caution the individual to learn to control his fear when breathing comes hard. Teach the individual certain relaxation techniques or hypnotic cues beforehand. Also, make sure that the patient is always attended by a respiratory therapist. By teaching the nurse or therapist massage techniques, combined with hypnosis, one can immeasurably facilitate the process of weaning. Finally, tranquilizers can be used when the weaning response is not modified by the methods already suggested.

Burn Units

The technique for handling body burns has improved over the last decade to the point now where an individual who sustains 80 percent of third degree body surface burn can still survive. The cure does not come without a cost. Delirium is not only a common problem in the burn unit, it is nearly a universal problem. Anyone who has worked on a burn service knows that close to 100 percent of all badly burned individuals are delirious for the first two to three weeks of their inpatient care. Sometimes the delirium is accompanied by vivid hallucinations, usually of a frightening sort, but only rarely do they involve flames. The treatment for the delirium is round-the-clock orientation by personnel, having a large timepiece in the immediate line of vision and a calendar clearly marked for the day, and access to daylight if possible. The nurses and doctors alike should be taught the technique of round-the-clock orientation, which consists of little more than reminding the individual morning, noon and night of the date, including the year and month, and the time. Nothing more need be done for the delirious state unless it becomes disruptive, in which case haloperidol can be administered. Frequent visits on the part of the relatives should be encouraged much in the manner of the death watch—round-the-clock for the weeks of delirium. It should be explained to the relatives and to the patient alike that delirium is normal and that it is self limited (23, 24).

The next most important problem in the burn unit, one that is far more important to the patient and to the medical attendants than delirium, is that of pain with the changing of the burn dressings. Each day the burns are dressed and the bandages reapplied. The area is continually soaked in silver nitrate and badly burned extremities are amputated within the first week or two. There are a number of ways to deal with pain. The most important is to insure that the individual obtains adequate analgesia. It is a fact that surgeons and medical physicians are inclined to under-medicate their patients. The reasons for this are complex. The fear of addiction is the one most frequently mentioned, but this seems hardly worth considering when the illness is limited in time and the patient is closely supervised. Adequate narcotic medication should be given and properly potentiated. The potentiators most frequently employed are chlorpromazine, the benzodiazepines, or the amphetamines. Along with the narcotic, aspirin or Tylenol can be used, as these are surprisingly effective at times.

The use of hypnosis and the teaching of autohypnosis can be of great help (25). The nurses on the burn unit, those who change the dressings, are, more often than not, anxious to learn hypnosis because if it is effective, their role can be transformed from that of a tormentor to one of a healer. Autohypnosis can be taught so that the patient can ease his own pain. This can be supplemented by the use of cassette tapes containing hypnotic instruction.

Some of you may recall the story of the first ovarian cyst that was removed by Ephraim McDowell on Christmas Day at Danville, Kentucky in 1809. He removed a 22-pound ovarian cyst from the abdomen of Mrs. Thomas Crawford without the use of anesthesia. Instead, they sang hymns together. Singing while changing burn dressings, shouting and cursing in rhythm, stamping, beating, encouraging the patient to shriek often provide a sense of relief and release that lowers the pain. Of course it should be done away from the other patients.

Next to delirium, depression is a common psychiatric finding on burn units. Most of these individuals are depressed. The depression depends on the premorbid personality and upon the functional and cosmetic loss. The first avenue of treatment is psychotherapy. Listen, encourage, bolster optimism, point out what is left as well as what has been taken away. Next comes the use of antidepressants, which we have found to be surprisingly effective in the burn unit. The third therapeutic avenue is mobilizing the supporting social systems by encouraging visits by friends and family. The use of stimulants is often helpful in getting a burn patient to move when it comes time to do so and to participate in a program of rehabilitation. We use methylphenidate (Ritalin), 10 mg to 20 mg once a day, or Dexedrine, 5mg once or twice a day for a period of three weeks.

It is important to deal with the family to make sure that their expectations for the future are in line with the truth. Occasionally, we hold staff meetings to include the family, all patients, and everybody on the ward. These are sometimes like a three-ring circus but they do seem to have a positive effect. We also have staff meetings about patient care to continue to keep the ward morale high as was described before. Finally, it is important to consider accident proneness in burn victims. Is the burn part of an accident process that would require continuing psychotherapy? If one suspects this to be true, outpatient psychotherapy would be recommended.

SURGICAL INTENSIVE CARE UNIT (SICU)

Coronary artery bypass graft (CABG) surgery has become one of the most popular major cardiac procedures in large teaching hospitals in this country today. The amount of attention given to preparing the patient for surgery in terms of reducing post operative confusion and delirium is variable. Unfortunately, preparation of this sort it is by no means commonplace. In fact, in some of the better known medical centers, scarcely any attention is given to the emotional aspect of undergoing open heart surgery. Although we have taken no survey of teaching hospitals where cardiac procedures are performed, we have spoken to representatives from approximately 15 such hospitals and would say that half provide some teaching in the form of a pre operative visit by a nurse or a nurse clinician. Of this half, about three quarters have a more elaborate program including diagrams of what is to be done and talks with former patients who have had the surgery. As will be explained, there is reason to believe that preoperative education and clarification could be of great value to the patient after surgery.

There are three stages to consider in the open heart surgical experience: the presurgical, the immediate postsurgical and the convalescent. There is also not one, but two areas of attention for the therapist to explore. The first is the patient himself and the second is his spouse or immediate family. Since this surgical enterprise is always a serious one with very much at stake, the spouse and children play a much more important part than they would in less grave procedures.

In the presurgical stage, there have been two studies that have given some evidence that a visit by a psychiatrist prior to surgery can lower the incidence of post operative delirium (26, 27). The difficulty with these investigations is that neither was planned as an intervention study. As a consequence the finding of reduced delirium on the part of those who had seen a psychiatrist came as an incidental result and important variables had not been controlled. Furthermore, neither study makes clear exactly what the psychiatrist does in the pre operative visit and one could get the impression that it is little more than a laying on of hands.

It is our opinion, based upon a considerable amount of clinical experience, that a psychiatrist can serve an important function in a pre operative visit. The patient's affect can be checked to see if it is overanxious, depressed, or appropriate. Anxiety can usually be calmed by education and support. Depression, if severe enough, may constitute a reason to delay surgery until the patient's state of mind improves. As important as making these diagnoses is the psychiatrist's ability to insure that the patient knows clearly what to expect as a result of surgery. Misconceptions can be corrected. At least one conjoint interview should be arranged with the spouse present; both should be encouraged to ask questions. If these are not forthcoming, the therapist should ask simple questions, such as, "What do you imagine the recovery room will be like?" "Do you expect to be in much pain?" The individual is told there will be pain. Following the advice of Egbert (28) the patient is told that pain is normal and does not mean that the surgery was faulty or that something like a sponge was left behind. We believe it is better for the patient to come away from the surgical experience stating that he had less pain than he was told he would have, than more.

A pre operative visit to the SICU with the patient is valuable particularly if he can be introduced to the nursing staff and he can be shown where he will be cared for. The clock, the calendar, the respiratory assist apparatus, and other articles of furniture and equipment can be described and explained.

It has been our custom to anticipate with the patient that he will become delirious following surgery. This is a result of our experience with the black patch delirium and so far it has worked out sufficiently well to encourage us to continue its use (29). Simply stated, the patient is told the delirium begins with a sense of strangeness, then a loss of time sense, often followed by suspicion, fear, and confusion. He is told that this takes place in practically all patients who have the surgery and, like an unpleasant dream, is bound to pass off by itself. Furthermore, he is told that when the psychiatrist visits him in the immediate post operative phase he will be reminded that the delirium might occur. Should it do so, the patient will know that it is a normal happening, soon to end.

The patient is shown word charts in case he is unable to speak and taught to communicate by blinking his eyes, nodding his head, or forming lip syllables. In this fashion, he is prepared for intubation. Sometimes it is possible to have a former patient who has undergone the entire experience help in explaining the forthcoming surgery. It is advisable however, to be certain of the former patient's performance before introducing him to the patient. Some are much better than others and it is best to have them in attendance rather than make them the primary teacher.

The importance of an uninterrupted pre operative night of sleep can not be overemphasized. In an informal poll taken two years ago, it was estimated that over 70 percent of patients facing CABG surgery spent a restless night before surgery (30). Since the majority of these individuals have been taking sleeping medication for some time, it is well to ask the usual dose they can depend upon for sleep and then to add 50 percent more.

We maintain an attitude of optimism, emphasizing the low rate of operating room mortality, stressing the fact of survival and the short duration of SICU discomfort; however, we never underemphasize the degree of discomfort.

The immediate post operative phase begins as soon as the patient returns to the SICU. If possible, we arrange to visit shortly after the patient arrives or soon after he regains consciousness. If nothing more, we sit at his bedside, talk to him in a reassuring way, touch his forearm or his hand, remind him of some of the things that were said to him, and ask if there is something we can do. We make sure the nurses have been instructed in the technique of round-the-clock orientation. We also try to let them know something special about the patient, something that will make him more of a human being than a physiological preparation. If an individual is an angler, a rose fancier, a real estate agent, or a mechanic, we do our best to imprint the nursing staff with this stamp of his individuality. Frequent visits by the family in the SICU are sometimes prohibited. In our opinion, this is a mistake. Usually, the most diligent and vigilant companions are family. A small portion of family cannot tolerate the environment of the SICU and should not be forced to do so. Most are delighted to participate.

It has long been our habit to instruct the SICU personnel to address the patient by his proper name. Referring to him in the familiar form as Jack or Billy can be demeaning when he has been accustomed to being called Mr. Smith. Maintaining dignity is extremely important to a patient with fragile reality testing.

If a delirium becomes apparent and the patient grows disruptive, he is placed in light restraint and is given haloperidol. Usually, a dose between 5mg and 12mg 3 i.d. will be enough to stop any kind of disruptive behavior. Haloperidol is particularly important because it has such a low incidence of cardiovascular side effects.

Convalescence begins when the patient has left the SICU, returned to the ward and is thinking about being discharged. We use as an operational definition of convalescence the time when all of the complications of surgery have ended and when the patient can think about ambulating and resuming previous activities. The one cardinal feature here is an explanation of what has actually been done. What does the bypass graft consist of? Have the patient draw a heart and then correct him by your own drawing or by an illustration.

Make sure that an activity program has been planned for the patient. Activity is one of the best antidotes for depression. Too seldom does the physician realize that few patients know how to pace their daily activities. Most of us are dependent upon our jobs to do the pacing for us and we must be literally told how far to walk in the morning, how fast, when to rest, and how long. The diet has to be spelled out. Planning the educational program during convalescence is an ideal way to explain what can be done in the way of habit modification, such as decreasing the amount of fat intake, or stopping cigarettes through a habit alteration program. Important in all of this is including the spouse and family. Psychotherapy may be needed in those cases where mobilization and return to work and socialization do not follow the expected course.

Psychiatry has provided acute medicine with a good deal of liaison work. As yet, we can not measure its usefulness in terms of reducing psychiatric morbidity or human suffering. In lieu of that, we have other modalities of measurement—money acceptance. I know of three hospitals where the departments of medicine and surgery have pooled resources to fund a full-time psychiatric position in intensive care. I know of two psychiatrists who are on the editorial board of ICU Journals. At our hospital, a psychiatrist is chairman of the committee on life support systems—when to discontinue life maintenance. These signs of progress should signal to psychiatrists that we are still very much part of the medical brotherhood.

REFERENCES

1. HAY, D. and OKIN, D.: The Psychological Stresses of Intensive Care Unit Nursing. *Psychosom. Med.*, 32:109, 1972.
2. GENTRY, W. D., FOSTER, S. B. and FROEHLING, S.: Psychologic Response to Situational Stress in Intensive and Non-Intensive Nursing. *Heart & Lung*, 1:793-796.
3. HACKETT, T. P. and WEISMAN, A. D.: Psychiatric Management of Operative Syndromes: I. The Therapeutic Consultation and the Effect of Non-Interpretive Intervention. *Psychosom. Med.*, 22:267-282, 1960.
4. LINN, L., et al.: Patterns of Behavior Disturbance Following Cataract Extraction. *Am. J. Psychiat.*, 110:281-289, 1953.
5. TITCHNER, J. L. and LEVINE, M. L.: *Surgery as a Human Experience.* New York: Oxford University Press, 1960.
6. JANIS, I. L.: *Psychological Stress.* New York: John Wiley & Sons, Inc., 1958.
7. ABRAM, H. S. and GILL, B. F.: Predictions of Post Operative

Psychiatric Complication. *N. Eng. J. Med.*, 265:1123, 1961.

8. KIMBALL, C. P.: The Experience of Open Heart Surgery, III. Toward A Definition and Understanding of Post Cardiotomy Delirium. *Arch. Gen. Psychiat.* 27:57, 1972.

9. TUFO, H. M. and OSTFELD, A. M.: Abstract presented at the American Psychosomatic Society, 1970 Meeting.

10. MORSE, R. M. and LITIN, E. M.: Post Operative Delirium. A Study of Etiologic Factors. *Amer. J. Psychiat.*, 126:388, 1969.

11. SURMAN, O.: Psychological Care of the Surgical Patient. Chapter in T. P. Hackett and N. H. Cassem (Eds.), *The MGH Handbook of Psychosomatic Liaison Psychiatry.* St. Louis, Missouri: The Mosby Company. In Press.

12. KILPATRICK, D. G., MILLER, W. C., ALLAIN, A. N., HUGGINS, M. B. and WILLIAMS, L. H.: The Use of Psychological Test Data to Predict Open Heart Surgery Outcome: A Prospective Study. *Psychosom. Med.*, 37:62, 1975.

13. BROWN, I. W. and HACKETT, T. P.: Emotional Reactions to Threat of Impending Death: A study of patients on monitor cardiac pacemakers. *Irish J. Med. Sc.*, 6:(496):177-187, 1967.

14. WEISMAN, A. D. and HACKETT, T. P.: Predilection to Death: Death and Dying as a Psychiatric Problem. *Psychosom. Med.*, 23:232-256, 1961.

15. HACKETT, T. P., CASSEM, N. H. and WISHNIE, H. A.: The Coronary Care Unit: An Appraisal of its Psychologic Hazards. *New Eng. J. Med.*, 279:1365-1370, 1968.

16. CASSEM, N. H. and HACKETT, T. P.: Psychiatric Consultation in a Coronary Care Unit. *Ann. Int. Med.*, 75:9-14, 1971.

17. DRUSS, R. G. and KORNFELD, D. S.: Survivors of Cardiac Arrest: A psychiatric study. *J. Am. Med. Assoc.*, 201:291-296, 1967.

18. DOBSON, M., TATTERSFIELD, A. E., ADLER, M. W. and McNICOL, M. W.: Attitudes in Long-term Adjustment of Patients Surviving Cardiac Arrest. *Brit. Med. J.*, 3:207-212, 1971.

19. CASSEM, N. H., WISHNIE, H. A. and HACKETT, T. P.: How Coronary Patients Respond to Last Rites. *Postgrad. Med.*, 45:147-152, 1969.

20. ROSEN, J. L. and BIBRING, G. L.: Psychological Reactions of Hospitalized Male Patients to a Heart Attack: Age and social class differences. *Psychosom. Med.*, 28:808-821, 1966.

21. HACKETT, T. P. and CASSEM, N. H.: White and Blue Collar Responses to Heart Attack. *J. Psychosom. Res.*, 20:85-95, 1976.

22. KENNEDY, J. A. and BAKST, H.: The Influence of Emotions on the Outcome of Cardiac Surgery: A predictive study. *Bulletin of New York Acad. of Med.*, 42, 811-845, 1966.

23. ANDREASON, N. J. C., et al.: Management of Emotional Reactions of Seriously Burned Adults. *N. Eng. J. Med.*, 286:65-69, 1972.

24. BERNSTEIN, N. R.: *Emotional Care of the Facially Burned and Disfigured.* Boston: Little Brown, 1976.

25. SCHAFER, D. W.: Hypnosis Used on a Burn Unit. *Internat. J. of Clin. and Exper. Hypnosis.*, 23:1-14, 1975.
26. LAZARUS, H. R. and HAGGENS, T. H.: Prevention of Psychosis Following Open Heart Surgery. *Amer. J. Psychiat.*, 124:1190, 1968.
27. LAYNE, O. J. and YUDOFSKY, S. C.: Post Operative Psychosis in Cardiotomy Patients. The role of organic and psychiatric factors. *N. Eng. J. Med.*, 284:518, 1971.
28. EGBERT, et al.: Reduction of Post Operative Pain by Encouragement and Instruction of the Patient. *N. Eng. J. Med.*, 270:825, 1964.
29. WEISMAN, A. D. and HACKETT, T. P.: Psychosis After Eye Surgery: Establishment of a specific doctor/patient relationship in prevention and treatment of black patch delirium. *N. Eng. J. Med.*, 258:1284, 1958.
30. SURMAN, O. S., et al.: Efficacy of Psychotherapy for Patients Undergoing Cardiac Surgery. *Arch. Gen. Psychiat.*, 30:830, 1974.

7

Psychosomatic Theories and Their Contributions to Chronic Illness

Chase Patterson Kimball, M.D.

INTRODUCTION AND ORIENTATION

In an era when biochemical concepts have come to hold dominance as the ultimate explanation for behavior, liaison psychiatrists often occupy the last bastion in the academic arena where a developmental approach to illness remains. That an event happens to an individual along the course of life and that this individual suffers this event because of something peculiar and specific in his life at that time and reacts to this event both because of this and because of processes laid down from the moment of conception and may continue to react in this way is perhaps the hallmark of the psychosomaticist's mode of thinking. In this approach the individual is neither psyche nor soma alone nor both of these together, but also an integral part of a social milieu which potently and mutually interacts with him.

In this synthetic as opposed to analytic approach to the individual *in* the social milieu, the psychosomaticist to a greater extent than most physicians needs to be versed in the theories and the application of the many different language systems that address themselves to behavior—essentially those embraced by the parent disciplines of

259

biology, psychology and social science. Even in writing this, I would prefer to use another term for biology so as to embrace physics and mathematics because some of our thinking in psychosomatic medicine, I think, approaches more the relativism of physics than the taxonomic approaches of biology. Likewise, the term psychology has lost designatory meaning today and has been replaced by the more amorphous term, behavioral science. Thus, I use the former terms in a broad rather than a specific sense.

Despite the theoretical complexities and ambiguities that have marked the historical development of psychosomatic medicine (1, 2) the practitioner of this discipline is a pragmatic individual who in this day of technology might be most likened to a general systems analyst (3) who uses those theoretical approaches that fit best at a particular time in a particular place leading to the most pragmatic approach to the specific problem at hand. In his hands, the approach that works fits best as the explanation at a given point in time. Indeed, with study, that approach in its idiosyncratic circumstance may contribute to studies that will amend and evolve theory. In the latter way, the psychosomaticist is like a naive anthropologist (i.e. unbiased observer) who branches out from his belief system in emphasizing as unbiased an observational approach as possible before resorting to theoretical concepts for explanation. He is first and foremost an observer who formulates his observations in terms of naive questions which would seek further data utilizing whatever theoretical orientations that suggest where the most results will be forthcoming. The generalizations that he will eventually extrapolate from these individual forays into this situation at this time remain only in the broadest sense the approach to another situation at another time and place. In other words, the various kinds of specificity that have dominated psychosomatic thinking in the past are not formulations to be glibly applied to groups of individuals with similar disease processes but serve only as beacons to suggest a plausible approach for investigating this individual situation at this time.

In this sense, a global synthetic approach toward understanding a situation necessitates an analytic approach utilizing several theoretical disciplines to explain naive observations. In our technological world we tend to observe from theoretical approaches rather than explain after the observation. Whereas all of this may seem self-obvious inasmuch as it is essentially what we all think that it is what we do, it is in observational fact exactly what we do not do. We live in a society that conditions us, through payments, to look at objects from a specific theoretical approach, thereby compromising unbiased observation. In what follows, I shall discuss paradigms which are sometimes helpful in keeping our observational processes open as opposed to closed in our approach to situations along a spectrum of illness. At all times we will need to take our observations and formulate them in terms of environmental, psychological and biological formulations. In doing this, we also need to be cautious in our natural predispositions to apply two-dimensional and linear relationships between our different theoretical schemes of explaining our observations. As a last caution, if simplicity is what was desired, we individually and collectively would have stayed in the warmth of our original ideological cages which 19th century science provided us. For idiosyncratic reasons known only to our individual selves have we ventured forth into this wild and spectacular land.

The Developmentalist's Approach

The graphic in Figure 1 is a two-dimensional map to guide us to the three-dimensional individual existing in a four-dimensional world. We greet the central character alone, but in reality he exists and has existed at all times in a social milieu and comes to us with a host of cohorts who in one way or another invade his space and affect his behavior as he will tell us, should we give him an opportunity. We greet this individual, as it were, at some predetermined way station between conception and death (or everlasting life). Something has happened. There has occurred a change in his and/or the environment's sense of himself as a functioning entity which is called illness. He comes/is taken for help. His experience of illness is expressed in terms of social dysfunction, somatic discomfort, and emotional distress. Occasionally (when he is taken), these are denied by the individual, either requiring some other explanation of us, and/or our

FIGURE 1

The Stages of Illness

GENETIC	DEVELOP-MENTAL	PRE-ILLNESS SITUATION	ILLNESS ONSET	ACUTE (ICU)	CONVA-LESCENT	REHABILI-TATIVE
Family Hx Aroused Patterns (Precursors of disease)	Personality Behavior Patterns (Associates of disease)	Stresses & Strains (Immediate correlates)	Experience of Symptoms Response to Symptoms	Anxiety Sadness Delirium	Grief Restitutive	Adaptation & Coping

Pre-Illness ‿‿‿ Hospital ‿‿‿ Altered Organism

attention toward those who have or would bring him to our attention. Then, our approach is first to the latter's discomfort in the anticipation that it will lead us into the system of the former. Immediately, as we begin our approach into the situation, we are led into the past system (determinants) of the identified patient, the present alteration of the individual and immediate environment (including family, friends, job), and the future expectations of the patient in the environmental milieu (prognostication, consequential). Thus, we have already evoked deterministic, evolutionary, and consequential modes of how we shall think about this situation; these modes impose upon us and our observations specific biases inasmuch as we will look for causes, we expect change over time, and we anticipate consequences for all involved in this situation. Therefore, we have *a priori* arranged our thinking and will look for a series of things that we shall attempt to string together in a connected (usually causative) way.

The Illness-Onset Situation

Most immediately and usually, we focus on the question "What has happened?" based on the premise *something happened* (4). We dress this up by calling it the Illness-Onset Situation and we look at it from the vantage point of the individual and significant others in the three dimensions of place and of time. However, mathematically, we have a more complex set of relationships inasmuch as we have three-dimensional persons bringing with them their pasts, present, and anticipated futures, existing in a present spatial situation and the interrelationships that these suggest. In order to get ourselves oriented, we seek out points of departure for our orientation in our questions that suggest that something happened, something must have happened to occasion change, and we suggest that this something must have occurred in some proximity to the change. This is based on data viewed in an empirical way. But it is dependent on how and whether or not we have developed psychologically (5) in a culture (6) which fosters an empirically-based cause and effect mode of thinking. A correlate of this mode is the idea of *specificity,* i.e., that certain kinds of events or situations lead to specific reactions and frequently enough so for statistical validity (also intrinsic to this mode of thinking).

Figure 2

Social Readjustment Rating Questionnaire

Events	Values
1. Marriage	500
2. Troubles with the boss	—
3. Detention in jail or other institution	—
4. Death of spouse	—
5. Major change in sleeping habits (a lot more or a lot less sleep, or change in part of day when asleep)	—
6. Death of a close family member	—
7. Major change in eating habits (a lot more or a lot less food intake, or very different meal hours or surroundings)	—
8. Foreclosure on a mortgage or loan	—
9. Revision of personal habits (dress, manners, associations, etc.)	—
10. Death of a close friend	—
11. Minor violations of the law (e.g. traffic tickets, jay walking, disturbing the peace, etc.)	—
12. Outstanding personal achievement	—
13. Pregnancy	—
14. Major change in the health or behavior of a family member	—
15. Sexual difficulties	—
16. In-law troubles	—
17. Major change in number of family get-togethers (e.g. a lot more or a lot less than usual)	—
18. Major change in financial state (e.g. a lot worse off or a lot better off than usual)	—
19. Gaining a new family member (e.g. through birth, adoption, oldster moving in, etc.)	—
20. Change in residence	—
21. Son or daughter leaving home (e.g. marriage, attending college, etc.)	—
22. Marital separation from mate	—

Most in vogue today is to view this "something" as stress (7), conceptualized by Holmes and Rahe as an event that would occasion the most readjustment (in terms of getting used to, coping with, maintaining present stability, etc.) on the part of the individual sustaining that stress. On a statistical basis, a universal list of those events which would require the most readjustment in descending order has been established for adults (Figure 2), others for children (8), and

FIGURE 2 *(continued)*

Events	Values
23. Major change in church activities (e.g. a lot more or a lot less than usual)	—
24. Marital reconciliation with mate	—
25. Being fired from work	—
26. Divorce	—
27. Changing to a different line of work	—
28. Major change in the number of arguments with spouse (e.g. either a lot more or a lot less than usual regarding child-rearing, personal habits, etc.)	—
29. Major change in responsibilities at work (e.g. promotion, demotion, lateral transfer)	—
30. Wife beginning or ceasing work outside the home	—
31. Major change in working hours or conditions	—
32. Major change in usual type and/or amount of recreation	—
33. Taking on a mortgage greater than $10,000 (e.g. purchasing a home, business, etc.)	—
34. Taking on a mortgage or loan less than $10,000 (e.g. purchasing a car, TV, freezer, etc.)	—
35. Major personal injury or illness	—
36. Major business readjustment (e.g. merger, reorganization, bankruptcy, etc.)	—
37. Major change in social activities (e.g. clubs, dancing, movies, visiting, etc.)	—
38. Major change in living conditions (e.g. building a new home, remodeling, deterioration of home or neighborhood)	—
39. Retirement from work	—
40. Vacation	—
41. Christmas	—
42. Changing to a new school	—
43. Beginning or ceasing formal schooling	—

(from T. H. Holmes and R. H. Rahe: The Social Readjustment Rating Scale. *J. Psychosom. Res.*, 11:213-218, 1967.)

still others for specific populations (9). Common to these lists in terms of meaning of stress appears to be something that implies a symbol of object loss which in Schmale's (10) terms may be real, threatened, or imaginary.

Whereas the definition of stress and the computations attempting to demonstrate statistical relationship between stress and physiologic dysfunction in terms of disease have become almost independent exercises in themselves, this relationship, whether causal or merely coincidental, is of importance to the clinician who would care for his patient with a knowledge of what other things have occurred in the patient's life in addition to this most recent somatic problem. Factors such as a business failure, a marital dispute, an investigation by the Internal Revenue Service certainly may influence the patient's response in one way or another, e.g., compliance with medical regimen, desire to get well, or attention to the present problem.

As suggested above, there are difficulties with the present stress hypothesis when viewed as a causative relationship to somatically conceptualized illness. First is the problem of the universality of stress. Not all stresses are preceived as stresses of the same magnitude by different individuals. Second, psychological factors may intercede to alter the reaction to what might have been perceived as a stress initially, including such phenomena as denial and learned coping behavior. Thus, a stress may not be perceived as a stress or reacted to as a stress or it might be perceived as a stress while at the same time both psychologically conceptualized and behaviorally conceptualized coping mechanisms intercede, thereby diluting or aborting a demonstrable somatic response to the stress. Another difficulty in stress research that would look only at physiological response is the fact that response is frequently not looked for in other aspects of behavior such as in the psychological or the social reference spheres. A further difficulty is our medical bias of looking for negative response patterns and pathology. Changed behavior that may at first be seen as pathological may be adaptive and protective in terms of the total organism.

Reaction to Stress

This area of investigation is in its infancy and is fraught with some of the same conceptual difficulties identified above. For a stress to be a stress, it may first have to be perceived as such on one level or another—that is, conscious or unconscious. On this basis, there are a relatively large number of different pathways this reaction might take depending on the sophistication of one's psychological, physiological, and social repertoires. Most basically, the percept on one level or another can be screened out, as appears to be the situation in some patients with hypertension (11, 12) at one phase of the illness. The mechanism of this screening out might be seen as a psychologically conceptualized denial. In time, a physiological explanation may make this process clearer. In some situations it may depend simply on arousal threshold. With or without this screening out process may be sequential behaviors viewed as means of coping with the perceived stress, each with its biological, psychological, and socially observed correlates. The extent to which these are adaptive or maladaptive, I suggest, relates to a value system intrinsic to each of these disciplines and their subdisciplines rather than being absolute in their own right. The only common denominator perhaps is that there is always a price to pay for experience even if that experience contributes to growth, further development, and aging.

Rahe (13) has suggested that a stress is a stress to the organism when it results in a strain in the individual. Using this concept, it would seem that a strain is a measurable response in one system or another, recording the impact of that stress on that system. Again, this gives a wide array of systems and subsystems to evaluate. In terms of biological responses, we would look first at the entire organism for multiple organ-system involvement and then more closely at specific organ system involvement. The idea of specificity is an old one and keeps turning up again in many forms. Alexander (14) proposed not only a psychological specificity but an equally important biological specificity to explain specific organ system involvement in disease. This was the concept of the vulnerable organ. Although he did not define this in detail, it seems as though he would resort to a genetic explanation for this vulnerability. Bridger (15) has observed that neonates respond to a specific stimulus with a physiological variation in a specific organ system that remains constant for that individual over time, although different neonates respond to the same stimulus with a different response in the same organ system or in a different organ system. To what extent this depends on genetic factors or *in utero* conditioning vis-à-vis maternal behavior remains unexplored.

The idea of vulnerable organ specificity gained momentum with the Alexandrian- and Mirsky-inspired (16) work of Weiner et al. (17) in a prospective study of individuals presumed to be vulnerable for peptic ulcer disease by virtue of a biological marker, elevated serum pepsinogen levels, who were under the presumed-to-be stressful situation of boot camp. Not only did these investigators demonstrate the development of a significant percent of peptic ulcers in this group as opposed to a contrast group of inductees who had low serum pepsinogen levels, but they also demonstrated that those individuals with the more pathological scores on psychological tests and psychiatric interviews correlated with which individuals among the hypersecreters developed ulcers.

Biological vulnerability and specificity concepts are helpful in assisting the clinician in anticipating which systems are at risk in terms of the individual's most recent vulnerability, that is, the present illness. Knowing that an individual has a vulnerable cardiovascular system will alert the physician to the possibility of intercurrent changes in this as a response to illness regardless of the present illness. In other words, the physician treating a patient who has multiple fractures as the result of an automobile accident would monitor the individual with a history of peptic ulcer disease or coronary artery insufficiency for those processes, respectively.

The concept of both psychological and physiological specificity continues to intrigue us. Friedman and Rosenman (18) have identified a correlation between Behavior Pattern Type A (as distinct from a more amorphous Behavior Pattern Type B) and coronary artery disease. Initially their observations included physiologic and biochemical factors in the definitions of this pattern (i.e., elevated cholesterol and tri-glyceride levels, elevated blood pressure levels) as well as behavioral factors that Rosenman believes are best symbolized by a forearm with a clenched first and a stop-watch strapped to the wrist. This description, with its emphasis on conscientiousness, industriousness, sense of urgency, competitiveness, and physical activity, obviously includes obsessive and compulsive characteristics and takes us back to some of Dunbar's (19) earlier observations and suggestions that individuals with specific personalities were vulnerable to specific diseases. This hypothesis enjoyed a brief popularity partly because it was too global and did not identify specific enough characteristics subject to quantification. It also did not contribute to a medicine that was becoming increasingly preoccupied with the mechanisms by which these characteristics worked in effecting alterations in physiology.

Ruesch's (20) observations, at the same time, led to the formulation of an infantile personality as the core personality for psychosomatic disease—Alexander's Holy Seven. Others have more recently introduced the idea of a similar personality for individuals reacting to stressful situations with primarily fixed pathophysiologic processes (Sifneos' Alexithymia (21), Marty's & de'Uzan's Pensée Opératoire (22)). These core personalities seem too generalizable and non-specific for correlation with individuals with specific pathophysiologic response patterns. Besides, they tend to belie clinical observations identifying different levels of sophistication in the cognitive, emotional, and social processes in individuals with different pathophysiologic disturbances or the changes in these responses at different phases in the illness. As an example of the latter, Engel (23) has shown the presence of different emotional presentations and defensive patterns during the exacerbation as opposed to the remission phases of ulcerative colitis. The essential feature linking these various observations together may be more the fluidity and capacity for psychological regression and reconstitution in individuals particularly prone to experience stress via pathophysiologic processes than a fixed personality concept. Some aspects of the Alexithymic and of the Infantile Personalities are close to those of the Borderline Personality (24, 25). A variety of, although not necessarily specific, pathophysiologic reactions are seen in these individuals correlated with fluctuations in psychologically conceptualized defensive systems.

Engel and Schmale (26) have proposed a specific response state to stress that puts the individuals at risk for psychological and/or physiologic dysfunction depending upon that individual's specific vulnerability potential (Figure 3). This state, the GU^2 (giving up-

FIGURE 3

The Giving Up—Given Up State

1. An unpleasant affect of helplessness or hopelessness.
2. A sense of inadequacy; an inability to cope.
3. A sense of diminished relationships with others.
4. A diminished sense of future.
5. A preoccupation with the past, especially the misfortunes of the past.
6. A perception of the present environment as alien and of no longer providing guidelines for behavior.

given up) is described as an initial response to a stressful situation. As such, it is an *in limbo* state. Much of their description is not unlike those identified as Stress Reactions (reactions to major civilian catastrophes, natural disasters, battlefield siutations) by other investigators (27). Individuals reacting in this way are characterized by an affect of helplessness or hopelessness, an expression of inadequacy, an inability of coping, a sense of futility, a diminished sense and orientation to the future, and a preoccupation with the past— notably the misfortunes of the past. Some would see this as a reactive depression or as a grief reaction, but its essential component is perhaps its identification as a dynamic state. The individual may recoup at any point or may go on to some decompensation of behavior psychologically, physiologically or socially. The importance of this concept in working with a patient already sustaining a major pathophysiologic process is that this process in and of itself may lead to such a state.

The work of Cassem and Hackett (28) in their study of patients sustaining myocardial infarction suggests that at least some of the early reactions of these patients suggest the GU^2 state (Figure 4). They note that patients in the Coronary Unit first manifest behavior associated with anxiety. There is sometimes denial of illness, the emotions around illness, and/or the consequences of it. This may be

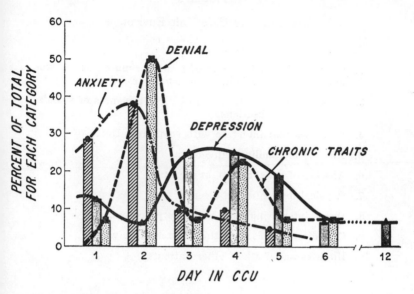

FIGURE 4. Psychological responses in a coronary care unit. From N. Cassem and T. Hackett, *Ann. Int. Med.*, 75:9-14, 1971.

associated with impulsive behavior and demands to sign out of the Unit. Most directly, anxiety is related to the severity of the patient's condition and pain. Anxiety as the predominant experience peaks about the second day and is gradually replaced by depression, which in their study they identify as peaking on the fourth day. These studies based on observations and patients' self-reports depend on a number of factors—the backgrounds of the patients under study, the previous illness experience, personality characteristics, the orientations of patients toward physicians and nurses, and the hospital environment.

Kornfeld et al. (29) have stressed the strangeness and oftentimes bizarreness of the intensive care unit environment as seen by the patient not previously familiar with hospitals (Figure 5). They identi-

FIGURE 5

The Intensive Care Unit Environment

1. An alien environment.

2. Overstimulation in terms of sounds, number of individuals attending patient, other senses assaulted.

3. Sensory monotony in terms of repetitiousness of sounds, sights, other sensations.

4. Processes that interfere with communication.

5. Absence of familiar individuals.

6. Absence of usual day-night sequence.

7. Physical discomfort of disease.

8. Drugs interfering with cognitive processes.

9. Crowding of beds, resulting in lack of privacy.

10. Illnesses and death of other patients.

fied these environments as relatively small areas in which beds are crowded close together, through which large numbers of nurses, physicians, aides, students, and family members are constantly moving. There is frequently no differentiation between nighttime and daytime in these windowless environments in which the lights are usually on. Patients lie next to each other, each attached to intravenous feeding units, cardiac monitors and automatic blood pressure recorders. In some intensive care units, such as those in which patients are recovering from open heart surgery, most patients are intubated rendering speech impossible; some are placed on water cooled mattresses in order to lower temperatures. In other units, such as burn units (30), patients may lie in isolation behind windows in special environments where they may be unclothed and in which they experience relative isolation from others. It is little wonder that in these environments, with the overstimulation of the senses on one hand and monotonous repetition on another, patients experience not only emotional reactions but oftentimes altered states of consciousness (Figure 6) associated

FIGURE 6

Altered States of Consciousness

1. Cognitive deficits: orientation, memory, concentration, abstraction (concreteness).

2. Emotional lability.

3. Environment.

4. Illness and injury: CNS, CV, GI, Resp., GU, Endocrine, Hematologic, Metastatic.

5. Drugs: sedatives, analgesics, mild tranquilizers, steroids, specific drugs.

6. Sleep

7. Withdrawal states: alcohol, narcotics.

8. Previous episodes of ASC.

both with the environments and the underlying condition for which they are being treated. Specific factors that have been correlated with confusion, disorientation, impairment of memory and judgment, emotional lability, and inattention have been interference with sleep, narcotics, sedatives, minor tranquilizers, the absence of orienting stimuli (calendars or clocks), the cacophony of unfamiliar sounds, the frequent crises in the environment, the continual changes of staff, and the anxiety aroused by what is going on.

There are several important considerations regarding alteration of consciousness states (31). Many psychiatrists, acting as consultants, misconceptualize these as acute psychotic states because of the delusions and hallucinations which are frequently associated with them especially in their most severe forms. While this characterization may be descriptively appropriate, it errs in failing to alert physicians to etiologic factors which most often are multifactorial, not the least of which are iatrogenic agents such as analgesics and sedatives. Furthermore, a functional diagnosis adds an unnecessary burden on both the patient and his family. From a diagnostic point of view, there are a number of significant findings that separate these states from functional ones: a) they are usually of brief duration, 5-7 days when untreated; b) the delusions and hallucinations are more likely to be ego-alien as opposed to ego-syntonic; c) they are responsive to relatively small amounts of phenothiazine; and d) they are responsive to relatively minor supportive forms of psychotherapy. From a theoretical view, these differences might be considered in terms of their relatively abrupt onset and limited duration so that what is observed is an incipient stage of a process that bears a similarity to diseases considered functional in nature, but is lacking in some of the other factors usually associated with them.

These acute states (32) are potentially hazardous ones for the individual, the hospital staff, and other patients. In the acute phases, individuals may act upon the delusional and hallucinatory components, bringing harm to themselves and others. Experience has shown that these acute stages have prior stages preceding from hyperalertness and irritability through mild to moderate states of confusion (Figure 7). These states usually go undetected so that the acute agitated stage appears to develop suddenly rather than as a

FIGURE 7

Stages of Altered States of Consciousness

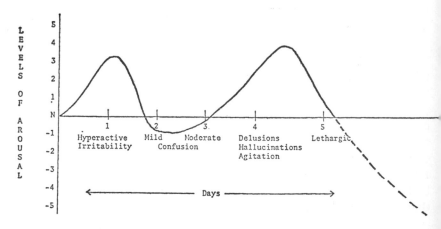

FIGURE 8

Treatment of Altered States of Consciousness

1. Do not leave patient alone!
2. Nurse's Aide.
3. Direct simple repeated orienting reassuring remarks.
4. Review medications, chemistries.
5. Identify other possible causes.
6. Reduce environmental confusion; change.
7. Phenothiazines.
8. Assess for further therapy.

more severe sequence of the previous stage. Patients in acute stages of delirium should not be left alone (Figure 8). The best attendant is usually a nurse's aide who can handle the patient in a matter-of-fact manner, simply reiterating orienting information concerning who the patient is, where he is, and what has occurred, while saying that everything will be all right in a little while. Meanwhile, it behooves the physician to seek out those factors that may be contributing to the delirium. Small amounts of a phenothiazine repeated hourly three to four times usually alleviate the agitation seen with these states and ameliorate the degree of confusion. Generally, when there are no major contraindications, it is best to maintain the patient on the phenothiazine for a week to 10 days in order to give him some distance from the psychic upheaval he has experienced. A small number of individuals sustaining such states will require subsequent psychiatric counselling.

Impulsive behavior observed during the acute stage of illness is infrequent, but when it occurs it may be a matter for speedy resolution, especially when it involves a patient in the Intensive Care Unit attempting to sign out against medical advice. Such individuals are usually not suffering from an altered state of consciousness, but rather are reacting characterologically to a state of heightened anxiety occasioned by an abrupt onset or exacerbated stage of illness. These individuals respond best to a benign authoritarianism, one that is straightforward, matter of fact, and definitive. Patients with obsessive traits will require elaborate explanation of what has occurred and of what to expect before demonstrating a willingness to comply with the medical regimen to perfection. Patients with hysteric traits may need permission to "carry on" in order to get through the denial and ventilate their anxiety. Thus, a knowledge of and a sensitivity for the defensive reactions of individuals with specific personality styles under stress (33) are essential for the clinician in his care for the patient at this stage in illness.

Knowledge of the patient's previous reactions to stressful experiences, including illness, is frequently helpful to the physician in anticipating reactions of patients to the present illness experience. Greene et al. (34) have observed patients undergoing cardiac catheterization, defining four specific behavioral patterns with physiologic and biochemical correlates that they feel may be indicative of the behavior to be anticipated during subsequent cardiac surgery. Some investigators (35) have correlated a history of a previous delirium with the post operative delirium in cardiac patients. Klein (36) studying patients in the coronary care unit has correlated behavioral measurements with urinary catecholamine metabolites as potential indicators of adverse cardiac function. He has also noted that not only are patients vulnerable to intensive care units, but some patients are sensitive to the anticipation of being transferred from them (37), expressing the feeling that they are being let loose and will no longer have the close attention that they have had. Anticipating this kind of response in some patients has led physicians and nurses working in this environment to prepare patients for transfer by listening for their expectations and hesitations. This is an increasingly important consideration in hospitals where patients may be transferred every few days through a gradation of lesser intensive care units, requiring a constant readjustment to changed environments, personnel and regimen.

It is not infrequent to observe in patients who have had a relatively benign course in the intensive care unit situation to sustain both psychological and physiological decompensation following or near the end of this phase of illness. This appears to be particularly true of individuals who use a denial of affect and sometimes of the severity of illness as the major defense during the initial phase. In post operative situations, these patients may manifest acute anxiety attacks, fevers of undetermined origin, acute gastric hemorrhages, pains of undetermined derivation (38). For the consulting psychiatrist, these occurrences may suggest a displacement of the patient's feelings through somatic processes. Dreams, which are particularly vivid at this time of convalescence, are useful in assessing the emotional status of these patients.

Convalescent Phase

The convalescent phase of illness commences with some stabilization in the patient's physiologic course where less moment-to-moment monitoring is required. As suggested above, this transition point is greeted by patients in varying ways. Some patients may greet this with relief, as the end of an ordeal; others with enthusiasm and optimism; and still others with apprehension and trepidation. As the transition evolves, most patients settle into convalescence with a diminution of anxiety that is replaced by a sense of enforced confinement. To the observer, this may appear as depression, but perhaps the term conservation-withdrawal (39) is more apt. When feelings are verbalized, patients say they are relieved, they can let go a bit, settle back, rest, and put worries out of their mind for a bit. In this phase, they are less enthusiastic than their physicians, nurses and family. They are more interested in turning to the wall, refusing visitors, and sleeping. They tend to fatigue easily, to show unsustained concentration, to pick at their food, and demonstrate a sense of feebleness. In some, this phase is of limited duration and is followed, in postcoronary patients at least, by a period of exuberance which is expressed in terms of a sense of wellbeing, demonstrated by increased energy and a regrasping of the business of living, catching up on the news, renewing business contacts, and getting reorganized. On the other hand, others may adopt a sick role that threatens to become chronic (40). The liaison psychiatrist in alerting the staff to these

FIGURE 9

The Grieving Process

Day			
1	SHOCK:	Disbelief, Denial, Numbness	
2	VENTILATION:	Anxiety	regression
3		Anger	introjection
			projection
		Sadness	identification
4			undoing
		Shame	reversal
5	DEFENSIVE:		isolation
			reaction formation
6		Guilt	rationalization
			intellectualization
7			
8			
9			
10		Depression	(turning around on oneself)
11			
12			
13			
14	REHABILITATIVE: Coping Adaptation	Hope	displacement
			sublimation
			(repression)

particular patterns in individuals can assist them in trying to understand what is going on and whether or not one or another kind of intervention is required.

This phase of illness, from a psychological viewpoint, lends itself to a grieving process model (41) (Figure 9). Frequently, it is not until this time that the patient begins to accept, rather than just endure, the fact of illness. This acknowledgment of illness and of the real, threatened, and imagined impositions it places on life is the beginning of recognition and reckoning. In order to embark on these processes, emotions frozen or trapped during the acute phase may need to be released, especially those of anxiety, anger and sadness. It is not until this phase that many patients come into an awareness of their vulnerability and of the possibility and probability of death at some point in the future. They may need to talk about this, but find themselves in the midst of individuals who exalt life and deny death. While discussions of, indeed preoccupation with, death and dying have joined the economic currents of our times for the well, these have less to do with the reality of the anxieties about death for the ill. For those of us on the front lines, patients in acute situations seem eager to be cared for and have their pains ameliorated rather than preoccupied with seeking some promise of eternal life. During the convalescent stage of the acute illness, they often appear to gain greater relief after talking about their anxieties about death and grieving for what might have been and in turn knowing better than ever what will be, and to regain control over their remaining life by getting things in order, including wills and arrangements for dependents and spouses.

Anger observed at this period first is directed at the self and takes the preoccupation of guilt over what the patient has done to bring this event on himself. Frequently, it is projected onto the physician, nurses and family, which is always painful for these individuals. This may be an important transitional phase and these recipients may need to be primed to endure it, while enabling the anger to become directed in more constructive ways. Similarly, sadness in the form of self-pitying is better shared with significant others than endured alone. The sadness may be viewed as for what might have been (death) as well as for what has been and will. When this is ventilated, for which permission first and facilitation second are required of the staff and family, the patient is freed to resort to his more characterological defensive patterns to cope with his changed state of being. During this phase of illness, patients may benefit from family conferences and group meetings with other patients and their spouses with similar disease processes. The value of these situations will depend on the individuals and families involved. Group processes have been found helpful in patients with tuberculosis (42), myocardial infarction (43), and chronic pulmonary disease (44), in adolescents with diabetes, etc. These groups are frequently run by nurses, chaplains, dieticians, and physiotherapists under the guidance of a physician and a liaison psychiatrist. All of these not only know their specific disciplines but have had long experience with the population under study. In these sessions, there is the recognition by the patient and his spouse first, that he is not the only one in this situation, and second, that there are many common problems to be faced which may be ameliorated by being shared. In the course of these sessions, there is an opportunity for much didactic communication about the illness from the staff. Questions raised by patients and their spouses, frequently on the basis of anxiety, can lead to clarification as well as an opportunity for group ventilation. Reassurance when appropriate can be forthcoming. When controlled by experienced therapists, confrontation can be utilized as part of the group process (45).

Self-help groups such as Mended Hearts, Colostomy Clubs, Cancer groups, Weight Watchers, etc., have proved helpful for some patients with chronic disease processes in their endeavors to live active and involved lives despite chronic disease processes. Obviously, while these appear helpful for some, they may prove anxiety-provoking for others, who may need a more intensive individual therapeutic experience with a personal counselor. When there are other problems in the family, a family therapist may be essential in order to help this already disturbed unit integrate yet another stress. Particularly vulnerable individuals are subject to more serious changes of behavior which will require specific intervention by psychiatrists for further assessment, evaluation and treatment. Some patients may experience depressive reactions; others develop chronic anxiety states; some express a wish no longer to live (46). There has been increasing awareness of the psychological morbidity that is associated with chronic illness and that is related to the extent of the functional incapacity in the home and at work (47). Some of these individuals develop functional symptoms not dissimilar from those associated with the underlying illness. For example, an individual with angina

FIGURE 10

Conversion (Modified Concept)

1. Atypical presentation
2. Bizarre description
3. La belle indifference
   Exaggerated affect
4. Model
   Self
   Significant other
5. Stress (real, threatened, imagined, object loss)
6. Specific Psychopathology—depression (treatment)
7. Secondary gains

secondary to coronary artery disease may in stressful situations develop pre-cordial pain in which there is no demonstrable evidence of coronary arterial insufficiency (48). Post operative cardiovascular patients may have episodes of hyperventilation which they relate to their underlying illness, but which are found to represent the repressed experience of breathing difficulty following surgery and anesthesia. Many of these reactions, which are at first reacted to as an emergency, are best conceptualized as modified conversion reactions (49) and can be identified positively by obtaining a more precise description of the symptom, the situation in which it occurs, and the reaction of the individual and significant others to it (Figure 10). The description is frequently atypical and differs from the somatically associated phenomenon; it is frequently presented with either exaggeration or indifference; it occurs in proximal relationship to a situation perceived as stressful, frequently one that threatens loss of support by a significant other; it may occur as a phenomenon masking depression or other psychiatric illness; and identifiable secondary gains may be easily ascertained.

In discussing the reactions to illness during the convalescent and rehabilitative phases, it is important to stress that objectified data of these processes are scanty. What has been mentioned above and what will be identified below are examples from relatively few intensive studies from which generalizations have been made. Each illness situation, as well as the environments in which it is handled, requires careful exploration and statistical analysis if we are to know enough to participate in these environments with maximum effectiveness. We need to use our eyes and ears as well as those of the individuals who consult us in order to develop hypotheses that further observations will help us sustain and amend in order to fill in the voids where experience and knowledge are presently lacking.

The Rehabilitative Phase

This phase of illness has only recently come under the increased scrutiny of researchers interested in coping and adaptation. Their vocabulary has been borrowed from all of the behavioral sciences. Among the patient groups studied have been: a) those with severe burns (50); b) those with poliomyelitis (51); c) parents of children with leukemia (52); d) patients undergoing surgery (38, 53); and e) patients undergoing chronic hemodialysis (54). The tasks seen as necessary for coping and adaptation include (55): a) maintaining a sense of personal worth; b) keeping distress within manageable limits; c) maintaining or restoring relationships with significant people; d) enhancing the prospects for recovering bodily functions; and e) increasing the likelihood of working out a personally valued and socially acceptable life style after maximum physical recovery (Figure 11). Essential psychological components for accomplishing these tasks depend on the individual's capacity for autonomy and mastery, adaptive ego mastery, and progressive differentiation in development. Indeed, the process of adapting to chronic illness and an altered sense of functioning is seen as a phase of individual development not unlike leaving home, marriage, and aging. Although the adaptive potential is partially related to the individual's past abilities in adjusting to stressful events, the current situation presents a challenge that offers new patterns for development. Adaptation is seen less in terms of compromise and conformity and more in terms

FIGURE 11

Tasks of Coping and Adaptation

1. Maintaining a sense of personal worth.

2. Keeping distress within manageable limits.

3. Maintaining, restoring relationships with significant persons.

4. Enhancing the prospects for recovering bodily functions (or alternatives).

5. Identifying the possibility and working toward an acceptable altered life style.

6. Emphasizing an opportunity for growth, the development of new skills.

7. Communication and demonstration of these capacities to other.

of an individual's capacity for finding new and unique ways of meeting the demands of his infirmity. Essential to this new phase of growth (in addition to the patient's outlook) is the presence of others who begin to work with the patient from the earliest phases of his incapacity and who relate to him as a person as opposed to a patient, an amputee, a burn patient, a cardiac, a chronic lunger, etc. On the other hand, through experience, these workers need to know at first hand the phenomena—biological, psychological, and social—specific for a specific disability (Figure 12).

TACTICS FOR THE CONSULTANT DERIVED FROM SPECIFIC STUDIES OF COPING

There are several areas where efforts to study individuals under the stress of physical illness have resulted in suggesting the unique and specific problems faced by these victims, the different kinds of coping devices utilized, and potential therapeutic interventions. These include poliomyelitis—the scourge of the late 1940's and 1950's—burns, severe spinal cord injuries resulting in quadraplegia and paraplegia, hemodialysis and renal transplant, and cancer. The

FIGURE 12

Specific Aids to Coping

1. Empathic, experienced helpers.

2. Provision for helpers, communication with each other, with skilled professionals.

3. Self-help groups: mended hearts, colostomy clubs, cancer groups.

4. Availability of family counselling and therapy (remember the spouse!).

5. Models for identification.

6. When possible, the resumption of former routines, functions and relationships.

7. Attention to the "cosmetic" deficits and changes.

8. An opportunity to review and communicate past achievements.

9. Medication: analgesics.

10. Hope, determination, faith.

results and implications of these studies will be briefly reviewed not only because of the specific suggestions for management of patients with specific conditions, but also for those principles of management extrapolated from one group to another.

Hamburg and Adams (56) identified 17 transition points, some inherent to the life cycle and others intrinsic to urbanized, technologically complex societies. There are: 1) separation from parents in childhood; 2) displacement by siblings; 3) childhood experiences (57); 4) illness and injuries of childhood; 5) illness and death of parents; 6) severe illness and injuries of adult years; 7) initial transitions (40); 10) competitive graduate education; 11) marriage; 12) pregnancy; 13) menopause; 14) periodic moves; 15) retirement; 16) rapid technological and social change; and 17) wars and threat of wars. Death of spouse, divorce, and job loss could be added at this time. The authors review the sources for what is presently known about coping: 1) severe injuries; and 2) the parents of fatally-ill children.

In their studies of severe injuries, they identify: 1) the resourcefulness of the individual; 2) the relatively large number of individual means of coping; 3) the spectrum of adjustment over time; and 4) the importance of group membership. Along the spectrum of adjustment, they suggest that initially, victims (and probably their caretakers) exhibit efforts to minimize the impact of the disaster and its potential consequences. Individuals deny the nature of illness, its seriousness and probable consequences. These are viewed as avoidance defenses preventing overwhelming catastrophic reactions and allowing for a gradual acceptance of facts preparing for the transition to the tasks ahead. As the individual begins to come face to face with his condition, he seeks information relevant to treatment and recovery. There begins the assessment of long-term limitations. At times during this phase painful reality becomes associated with episodes of depression. Gradually, there is an increasing identification with groups. In a ward or unit situation where patients have identical or similar illnesses, there develops a firm sense of belonging. As the individual attempts to redefine his role vis-à-vis his altered physical state, there occurs the testing of significant others in terms of their support, interest, and attachment. These are first made with the caring staff, frequently with staff of the opposite sex. They then are made with spouses, fiancés, and other family members. Subsequently, they are made with work colleagues and supervisors.

In the studies of the parents of fatally-ill children (58), workers again have identified a spectrum of reactions. During the initial shock phase following news of the diagnosis of lymphoma from the physician, parents were only interested in the information that aided in handling the immediate situation and in making decisions about the immediate care of their child. Over time, often months, when the implications of the diagnosis had been assimilated, and during a second stage in which parents blamed themselves for not having paid attention to suggested earlier signs and symptoms, parents demonstrated information-seeking behavior from many sources. Knowing may be seen as a more active approach to coping in terms of preparing the individual for the future. At the same time, the searching for information carried with it a fervent hope that it would lead to discoveries. Over time, hope for a miracle in terms of a cure became attenuated to a hope for a remission or that the child would be well enough to go home for a weekend or for a birthday party. As prognosis for recovery diminished and death loomed closer, parents were observed to enter a phase of anticipatory grieving (59) during which they experienced preoccupation with many somatic symptoms: weakness, sighing, crying, insomnia, decreased libido, impotence, and increased motor activity, as well as withdrawal from usual social and professional activities.

The success of coping in these situations, while different at different life phases, may be addressed in terms of: 1) the effectiveness with which the task is accomplished; and 2) the cost to the individual of this effectiveness. It depends on the likelihood that the tasks can be accomplished according to standards tolerable to the individual and the group in which he lives. It includes seeking advanced information about the new situation, trying out new forms of behavior in anticipating new roles, and worrying about possible future difficulties. It is assisted by interpersonal closeness in which projected ideas, new patterns of behavior, and altered relationships are discussed openly. In these interpersonal situations, the ward, outside groups, and family, there is the opportunity for pooling of information, support, ventilating, trying out new ideas, and testing out new models of role complementarity. This active effort supports the capacity for optimism and may overcome passivity and inactivity which may lead to pessimism. These tasks of coping for a specific individual may be formulated by four questions: 1) How can stress be relieved? 2) How can a sense of personal worth be maintained? 3) How can rewarding continuity of interpersonal relationships be maintained? 4) How can the requirements of the stressful task be met or opportunities utilized?

Kiely (60) views severe illness as a psychological stress depending upon the perception and cognitive appraisal and meaning attached to stress as modified by each other and the emotions aroused. The perceived stress is that of: 1) loss or threat of loss of psychic objects, which include body image, personal relationships and body image; 2) injury or threat of injury to body, including pain and mutilation; and 3) frustration of biological drive satisfaction, especially basic nurturement, libidinal needs, and avenues of aggressive discharge. Determinants of coping depend on: 1) personality which may include stress-response patterns, reaction time, vectors of response (approach-avoidance); 2) disease-related factors; 3) the life setting; and 4) the hospital environment. He suggests that cognitive coping styles include minimalization with selective inattention, ignoring, rationalization of the facts, and selective misinterpretation sometimes leading to psychic delirium with hallucinations and distortional interpretations. Vigilant focusing in terms of obsessiveness and hypervigilance is another component of cognitive coping which leads to information about the environment during the first stages of incapacity. Concurrent with cognitive coping styles are affective coping responses which include dysphoric affects in which women frequently focus concern over alteration of body image, while men may be distraught over their physical helplessness and dependency on others. During this period, manifestations of fear and doubt are ubiquitous. Associated with affective coping responses are behavioral coping patterns suggested by Lipowski (61) which include active tackling of tasks imposed by illness or injury; capitulating, characterized by passivity, inactivity, and helpless dependency on others; and avoidance, an active effort to free oneself of the constraint implicit in the acceptance of illness or injury. A fourth component of coping identified by Kiely is that of the "courage to be," dependent upon the will of the individual and his capacity to change, characteristics that are probably rooted in very early development.

Poliomyelitis

Although poliomyelitis is no longer the threat that it was in the 1940's and 1950's, the studies by Visotsky et al. (51) and Davis (62) serve as important keys to our present approaches to patients with severe limitations of physical function in unfamiliar surroundings. During the early phases, the individual's concerns are: a) the lack of information; b) fear of worthlessness; c) severe depressions; d) restlessness; e) boredom; f) loneliness g) fear of rejection by family; h) helplessness; i) fear of respirators and other mechanical equipment; j) concern over future prospects, physical and economic. Later, during the rehabilitative phase, patient concerns are about: a) financial; b) future education; c) occupational opportunities; d) marital relationships; e) permanent disfigurement; and f) family and community relationships.

In approaching the patient with a chronic illness, the liaison psychiatrist needs to know: 1) the specific and common disability and burdens of the illness; 2) the pre-illness personality of the individual and the situational context in which the illness occurs; 3) that occasional individuals find paradoxical benefits in the illness since some aspects of it may mesh with pre-existing personal needs; 4) the usual and specific psychosocial consequences of the disease. In the latter context, he needs to assess how the noxious impact of the illness is commonly detoxified; whether there are patterns of long-term learning processes that lead to increased resourcefulness; and what kinds of personal development result from such experiences.

Responses of patients during the acute phase are ones of avoidance and minimalization, concern over relationship with spouse and family, and specific aspects of the illness, including altered states of consciousness. Avoidance is again seen in later stages of the illness course at times of corrective surgery. This is more common in adolescents. Preoccupation with relationship with family also recurs during the chronic and rehabilitative phase. However, these are likely to be more specific about the problems of carrying out role responsibilities in the family during hospitalization. Also during the convalescent period, concerns extend to those of economic security, maintaining a connectedness with the community, religion, and specific interactions with physicians and other treatment personnel. Depending upon the extent that the patient is able to feel an individualized relationship with a therapist, he will be able to project his concerns, express his anxieties, and try out various defenses and coping strategies for review. When this possibility does not exist, anxiety and depression frequently occur.

The patient's determination to improve, while self-generated and probably related to early developmental factors, is significantly aided by family, staff and the ward community. Most patients are slow to accept the fact that there will be permanent disability. In this regard, the patient is in a pivotal situation. Too rapid an acceptance of disability may lead to despair and despondency which may result in lack of maximum participation in the treatment program. On the other hand, expectations that are maximally discordant with reality may result in dashed hopes and total resignation at a future time, with failure to accept a limited recovery.

The therapists working with these patients obviously walk the tightrope of portraying optimism while not promising more than what is realistically expectable. When this is achieved, the combination of a competent treatment program and a cooperative patient improves the chances of decreasing ultimate disability. When there is demonstrable physical progress, encouragement is given for further progress. While that still biologically elusive phenomenon called hope is recognized as an essential component for rehabilitation in the face of adversity, when it is unrealistic it may lead to failure to accept disability and consequently to inappropriate behavior. Time which includes patience has an immunizing effect not only for patients but also for the caring staff and relatives. Perhaps of greatest importance is the interaction with other patients with similar disabilities and illnesses which leads to overcoming the sense of isolation and loneliness and assists in the development of a sense of security. Open wards facilitate this kind of interaction. In these situations, it is important for the staff to be aware that this communal-like situation for the patient may lead to a sense of isolation and alienation for the spouse who is estranged from this enormous room while bearing the burdens of increased responsibility and worry, oftentimes alone. Attempts to involve the spouse in group activities with other spouses on the unit are sometimes helpful in overcoming this likelihood.

In the rehabilitative phases of chronic illness, Visotsky et al.'s study of Respiratory Centers observed the interaction with the staff, noting that after the initial contacts there was frequent testing of the staff which often was ignored. The testing was based upon positive and negative relationships in the previous treatment facility. This testing was a two-way process, for the staff also was quick to pigeonhole patients on the basis of early observations into categories based on its experience with previous patients. Such early designations, without further specific objectification, frequently place a heavy and unnecessary burden on both patients and staff. These differential responses of patients to staff and staff to patients who are likely to be together for a long time include personality and cultural differences which may need to be to be addressed over time. This redressment frequently falls to the consultant psychiatrist who comes from the outside and is at a bit of a distance from the day-to-day operations of the unit. The consultant may find himself in the role of confidant to both staff and patient; oftentimes when there is conflict he becomes the mediator between the two. In this phase, the consultant's role is also one of encouraging the spirits and optimism of the staff burdened daily with heavy and emotionally-laden problems, identifying dysphoric and emotional restricted responses in patients, and facilitating interactions of both patient and staff with each other and among themselves.

Interaction with family, friends, and professional associates is crucial to the future adjustment of the patient. These individuals are initially uncomfortable and fearful of their own health in hospital environments. Attention to these fears through the matter-of-fact presentation of facts about the patient's illness is important. As trust is gained, the staff can begin to listen to the specific concerns of family members and friends, not only in regard to the patient but for themselves.

The interaction of patients with other patients may present a two-edged sword since a comparison of deficits and eventual competition are introduced which provides patients with a sense of mutuality while also emphasizing differences, setting up conditions for a recrudescence of repressed sibling rivalries. The extent to which these are successful will depend on the individual's readiness for integration into a group and the presence of individuals competent in managing group processes. For the extremely handicapped, there may need to be protection by staff members until the group can begin to effect such support. There is the problem of in-groups and out-groups. There is above all the problem of limited knowledge about the interactions of groups, especially of those with chronic problems. It is likely that there are individual differences affecting the extent to which help may be forthcoming from a specific group, so that an individual's group experience may need to be titrated according to his needs.

Following discharge from active treatment units, patients experience an emotional letdown, including an increased awareness of limitations in physical recovery and sense of loss from the support of the ward. There is concern with the slowness of physical progress, the unsureness about previous relationships, questions about one's own usefulness at home and in the community, and economic security. Through the persistence of effort, including self-care and the encouragement of medical help, the individual gradually develops new interests and comes to take a measure of pride in his perseverance, stoicism and strength. Through a process of settling for short and intermediate term goals, the individual may continue to derive hope from more gradual progress.

Mastery in coping includes: 1) keeping distress within manageable limits; 2) generating encouragement and hope; 3) maintaining and developing a sense of personal worth; 4) maintaining or restoring relations with significant others; 5) enhancing prospects for physical recovery; and 6) enlarging prospects for favorable future situations.

Burns

Hamburg et al. studied the responses of severely burned patients through the rehabilitative stage (63). Seen as a problem in adaptation was the struggle of each patient with his personal problem, related not only to the extent of the injury itself but also to the interpretation of it. Also affecting adaptation were the life-threatening nature of the illness, pain, uncertainty about course of illness, toxicity, sedation, analgesia, and the effects of these anxieties and therapies on the mental apparatus. Adaptation was further influenced by internal psychological processes, two-person relationships, and group processes.

Emotional problems during the acute phase were minimalization followed by a marked concern which was addressed during the first several weeks to survival and subsequently to the extent of suffering. Concerns during this time frame are those of separation from home, doubt about future relationships with significant others, preoccupation with responsibility for the accident which included both self-blame and blame on others, and adequacy of communication with the physician and hospital staff.

In the emergency situation there were frequently clouding of the sensorium (exacerbated by narcotics), emotional constriction with tight control over recognition and expression of emotions, a manifestation of a "blah" attitude, resignation, and the sense of "one must take what comes without complaining." Specific defensive mechanisms included: 1) *repression and suppression*: a conscious effort to avoid thinking of unpleasant experience, an automatic exclusion from consciousness of affect associated with the acknowledged and recalled traumatic experience; 2) *denial*: a rejection by the individual of some easily recognizable and consensually validated aspect of external reality so that the victim thought, spoke, or acted *as if* this aspect of reality did not in fact exist; 3) *illusion, delusion and hallucination*: occurring gradually over time and related to both psychological processes and physical course; 4) *regression*: the presentation of demanding, complaining, attention-seeking behavior—markedly dependent relationships reminiscent of infantile dependence, an expressed need for frequently repeated reassurance from others; and 5) *re-working*: repetitive rumination over the traumatic experience in an effort to relieve residual tension. Less frequent and usually less severe defenses included withdrawal, religiosity, rationalization, and conversion reactions.

Concerns during the later stages of treatment related to a more objective assessment of the severity of the injury, the extent of residual damage, disfigurement, change of life plans, and finances. In addition, concerns were expressed about residual problems prior to the accident; the inability to participate in important tension-relieving activities which had been satisfying, gratifying, and enhancing to self-esteem; the threat to the capacity to be loved by others; disfigurement; dependency on others; possible impairment of sexual function; and handling of aggression, hostility, and anger while in the dependent position.

Recovery mechanisms that facilitated recovery were: 1) mobilization of hope: frequently derived by interaction with other patients with burns and members of the staff who were capable of helping; 2) the restoration of interpersonal relationships through personal assistance (nurses, physicians, Gray Ladies, Red Cross) and group activities (patient and staff). Group processes facilitated a mutuality of experience in which intimacy was attained. In these processes, there was little attempt to mobilize sympathy. Humor was utilized as a basis for more communication, overcoming personal positions, and restoring self-esteem through positive interactions with others. There occurred the testing of key individuals in the environment, especially staff members of the opposite sex. Pride was taken in active participation in the recovery process.

Andreason et al. (64) also noted the presence of anxiety, depression, fear of deformity, and delirium in adult patients during the acute phases. These were accompanied by refusal to eat, removal of grafts, and hostility expressed toward relatives and staff. Such behavior was frequently exacerbated at times of surgical procedures. In several patients, they identified the loss of a will to live that led to a disengagement with staff and other patients and minimal compliance with the treatment regimen.

Seligman et al. (65), studying the emotional responses of children with burns, identified these as depending on pre-burn factors: 1) emotional stability; 2) the "accident" in which the burn occurred; and 3) the history, personality, and family situation of the child.

Positive factors in survival related to early denial and withdrawal. However, subsequent studies suggest that while these may be adaptive in some children they are not so in all and behavior such as protest may be more advantageous in others depending on timing, other losses and parent-staff responses. Survival also related to the somatic responses (hypertension, ulcers, seizures, and infections), an interesting observation that requires further attention. The authors emphasized the need for psychiatrists and social workers to work with family and the nursing staff attending burned children.

Quinby and Bernstein (66) addressed the difficulty of new nurses working in burn units, noting the difficult challenge to their personal and professional identity which was derived from the discrepancy between their idealized expectations, their conflict between these goals and reality, and their resolution of this conflict.

Quindlen and Abram (67) have noted the frequency of delirium in burned patients, identifying: 1) a disturbed metabolic equilibrium; 2) altered neurologic function; 3) overstimulation by constant pain, surgical procedures, dressings, etc.; 4) lack of orienting stimuli—visual and auditory, aseptic isolation, and an inability to move; 5) emotional trauma due to a disfigurement and disability, and 6) inability of the patient to handle previous emotional problems. In patients with neurologic damage, they note the similarities between delirium of burns and Wernicke's encephalopathy in terms of the clinical symptoms and the pathologic changes. In both there appear cellular change in the grey matter, especially in the hypothalamus.

Sophistication has rapidly developed in the treatment of burns. Special environments and new methods of handling patients with burns have led to an array of specific problems. One of these, much noted but still under study, is the effect of the isolation of patients in order to prevent infections. In these units, patients are frequently unclothed, do not have direct communication with relatives, are often attended by masked and garbed staff, and are subject to a monotonous and unfamiliar environment. Burn centers are often distant from the patient's home so that contact with family members is infrequent and sporadic. In these situations, it is important to develop an ancillary staff of workers who are able to stand-in for the absent family and who are capable of writing letters, reading, chatting, and playing games. For the staff working in these special units and hospitals, support through group sessions led by psychiatrists and psychologists is helpful in bringing out the anxieties, and despondencies that arise around patients and between staff persons.

Severe Spinal Cord Injuries

About 5000 individuals per year are left quadraplegic or paraplegic secondary to cervical trauma, resulting in a total living population of such persons estimated at 150,000 (68). The average life expectancy of these individuals is seven years, with 77 percent of those under 25 and 55 percent of those between 25 and 34 surviving more than 10 years. Life expectancy is first determined by the completeness of the lesion. Lesions to the first three cervical levels are rapidly fatal because of respiratory paralysis. C-4 lesions are marked by total dependency and a short life span because of respiratory complications. C-5 lesions allow for neck motion, partial shoulder motion, and weak elbow flexion; there is better respiratory excursions and life expectancy therefore is increased. C-6 lesions provide for full innervation of shoulder motion, elbow flexion, weak wrist extension, and poor grasp. C-7 lesions provide for elbow extension which permits push-ups from a wheelchair and other transfer maneuvers; there may be some digital extension.

The greatest cause of death in quadraplegics is renal failure secondary to urinary tract infection. Suicide, either as an overt action or as "physiologic suicide," is common. In the latter situation, the patient neglects his personal and medical care, succumbing to decubiti, infections, and respiratory, cardiac, and renal failure. However, individual responses vary resulting in different outcomes. A major national example is that of the new head of the Veterans Administration who suffered the amputation of both legs and his right arm by a grenade during the Vietnam War. He demonstrates an individual's response through perseverance and motivation to newer rehabilitation techniques. Many of the latter have been pioneered by Howard Rusk (69) at the New York University Rehabilitation Unit. Rusk believes that an optimistic attitude of the physician and others is all important. Rehabilitation should be started early and carried on dynamically to the highest possible level of self sufficiency. The quadraplegic's existence consists of two phases, the bed and the wheelchair. Transfer from one to the other requires the help of an attendant. Constant problems include the potential for decubiti, blood pressure changes, proper nutrition, urine output, possible fractures and contractures, ankylosis, constipation, and renal infection. Frequent medical follow-ups and laboratory tests are necessary.

Despite severe impairment, with the assistance of special devices and through operant conditioning the patient can learn a number of skills increasing independence of function (70). After discharge, comprehensive home care is needed. The best asset of the quadraplegic is a strong, unified, resourceful family. However, such a resource is frequently lacking; nursing homes are usually inadequate and comprehensive specialized centers are few in number.

The acute phase of injury is manifested by spinal shock, the disappearance of all neural reflex below the transaction. There is a flaccid paralysis which later is followed by a spastic or hypertonic state of the skeletal muscles. Since spinal shock also affects the autonomic nervous system, there are marked variations in heart rate, respiration, regulation of blood pressure, control of temperature, lack of bladder and bowel control. With return of reflex activity, the subacute phase is initiated. This is characterized by: 1) spasticity and contractures, both of which are influenced by emotional attitudes as well as physical factors; 2) management of elimination tracts; 3) decubiti; 4) blood pressure irregularities; 5) respiratory complications; 6) osteoporosis; 7) autonomic hyperreflexia; 8) phantom pains and sensations; 9) impaired sexual function.

The predominant psychological aspect of quadraplegia is social atrophy (71), the extent of which interrelates with personal motivation. Nagler (72) has identified seven distinct psychological reaction types to severe cord injury: 1) early anxiety and reactive depression with initial failure to adjust to situation with subsequent change; 2) psychotic reaction with paranoid features associated with pre-morbid personality; 3) hopeless indifference occurring most frequently in the less intelligent; 4) a psychopathic reaction characterized by hostility; 5) extreme dependency, emotional immaturity associated with subsequent addiction; 6) an emotional explosive response with difficulty of channeling aggressive drives into productive accomplishments; and 7) an acceptance of disability, with good insight into limitations and potentialities.

Shoutz (73) has classified negative, neutralizing, and positive reactions in individuals with quadraplegia, which are useful in viewing a patient's willingness to participate in rehabilitation. Negative reactions include: gross confusion and uncertainty; panic or non-specific anxiety; nightmares; fear of loss of sanity; fear of death or dying; fear of becoming a physical, emotional or financial burden; feeling different from others and shame on exposure; vulnerability to rejection, emotional or physical attack; feelings of self-punishment; suicidal thoughts and death wishes; uncontrollable hostility; rejection by friends, family and society; feelings of being at the mercy of a cruel or unjust fate; feeling that the adult status is completely lost; and worry over the availability of physical assistance. Neutralizing reactions are: intellectual denial of illness; withdrawal from emotional reactivity through conversion of unpleasant affect; relief from responsibility of life; decentralizing the disability in relation to total personality; a feeling of having paid one's debts for past sins; and exploiting others. Positive reactions are: fantasizing future success; thinking of the disability as a new opportunity to correct old errors; full appreciation of life by almost dying; faith and hope for a miracle cure; a feeling of interpersonal worth derived from the care of others; a feeling of being selected for spiritual trials of suffering; and developing good values from non-physical aspects of existence.

Masterman (74) identified the following characteristics interfering with the rehabilitative process: academic underachievement; anxiety; dependency; depression; fantasy; guilt; hostility; hypochondriasis; interpersonal difficulties; inadequate emotional control; lack of self-confidence; lack of parental understanding; need for tender emotion; overprotection; projection of blame; psychosexual problems; reaction to standards; resentment of authority; reflexion; social withdrawal; thinking insufficiency; and unrealistically high goals.

In reviewing these observations, it is important that the presence of any one of these characteristics is likely to be observed in an individual at one or another phase of the illness. It is not the occasional occurrence of any one of these reactions but rather a sustained response that bodes for good adjustment or maladjustment over the long haul. When certain characteristics interfere with therapy, attention is indicated. Although an individual's previous personality has been stressed as a major factor in his subsequent adjustment to traumatic injury, it is not uncommon to observe major alterations in an individual's personality, suggesting growth and maturational processes that accompany major stress and challenges (75).

The typical reactions to quadraplegia can be identified by stages and the specific disabilities each individual faces. There are usually a withdrawal and isolation mechanism which minimizes the focus on self, a lack of spontaneity and initiative, a situational depression associated with disability and the future life role, a tendency toward ambivalence, indecision and passive submissive behavior, unrealistic thinking, and immature emotional expression (76). There follows an attempt to compensate for loss of a sense of self which includes the physical, sexual and personal, and a resulting dependency on others. Low self-esteem relates both to these losses and the debilitating aspects of the illness, including shame, anxiety, and guilt over excretory functions. As in other illnesses, the first phase is one of anxiety, depression, denial, grief, and mourning, accompanied by passivity and passive-aggression. Following this, there is an attempt to recrystallize the self, which may include the development of a new image based on acceptance and hope rather than hate. Aggression may be positively used in developing an active and constructive approach to the problems ahead (77). Successful rehabilitation depends on: 1) realism and clarity of goals; 2) suitable value standards and behavior; 3) adequate tolerance for frustration; 4) increasing degrees of autonomy (78). The key factor underlying this is motivation focused on a positive reason for living. Motivation can be encouraged, if not instilled, through strong relationships and trusting ties among therapists, relatives, and the patient. All attending the patient need to exude realistic confidence, hope, and direction. While only 10 percent of all patients with quadraplegia reach viable vocational goals, those who are younger, with higher educational levels, good premorbid work histories, ability to transport self, the ability to use special devices, and motivation have found work in clerical, sales, personnel, professional, technical, and managerial positions (79). Presently, sheltered workshops offer the most suitable environment for the severely disabled individual. With increased attention to the environmental needs of these individuals, opportunities in the open market place can be developed.

MacRae and Henderson (80) have stressed the need to teach patients with para- and quadraplegia how to handle their sexual limitations. Such instructions include: precise identification of neurophysiologic alterations, including motor and sensory; the increased need for rest, comfort, and avoidance of pain; attention to the esthetically distressing aspects of bowel and bladder functions; and prolonged counselling relating to the psychosocial aspects of altered sexual functioning, including learning a variety of new techniques and unfamiliar performances. On the other hand, Hanson and Franklin suggest that staff have tended to overemphasize the importance of sexual loss in men with spinal cord injuries as related to other functions (81). However, regardless of the extent of the individual's desire to become sexually re-engaged, there remains the need for the staff working most intimately with the patient to assist him or her in giving expression to fears, anxiety, frustration, shame, fantasy, and wishes. More general sexual counselling may be given by informed individuals in group sessions with patients and spouses. The use of written and audio-visual materials may help in patient education and in drawing out emotional feelings around sexual problems.

Wing (82) has studied the later stages of rehabilitation in terms of vocational training for severely incapacitated individuals, finding: 1) initial lack of confidence in ability to obtain and hold down a reasonable job; 2) improvement in confidence correlated with experiences on the unit and accompanied by a decrease in self-rated anxiety and depression; and 3) increase in confidence correlated with sustained employment after discharge. Improvement depended on: 1) an individual's ability to approach difficulties constructively; 2) a demonstration of the handicap's residual capacities; and 3) social influences such as a community where self-confidence in the face of severe difficulties was valued. Lack of improvement correlated with: 1) passive or casual approaches to rehabilitation; 2) strong idiosyncratic and unconstructive drives; and 3) higher magnitudes of psychiatric disorder.

Concepts of functional behaviorism may be applied particularly in the area of rehabilitation. Goldiamond (83) describes this approach as dealing with "the meaning or motivation of behavior in terms of its maintaining consequences." This pattern may be required for these consequences to occur. The behavior-consequence language deals directly with observables and potentially manipulatable events. The meaning of current behavior is assessed, *e.g.*, it is determined to be attention-getting, it is directed toward attaining a specific object, etc. On the basis of this, if the consequence is viewed as desirable, a program is developed which will alter the present methods by such techniques as negative reinforcement and encourage substitute patterns by such techniques as positive reinforcement. On the other hand, it may be necessary for patient and therapist to agree on an alternative goal. Once the goal has been mutually agreed upon, the therapist "develops a program which converts the current repertoire to the desired repertoire in a step-by-step manner." Programming includes programmed instruction, behavior modification, and biofeedback. Designing a program includes identifying: the starting point, the present behavior pattern of the patient, *i.e.*, his *current relevant repertoire;* the steps required to reach the target. In turn, the *target relevant repertoire* may become the current relevant one for the next target. A program requires a system of a *response-contingent-consequences* in which a "reward" is contained. Goldiamond has proposed a constructional approach as opposed to a pathological one by concentrating on the behavior to be established rather than on the one to be eliminated (84). In behavioral analysis, the focus is on goals rather than obstacles. Problem-solving begins with the raising of questions based first on what the goal is and subsequently on what is presently available and what needs to be provided in order to attain that goal.

Other Neurological Disorders

To a varying extent, the reactions of individuals to other neurological disorders pattern themselves after those observed in patients with quadra- and para-plegia. In most of these, at least initially, the extent of incapacitation is usually less catastrophic. On the other hand, the onset may be insidious and the course of the illness marked by remissions and exacerbations, each cycle leaving the individual further incapacitated. Consequently, individuals with progressive neurological disorders usch as amyotrophic lateral sclerosis and multiple sclerosis live in constant awareness of further deterioration and incapacitation. There are also more or less specific characteristics related to different neurologic disease. In ALS, for instance, the course may be marked by serious depression, sometimes of psychotic proportions whereas in many individuals with multiple sclerosis, there is a peculiar *la belle indifférence* that characterizes the process. The initial phases of the illness in these progressive kinds of disorders are marked by much anxiety over the still unknown basis of the early symptoms, their fluctuating presentations, the uncertainty of the diagnosis, and the elaborate examinations necessary for ascertaining the diagnosis.

Individuals experiencing subarachnoid hemorrhages and occlusive cerebrovascular disease have an intermediate course between the sudden cervical trauma in quadraplegia and the progressive diseases (85). About 5000 patients per year are admitted to hospitals with a diagnosis of subarachnoid hemorrhage. Fifty percent of conservatively managed patients die during the initial hospitalization, frequently because of recurrent hemorrhage. Those surviving the initial episode have a 20 percent risk of dying of recurrent hemorrhage in the next six months. Newer surgical techniques and active management during the acute phase have reduced these figures. Individuals with intracerebral hemorrhages are at greater risk when conservatively managed. Thrombotic strokes constitute the most common type of cerebrovascular accidents. When these events are secondary to extracranial occlusive cerebrovascular disease, surgical intervention is increasingly successful. Prognosis for return to previous function is better in those surviving subarachnoid hemorrhage than for those surviving thrombotic disease (86). Ford et al. identify that prognosis for survival can be made within the first few days after strokes (87). Factors associated with early death are: hemorrhage, advanced age, coma, signs of damage to extensive or critical areas of brain, and presence of cardiovascular disease. Functional recovery occurs most during the first month, with about half of the survivors regaining independence and up to 20 percent requiring complete care. Over five years, mortality reaches 50 percent.

Storey followed 261 patients six months to six years after subarachnoid hemorrhage (85). Forty-one percent demonstrated personality impairment while five percent showed improvement, possibly because of a leucotomy effect. Impairment correlated with the amount of brain damage, CNS signs and middle cerebral artery aneurysms. Most frequent changes were increases in anxiety and irritability with loss of vitality. Goldstein (88) noted the high presence of catastrophic reactions in patients sustaining irreversible CNS damage. These reactions included marked emotional lability in patients with deficits in cognitive functions when confronted by a novel situation. Individuals with such disorders require careful attention and protection from overwhelming stimulation requiring quick and novel adjustment. Individuals attending such patients need to be succinct, direct, clear, calm, patient, and matter of fact in their relationship. The great lability of affect needs to be met with calmness and soothing reassurance rather than confrontation.

Feldman et al. (89) compared functionally oriented medical care and formal rehabilitation management of patients with hemiplegia due to cerebrovascular disease. They concluded that the great majority of hemiparetic stroke victims can be rehabilitated adequately without formal rehabilitation services if proper attention is given to ambulation and self-care activities.

Pain

Patients with pain for whatever reason require a complete and detailed psychosocial evaluation in order to assess the relative influences of organic, psychological, and environmental factors affecting it (89). Pain has both a public and private meaning. The public meaning is that of scientific medicine that attempts to analyze it in terms of vectors: intensity, location, duration, radiation, quality, timing of onset, etc. These are then related to pains generally characteristic of organ system pathology. The private meaning of pain extends to all the painful experiences that the individual has ever had and the specific memories and interpretations which he relates to them. Generally, pain is seen as bad and frequently is associated with punishment, guilt, anger, sadness, and specific memories attending these kinds of feelings. It is also attended by the fantasy or expectation of obtaining relief not only through physical means but through the kinds of ministrations rendered by kind and empathetic parents. Whether or not there is a physical explanation for pain, the emotional sides need to be explored and suitably accommodated. When these aspects of pain have been attended to, the need for physical models of intervention is frequently of less magnitude (91).

Egbert et al. (92) in a controlled evaluation of 97 surgical patients undergoing elective procedures demonstrated that with encouragement and education in terms of learning what to expect during the postoperative period, how to relax, how to take deep breaths, how to move so as to remain comfortable after operation, the need for postoperative narcotic requirements was reduced by half and discharge time was 2 and 7/10 days earlier than that of the non-treated group. Similar observations have been made for patients undergoing amputation and radical breast surgery.

Zborowski (93) has addressed the cultural, sexual, and age differences in the expression of pain in a comparison of four ethno-cultural groups—Jewish, Italian, Irish, and "Old American" stock. Members of the former two groups are described as emotional in their responses to pain. Differences between these two suggested that while individuals of Italian extraction were concerned with immediacy of the pain experience and were disturbed by the actual sensation which they experienced in a given situation, patients of Jewish origin focused on the symptomatic meaning of pain and upon the significance of pain in relation to their health, welfare, and eventually the welfare of the families. These attitudes relate to drug acceptance and pain relief. The Italian calls for pain relief, is concerned with its analgesic effects, and on relief easily relinquishes his sufferings and manifests a happy and joyful disposition. The Jewish patient is reluctant to accept the drug and fearful of the effect of the drug on his general health, its habit-forming potential, and the fact that the drug does not cure. Such differences, when verified in the individual, suggest that in the first instance it is important to relieve the actual pain by medication first, whereas in the second, it is first indicated to relieve the anxieties with regard to the sources of pain. These two groups also tended to view physicians differently, the Italian group displaying a confident attitude, reinforced by the latter administering a pain-relieving drug, the Jewish group maintaining a skeptical attitude feeling that the mere relief of pain by the doctor's drugs does not testify to his skill to take care of the underlying illness.

"Old Americans," on the other hand, attempt to minimize pain; they avoid complaining and provoking pity, withdrawing when pain becomes too intense. In their relationships with the physician they tend to give matter-of-fact descriptions of the pain and assume the detached role of an unemotional observer. However, they are concerned about the significance of the pain which correlates with a pronounced health consciousness. The "Old American" patient in contrast to the Jewish one is optimistic as opposed to pessimistic in his future-orientation. The former's anxiety is greatly relieved when he feels something is being done about it in terms of specific activities and treatment. Irish patients on the other hand were depicted as stoical individuals capable of sustaining a great deal of pain. Intra-group variations were observed and were related to: the degree of Americanization; socio-economic background, education, and religiosity. The role of family in transmitting attitudes and emotional expression was also important in the reaction to pain by individuals. Hence, a knowledge of group attitudes toward pain is important to an understanding of an individual's reaction, a principle underscored by Wolff and his co-workers (94) in their early studies.

Cancer

Although cancer probably is not a unitary disease in terms of a single causative agent, but rather depends on a host of perhaps different factors operating together over time, the phenomenon of cancer as it is regarded by our present society is that of a more or

less relentless and progressive disease ultimately resulting in prolonged suffering and death. The fear of and reaction to this phenomenon in Western society is perhaps greater than to any other
illness. Although progress in terms of early diagnosis (carcinoma of
the cervix) and various therapeutic approaches to other organ cancers
have resulted in increased survival and five-year cures, there remains
a large number of cancers in which little progress in these dimensions
has occurred. The absence of an identifiable single agent increases
the anxiety that occurs when rational explanations are lacking and the
unknown looms large. In a very real sense, fear and anxiety in the
minds of healer and patient alike are oftentimes synonymous with
cancer.

Over the years, there have been attempts to identify specific personality characteristics for the individual vulnerable to developing
cancer. LeShan and Worthington (95, 96) identified pre-cancerous
traits which included a sense of despair and an inability to express
hostile feelings and emotions in self defense. Thomas (97) in her
prospective study of health and illness in Johns Hopkins medical
students found no overt characteristics for individuals who subsequently developed cancer. Rather, intrigued by this being the only
group for which she was unable to find a biological or psychological
marker or predictor of subsequent illness, she attributed this finding
to the individual's capacity for concealing feelings and emotional
expression. Later, Harrower (98), in a study of figure drawings by
these students, identified a characteristic pose for those who subsequently developed cancer. This was a pose of "ambivalence" in which
the figure had one arm extended outward and the other arm held in
against the body. Kissen (99) has studied the personalities of
individuals who smoke, suggesting that this behavior is utilized as a
means of suppressing emotional expression. Goldfarb et al. (100)
have observed that patients with malignancies survive longer when
they can decrease their anxiety by outward action. Koroljow (101)
correlated the treatment of depression with temporary cessation of
tumor growth in patients with cancer. Mueller and Watkin (102)
correlated plasma free fatty acid with rate of growth of malignancy,
similar to patterns in patients with fear, repressed anger and depres-

sion (103). These inconclusive and sporadic findings do not justify postulating emotions as an etiologic factor in malignancy, but suggest reactions commonly enough found among cancer patients to alert the clinician to consider therapy for them.

Several authors have noted the delay exhibited by patients with cancer in seeking medical attention (104, 105). Henderson related a previous experience of cancer affecting members of family, friends, or acquaintances as a factor in delay as well as personal anxiety. Relationship with a supportive physician and information were effective in bringing patients for diagnosis and treatment early. Hackett et al. found: detection of cancer through routine examination ensured the least delay; worry about the condition reduced delay time more than pain, incapacity or other factors; patients of higher social class sought help significantly sooner than the less privileged; and delay was less in patients who referred to their condition as cancer, tumor, or growth. Since early detection is considered the prime factor in the effective treatment of cancer, attention to the mechanisms of delay in patients with symptoms becomes the obligation of all physicians involved in the care of patients, including the psychiatrist.

Hinton (106) describes patients "bearing cancer" as showing an initial preoccupation with physical symptoms, especially pain, disfigurement, concern over the future, loss of work, dependency, alienation, depression, anxiety, and aggression. Coping mechanisms included minimalization, vigilance, and repressive ego defenses, including repression, guilt, and projection. Suicidal attempts as messages of appeal, anger, and despair were relatively frequent. As opposed to rejection, some patients could accept cancer with a quiet courage or even a sense of bearing aloft.

Milton (107) describes several stages in the course of the patient with malignant disease. The first is the realization of a disease; the second begins with the diagnosis of the malignancy and denial, followed by the "why me" reaction. There is then the preoccupation with the treatment of the disease and its effects such as radical mastectomy, colostomy, and radical lymph node dissections. The third stage is that when incurability is realized. The fourth stage is that of the dying patient. The patient's fears include those of losing dignity and of becoming a thing. The initial defense of denial is followed by withdrawal and subsequently by accepting reality. Later, there may be rejection of consequences, false jocularity, and progressive feelings of rejection and rejection of others. Solzhenitsyn (108) has expressed the latter as "growing like a wall behind me, the patient on one side—friends, family on the other." For specific diseases, there are specific reactions such as the loss of a symbolic organ. Renneker and Cutler (109) review the experiences of patients to the loss of a breast. This was frequently experienced as an end to productive motherhood, a punctuation to sexual attractiveness and activity. While these feelings may be less expressed today, they are still present beneath the surface in many individuals and their spouses. Asken (110) cites the need for pre operative counselling and post operative rehabilitation in patients undergoing mastectomy.

At different ages the management of cancer in the patient by the physician varies. Since, at least initially, the idea of having cancer is equated by many individuals with having a "terminal illness," the reactions of individuals are partly based upon the attitude of death. The idea of death is different at different ages (111). Nagy has written of the child's idea of death (112). At age five and under, death is seen as like going to sleep. It is not permanent. The dead return. Close to the age of 10, death is seen like going to another land after a short period, several days of stillness. The other land is described in heaven-like terms. The adolescent's concept of death cognitively is closer to the adult's, but affectively the adolescent has little relatedness with the concept. Even in the face of great illness, the idea of one's own vulnerability and ultimate destructibility is frequently held as absurd. Much of adolescence may be seen as death-defying acts of bravado both by the ill and the well. Only slowly during the early adult years, does a more adult-like response to the inevitability of death occur. Marriage, the birth of children and the ultimate death of parents give real testimony to the progression of generations and are documented by vows, buying of insurance policies, and the writing of wills.

As the body of the individual or those of his friends begin to give way to the progressive and degenerative diseases of middle age, a more final acknowledgment of the death of the individual emerges and begins to shape the way in which the individual chooses to live his remaining life. This is true for both the ill and well. For the ill, the urgency to live as fully as possible, to complete those major tasks that have been undertaken, and to leave something behind are paramount. Such desire and activity may paradoxically interfere in the vital life relationships that the individual also wishes to leave behind, especially the personal legacy for one's children. For the older individual, the thought and subject of death, while omnipresent, are less the focus of interest. It takes a distant second place to life, despite protests to the contrary. Illness and its potential threats to life may be more easily taken in stride, the individual bargaining to get as much out of his remaining life as he can. Thus, the attitudes that one has toward death have much to do with the acknowledgement and acceptance of illness. This is further colored by the life phase the individual is in and the life tasks before him.

What the physician tells the patient as well as how he does this will depend on where that individual is in his developmental course, what he can hear, what he can understand, what he can handle, what he must handle to carry out his responsibilities to significant others and to himself in terms of the legacy he would leave behind. The physician takes his first cues from the patient, allowing open communication and discussion. He can go no faster than the patient. The child's questions that may sound the same as the adult's are different. They demand different answers. The adolescent's dilemma is perhaps the most difficult for the physician, as are most adolescent dilemmas. Not only is it fraught with the physician's own counter-transference in terms of his own adolescence, but he finds it difficult to accept the idea that the completion of adolescent tasks is as essential to the latter's life as the treatment of the disease. The management of these two courses frequently seem at opposite ends of a spectrum of life. In the adolescent much of the concern about death is manifested by the problems about living the life of the adolescent. Concern displaced onto seemingly mundane concerns: Can one still wear a bikini? What about a wig? Death like sex is a very private and personal matter, one which is obvious and not obvious at the same time. The behavior of the individual will frequently appear to be contrary to the best interest of himself as patient. The resolution of this dichotomy is not always easy. Nor is it with any problem of any adolescent.

In the adolescent (113) personality integration has not been completed nor have adult defense mechanisms been fully evolved thereby interfering with adult-like adjustment. Alterations in self-concept are frequent, resulting in a sense of being different and no longer belonging. Coping processes often reflect denial of illness, overcompensation, intellectualization, and anger. Dishonesty on the part of physicians, parents, or others is not tolerated. Periodic depressions occur, but are brief. Alterations in body image relates to disfigurement incurred during the course of treatment: alopecia, radiation, dermatitis, and amputation. Interpersonal relations are compromised by fear of rejection, distrust, and overprotection by parents. Concerns over the future exist and interestingly are those about college, marriage, and children. Fears of sterility as well as sexual unattractiveness may lead to behavior resulting in out-of-wedlock pregnancy. Many of the problems observed are the results of failure by parents and other adults to view the adolescent as an individual in the stage of development with many of the preoccupations and aspirations of his peers. Death, when even acknowledged, is viewed differently from that of an adult. Denial in this age group, when it does not lead to neglect of treatment, frequently appears to be a useful coping device. It is not unusual to observe the adolescent taking care of his parents while seeking his own courageous reaching out and relating with peers similarly afflicted and often of the opposite sex.

In the adult patient, the physician's task is to support the life-appointed tasks that the patient has wittingly or unwittingly taken upon himself. These may be the ordering of business affairs, attention to present and future family affairs, and attempts to plan a course through a prolonged and progressive illness. He may need the assistance of experts other than those of the physician. A major task for mothers is the projection of her care of her children onto others for the future. These tasks are neither easily nor rapidly accomplished, but are pursued deliberately and sometimes silently over many months. In the resolution of these problems, psychiatric counselling is frequently advisable. Norton's (114) account of her work with a dying mother of two is a graphic picture of one role that a physician can fulfill in the care of a patient.

Stehlin and Beach (115) outline four processes in the work of the physician with a patient with cancer. First is the assessment of the patient's attitude toward cancer. This depends upon an open discussion which cannot be pursued until ventilation of affect has been facilitated. In this, the physician can use didactic knowledge, such as: suggesting that the cancer did not begin yesterday; that the patient has already lived with it a long time; that while there is much that is known, there is also much that is not; that the spread of cancer is related to many individual factors that include optimism, hope, determination; that so long as life continues, one lives and can live as fully as possible. Second, he needs to clarify and explain the physical factors associated with the disease and the methods available for treatment. In doing this, he needs to stay with the patient, not going beyond what the patient is able to hear or understand. In doing this, he is communicating a sense of control. A third exploration involves an elicitation of the patient's attitudes toward life in general, his sense of self, of his will to live, and of his attempt to realize the full potential of this life by living as fully as possible at the present. The fourth dimension relates to the attitudes and personality of the physician: his ability to communicate that both he and the patient are in this world together; are potential victims of the same fate; that each of their lives is vital and directed, and in this instance, allied against the disease in the patient; and that this too is part of living.

Davies et al. (116) have emphasized the organic factors affecting psychological adjustment in patients with cancer. Mild intellectual impairments are associated with better adjustment and longer survival. These are associated with less anxiety and despair. An apathetic-given-up attitude correlated with earlier death and greater illness. Many of the patients observed in this study were more concerned about their illness, pain and its relief, and getting home for a weekend than in talking about dying and death.

Schonfeld (117) identified coping and return to work in patients successfully treated for cancer with lower scores on the morale loss scale and higher scores on the well-being scale of the MMPI than those not returning to work. There were also lower scores on the measure of covert, although not of overt, anxiety from those not returning to work. The latter scored highest on situational fears. For many kinds of illness, seemingly successful management of the physical factors does not correspond with high levels of social readjustment, such as return to work. This has been documented in patients with mental illness and cardiac problems as well as others. Many of the factors influencing this are still in need of identification. Among the factors seemed to be those related to the anxieties and fears of the unafflicted; their efforts to put themselves at a distance from illness; the impetus for employers to maintain low company paid health and death benefit plans; and the failure of private and public employers to make adequate accommodations for the handicapped. However, studies also suggest that much of the failure for coping relates to the altered sense of self in the individual. Repeatedly, anxiety and depressed stages have been identified, although the extent and variations of these are often left undescribed. Identification and treatment of these are also left undescribed. Identification and treatment of these stages appears unsystematic, oftentimes ignored and unsuspected. Following treatment procedures, medical facilities and physicians usually make only cursory examination as to social, business, and family readjustment.

More recently group therapy for patients with various illnesses has been proposed. Bilodeau and Hackett (118) have described this for patients sustaining myocardial infarction and for their spouses. Yalom (119) has recently reported on group therapy for cancer patients. In these situations, he emphasizes that the psychiatrist must accept the anger of patients, their sense of vulnerability and impatience in the face of the disease and death, theirs and their patients. The patient's irrational anger is frequently displaced. Patients expect physicians to meet unrealistic demands, to be all-knowing, all-protecting and the ultimate rescuers. Rational anger was directed toward oncologists and surgeons who had left them uninformed and excluded them from decisions affecting treatment. Patients felt that they had been abandoned at a time when support was most needed. The open group expression and confrontation were seen as allowing patients to move into a richer mode of experience. Yalom suggests that several months' experience as an apprentice is essential for most psychiatrists to participate in such group processes. More recently, Yalom and Lieberman have collaborated in a study of self-help groups, such as ileostomy clubs, mended-heart societies, groups of individuals with hemophilia, ureterostomies, mastectomies, etc., in an attempt to evaluate their roles in individual adjustment and coping.

Chronic Hemodialysis and Renal Transplant

Presently, there are about 7000 individuals on hemodialysis. This level is expected to increase to a level between 15,000 and 30,000 individuals annually. The cost of maintaining this number on hemodialysis and a smaller subpopulation for one or more renal transplants each will compete for an increasing part of the health dollar. The ethical dimensions of this aspect of the problem has and will continue to concern all who are involved with it (120). Since hemodialysis was first instituted, many physical and emotional problems have been observed in patients undergoing this procedure. Because of these two factors, scarce medical resources and difficulties in adapting and surviving in hemodialysis, attempts have been made to identify those factors which correlate with a good prognosis. Patient assessment is made on: 1) capacity for self care, based on previous emotional stability, stable behavior, wish to survive and acceptance of authority; 2) capacity for rehabilitation, based on motivation, ability to adapt, firm identifications with family, friends, and occupation, and high self-esteem; and 3) capacity to adapt to stress (121). Successful adaptation correlates with: 1) high intelligence; 2) less defensive attitude; 3) less reliance on somatic defenses (hypochondriasis and hysteria); and 4) emotional support from family. Evaluation observes: 1) past and present level of functioning, especially in marriage and job; 2) ego resources for successful adaptation to increased demands; and 3) anticipated approaches to solving psychological problems occasioned by the treatment.

A number of observers have identified that adaptation occurs in a stepwise process (122, 123, 124). The initial evaluation of suitability occurs in the first stage when the patient is in a severely toxic state, manifesting fatigue, apathy, drowsiness, inability to concentrate, depression, and emotional instability. This toxic state is directly related to the multiple metabolic imbalances that occur with decreased renal function and the resulting uremia. When the renal dysfunction has been prolonged, there may also be anemia which will contribute to the altered state of consciousness with its cognitive deficits in the areas of orientation, memory, concentration and abstraction, emotional lability, and visual motor incoordination.

The second phase commences with the first hemodialysis and lasts one to three weeks during which the patient reaches physiological equilibrium: a decrease in blood urea nitrogen and improved electrolyte balance. This is accompanied by a decrease in apathy, an increased sense of well-being and sometimes euphoria, sometimes identified as the honeymoon phase. It ends with the patient's awareness of his responsibility in assisting in the program and progressively to take up his social and professional responsibilities. Associated with the dialysis experience, there may be transient episodes of anxiety and insomnia. A third phase, one of equilibrium, during which disenchantment and discouragement are present, occurs between the third week and the third month. During this time, the dialysand is physically weak, often anxious, and sometimes depressed, demonstrates conflicts over dependency on the machine and the staff, and experiences headaches and episodes of vomiting related to the dialysis.

Perhaps not enough attention has been paid to the relatively rapid and marked change in consciousness that occurs over the period of dialysis, with the individual reverting from a relatively lethargic state to one of hypervigilance and alertness following the electrolytic corrections. Electroencephalograms that have been taken throughout the dialysis correlate this physiologically. Since the beginning of chronic dialysis, much has been written describing the neurological disorders that have been observed during treatment. Wakim (125) has described a dialysis disequilibrium syndrome as including: headache, vomiting, muscular twitchings and tremors, disorientation, convulsive seizures, episodes of ventricular tachycardia and other cardiac irregularities. He has correlated these symptoms and discusses their etiology in terms of cerebral edema caused by a reverse urea effect; hypoglycemia, alterations in carbon dioxide tension; change in potassium and calcium levels; shifts in other electrolytes; and dehydration. Tyler (126) described neurologic disorders occurring with infections and unusual central nervous system tumors of possible reticuloendothelial origin, possibly related to immunosuppressant therapy in patients receiving renal transplants. Savoy (127) and others have observed hyperparathyroidism in patients on chronic dialysis presenting with pruritus and emotional changes, including irritability, depression, and paranoid delusions. Raskin and Fishman (128) noted the occurrence of neurological disorders in renal failure as including subdural hematoma, Wernicke's encephalopathy, mycotic and cytomegalovirus infections. Mahurkar (129) describes a syndrome he calls dialysis dementia as a progressive mental deterioration with dyspraxia, facial grimacing, myoclonus and general seizures. Alfrey (130) finds evidence to suggest that the dialysis encephalopathy syndrome may relate to high central nervous system levels of aluminum as a result of the dialysate.

Thus it would seem that it is difficult to separate specific metabolic factors from specific emotional ones in attempting to interpret the reactions of patients on dialysis during these two phases. Since the mid-sixties, investigators have been describing the psychological reactions of patients to dialysis (131). Abram (132) discussed the stress of dialysis in terms of the emotional conflicts raised around dependency-independency which frequently led to rebellion against the medical regimen. He stressed the need for criteria to be used in a process of selecting candidates. He identified the need of the psychiatrist to examine with the patient the meaning of prolongation of life for that patient while attempting a resolution of the conflict between dependency on the machine and staff with the inherent independence in maintaining a "normal" life. DeNour (133) described uniform defenses of denial, displacement, isolation, reaction formation, and projection in nine patients undergoing dialysis over a year's time as being adaptive, but leading to ego restriction that compromised interactions with others and adjustment to pre-illness life patterns. This study noted the dependency of patients on the machine and the difficulty in handling the aggression resulting from this dependency. Brain dysfunction was also identified as a compromising factor to successful adaptation. Beard (134) described the fear of imminent death as an immediate, initial and recurring phenomenon at the time of diagnosis and throughout the spectrum of dialysis and transplantation. Discouragement, sadness, self-depreciation, hopelessness, resentment, and loneliness were accompaniments of the dialysis. On the other hand, fear of living related to a view of the less than satisfactory life, the sense of chronic debilitation, and the identification by self and others of the individual as a handicapped individual. Successful coping related to an ability to share, enter into and maintain relationships with others, maturity and a capacity for flexibility.

Short (135) described the unusual demands placed on the patient, family and dialysis team, emphasizing the ubiquitous presence of denial, and suggesting that at least initially it served as an effective mental mechanism helping the various individuals to cope with a continuing unsatisfactory situation. While it may be appropriate for the individual and family at some stages, it is inappropriate for the dialysis team both in terms of themselves as well as in terms of addressing non-compliance and other kinds of reactive behavior in patients and families. Halper (136) in an excellent brief review article noted the multiple difficulties encountered by patients in dialysis programs, including the fluctuation in cognitive functioning during dialysis, leading oftentimes to permanent deterioration. He identified denial, oftentimes seen as adaptive in the early stages of illness, to be restricting during later stages, especially in the ventilation of the anger, pain, discomfort, and frustration that individuals on dialysis experience. He associated denial with suicidal behavior and the wish to no longer live, a phenomenon also identified by others. Abram (137) correlated suicide with the death of a parent, divorce, and the relative threat of passivity and inactivity in the male. Goldstein (138) noted its relationship to the lack of adherence to a treatment protocol as an attempt to reduce the anxiety resulting from the patient's recognition of his heavy responsibility in the program. McKegney (46) saw these patients as having had repeated losses, the most recent of which was renal failure, who had essentially given-up. He also identified the cognitive dissonance between patient and staff relative to objectives, goals, values, and the problems of life on dialysis. When such behavior and patients are identified, the option of ceasing dialysis by conscious decision needs to be addressed openly and individually with the patient. Glassman (139), using the California Personality Index and the Shipman test, described the discordance between test scores, revealing a high sense of well-being and low scores for anxiety and depression, respectively, and the clinical observations of lethargy, depression, pruritus, peripheral neuropathy and shunt infections. Massive denial, they felt, contributed to a delusional process that led to eating and drinking binges and decreased survival. DeNour (140) correlated non-compliance with the medical regimen with low frustration tolerance, primary and secondary gains from the sick role. Acting-out behavior, while present in both compliers and non-compliers, was greater in the latter.

A fourth phase of adjustment occurs between the third and sixth months for some, but not all, patients. In this phase, the problems encountered relate to living rather than dying. Patients have come to assume increasing responsibility for their care, and learned to be aware of imminent complications and the hazards of deviation from the prescribed regimen. There is also the recognition of the progressive deterioration and alterations that occur with chronic dialysis. Lindner (141) has described the accelerated atherosclerosis in these patients; Lim (142) the presence of gonadal dysfunction in uremic men; and Levy (143) impotence and diminished orgasm as related to emotional factors. The conflicts around sexuality involve the symbolic significance of the urinary tract: the functional relationship to the uro-genital system, urination, and genital activity. Viederman (144) sees the whole process of hemodialysis as evoking conscious and unconscious fantasies relating to early developmental stages, especially related to the mother-child interaction and hopeless dependency. He feels that the treatment situation requires a regression (adaptive or maladaptive) to early life stages, suggesting that the quality and degree of conflict which reemerges and the past solutions to early conflicts will affect the quality of the adaptation to treatment. Patients will do poorly unless they have developed a particularly gratifying infantile mutuality with the mothers which engendered a deep sense of basic trust, and hope which persists in the face of severe frustration.

Most investigators have focused on the social environment of the patient undergoing dialysis, citing relationships with staff and family. Foster (145) correlated survival with affiliation with the Roman Catholic faith and continued presence of both parents, as well as with low mean blood urea nitrogen levels. Length of survival correlated with the constraint scale on the Miller-Quinlan Boundary Image Test. Gillum (146) suggested that compliance depended upon four factors: 1) psychological; 2) environmental and social; 3) characteristics of the treatment regimen; and 4) patient-physician interaction. DeNour (147) predicted adjustment to dialysis in terms of compliance with diet, rehabilitation to social and work situations and the patient's psychological condition as reflected by four aspects—depression, suicidal tendencies, anxiety, and psychotic complications. In comparing results on the research unit with other groups, she found the studied patients fulfilled their potential for adjustment to a greater degree than the controls, who showed more depression and more non-compliance. She suggests that this related to the presence of a psychiatrist and a social worker on the unit, but questioned whether this was the result of direct interactions with patients or through indirect work with physicians and staff.

Marshall (148) addressed the effective use of a psychiatric consultant on a dialysis unit in group meetings of patients, staff meetings, the evaluation of patients, and ward routines. MacNamara (149) identifies the role of the social worker on the dialysis and homotransplant units working with transplant donors and recipients. She found that the focus of psychiatrists has frequently been only on the hospital course of the patient, with less attention to the family, donors, and even staff. First and foremost, she felt the essential need imposed by the illness on the patient was one of self-control. Patients were concerned about: the reactions of spouses and children; loss of status; deprivation of formerly gratifying activities—eating, drinking, sexual relations; emotions of anger, guilt, and anxiety; and especially in finding outlets for tension and aggression. Crammond (150) defined the role of the psychiatrist as: 1) assessing and assisting patients, staff and family responses under stress; 2) educating staff as to the emotional responses of patients and families to the frequent changes in staff; 3) selection of patients for dialysis and transplant; 4) involving the community in the selection process of dialysis candidates; and 5) working with patients and families about the anxieties and hopes regarding transplant. Shambaugh (151) studied spouses under stress, noting a progressive lessening of panic and denial and increasing openness and interaction leading to a sense of emotional separateness from partners. This would seem to be a double-edged sword were it to result in withdrawal from the partner's needs.

Home Dialysis

In order to accommodate the increasing numbers of individuals requiring dialysis, with the expense and inconveniences imposed upon families and patients, home dialysis has become increasingly common. It is not without its specific hazards and specific problems. Smith (152) in discussing the advantages and disadvantages noted that the idea of home dialysis needs to be part of the initial contract with the patient. Patients where this had not been discussed had difficulty in transferring from the hospital to the home situation. Also noted were the frustrations for patients and staff over delays caused by administrative decisions, obtaining the equipment, and educating patient and spouse. Success or failure depended upon not only the presence of a spouse, but of an individual capable of withstanding the heavy responsibility and onerous duties imposed.

Brown (153) identifies four factors relating to the success of home dialysis: 1) extent of change in physical and emotional state secondary to the disease; 2) source and extent of financial support; 3) role and relationship of helper to the patient; and 4) the importance that the patient perceived dialysis had to his daily life. Success depended on the recognition by patient and spouse of the imposing roles demanded by dialysis incompatible with the pre-existing ones, as well as on the ability to accept these changed relationships. Success also depended on an ability to gain a sense of independence from the machine and redevelopment of social contacts and interests. Staff as well as patients and families should realize that a full-time job is neither important nor possible for all dialysands. Blagg (154), focusing on the physical complications of dialysis previously mentioned, emphasized problems with anticoagulation, infections, shunts and fistulas, and equipment in home dialysis. He noted that psychologic problems were greater in the young than in the old who had less difficulty adjusting to the rigid schedule demanded by dialysis. Fishman (155) reported on adjustment to home dialysis as relating to psychometric variables established during the first week of dialysis rather than to background variables. For the patient, elevated MMPI and MAACL scores on anxiety, depression, hostility scales correlated with more numerous complaints of physical symptoms on dialysis. For the relative, high scores on anxiety, depression, hostility, competitiveness, and introversion likewise correlated with more complaints of physical symptoms while on dialysis by the patient. First year on dialysis adjustment correlated with present problem-solving ability rather than past learning as measured by the Shipley-Hartford I.Q. Scale. However, the physical health of the patient after the initial week on dialysis did not correlate with emotional adjustment but with survival.

Transplant

Although the socio-psycho-biological aspects of transplants have frequently been grouped with those of dialysis, there are specific additional problems relating to the donor or the cadaver donor's family and his relationship to the recipient (156). Again, this is a transitional relationship with changes occurring over time. There is, first, anxiety over finding a donor, then over making a specific request of the donor, the multiple pressures on the donor both internal (obligation) and external (the family), the sense of obligation of the recipient to donor or donor's family, the sense of guilt by the recipient in the event of rejection, the specific hazards of immunosuppressant and steroid therapy to the physical and emotional state of the patient, the changing focus of attention by all directed at one stage to the donor back to the recipient; and, finally, the ordeal of second and even third transplants in the event of rejection (157, 158, 159).

Psychotherapy with patients on chronic hemodialysis is not only possible but necessary and involves not only the patient, but family, staff, and potential donors and their families. Hence, the complexities are great in terms of who is the identified object for therapy and who is the identified therapist at any point in time. There is further the question of individual therapy in addition or as opposed to group therapy. There is always the ethical issue of confidentiality and the almost certain infringement on the usual patient-physician relationship. Therapy will follow and relate to the stresses of dialysis identified above. These include: 1) alteration in body concept by threatened loss, dysfunction and presence of shunt; 2) dependency on machine; 3) threat of death; and 4) frustration in coping with drives (aggression) or loss of drive (sexual). Therapy addresses denial, the marked ego restriction and personality impoverishment observed in these patients. The extent of therapy will depend on the patient's resistance, tolerance for increased anxiety, ability to form interpersonal relationships, and the capacity of the therapist to get involved with life-threatening and debilitating problems. The focus of therapy is frequently that of addressing: a) the issue of dependence-independence; b) bringing out and channeling aggression; c) coping with the threat of death; d) acceptance of time-limited regression; and e) accepting an altered sense of body image (54).

As implied in the preceding overview, the phenomenon of dialysis and organ transplant occurs in an environment that transcends the usual physician-patient dyad focusing on specific physical or emotional problems, but rather involves many individuals and many problems relating to modern society and technology and its values that directly and indirectly affect the patient-physician interaction. These are best considered by Fox and Swazey (160) in *The Courage to Fail.*

THE FAMILY AND ILLNESS

Throughout the preceding sections, we have focused on the individual's experience of illness as occurring in and relating to an environment, dependent not only on his past existence but on the support of those individuals around him, most of all the family. In more recent times, we have come to think and speak less of illness in the individual and more about illness in and of the family. For illness, whether it is specified as being in a a specific individual or not, seems to always relate to preceding or concurrent illness in the family. When illness occurs in the family, Anthony (161) observes: 1) changes in intrafamilial dominance; 2) a reevaluation of family member roles; 3) shifts in the strength and directions of feelings between family members; 4) alterations in sexual patterns; 5) new patterns of maintaining discipline; and 6) reordering of home routines. Illness and incapacitation of the father result in his becoming a relative non-entity with a disregard for his rulings. Even upon recovery, he failed to regain all of his former dominance.

Jackson (162) noted four patterns of adjustment to the crisis of illness: 1) the family may return to its normal level of adjustment; 2) the family may fail to recover for a while, if it has previously been a poorly organized unit; 3) with repeated illness, the lack of family interaction is chronically impaired with further deterioration after each episode; and 4) the level of interaction is frequently higher following illness. Koos (163) describes the extrafamilial effects of illness as withdrawal from active contact with the outside world so that affiliations and relationships are gradually discarded. Shame is important in bringing about such withdrawal from active contact. This may become amalgamated with guilt reactions already provoked in individual family members as a consequence of assumed responsibility for the illness. Parsons and Fox (164) view illness as a form of deviant behavior and as an escape from the pressures of everyday life. Small families are vulnerable to the strains of illness and members exploit it. Frequently, it "provides" a solution for life problems of individual family members. Families overreact to the passive, dependent nature of illness and its inferior childlike status by being more sympathetic, supportive, indulgent, and persuasive than they need to be, because they project their own regressive needs on the sick individual. Thus becoming sick entails the learning of a sick role. Anthony, viewing illness in the family as a challenge, adopts Toynbee's analysis of growth, breakdown, and disintegration in social groups as including the potential for: 1) growth and differentiation; 2) breakdown and rally; and 3) rout and disintegration. Spiegel (165) identifies three stages of accommodation of a family to illness in one of its members. The first is one of manipulation in which the family exercises role induction measures such as coercing, coaxing, evaluating, unmasking, and provoking, only to be met by the patient's counterinduction or neutralization measures of defying, withholding, denying, masking, and postponing. Subsequently, role reversal techniques will be used which may lead to role modification, using measures such as joking, referral, exploring, compromising, and consolidating.

These studies emphasize that the care of the patient with a chronic illness necessitates care and attention of the family as well. Oftentimes, family members are left to shift for themselves under the burden of illness, isolated both from the attention to the patient by the physician or the concern of other family members and friends. Group and family therapeutic methods are frequently useful in detecting and alleviating distress resulting from illness in the family. Individual attention by the physician and/or consulting psychiatrist, however brief, may serve to elicit unsuspected tensions and conflicts within the family. No evaluation or treatment of an individual is complete until at least one other member of the family has been interviewed.

FIGURE 13

The Role of the Liaison Psychiatrist

1. Know the patients: Listen to them.
2. Know the field: Have an internship.
3. Know the staff: Eat with them.
4. Be seen: Go on the ward.
5. Be available: At office and home.
6. Know your limits: They want you for *your* expertise.
7. Make no promises: Above what you can give.
8. Communicate simply: In English.
9. Stick to empirical
   data, not theory: Theory is fine in conferences.
10. Be ethical: Confidentiality.

SUMMARY

The approach to the patient (Figure 13) with illness resulting in chronic disability demands first a knowledge of the patient's previous life situation, his early development, his adjustment to the stresses of that environment, the major behavior and personality characteristics that developed in that environment, the present life situation of the person (166) when he became ill, his reactions to the acute and convalescent phases of illness, an assessment of the environmental resources available to the individual at the present time, especially significant others. Most important, perhaps, is the patient's capacity (167) for optimism and faith in learning new ways for survival.

REFERENCES

1. KIMBALL, C. P.: Conceptual Developments in Psychosomatic Medicine: 1939-1969. *Ann. Int. Med.*, 73:307-316, 1970.
2. KIMBALL, C. P.: Languages of Psychosomatic Medicine. Presented at the 11th European Conference for Psychosomatic

Research at the University of Heidelberg, Sept. 16, 1976. In Press: Basel: S. Karger.

3. GRINKER, R. R. (Ed.): *Toward a Unified Theory of Human Behavior: An Introduction to General Systems Theory.* 2nd Edition. New York: Basic Books, 1967.

4. HELLER, J.: *Something Happened.* New York: Random House-Ballantine Books, 1975.

5. SHAPIRO, D.: *Neurotic Styles.* New York: Basic Books, 1965.

6. LEVINE, R. A.: *Culture, Behavior and Personality.* Chicago: Aldine Publishing Co., 1973.

7. HOLMES, T. H. and RAHE, R. H.: The Social Readjustment Rating Scale. *J. Psychosom. Res.*, 11:213-218, 1967.

8. CODDINGTON, R. D.: The Significance of Life Events as Etiologic Factors in the Diseases of Children, I. *J. Psychosom. Res.*, 16:7-18, 1972.

9. PAYKEL, E. S., PRUSOFF, B. A., and UHLENHUTH, E. H.: Scaling of Life Events. *Arch. Gen. Psych.*, 25:340-347, 1971.

10. SCHMALE, A. H.: Relationship of Separation and Depression to Disease. I. A Report on a Hospitalized Medical Population. *Psychosom. Med.*, 20:259-277, 1958.

11. SAPIRA, J. D., SCHEILP, E. T., MORIARTY, R., and SHAPIRO, A.: Difference in Perception Between Hypertensive and Normotensive Populations. *Psychosom. Med.*, 33:239-250, 1971.

12. REISER, M. F.: Theoretical Considerations of the Role of Psychological Factors in Pathogenesis and Etiology of Essential Hypertension. In M. Koster, H. Musaph, and P. Visser (Eds.), *Psychosomatics in Essential Hypertension. Bibl. Psychiat.*, 144:117-124, 1970. Basel: Karger.

13. RAHE, R. H.: Stress and Strain in Coronary Heart Disease. *J. So. Carolina Med. Assoc.*, 72:7-14, 1976, No. 2 Supplement.

14. ALEXANDER, F.: *Psychosomatic Medicine.* New York: W. W. Norton & Co., 1950.

15. BRIDGER, W. H.: Sensory Discrimination and Autonomic Function in the Newborn. *J. Amer. Acad. Child Psychiat.*, 1:67-82, 1962.

16. MIRSKY, I. A.: Physiologic, Psychologic and Social Determinants in the Etiology of Duodenal Ulcer. *Amer. J. Dig. Dis.*, 3:285-314, 1958.

17. WEINER, H., THALER, M., REISER, M. F., and MIRSKY, I. A.: Etiology of Duodenal Ulcer. I. Relation of Specific Psychological Characteristics to Rate of Gastric Secretion (Serum Pepsinogen). *Psychosom. Med.*, 19:1-10, 1957.

18. FRIEDMAN, M. and ROSENMAN, R. H.: Association of Specific Overt Behavior Pattern with Blood and Cardiovascular Findings. *J.A.M.A.*, 169:1286-1296, 1959.

19. DUNBAR, H. F.: *Emotions and Bodily Changes: A Survey of Literature on Psychosomatic Interrelationships.* New York: Columbia Univ. Press, 1954.

20. RUESCH, J.: The Infantile Personality: The Core Problem of Psychosomatic Medicine. *Psychosom. Med.*, 10:134-144, 1948.
21. NEMIAH, J. and SIFNEOS, P.: Affect and Fantasy in Patients with Psychosomatic Disorders. In O. W. Hill (Ed.), *Modern Trends in Psychosomatic Medicine*, Volume II. London: Butterworths, pp. 26-34, 1970, Chapter 2.
22. MARTY, P. and DE'UZAN, M.: La "pensée opératoire". *Rev. Franc. Psychoanal.*, Vol. 27, Suppl. 1345, 1963.
23. ENGEL, G. L.: Studies of Ulcerative Colitis. V. Psychological Aspects and Their Implications for Treatment. *Amer. J. Dis.*, 3:315, 1958.
24. KERNBERG, O. F.: Prognostic Considerations Regarding Borderline Personality Organization. *J. Amer. Psychoanal. Assoc.*, 19:595-635, 1971.
25. GRINKER, R., WERBLE, B., and DRYE, R.: *The Borderline Syndrome*. New York: Basic Books, 1968.
26. ENGEL, G. and SCHMALE, A.: Psychoanalytic Theory of Somatic Disorder: Conversion, Specificity and the Disease-Onset Situation. *J. Amer. Psychoanal. Assoc.*, 15:344, 1967.
27. RABKIN, J. G. and STRUENING, E. L.: Life Events, Stress and Illness. *Science*, 194:1013-1020, 1976.
28. CASSEM, N. H. and HACKETT, T. P.: Psychiatric Consultation in a Coronary Care Unit. *Ann. Int. Med.*, 75:9-14, 1971.
29. KORNFELD, D. S., ZIMBERG, S., and MALM, J. R.: Psychiatric Complications of Open-Heart Surgery. *New Eng. J. Med.*, 273: 287-292, 1965.
30. SELIGMAN, R., MACMILLAN, B. G., and CARROLL, S.: The Burned Child: A Neglected Area of Psychiatry. *Amer. J. Psychiat.*, 128:84-89, 1971.
31. ENGEL, G. L. and ROMANO, J.: Delirium, A Syndrome of Cerebral Insufficiency. *J. Chron. Dis.*, 9:260-277, 1959.
32. KIMBALL, C. P.: Delirium. In Howard F. Conn (Ed.), *Current Therapy*, pp. 833-835, 1974.
33. KAHANA, R. J. and BIBRING, G. L.: Personality Types in Medical Management. In N. Zinberg (Ed.), *Psychiatry and Medical Practice in a General Hospital*. New York: International Univ. Press, pp. 108-123, 1964.
34. GREENE, W. A., CONRON, G., SCHALCH, D. S., and SCHREINER, B. F.: Psychological Reactions with Changes in Growth Hormone and Cortisol Levels: A Study of Patients Undergoing Cardiac Catheterization. *Psychosom. Med.*, 32:599-614, 1970.
35. QUINLAN, D. M., KIMBALL, C. P., and OSBORNE, F.: The Experience of Open Heart Surgery. IV. Assessment of Disorientation and Dysphoria Following Cardiac Surgery. *Arch. Gen. Psychiat.*, 31:241-244, 1974.
36. KLEIN, R.: Behavioral Patterns and Catecholamine Excretion in Acute Myocardial Infarction. *Psychosom. Med.* (Abstract), 31:449-450, 1969.

37. KLEIN, R. F., KLINER, V. A., ZIPES, D. P., et al.: Transfer from a Coronary Care Unit. *Arch. Int. Med.*, 122:104-108, 1968.
38. KIMBALL, C. P.: Psychological Responses to the Experience of Open Heart Surgery. I. *Amer. J. Psych.*, 126:348-359, 1969.
39. ENGEL, G. L.: *Psychological Development in Health and Disease.* Philadelphia: W. B. Saunders, 1962.
40. MECHANIC, D.: Response Factors in Illness: The Study of Illness Behavior. *Soc. Psychiat.*, 1:11-20, 1966.
41. LINDEMANN, E.: Symptomatology and Management of Acute Grief. *Amer. J. Psychiat.*, 101:141-148, 1944.
42. PRATT, J. H.: The "Home Sanatorium" Treatment of Consumption. *Boston Med. & Surg. J.*, 154:210-216, 1906.
43. BILODEAU, C. B. and HACKETT, T. P.: Issues Raised in a Group Setting by Patients Recovering from Myocardial Infarction. *Amer. J. Psychiat.*, 128:105-110, 1971.
44. AGLE, D. P., BAUM, G. L., CHESTER, E. H., et al.: Multidiscipline Treatment of Chronic Pulmonary Insufficiency. I. Psychological Aspects of Rehabilitation. *Psychosom. Med.*, 35:41-49, 1973.
45. CASTELNUOVO-TEDESCO, P.: *The Twenty-Minute Hour. A Guide to Brief Psychotherapy for the Physician.* Boston: Little, Brown & Co., 1965.
46. MCKEGNEY, F. P. and LANGE, P.: The Decision to No Longer Live on Chronic Hemodialysis. *Amer. J. Psychiat.*, 128:267, 1971.
47. CROOG, S. H. and LEVINE, S.: Social Status and Subjective Perceptions of 250 Men After Myocardial Infarction. *Pub. Health Reports*, 84:989-997, 1969.
48. WHITE, K.: Angina Pectoris and Angina Innocens. *Psychosom. Med.*, 17:128-138, 1955.
49. ENGEL, G. L.: Conversion Symptoms. In C. M. MacBryde (Ed.), *Signs and Symptoms: Applied Physiology and Clinical Interpretation*, Chapter 26, 5th Edition. J. B. Lippincott, 1969.
50. HAMBURG, D., HAMBURG, B., and DEGOZA, S.: Adaptive Problems and Mechanisms in Severely Burned Patients. *Psych.*, 16:1-20, 1953.
51. VISOTSKY, H. M., HAMBURG, D. A., GOSS, M. E. and LEBOVITS, B.: Coping Behavior Under Extreme Stress. *Arch. Gen. Psychiat.*, 5:27-52, 1961.
52. FRIEDMAN, S. B., MASON, J. W., and HAMBURG, D. A.: Urinary 17-Hydroxycortico-Steriod Levels in Parents of Children with Neoplastic Disease: A Study of Chronic Psychological Stress. *Psychosom. Med.*, 25:364-376, 1963.
53. JANIS, I. L.: *Psychological Stress: Psychoanalytic and Behavioral Studies of Surgical Patients.* New York: John Wiley & Sons, 1958.
54. KAPLAN DE-NOUR, A.: Psychotherapy with Patients on Chronic Hemodialysis. *Brit. J. Psychiat.*, 116:207-215, 1970.

55. ADAMS, J. and LINDEMANN, E.: Coping with Long-Term Disability. In G. V. Coehlo, D. A. Hamburg, and J. E. Adams (Eds.), *Coping and Adaptation.* New York: Basic Books, 1974.

56. HAMBURG, D. A. and ADAMS, J. E.: A Perspective on Coping Behavior: Seeking and Utilizing Information in Major Transitions. *Arch. Gen. Psych.,* 17:277-284, 1967.

57. MURPHEY, E., et al.: Development of Autonomy and Parent-Child Interaction in Late Adolescence. *Amer. J. Orthopsychiat.,* 33:643-652, 1952.

58. CHODOFF, P., FRIEDMAN, S., and HAMBURG, D.: Stress, Defenses and Coping Behavior: Observations in Parents of Children with Malignant Disease. *Amer. J. Psychiat.,* 120:743-749, 1964.

59. SCHOENFIELD, B., GOLDBERG, I., CARR, A., and PERETZ, D.: *Anticipatory Grieving.* New York: Columbia Univ. Press, 1974.

60. KIELEY, W. F.: Coping with Severe Illness. Chapter 6 in *Advances in Psychosomatic Medicine, VIII.* Basel, N. Y.: S. Karger AG, 1971.

61. LIPOWSKI, Z. J.: Physical Illness, the Individual, and the Coping Process. *Psychiat. in Med.,* 1:91-102, 1970.

62. DAVIS, F.: *Passage Through Crisis: Polio Victims and Their Families.* New York: The Bobbs-Merrill Co., 1963.

63. HAMBURG, D., HAMBURG, B. and DeGOZA, S.: Adaptive Problems and Mechanisms in Severely Burned Patients. *Psychiat.,* 16:1-20, 1953.

64. ANDREASON, N. J., NOYES, R., HARTFORD, C., GRODLAND, G., and PROCTOR, S.: Management of Emotional Reactions in Seriously Burned Adults. *N.E.J.M.,* 286:65-69, 1972.

65. SELIGMAN, R.: Emotional Responses of Burned Children in a Pediatric Intensive Care Unit. *Psych. in Med.,* 3:59-65, 1972.

66. QUINBY, S. and BERNSTEIN, N.: Identity Problems and the Adaptation of Nurses to Severely Burned Children. *Amer. J. Psychiat.,* 128:58-63, 1971.

67. QUINDLEN, E. A. and ABRAM, H. S.: Psychosis in the Burned Patient: A Neglected Area of Research. *South. Med. J.,* 62:1463-1466, 1969.

68. O'CONNOR, J. A.: Traumatic Quadraplegia: A Comprehensive Review. *J. Rehab.,* May-June 1971, pp. 14-20.

69. RUSK, H.: *Rehabilitation Medicine.* St. Louis, Mo.: Mosby Co., 1964.

70. TROMBY, C.: Principles of Operant Conditioning Relating to Orthotic Training of Quadraplegic Patients. *Amer. J. Occ. Rehab.,* 49:592-597, 1968.

71. ALBRECHT, G. L. (Ed.): *The Sociology of Physical Disability and Rehabilitation.* Pittsburgh: Univ. of Pittsburgh, 1976.

72. NAGLER, B.: Psychiatric Aspects of Cord Injury. *Amer. J. Psychol.,* 107:49-55, 1950.

73. SHOUTZ, C.: Severe Chronic Illness. In J. Garrett and E. Levine

(Eds.), *Psychological Practices with the Physically Disabled.*
New York: Columbia Univ. Press, 1962.

74. MASTERMAN, L.: *Psychological Aspects of Rehabilitation.* Kansas
City, Mo.: Community Studies, Inc., 1961.

75. KAPLAN, L., et al.: *Comprehensive Follow-up Study of Spinal
Cord Dysfunction and Its Resultant Disabilities.* N. Y. Insti-
tute of Rehabilitation Medicine, N. Y. University Medical
Center, 1966.

76. MUELLER, A.: Personality Problems of the Spinal Cord Injured.
J. Consult. Psychol., 14:189-192, 1950.

77. SILLER, J.: Psychological Situation of the Disabled with Spinal
Cord Injuries. *Rehab. Lit.,* 30:290-296, 1969.

78. RABINOWITZ, H.: Motivation for Recovery—Four Social Psychologic Aspects. *Arch. Phys. Med. Rehab.,* 42:799-807, 1961.

79. LEVENSON, B. and GREEN, J.: Return to Work After Severe Disability. *J. Chron. Disabil.,* Vol. 18, 1965.

80. MACRAE, I. and HENDERSON, G.: Sexuality and Irreversible
Health Limitations. *Nursing Clin. No. Amer.,* 10:167-180, 1975.

81. HANSON, R. W. and FRANKLIN, M. R.: Sexual Loss in Relation
to Other Functional Losses for Spinal Cord Injured Males.
Arch. Phys. Med. Rehab., Vol. 57, 1976.

82. WING, J. K.: Social and Psychological Changes in a Rehabilitation Unit. *Soc. Psychiat.,* 1:21-28, 1966.

83. GOLDIAMOND, I.: Coping and Adaptive Behaviors of the Disabled.
In G. L. Albrecht (Ed.), *The Sociology of Physical Disability
and Rehabilitation.* Pittsburgh: Univ. of Pittsburgh, 1976.
Chapter 5, pp. 97-138.

84. GOLDIAMOND, I.: Toward a Constructional Approach to Social
Problems. *Behaviorism,* 2:1-84, 1974.

85. STOREY, P. B.: Brain Damage and Personality Change After
Sub-arachnoid Hemorrhage. *Brit. J. Psychiat.,* 117:129-142,
1970.

86. BROWNE, T. R. and POSHANZER, D. C.: Treatment of Strokes.
N.E.J.M., 281:594-602, 650-657, 1969.

87. FORD, A., KATZ, S., CHIN, A., and NEWILL, V.: Prognosis After
Strokes. *Med.,* 45:223-246, 1966.

88. GOLDSTEIN, K.: The Effect of Brain Damage on the Personality.
Psychiat., 15:245-260, 1952.

89. FELDMAN, D. J., UNTERECHER, J., LLOYD, K., RUSH, H. A., and
TOOLE, A.: A Comparison of Functionally Oriented Medical
Care and Formal Rehabilitation in the Management of Patients
with Hemiplegia Due to Cerebrovascular Disease. *J. Chron.
Dis.,* 15:297, 1962.

90. ENGEL, G. L.: Psychogenic Pain and the Pain-prone Patient.
Amer. J. Med., 26:899-918, 1959.

91. SZASZ, T.: *Pain and Pleasure.* New York: Basic Books, 1975.

92. EGBERT, L. D., BATTIT, G. E., WELCH, C. E., and BARTLETT, M.

K.: Reduction of Post-Operative Pain by Encouragement and Instruction of Patients. *N.E.J.M.*, 27:825-827, 1964.

93. ZBOROWSKI, M.: Cultural Components in Responses to Pain. In D. Apple (Ed.), *Sociological Studies of Health and Illness.* McGraw-Hill Book Co., The Blakiston Div., 1960, pp. 118-133.

94. HARDY, J. D., WOLFF, H. G., and GOODELL, H.: *Pain Sensations and Reactions.* Baltimore: Williams & Wilkins Co., 1952.

95. LeSHAN, L. I. and WORTHINGTON, R. E.: Personality as Factor in the Pathogenesis of Cancer: A Review of the Literature. *Brit. J. Med. Psychol.*, 29:49-56, 1956.

96. LeSHAN, L. I.: An Emotional Life-History Pattern Associated with Neoplastic Disease. *Ann. N. Y. Acad. Sci.*, 125:780-793, 1966.

97. THOMAS, C. E. and GREENSTREET, R. L.: Psychobiological Characteristics in Youth as Predictors of Five Disease States: Suicide, Mental Illness, Hypertension, Coronary Heart Disease and Tumor. *J. Hopkins Med. J.*, 132:16-43, 1973.

98. HARROWER, M., THOMAS, C., and ALTMAN, A.: Human Figure Drawings in a Prospective Study of Six Disorders. *J. Nerv. Ment. Dis.*, 161:191-199, 1975.

99. KISSEN, D. M., BROWN, R. I. F., and KISSEN, M.: A Further Report on Personality and Psychosocial Factors in Lung Cancer. *Ann. N. Y. Acad. Sci.*, 164:535-544, 1969.

100. GOLDFARB, C., DRIESEN, J., and COLE, D.: Psychophysiologic Aspects of Malignancy. *Amer. J. Psychiat.*, 123:1545-1552, 1967.

101. KOROLJOW, S.: Two Cases of Malignant Tumors with Metastases Apparently Treated Successfully with Hypoglycemic Coma. *Psychiat. Quarterly*, 36:261-270, 1962.

102. MUELLER, P. and WATKIN, D.: Plasma Unesterified Fatty Acid Concentration in Neoplastic Disease. *J. Lab. Clin. Med.*, 57: 95-108, 1961.

103. CARDON, P. V., Jr. and MILLER, P. S.: A Possible Mechanism: Psychogenic Fat Mobilization. *Ann. N. Y. Acad. Sci.*, 125:924-927, 1966.

104. HACKETT, T. P., CASSEM, N. H. and RAKER, J. W.: Patient Delay in Cancer. *N.E.J.M.*, 289:14-20, 1973.

105. HENDERSON, J. G.: Denial and Repression as Factors in the Delay of Patients with Cancer Presenting to the Physician. Proc. Conf. Psychophysiol. Aspects of Cancer. *N. Y. Acad. Sci. Ann.*, 164: 1969.

106. HINTON, J.: Bearing Cancer. *Brit. J. Med. Psychol.*, 46:105-113, 1973.

107. MILTON, G. W.: Thoughts in the Mind of a Patient with Cancer. *Brit. Med. J.*, p. 221-223, 1973.

108. SOLZHENITSYN, A.: *Cancer Ward.* Harmondsworth: Penguin Books, 1972.

109. RENNEKER, R. and CUTLER, M.: Psychological Problems of Adjustment to Cancer of the Breast. *J.A.M.A.*, pp. 833-838, 1952.

110. ASKEN, M. J.: Psychoemotional Aspects of Mastectomy: A Review of the Literature. *Amer. J. Psychiat.*, 132:56-59, 1975.
111. KIMBALL, C. P.: Death & Dying: A Chronological Discussion. *J. Thanatology.* 1:42-52, 1971.
112. NAGY, M. H.: The Child's View of Death. *J. Genet. Psychol.*, 73:3-27, 1948.
113. MOORE, D. C., HOLTON, C. P., and MARTEN, G. W.: Psychologic Problems in the Management of Adolescents with Malignancy. *Clinic. Ped.*, 8:465-473, 1969.
114. NORTON, J.: Treatment of a Dying Patient. *Psychoanal. Study Child.* New York: International Universities Press, Inc., 18: 541-560, 1963.
115. STEHLIN, J. S. and BEACH, K. H.: Psychological Aspects of Cancer Therapy. *J.A.M.A.*, 197:100-104, 1966.
116. DAVIES, J., QUINLAN, D. M., McKEGNEY, F. P., and KIMBALL, C. P.:Organic Factors and Psychological Adjustment in Advanced Cancer Patients. *Psychosom. Med.*, 35:464-471, 1973.
117. SCHONFELD, J.: Psychological Factors Related to Delayed Return to an Earlier Life Style in Successfully Treated Cancer Patients. *J. Psychosom. Res.*, 16:41-46, 1972.
118. BILODEAU, C. B. and HACKETT, T. P.: Issues Raised in a Group Setting by Patients Recovering from Myocardial Infarction. *Amer. J. Psychiat.*, 128:73-78, 1971.
119. YALOM, I. D.: The Terminally Ill with Cancer Find Support in Group Therapy. Roche Report. *Frontiers of Psychiatry*, 7, February 15, 1977, #3.
120. RAMSEY, P.: Choosing How to Choose: Patients and Sparse Medical Resources. In *The Patient as Person.* New Haven: Yale Univ. Press, 1970.
121. SAND, P., LIVINGSTON, C., and WRIGHT, R. G.: Psychological Assessment of Candiates for a Hemodialysis Program. *Ann. Int. Med.*, 64:602-610, 1966.
122. SAND, P.: cf., above.
123. ABRAM, H. S.: The Psychiatrist, the Treatment of Chronic Renal Failure, and the Prolongation of Life II. *Amer. J. Psychiat.*, 125:157-167, 1969.
124. REICHMAN, F. and LEVY, N. B.: Problems in Adaptation to Maintenance on Hemodialysis: A Four Year Study of 25 Patients. In N. Levy (Ed.), *Living or Dying: Adaptation to Hemodialysis.* Springfield: Charles C Thomas, 1974.
125. WAKIM, K. G.: The Pathophysiology of Dialysis Equilibrium Syndrome. *Mayo Clin. Proc.*, 44:406-429, 1969.
126. TYLER, H. R.: Neurologic Disorders Seen in Uremic Patients. *Arch. Int. Med.*, 126:781-786, 1970.
127. SAVOY, G. M., YIUM, J. J., JORDAN, P. H., and GUINN, G. A.: Hyperparathyroidism in Patients in Chronic Hemodialysis. *Amer. J. Surg.*, 126:755-757, 1973.

128. RASKIN, N. H. and FISHMAN, R. A.: Neurological Disorders in Renal Failure. *N.E.J.M.*, 294:204-210, 1976.
129. MAHURKAR, S. D., SALTA, R., SMITH., E. C., DHAR, S., MEYERS, E., and DUNEA, G.: Dialysis Dementia. *Lancet*, 1973, pp. 1412-1415.
130. ALFREY, A. C.: The Dialysis Encephalopathy Syndrome. *N.E.J.M.*, 294:184-188, 1976.
131. SHEA, E. J., BOGDAN, D. F., FREEMAN, R. B., and SCHREINER, G. E.: Hemodialysis for Chronic Renal Failure. IV. Psychological Consideration. *Ann Int. Med.*, 62:558-563, 1965.
132. ABRAM, H. S.: The Psychiatrist, the Treatment of Chronic Renal Failure and the Prolongation of Life. I. *Amer. J. Psychiat.*, 124:1351-1358, 1968.
133. DeNOUR, A. K., SHALTIEL, J., and CZACZKES, J. W.: Emotional Reactions of Patients on Chronic Hemodialysis. *Psychosom. Med.*, 30:521-533, 1968.
134. BEARD, B. H.: Fear of Death and Fear of Life. *Arch. Gen. Psychiat.*, 21:373-380, 1969.
135. SHORT, M. J. and WILSON, W. P.: Roles of Denial in Chronic Hemodialysis. *Arch. Gen. Psychiat.*, 20:433-437, 1969.
136. HALPER, I.: Psychiatric Observations in a Chronic Hemodialysis Program. *Med. Clin. No. Amer.*, 55:177-191, 1971.
137. ABRAM, H. S., MOORE, G. L., and WESTERVELT, F. B.: Suicide Behavior in Chronic Patients. *Amer. J. Psychiat.*, 127:1199-1204, 1971.
138. GOLDSTEIN, A. M. and REZNIKOFF, M.: Suicide in Chronic Hemodialysis Patients from an External Locus of Control Framework. *Amer. J. Psychiat.*, 127:1204-1208, 1971.
139. GLASSMAN, B. M. and SIEGEL, A.: Personality Correlates of Survival in a Long-term Hemodialysis Program. *Arch. Gen. Psychiat.*, 22:566-574, 1970.
140. DeNOUR, A. K. and CZACZKES, J. W.: Personality Factors in Chronic Hemodialysis Patients Causing Non-Compliance with Medical Regimen. *Psychosom. Med.*, 34:333-344, 1972.
141. LINDER, A. and CURTIS, K.: Morbidity and Mortality in Association with Long Term Hemodialysis. *Hosp. Proc.*, Nov., 1974, pp. 143-150.
142. LIM, F.: Gonadal Dysfunction in Uremic Men. (In press).
143. LEVY, N. B.: Sexual Adjustment to Hemodialysis and Transplantation. In N. E. Levy (Ed.), *Living or Dying: Adaptation to Hemodialysis*. Springfield: Charles C. Thomas, 1974.
144. VIEDERMAN, M.: Adaptive and Mal-adaptive Regression in Hemodialysis. *Psychiat.*, 37:68-77, 1974.
145. FOSTER, F. G., COHN, G. L., and McKEGNEY, F. P.: Psychobiologic Factors and Individual Survival on Chronic Renal Dialysis: A Two-year Followup. I. *Psychosom. Med.*, 35:64-81, 1973.

146. GILLUM, R. F. and BARSKY, A. J.: Diagnosis and Management of Patient Non-Compliance. *J.A.M.A.*, 228:1563-1567, 1974.
147. DeNOUR, A. K. and CZACZKES, J. W.: The Influence of Patient's Personality on Adjustment to Chronic Dialysis: A Predictive Study. *J. Nerv. Ment. Dis.*, 162:323-333, 1976.
148. MARSHALL, J. R.: Effective Use of a Psychiatric Consultant on a Dialysis Unit. *Postgrad. Med.*, 55:121-125, 1974.
149. MACNAMARA, M.: Psychosocial Problems in a Renal Unit. *Brit. J. Psychiat.*, 113:1231-1236, 1967.
150. CRAMMOND, W. A., KNIGHT, P. R., and LAWRENCE, J. R.: The Psychiatric Contribution to a Renal Unit Undertaking Chronic Haemodialysis and Renal Homotransplantation. *Brit. J. Psychiat.*, 113:1201-1212, 1967.
151. SHAMBAUGH, P. W. and KANTER, S. S.: Spouses Under Stress: Group Meetings with Spouses of Patients on Hemodialysis. *J. Amer. Psych.*, 125:928-936, 1969.
152. SMITH, E., MCDONALD, S., CURTIS, J., and DEWARDENER, H.: Hemodialysis in the Home. *Lancet*, March 22, 1969, pp. 614-617.
153. BROWN, T. M., FEINS, A., PARKE, R., and PAULUS, D.: Living with Long Term Dialysis. *Ann. Int. Med.*, 81:165-170, 1974.
154. BLAGG, C., HICKMAN, R., ESCHBACH, J., and SCHRIBNER, B.: Home Dialysis: Six Years' Experience. *N.E.J.M.*, 283:1126-1131, 1970.
155. FISHMAN, D. and SCHNEIDER, C.: Predicting Emotional Adjustment. *J. Chron. Dis.*, 125:99-109, 1972.
156. KEMPF, J.: Renal Failure, Artificial Kidney, and Renal Transplant. *Amer. J. Psychiat.*, 122:1270-1274, 1966.
157. SHORT, M. and HARRIS, N.: Psychiatric Observations of Renal Homotransplantation. *South. Med. J.*, 62:1479-1481, 1969.
158. KEMPF, J., BERMANN, E., and COPPOLILLO, H.: Kidney Transplant and Shifts in Family Dynamics. *Amer. J. Psychiat.*, 125:1485-1490, 1969.
159. EISENDRATH, R.: The Role of Grief and Fear in the Death of Kidney Transplant Patients. *Amer. J. Psychiat.*, 126:381-387, 1970.
160. FOX, R. C. and SWAZEY, J.: *The Courage to Fail: A Social View of Organ Transplants and Dialysis.* Chicago: Univ. of Chicago Press, 1974.
161. ANTHONY, E. J.: The Impact of Mental and Physical Illness on Family Life. *Amer. J. Psych.*, 127:138-146, 1970.
162. JACKSON, D.: Family Interaction, Family Homeostasis and Some Implications for Conjoint Family Psychotherapy. In J. Masserman (Ed.), *Individual and Familial Dynamics.* New York: Grune & Stratton, 1959.
163. KOOS, E.: *Families in Trouble.* New York: King's Crown Press, 1946.
164. PARSONS, T. and FOX, R.: Illness, Therapy and the Modern Urban American Family. *J. Soc. Issues*, 8:31-44, 1952.

165. SPIEGEL, J.: The Resolution of Role Conflict Within the Family. In E. Greenblatt, D. Levinson, and R. Williams (Eds.), *The Patient and the Mental Hospital.* Glencoe: Free Press of Glencoe, 1957.

166. RAMSEY, P.: *The Patient as Person.* New Haven: Yale Univ. Press, 1974.

167. FRANK, J. D.: *Persuasion and Healing.* Baltimore: Johns Hopkins Univ., 1973.

8

Emotional Aspects of the Symptoms, Functions and Disorders of Women

Carol R. Nadelson, M.D. and
Malkah T. Notman, M.D.

The psychiatrist working in obstetrics and gynecology can be considered to have three kinds of roles. The first, as a consultant, includes the evaluation of patients with psychiatric symptoms such as depression, psychosis, and behavior problems, as well as those with functional disorders and psychosomatic illnesses (1, 2).

The second is the liaison role, in which the psychiatrist works in a more ongoing fashion and in a teaching relationship offering a psychiatric perspective for obstetrical-gynecological problems. This requires assimilating and integrating information in obstetrics-gynecology as well as psychiatry. Balint type groups, where gynecologists meet together with a psychiatrist to discuss cases, are an example of this type of role for the psychiatrist.

A growing body of recent information in areas such as contraception, pregnancy, abortion, sterilization, rape, menopause, and sexual functioning has challenged widely held myths and provided new insights and information, further expanding the liaison role of the psychiatrist. In these areas the psychiatrist is often not formally

334

consulted since the problems are not traditionally defined as psychiatric or psychosomatic disorders. Further differentiating the liaison psychiatrist's role in obstetrics-gynecology from his/her role in other medical specialties is the presence of a large population of "normal" patients, e.g., pregnant women.

The third role is a relatively new one. It constitutes those activities where the psychiatrist and obstetrician-gynecologist overlap in function, sometimes working conjointly, sometimes supplementing each other. This role has emerged particularly in sexual therapy and in the teaching of human sexuality, where the psychiatrist and gynecologist frequently function as co-therapists or teach as coinstructors, each with a special body of information and a particular perspective.

Historically, these roles have evolved from the psychosomatic model and from early work which considered the relationship between psychological experience and somatic manifestations. In this discussion we will focus primarily on those symptoms, functions and disorders which are related to obstetrics and gynecology.

In 1931 Horney (3) and Frank (4) published separate papers on premenstrual tension, and in 1939 Benedek and Rubenstein (5) first published their work correlating ovarian activity and psychodynamic processes. Lindemann (6), in 1941, reported on pre- and post-operative evaluations of women following hysterectomies. His emphasis on the specific meaning of the loss of the uterus was an impetus for investigations of women's responses to the range of physiological and pathological conditions involving reproductive organs. This work was expanded when, in 1952, Renneker and Cutler (7) stressed the meaning of the loss of the breast to women, and reported on the post-mastectomy mourning process. A vast literature has developed in this area, with several textbooks devoted to specific psychological phenomena related to women and their anatomy, physiology and pathology (8, 9, 10). However, Pasnau (11) in 1975 comments that "surprisingly little has been written about the role of the liaison psychiatrist working specifically with obstetrics-gynecology." Work in this area has clearly been more limited than consultation-liaison in medicine and surgery; even major reviews have not dealt with the subject, including Lipowski in his own book and in his listing of major areas of consultation-liaison work (12, 13). In addition, the paucity of existing consultation-liaison services within obstetrics-gynecology is noteworthy.

One consideration which may be important is that obstetrics-gynecology is often relegated to a separate and lower status in the medical hierarchy. Another factor is that the population treated is exclusively female, often with no "interesting pathology." Since the obstetrician-gynecologist functions as the exclusive physician of the majority of women during their reproductive years, and cares for them during a number of critical life phases, neglect of this area is especially significant. Mathis (14) comments:

> Sex, reproduction, and the reproductive system are almost synonymous with emotional reactions in our culture. The emotional charge invested in the genitalia makes that area peculiarly vulnerable to symptoms arising from any conflictual aspect of living. The woman who seeks medical attention for her reproductive system deserves a physician who understands the total significance of feminity as well as he knows the anatomy and physiology of the female. The physician who assumes this responsibility automatically becomes involved in emotional processes unequaled in any other branch of medicine, psychiatry not excepted.

The obstetrican-gynecologist physician is also vulnerable to his/her emotional responses to sexuality and reproduction and as a consequence may tend to avoid investigating these concerns with patients. Many refer emotionally related problems to the office nurse or to the hospital social worker. In medical school, students have generally been taught about these areas while studying anatomy, physiology and biochemistry, or as a part of the specific disciplines related to reproductive functioning, e.g., obstetrics-gynecology, urology, or medicine, but rarely as human sexuality. Much of this information has not been integrated in such a way that it relates to the kinds of problems faced by physicians in practice (15).

In addition to the resistance created by the emotional responses of the physicians, there is evidence from recent critical discussions by Parlee (16), Lennane and Lennane (17), Glasser (18), Pasnau

(11), and Bart (19) that much of the data on which attitudes are based and which has been cited in the past is questionable. For instance, the concept that a depression inevitably follows an abortion has been shown to be incorrect (20).

The psychiatrist working in obstetrics-gynecology is likely to be concerned with similar problems, as the consultation-liaison psychiatrist in any specialty. However, there are unique aspects as well. Lipowski summarizes the most frequent problems encountered in consultation-liaison psychiatry:

1) Suicide attempt or threat.

2) Grossly disturbed behavior.

3) Emotional over-reactions.

4) Refusal to cooperate with recommended procedures.

5) Delayed convalescence.

6) Conflicts between patient and personnel.

7) Patients with psychiatric history.

8) Psychiatric effects of drugs used for medical purposes, i.e. steroids.

9) Selection and/or preparation of patients for therapeutic procedures.

10) Disposition.

The specific patient problems of obstetrics-gynecology consultation-liaison include the social, legal and ethical implications, i.e., family planning, abortion, or sterilization which have an impact far beyond the individual patient. Treating sexual dysfunction involves at least two people in an intimate interaction where many aspects of an individual's personality and life are expressed. In areas such as these the consultation-liaison psychiatrist must be prepared to teach general psychiatric principles as well as to offer specific knowledge of the particular problem, be it the "normal" state of pregnancy or a complex surgical mutilative procedure. The consultation-liaison psychiatrist must distinguish between recommendations arising from his/her professional expertise and his/her own values.

Change in Reproductive and Sexual Patterns

In the past years major social changes have occurred affecting women and families. Birthrates have declined, families are smaller, more women choose not to mary, to marry late and/or to remain childless. An increasing number of young women (21, 22) are seeking sterilization. Many of these are nulliparous and in their early twenties.

The pregnant woman now has less social support available to her than she did 15 or 20 years ago, when prevailing social norms favored larger families and there were fewer non-domestic options for women. In fact, the shift in values has swung to the opposite pole; women who are having a third or fourth child describe outright hostility from peers, and occasionally encounter expressions of disapproval from their obstetricians as well.

Many women are postponing pregnancies until their education and training are completed or their careers have been established. The older pregnant woman often has difficulty gaining support from medical people. The liaison psychiatrist must keep in mind the changed social realities which are important to the patient. He/she may be in a position to constructively interpret these to the obstetrician-gynecologist who is concerned primarily with the medical priorities.

The fact that sexual mores have changed is by now self-evident. Sexual relations outside of marriage are more widespread. Lesbian relationships are more open, some as an expression of political ideology or as an explanation of alternate patterns of intimacy (23). The gynecologist has had to become accustomed to new realities— including the possibility of venereal disease in a wide cross section of patients, requests for contraceptive and sexual counselling for unmarried couples, and gynecological care of patients identifying themselves as bisexual or lesbian. The consultation-liaison psychiatrist must be sensitive to these issues and particularly to the potential conflict in values and its possible effect on patient care.

The Changing Doctor-Patient Relationship

Certain characteristics of the doctor-patient relationship emphasize the potential problem between gynecologists and their patients. The expectation that the doctor, who has usually been male, is informed, helping, authoritative, and protective fits especially well with the conventional view of women as naive, compliant and dependent. This parent-child model is frequently observed in this field and is discussed in some medical literature (24, 25), as well as being the subject of some feminist writing (26, 27, 28). These authors point out the depreciation inherent in this model (e.g., many gynecologists continue to call their patients "girls").

Communication fails (29) when the doctor-patient relationship is not a true partnership. Indeed, in many instances decisions about a patient's care have been and still are based on a paternalistic view of the doctor's understanding of the best interests of the patients. For instance, decisions about female sterilization and abortion have until recently been made largely on the basis of the physician's attitudes. They also have required the consent of a husband, reflecting traditional concepts of wives and children as the property of the husband. It is interesting to note that male sterilization generally had not required the consent of the wife. The discrepancy between requirements for men as compared with women is significant in this kind of situation.

There has been a move toward home delivery among some women, who have stressed their discontent with the institutional atmosphere of a hospital, and have also wanted to include husbands and other family members. Along with this trend has come a movement towards self-examination, and reliance less on trained medical personnel and more upon peers and oneself.

The obstetrician and gynecologist who is traditionally trained is apt to become defensive and frustrated. The self-help aspects threaten established medical roles and seem to dispense with valuable experience. The consultation-liaison psychiatrist must be able to help the obstetrician-gynecologist understand the reactions of women who feel anxious, excluded and put off by the stereotypes and attitudes which predominate in the field. While the nature of the doctor-doctor interaction and the style of consultation has often made it easier for male psychiatrists to operate in these roles collaboratively with male obstetricians-gynecologists, the presence of a woman physician is often helpful in understanding the responses of the patient. At the Beth Israel Hospital efforts have been made to have women take the major role in obstetrical-gynecological liaison psychiatry.

Since, as we have noted, the gynecologist-obstetrician is the physician to whom many women turn for primary health care, his/her role has been expanded to include counselling. The potential for a preventive approach in both physical and emotional health is also important in fields which are diverse and complex and accordingly require certain skills and psychological understanding which have not been part of the traditional training in obstetrics-gynecology.

The obstetrician-gynecologist should have an awareness of his/her attitudes and responses to patients. The example of teenage pregnancy illustrates this. Obstetricians delivering babies of teenagers find themselves both frustrated by the teenagers' seeming inability to use effective contraceptives, and uncomfortable in dealing with young women who may have a very different concept of pregnancy and motherhood than the one the obstetrician has grown accustomed to understanding. The psychiatrist is in a position to provide an important perspective, but must also have an understanding of adolescence, pregnancy and abortion as well as information and attitudes about teenage sexuality which will make him or her more helpful to the obstetrician-gynecologist as well as to the patient.

The Gynecologist

Since gynecology is a surgical specialty, many of the same considerations and approaches to patients that are important in surgery exist in this field. The gynecologist's work environment is similar to that of the surgeon. Schedules are grueling, communication is often minimal because of lack of opportunity, as well as the special pressures of practice, which may foster adaptations that are often antithetical to values held by psychiatrists, i.e., the value of mobilizing affect and making conflict and ambivalence more explicit.

Pasnau (11), in discussing some of the unique characteristics of obstetrics-gynecology, stresses the widely-ranging nature of the clinical setting: "It extends from the maternity ward-delivery room-pre- and postnatal clinics to the intensive care unit and oncology wards of the gynecology service. No other clinical specialty, unless it be family practice, comes to mind as crossing so many clinical settings and systems of care." He feels that great emotional demands are made of the obstetrician-gynecologist, who must be able to function in all of these settings. These factors, coupled with the action orientation of the surgeon and personality characteristics which may make them less at ease with emotional expression, may contribute to some of the difficulties in communication often reported by patients.

Hertz (24) stresses the polarization and dissonance often experienced by the gynecologist: He/she is oriented toward the maintenance of pregnancy, yet also interrupts it, and counsels about contraceptives, but on the other hand is also asked about artificial insemination, etc. Hertz feels that these demands may evoke unconscious conflict as well as obvious role conflict in the gynecologist.

Consultation-Liaison at the Beth Israel Hospital

At the Beth Israel Hospital, liaison with the department of Obstetrics-Gynecology has a long history. In 1955 a longitudinal study of the psychological processes in pregnancy was undertaken by Dr. Grete Bibring and an interdisciplinary staff including psychiatrists, psychologists, a pediatrician and a social worker together with the obstetrical-gynecological staff.

Subsequently, when abortions could be obtained only to save the life or preserve the health of the pregnant woman, the psychiatry service became involved in doing abortion consultations. At this time an overwhelming number of hospital abortions were performed for psychiatric indications. Thus, there developed a working liaison relationship which formed the basis of an ongoing collaboration and was based on need for joint policy decisions, in the face of changing consultation requirements. During this time a longitudinal study of the psychological effects of abortions was carried out by psychiatrists (20).

Another project which strengthened the liaison at Beth Israel Hospital has been the development of joint teaching in human sexuality. The obstetrics-gynecology residents and the medical students meet jointly with the liaison psychiatrist and the gynecologist who was trained in sexual counselling for lectures, films, clinical presentations and discussions of interviewing and sexual history taking. The liaison psychiatrist has supervised obstetrics-gynecology residents and staff personnel in the psychological aspects of sexual counselling. The gynecologist together with a psychiatrist has treated couples who are referred for sexual counselling. Some gynecology residents have also spent elective time on psychiatry to strengthen their diagnostic skills and to learn about the treatment of sexual dysfunctions.

These areas of joint collaboration create a working relationship with gynecologists which bridges the gap of differing orientations and of their approaches to patients. However, because of the changes in obstetrics-gynecology personnel and responsibilities, sustained relationships with everyone involved may be difficult to develop. The frequent changing of resident means that new relationships must be developed; those collaborative patterns earlier worked out with senior staff may not filter down to everyone.

Attendance at rounds provides a forum for teaching and discussion. At the Beth Israel Hospital a psychiatrist has attended informal discussion teaching rounds, oncology rounds and social service rounds at which the entire staff involved with a case is present. This latter has proven to be a particularly important setting for general teaching as well as for case discussion. The kinds of problems presented there include management questions on a variety of social-psychological problems. These have included patients with addiction, psychoses, disorganized families, different cultural backgrounds, those who have received fragmented care in the past, pregnant women with a history of child abuse, etc.

In the 18-month period between July, 1975 and November, 1976, a review of 63 consultation reports at the Beth Israel Hospital revealed five major areas:

a. Emotional reactions to an obstetrical or gynecological experience;   25%
    e.g., the birth of a defective child, or the diagnosis of malignancy

b. Patients presenting psychiatric symptoms which the obstetrician-gynecologist was concerned about or wanted documented. For some of these the request involved management, including information about appropriate medication.   37%
    e.g. bizarre ideation, depression, intense anxiety, and patients with a psychiatric history

c. Patients where someone, often a social worker, wanted help with management of emotional issues.   8%

d. Evaluations related to the performance of specific procedures;   20%
    e.g., abortions where the patient was ambivalent, tubal ligation in young women

e. "Psychosomatic" problems, somatic presentation, or forms of psychiatric disorders;   11%
    e.g., pelvic pain or abdominal pain, unexplained by organic disease

A diagnosis of psychosis was made for eight patients, primarily from category b. The largest group of consultations are those patients who present with psychiatric symptoms. Sometimes these people have a history of psychiatric illness, sometimes a worrisome depression. "Psychosomatic" problems are a small group. The data on these patients concur with that reported by Stoeckle and others who discuss the high level of "psychological distress" in medical patients (30). It also provides some information about the consultative use of the psychiatrist by the obstetrical-gynecological service. As might be predicted, the extent of the liaison function does not become apparent from the examination of formal consultation requests. However, without liaison activity it is likely that there would be considerably fewer consultations.

We will turn our discussion to some specific areas where recent information has made important changes in practice, illustrating the evolution and unfolding of the three roles of the consultation-liaison psychiatrist.

SEXUAL DYSFUNCTION

Complaints about sexual functioning are seen with increasing frequency by psychiatrists and other physicians as it becomes more socially acceptable to acknowledge sexual difficulties and as knowledge about the causes and treatment of these disorders is more widely disseminated.

Burnap and Golden (31) have reported on the types of sexual disorders seen by family physicians, internists, obstetrician-gynecologists, urologists and general surgeons (Table 1).

The authors point out that the types of problems least often reported were those that were most often included in medical school courses, while the most frequently appearing problems had been largely ignored. In addition, they state that the variability in the reported incidence of sexual problems encountered by the physicians studied was more related to the comfort of the physician than to the incidence of that type of particular problems in the population. Physicians who routinely obtained a sexual history, and were able to discuss sexual concerns with their patients, reported a higher incidence of sexual problems in their practice than those who failed to ask about sexual adjustment. Another finding of the study was that the majority of the physicians felt that their medical school preparation for assessing and treating patients with sexual problems was inadequate.

Ignorance and anxiety are frequently converted into questions

TABLE 1

Types of Sexual Problems Defined and Ranked
According to Frequency

The Problem as Stated to the Physician	Estimated Cases Seen Per Year by 60 Physicians
1. Lack of orgasm during intercourse	1,917
2. Frigidity, or lack of desire for intercourse	1,830
3. Frequency of intercourse, or concern of the patient over how often intercourse occurs	1,146
4. General sex information, no specific problem	1,438
5. Impotence, or lack of erection during intercourse	1,335
6. Dyspareunia, or painful intercourse	1,212
7. Lack of affection in intercourse, whether or not orgasm occurs	1,016
8. Premarital counseling	648
9. Extramarital intercourse, including premarital	633
10. Premature ejaculation	571
11. Sex education of children, including the parent who asks for advice	520
12. Lack of satisfaction with intercourse, whether or not orgasm occurs	419
13. Sexual problems with disease of surgery, such as a woman contemplating hysterectomy	414
14. Sexual problems related to the menopause	410
15. Homosexuality (presented to the physician as a problem)	85
16. Perversions, all types, except those given in No. 15 and in No. 17 through No. 20	35
17. Masturbation	32
18. Nymphomania, or excessive desire for intercourse by the female	16
19. Incest, or sex relations with other family members	5
20. Satyriasis, or excessive desire for intercourse by the male	5

about the relevance or validity of including courses in the diagnosis and treatment of sexual disorders in programs designed to train general physicians. However, it is important to note that patients with marital and sexual problems often go to psychiatrists last, not first.

Diagnosing Sexual Dysfunctions

Sexual complaints may be at the level of desire, performance or gratification. "Sexual dysfunctions" are specific disorders of coital performance caused by physical and/or psychogenic factors. Symptoms based on lack of interest in sexuality are more often psychogenic or interpersonal in etiology and are not dysfunctions. Symptoms of sexual dysfunction are non-specific, i.e., a particular physical syndrome or psychological characteristic is not necessarily responsible for a particular clinical picture. The same symptom in one person may well have a different, even opposite, cause in another. The evaluator must be aware of *both* psychological and physical impediments to sexual functioning.

An adequate sexual history and physical examination are necessary in order to eliminate any potential organic causes, or to assess the relevance of factors like age, pregnancy, cardiac disease, radical surgery, etc. It is often easier for those with psychological sophistication to obtain an accurate and detailed developmental history than to obtain basic data on the patients' sexual understanding, attitudes and functioning. Since sexual dysfunctions exist within relationships, both partners and the relationship must be evaluated. Factors to be considered in order to formulate appropriate treatment plans include psychopathology, motivation for therapy, and ego resuorces, including coping mechanisms.

Etiology of Sexual Dysfunctions

While sexual dysfunction symptoms are often multi-factorial, they can be divided into three basic groups:

1) Primarly organic in etiology (3-20 percent of sexual dysfunction) (32).*

2) Primarily psychogenic in etiology.

3) An existing organic problem results in psychologically based symptoms, i.e., the person with cardiac disease who loses interest in sex because of anxiety about the possible cardiac damage which may occur following coitus.

It is important to emphasize that in all of these conditions the psychological implications may be profound and contribute significantly to the problem, i.e., the person who has had radical surgery may have serious emotional problems regarding his "body image" which can result in sexual symptomatology.

1. Physical Causes of Sexual Dysfunction (32, 33)

These can be grouped according to the mechanism of action:

a) *Dysfunction related to biochemical-physiological factors producing systemic effects.* These include cardiopulmonary, hepatic, renal, endocrine and degenerative disease as well as systemic infections and malignancies. The effect on functioning is generally to decrease libido and thus to impair sexual arousal or potency because of general delibitation, pain or depresion. However, specific effects of hormonal changes related to the disease process or to the treatment may occur, i.e., estrogen or androgen shifts, or the overall effects of infections such as mumps and tuberculosis which have direct effects on the testis or ovaries. Tumors may invade certain organs and cause specific symptoms, in addition to general systemic effects.

---

* It is important to caution the reader to note the population base referred to when statistics are used since referrals are made selectively, i.e., the gynecologist sees many more organic problems than the psychiatrist, and he/she may overrate the incidence of problems in the category, while the psychiatrist may do the same with regard to psychological etiologies.

b) *Dysfunctions caused by anatomic or mechanical interference* primarily with local genital or adjacent structures. These include disorders producing pain, local damage or irritability such as infection, i.e., urethritis, prostatis, endometritis, vaginitis and pelvic inflammatory disease. In addition conditions like priapism, phimosis, clitoral adhesions, chordée, hypospadias, imperforate hymen, and allergic or radiation reactions may produce local discomfort or make intromission difficult. Approximately three-fourths of women treated with radiation for cervical cancer have sexual dysfunction following therapy (34). At times intercourse in advanced pregnancy may be uncomfortable.

c) *Dysfunctions occurring following surgical procedures.* These occur because of damage to genitals directly or by interfering with nerve supply or hormone production. Included in this group are problems related to prostatectomy (especially radical perineal), abdominal perineal resections, lumbar sympathectomies, abdominal aortic surgery, obstetrical trauma or the complications of hysterectomy. These may interfere with sexual response when there is pain, a patulous introitus or ejaculatory disturbance.

d) *Neurologically related dysfunctions.* These include disorders where there is damage to higher centers such as occur with temporal or frontal lobe damage, i.e., tumor, trauma, cerebrovascular accident; or when lower spinal damage occurs, i.e., amyotrophic lateral sclerosis, spina bifida, multiple sclerosis, surgery or trauma to sacral or lumbar cord, tabes dorsalis or combined systems disease. In the case of higher brain center damage the primary effect is an increase or decrease in libido. With spinal damage libido is generally not affected, but the ability to have erections, ejaculations or orgasm changes.

e) *Local vascular disorders.* Impairment of erectile functioning in males occurs because of interference with penile blood supply, e.g., thrombosis of penile veins or arteries (aortic bifurcation thrombosis or Leriche syndrome), leukemia, or sickle cell disease.

f) *Drugs and Medications.* Drugs or medications can affect sexual responses directly or indirectly by acting centrally and changing libidinal responses, or by interfering with peripheral mechanisms via the autonomic nervous system, the alteration of blood flow or muscular activity. The effects may be difficult to assess because mood, personality, and perception are variable; this is especially true with hallucinogens like LSD and marijuana. Patients may not consider that medications are drugs, or they may feel that the medication they are taking is for another purpose and therefore has no relationship to sexual functioning.

Drugs that are most frequently used and do alter sexual performance include:

1) Alcohol and barbiturates. Although usually considered depressants, in small amounts they reduce anxiety and inhibition, and thus can increase sexual responses.

2) Anticholinergics interfere with the parasympathetic nervous system, and thus with penile blood flow, inhibiting full erection. Since these drugs are used frequently in people with gastrointestinal disturbances, potency complaints may be related to these drugs.

3) Antiadrenergics interfere with sympathetic nervous system, and thus in the male may cause difficulties with ejaculation. Since these drugs are used for the management of hypertension, symptoms in men on these medications may be drug-related. Some ganglionic blocking agents used for the treatment of hypertension may act on both sympathetic and parasympathetic nervous systems.

4) Drugs which have indirect effects on sexual behavior include psychotropic medications. They may improve sexual behavior because of reduction of anxiety or depression, but they also have other effects, i.e., thoridazine produces "dry ejaculation" (retrograde ejaculation into the bladder) and haloperidol has been reported to produce potency disturbances. On the other hand, lithium may be perceived by the patient as depressing sexual functioning when it acts to diminish mania.

2. Psychological Aspects of Sexual Dysfunction

The psychological factors involved in sexual dysfunctions may be related to past and/or current factors. Traditional psychiatry has dealt more with the understanding and resolution of past life issues, and less with the immediate obstacles to adequate functioning. More recent therapeutic approaches, originating with Masters and Johnson (33) have attempted to modify the immediate antecedents of sexual problems, often ignoring the more remote causes. Kaplan (32) utilizes a multicausal and integrated approach with more limited goals than those of traditional psychotherapy or psychoanalysis. The attempt is to relieve the sexual dysfunction symptom, rather than effect personality change or marital harmony. Many of those who are seen for sexual therapy have had previous psychotherapy or seek it afterwards, probably related to the complexity of the symptomatology and what is uncovered during the therapy (32, 33, 35, 36).

Kaplan (32) considers impotence and other dysfunctions to be the physiological concomitants of anxiety (rather than a defense against the emergence of anxiety), resulting from the reactivating of oedipal feelings and fantasies. This psychosomatic concept implies a relationship between stress and symptom in any individual, and implies that some individuals are more vulnerable to certain types of stresses than others. The erectile mechanism may not function in stressful situations including illness, life-threatening situations, or even when the partner is not physically attractive.

Since sexual responsiveness is complex, and once initiated is a series of autonomically mediated visceral reflexes, sexual function is successful only if the person is relaxed, undistracted and not consciously monitoring or involved in obsessive ruminations. The psychogenic factors which are etiologic in the symptoms reported are related to:

a) Early sexual attitudes and experiences. These include:

    1) Lack of information because of: ignorance of technique, fear (of pregnancy, venereal disease, etc.), unrealistic expec-

tations (simultaneous orgasm), persistence of myths (men are always interested in having sex, but women are not).

2) Negative family or societal attitudes which may produce guilt, anxiety or dislike of sexual practices.

3) Past history of a traumatic sexual experience, i.e., rape, incest.

4) Early homosexual experiences which produce anxiety about sexual identity or choice.

b) Situational factors. Most often these include family or work stress, marital communication problems, infidelity, or boredom. Differences in life stage and interests between partners are often factors.

c) Problems related to intrapsychic and interpersonal issues. These range widely from simple performance anxiety when there has been a previous history of failure in sexual functioning, to serious depressions with sexual symptomatology serving as the entree into treatment. While an understanding of dynamics is essential, it is possible for a couple to learn to understand and appreciate each other, and re-explore their relationship without extensive exploration of unconscious issues. However, especially if the therapist is inexperienced, transference issues may prove to be obstacles to treatment.

The major problems producing sexual symptoms in this area are related to:

1. *Low self-esteem.* This may be manifested by fear of failure or rejection, performance anxiety, or concern about sexual identity.

2. *Dependency.* For the individual with dependency problems, the desire for a sexual relationship may be secondary to gratification of dependency needs.

3. *Depression.* This may be the major problem and it may manifest itself as a sexual dysfunction. It is critical that the depression be diagnosed and treated before any attempt at therapy for the sexual dysfunction is attempted (32). It is important to distinguish

between a depression caused by a sexual dysfunction, which can be treated by behaviorally-oriented and other specific techniques, and a depression which causes sexual problems, and must be treated primarily as a depression. Referrals for sexual dysfunction therapy are frequently made by other physicians when there is a significant underlying depression, and the symptom is a manifestation of this depression.

4. *Control issues.* When erotic feelings and orgasm are perceived as a dangerous loss of control, the individual may respond defensively. Patients often report that they go through the motions of sexual involvement but they are unable to experience sexual feelings. They become "spectators" or they develop obsessional and unrelated thoughts which diminish their sexual pleasure.

5. *Communication problems.* This may be primarily related to the physical and sexual aspects of the relationship, and amenable to a behavioral approach therapeutically, or it may be an indication of more extensive difficulty in the relationship, requiring another type of therapeutic approach. At times couples insist on direct sexual therapy, which may deteriorate rapidly since it produces pressure for communication and arouses the anxiety which had been masked by the symptom.

6. *Symptoms related to earlier unresolved conflicts.* This is classically seen in the madonna-prostitute dichotomy in men, where the man is unable to perform sexually with his spouse but he had been able to perform with other women. This symptom complex is frequently seen in the context of a pregnancy, when a wife symbolically becomes psychologically a mother, or a husband may psychologically become a father.

Sexual Response Cycle

The cycles of both female and male can be divided into four phases (33). Evidence from studies of the male cycle indicates that there is a biphasic response in terms of nervous system mediation whereby erection is primarily mediated by the parasympathetic nervous system and the emission phase of ejaculation by sympathetic nervous system and somatic nerves (32). Clinical evidence from dysfunctional syndromes in females suggests that similar mediation exists (37).

1) The *excitement* phase is characterized by increasing pelvic and penile vasocongestion which produces erection in the male, and vaginal lubrication and genital swelling in the female. In addition, there are changes in the position of pelvic organs and the vagina increases in size.

2) The *plateau* phase occurs when there is maximal enlargement and congestion of pelvic organs with shifting positions of organs, including elevation of the uterus. Immediately prior to ejaculation in the male is the period called ejaculatory inevitability at which time it is no longer possible to voluntarily inhibit ejaculation. There is no comparable period in the female cycle.

3) The *orgasmic* phase occurs with ejaculation. It consists, in the male, of involuntary 0.8 second contractions of the striated muscles surrounding the base of the penis, and of the smooth muscles of the penile urethra. The female response is similar with both striated and smooth perineal and adjacent musculature contracting at the same rate.

4) The *resolution* phase results in an abatement of local vasocongestion and a return to the basal state. For the male there is a refractory period, during which time the excitement phase cannot recur. This period of time varies primarily with age. It may last for a few seconds in adolescents, or it may take several days in a man who is over 70. There is considerable individual variation, and no specific "normal" time. For the female the absence of the refractory period means that multiple orgasms can occur in rapid succession.

Sexual Dysfunction of the Female

There is considerable confusion in the conceptualization and classification of female sexual dysfunctions. The term "frigidity" is a "catchall" term which has meant many things including failure to be erotically stimulated, and/or inability to achieve orgasm.

Kaplan's (32) classification scheme is based on the same biphasic sexual response cycle as exists in the male and also classifies disorders as primary or secondary.

1) *Sexual Unresponsiveness* (37). This category most closely approximates the more common usage of the term frigidity, and refers to inhibition of sexual arousal. The woman experiences a lack or inhibition of sexual feelings. Physiologically, she suffers from an impairment of the vasocongestive part of the cycle, so that she does not have sufficient vaginal lubrication or change in vaginal size. Etiologically, negative attitudes about sexuality, psychological or interactional problems are factors in symptom formation.

2) *Orgasmic Dysfunction* occurs in sexually responsive women who do not reach orgasm when aroused. It rarely has an organic basis, but it occurs most often in women with fear or anxiety about loss of control or unrealistic expectations about sexual performance, i.e., if the woman believes that orgasm should occur only via coitus, she may feel that she or her partner is inadequate. Anxiety appears to be mobilized at the moment of impending orgasm with the resurgent involuntary inhibition of the reflex.

3) *Vaginismus* is defined as the involuntary spastic contraction of the outer one-third of the vagina (vaginal and anal sphincter muscles). It can be considered a conditioned response, rather than specifically a hysterical conversion reaction; thus, it may or may not be related to serious intrapsychic pathology.

It may account for many of the cases of "imperforate hymen" seen in the past. Severe vaginismus may entirely prevent intercourse, and women with this symptom may avoid any attempt at coitus because they experience dyspareunia. A definitive diagnosis can only be made on physical exam. Since gynecologists are more likely to see patients with this problem initially, and those psychiatrists who do see it are unlikely to be able to make the diagnosis without a physical exam, it is clear that a good working relationship between physicians is of critical importance for appropriate assessment and treatment.

4) Dyspareunia or painful intercourse is perhaps the most common disorder causing sexual difficulties in women, seen by the gynecologist. The pain is frequently organic in etiology and thus requires a careful history and physical examination. An anatomic approach is perhaps the best way of understanding dyspareunia. Pain may result from organic lesions of the vaginal opening, clitoris, vagina, uterus, tubes and/or ovaries so that each area must be carefully explored. Other causes of dyspareunia may be related to insufficient lubrication because sexual excitation is minimal.

Therapeutic Principles

While there are a number of methods of treating sexual dysfunctions, we will consider the developments of the past decade beginning with the pioneering work of Masters and Johnson (33), since these illustrate the expanding role of the psychiatrist, and they yield better treatment results for situations with good indications than do other treatment modalities. We will not consider more traditional forms of individual, couples and group therapy, since the treatment of sexual dysfunctions by those modalities does not differ substantively from the general principles involving referral and psychiatric treatment.

The "new" sex therapies involve treatment procedures for specific dysfunctional syndromes, not for orientation or gender identity problems. The most successful model of treatment involves a synthesis of theory and procedure from several perspectives, with a focus on a basic psychodynamic understanding of the partners. An attempt is made to modify the immediate antecedents of sexual difficulties, recognizing that deeper roots exist, but assuming that resolution can occur at a more superficial level.

From a transactional systems viewpoint, the relationship itself, rather than the individual, is seen as the patient. An attempt is made then to clarify and resolve the reciprocal dynamics of the disorder. Learning theory principles are brought to bear in the process of identification of the mechanisms by which transactions are maintained and reinforced, in order to provide appropriate behavioral modifications. The symptom, then, may be considered the disorder, rather than the symptom of an underlying disorder. This is not inconsistent with, but can expand, a psychodynamic understanding. The interweaving of some of the perspectives derived from the role theory models is also useful in understanding and working with the complex interactions which derive from role definitions and expectations.

In order to succeed, the therapist must attempt to foster a sense of security in sexual functioning, to facilitate trust between partners, and to relieve excessive judgment, criticism, need for control, guilt and anxiety about performance. Since the treatment itself involves placing the patient in an anxiety-producing situation, the therapist must also help the patients tolerate this anxiety. The therapist essentially assumes an authoritative position, as the permissive parent or teacher and relieves the partners of that role. The relationship of the partners to the authority figure(s) can then be explored in the context of the progress of the therapy. Resistances arise rapidly in this form of treatment. Most often they appear as complaints about not having had time to do the assigned exercises; occasionally they may present as anger, attempts at sabotage or complaints that the exercises are too mechanical. These must be dealt with as resistances. The firm support of the therapist is most critical in overcoming them. However, since the interpersonal sensitivity of the situation may be especially high in some situations, i.e., where a direct role reversal in terms of activity-passivity may be expected, the therapist must be cautious and have a good understanding of each partner before proceeding.

There are several general operational principles in the approach to the therapy of sexual dysfunctions:

1) *Shared responsibility of the couple.* It is assumed that regardless of the specifics of the etiology, the treatment is a shared responsibility. It is not acceptable to place blame or to focus specifically on one partner as the one with "the problem."

2) *Permission for sexual enjoyment.* Sexuality is encouraged as a way of communicating, sharing and relaxing. Partners are encouraged to be spontaneous and less rigid in their definitions of acceptable sexual behaviors, or times for sexual enjoyment.

3) *Decreased pressure to perform coitus.* There is more emphasis on enjoyment of sensuality without requiring orgasm each time.

4) *Communication is emphasized.* Partners are encouraged to understand and accept each other's values, preferences and differences as "normal". Imputing motive or intention is interdicted, i.e., a partner cannot say, "You are rejecting me," but rather, "I feel that I am being rejected."

5) *A time limit* keeps the pressure to progress optimized, prevents falling into prolonged patterns of resistance, and prevents involvement in more complex dynamic issues which can be counterproductive for some couples. On the other hand, periodic reevaluations are important so that if the therapeutic approach is not effective it can be modified or changed. The use of these techniques in conjunction with psychotherapy has been debated and is not as yet resolved. Some therapists claim that it is not only helpful but important, while others see it as interfering with the psychotherapeutic process.

6) *Conjoint or co-therapy with a male/female therapy team.* This has also been debated. Masters and Johnson (33) feel that it is critical, since it provides the support of a partner of the same sex, and also decrease the intensity of the transference. Others, including Kaplan (32), feel that an experienced therapist of either gender, provided that person is well-trained in traditional therapies as well as sexual therapy, is suitable. Our experience indicates that it is important to have therapists of each gender when one of the partners demonstrates more extensive psychopathology and/or when the modification of treatment may take the form of individual meetings interwoven with couples meetings.

The question of the effect of one or two therapists on the transference is an important one. Rather than decreasing the intensity of transference reaction, two therapists, as parental figures, may increase it.

Treatment of Sexual Dysfunctions

The basic therapy format proposed by Masters and Johnson involves two weeks away from home and work, devoted totally to the treatment. While this has been extremely successful, it is not easily adaptable. The financial and time commitments for both patients and therapists may be prohibitive; in addition, their approach may not be applicable to some people. In our experience (36), those people who considered going to the Masters and Johnson clinic were already on their way to successful treatment.

Sex therapy clinics have arisen in all parts of the country, adapted to meet the specific problems and characteristics of the population involved, as well as the motivation and resistances of specific patients, i.e., active participation of both partners may be difficult in cultures where man may not tolerate any inference that their sexual performance is inadequate. The woman may be seen alone in these situations. It is important to keep in mind, however, that these reasons may also be resistances to treatment.

The therapeutic processes for the sexual dysfunctions have similar characteristics and principles. These include:

1. An initial period of coital abstinence to reduce performance anxiety and facilitate communication.

2. A focus on the substitution of giving and receiving pleasure for the exclusive goal of orgasm through systematic tactile stimulation and exploration.

3. Sequence and variation in sexual techniques which facilitate and reinforce success.

4. Specific suggestions and directions.

The following is a summary of some specific aspects of treatment.

1. *Sexual Unresponsiveness* (*Frigidity*)

The goal of therapy is to create an undemanding, relaxed and sensuous environment for sexual interaction to occur. These women often defend themselves against erotic feelings because of guilt or fear of rejection. They need support for sensual expression.

The treatment principles include:

a. Sensate focus exercises which emphasize pleasuring without demand for the first four to eight sessions.

Coitus and ejaculation are generally prohibited and the couple explores a variety of non-genital, and later genital kinds of stimulation. The emphasis is on enjoyment, the presence or absence of an erection is de-emphasized.

b. Dispelling obsessive thought.

Spectatoring is actively encouraged. Overconcern with the feelings or judgments of the partner prevent relaxation. Support and reassurances are important, as is permission for focusing on oneself and not on the partner.

c. Resumption of coitus.

Generally, after four to 10 sessions enough confidence is restored so that the couple can resume coitus.

The sensate focus exercise is a critical component. The permission and encouragement provided by this exercise may produce dramatic effects particularly if there is no specific sexual demand. It is important that it proceed slowly so that the woman can experience her own sexual feelings rather than perform as she feels she is expected to. She is encouraged to be more active in her participation. Coitus is introduced with slow, non-demand thrusting under her control, i.e., in a female superior position. Resistances are frequent, including negative reactions about what is felt, disbelief that there will be any positive effect, and/or obsessive thoughts. The therapist must refocus on sensual feelings.

2. *Orgastic Dysfunction*

The basic goal of this treatment is to enable the patient to release an overcontrolled response. This involves maximizing clitoral stimulation while at the same time diminishing the inhibitory factors. While the former is more straightforward, the latter is complex and requires a thorough understanding of the dynamics of the inhibition or the environmental interference.

The maximization of stimulation may initially involve removing the partner. The woman can be taught to bring herself to orgasm through masturbation manually or with a vibrator, providing that she is ready to accept this practice. Fantasies are encouraged. She may need to be reassured that they are not "sick" regardless of the content. Spectatoring is discouraged. As treatment proceeds her partner becomes involves first in non-coital stimulation. They proceed in a way which is similar to other dysfunctions with some modifications. The use of the "bridge technique" (33) may help with women who are primarily orgastic by clitoral stimulation, but not with coitus. This technique involves manual clitoral stimulation during coitus.

Approximately eight percent of the female population has been reported to be anorgastic by any means (32). A large percentage achieve orgasm by means other than coitus. For those women who are primarily anorgastic the major objective is to achieve the first orgasm. This dispels the fear that she is incapable of orgasm and facilitates further progress. Treatment proceeds on the premise that the reflex has been inhibited, not destroyed in these women. If the inhibition is related to unconscious determinants, then referral for psychotherapy may be necessary. Barbach has reported good results using group treatment techniques (38). Of 83 women in her program, 92 percent achieved orgasm after five weeks via masturbation, and were able to transfer to a partner within eight months.

3. *Vaginismus*

Treatment of this disorder involves progressive deconditioning of the involuntary spasm of the vaginal muscles. Before this can be done, the patient's phobic avoidance of vaginal entry must be alleviated.

Frequently this can be initiated in the gynecologist's office with a gentle pelvic exam and the use of graduated sized dilators. The presence or involvement of the partner may facilitate treatment. Encouragement and support are of primary importance. This is in contrast to the usual situation, where the partner may be angry and feel rejected, often not understanding the unconscious nature of the symptom, but interpreting it as willful. Psychotherapy in conjunction with this direct approach is sometimes indicated.

Treatment Results

Since this treatment modality is relatively new, and the patient populations are so variable, long-term follow-up data have been difficult to obtain. Treatment failures seem to occur when motivation is not evaluated.

It is clear that the liaison between therapists with physical and psychological expertise is especially critical in the evaluation and treatment of sexual dysfunctions. Patients are optimally treated if the therapists are available to each other or work directly together. This requires that the psychiatrist be more comfortable with the physical aspects of these disorders, while the gynecologist acquires a psychological perspective. Thus, the role of each is expanded.

PREGNANCY: SPECIAL ISSUES

The complex interaction of physical and psychosocial factors in pregnancy makes demands upon physicians which their training has often not addressed, and which may conflict with their individual values and attitudes. A paradigm for understanding the evolving role of the psychiatrist in gynecologic care is the problem of the pregnant teenager whose management requires a complex integration of expertise in a number of fields. The gynecologist is asked to help her make a decision about her pregnancy, and to treat her in a sympathetic, unbiased manner often without possessing the understanding or objectivity required. If she decides to abort the pregnancy, the physician is asked to perform a procedure which may not have been legal or ethical during his training and about which he may have conflicted feelings.

The psychiatrist has increasingly been involved as a consultant and teacher. Until recently the consultation/liaison function had largely involved answering questions about pregnancy which included the acceptance or rejection of the "feminine" role in pregnancy, and concerns about the likelihood of postpartum depression or psychosis. The questions which are important currently are considerably broader.

We will consider the kinds of information about pregnancy, motherhood and abortion which must be synthesized for effective consultation/liaison work to be done.

"Pregnancy is a 'disease' of nine months' duration, and women should be given adequate prophylaxis well in advance to mitigate some of the unfortunate sequelae associated with pregnancy, labor and delivery (39)." Thus begins a chapter on Marriage and Parenthood in a 1962 textbook. While important aspects of the pregnancy are also considered, it is the disease model which is striking and must be questioned.

Pregnancy is a normative function with special characteristics which make it similar to other developmental crises of the life cycle (40), i.e., puberty and menopause. These crises require adaptation. They confront the individual with new issues, and also precipitate the re-emergence of earlier unsettled conflicts. They offer the individual the possibility of further growth and maturation through mastery.

Pregnancy has been called a fulfillment and a creative act (41). It may also be a stressful time, requiring the woman to meet the challenges of pregnancy itself and the subsequent new identity which emerges. Bibring et al. (42) point out that pregnancy involves both physical and psychological changes that are immutable. Thus, like puberty and menopause, the issues involved in resolution of this stage are milestones. Once one is an adolescent one cannot be a child again, and once one has passed menopause one cannot bear children.

For most pregnant women, "routine care" including physical attention, factual information, and support are sufficient. However, for many women, the obstetrician may be the only person in a position to observe and respond to failing psychological defenses which may result in decompensation during a pregnancy.

The consultation/liaison psychotherapist has an important role. Bibring and Valenstein (43) described the development of a consultation/liaison team on the obstetric-gynecological service of a general hospital. The team interviewed newly-admitted patients in order to intercept and refer for psychotherapy where indicated. The team also served as an educational nucleus to alert and help train the obstetric personnel to recognize and care for patients who presented psychological problems for obstetric management.

Among the results of the study they conducted while working in this way was that a "surprising" number of young women were referred to them who were diagnosed as borderline personalities or considered to be seriously disturbed. They found that emotional instability was prominent and that archaic material was easily elicited. However they noted that therapeutic results could be obtained with greater ease than would have been expected from the severity of the presenting disturbances and that the adjustment to pregnancy and parenthood was not necessarily as difficult as had been anticipated. They concluded that pregnancy could be considered a developmental crisis and thus upheaval and even regression could be expected in the service of maturation.

When the diagnosis of pregnancy is made, even when the pregnancy is desired, fear and ambivalence are frequently experienced by the "normal" woman, as one would expect with any new and major life change. The beginning is simple, but the implications are lifelong, and the changes are permanent and progressive. Areas that had previously seemed conflict-free may no longer be experienced in the same way. Anxiety and questions may arise about one's future role and responsibility, about the marriage, and about career plans. Pregnant women often describe feeling alienated from a physician who does not acknowledge negative feelings or permit ambivalence. They feel criticized and guilty.

Other feelings which are basic to the experience of pregnancy are those concerning the woman's early relationships with her mother and the experience of having been mothered. There is a change in the relationship of the woman to her mother, as they change roles. Past difficulties may cause feelings of guilt, anger, ambivalence, and remorse (40, 41, 42, 43). Pregnancy has multiple meanings for both parents together, as well as for each of them individually. They must conceptualize themselves as parents, and deal with ambivalence and separateness. In addition the father may feel threatened if he sees the child as a potential competitor (44). The child's sex or position in the family may have particular meaning. Sexual problems are often manifested for the first time, related to feelings about the current pregnancy or future pregnancies, or because of the physical changes occurring during the prepartum and postpartum periods. Bearing a child represents a hastening toward adulthood.

Motivation for Pregnancy

The motivations for pregnancy are complex and multiple and are not limited to feelings about a specific relationship. They may be different from those relating to actually caring for children.

Concerns about the ability to love or be loved may be motivating factors. Women at times express the feeling that a child would guarantee them love. A pregnancy may occur as an attempt to resolve questions about the reality or endurance of a particular relationship (41, 45). A pregnancy may also serve to affirm sexual identity (41), especially in adolescent and younger women. However, while the occurrence of a pregnancy provides the physical evidence of femininity or adulthood, the psychological aspects of the pregnancy may not be resolved. In the adolescent, a pregnancy may be an attempt to facilitate separation from her parents, or to resolve long-standing conflicts in that relationship (46). A woman may want a child because she wants a mother (45) and needs to master an early life experience of deprivation. The pregnancy may provide, in fantasy, a means of having a child and being a child simultaneously. It may also be an unconscious attempt to seek a resolution of oedipal conflicts.

Pregnancy in the Adolescent

Although the incidence of pregnancy generally is decreasing and the high value placed on parenthood is changing, teenage parents are a rapidly increasing group. In 1968, a fourth of 20-year-old females had had at least one baby while in their teens (47, 48). The implications of this change are extremely important. In addition to the problems of superimposing two developmental phases, the long-term consequences for the teenage mother and her child must be considered. The question of whether a pregnancy is wanted or unwanted is far more complex to assess since the desire and the capability of fulfilling expectations at this life stage are less consistent.

The physical and psychosocial consequences are considerable. There is a higher risk of toxemia, premature birth, perinatal loss, pre- and postnatal infection, and complications of labor and delivery, which appear to be related to poor prenatal care, often correlated with socio-economic factors. The psychosocial risks include school dropout and repeated failures in jobs and life situations, with a high pregnancy recidivism rate (49). Menarche confronts the adolescent girl with irreversible physiological changes which have multiple implications and over which she has no control. Since the onset of menarche has been earlier in recent years, the physical events may take place in the emotional matrix of childhood. Thus the adolescent may not be prepared to cope with the "normal" adolescent changes, especially if other stresses have occurred during this phase.

Early in adolescence sexual fantasies and feelings are handled by direct expression in action, by symptom formation, or by repression, withdrawal or denial. At times the adaptive and defensive measures employed are extreme and severe regression may occur. Inconsistency, unpredictability, and ambivalence are the hallmarks of the evolutionary process toward the final maturational goals. In the course of the development of a self-concept, the young adolescent girl does not necessarily integrate the perception of herself as a physiological woman capable of procreation in the same way as would an adult woman. The consequences of sexual activity may be perceived in vastly different ways, and often there is little understanding of the repercussions of sexual acts. Pregnancy, for example, may be a vague, unintegrated and unreal possibility; a baby may be a doll to play with, it may express a regressive wish, it may be the representation of a childlike self-image, or it may be a plea for caring. Schaffer and Pine (49) discuss pregnancy in adolescents as an expression of and solution of the conflict between the wish to be mothered and the urge to be mothering. It may be a response to a loss especially of a parent. A pregnancy can be a way for an adolescent girl to announce her womanhood and invite acknowledgement of her sexuality. It may occur when more subtle communications are missed, or when parents fail to facilitate separation. It may be a way of avoiding loneliness and isolation.

Bernard (46) described the interplay of social and familial forces with the adolescent's internal strivings for independence and sexual maturation. She also pointed to the significance of disorganization and deprivation in the families of young pregnant adolescents.

Deutsch (41) emphasized unconscious motivation and mentioned flight from incestuous fantasies by means of intimacy with the first man encountered. Also important are passivity, identification with a pregnancy of mother or sister, revenge toward the family, and depression. She pointed out that no specific dynamic constellation is present for all pregnant adolescents and commented that the adolescent "ego is too weak to escape the dangers and temptations of the outside world or to achieve more favorable conditions under which to satisfy the urge for motherhood."

Young (50) noted the pregnant adolescent's failure to apply her sexual knowledge to herself was evidenced by non-use of contraception and lack of anticipation of pregnancy. The adolescent may be unwilling or unable to give up comforting and supporting fantasies and thus be unmotivated to avoid pregnancy. She may be terrified to face her own emptiness and inadequate resources. Repetition is more likely if the basic issues are unresolved.

The problems of loss are further intensified because the putative fáther (also frequently an adolescent) may abandon the girl or she may provoke rejection to alleviate her guilt and mollify her parents. The resultant feelings of despair and unworthiness result in further lowering of self-esteem.

For the adolescent, the conflict about her pregnancy, which must be resolved, resonates between the positive aspects of conception and pregnancy and the frustration and sadness of making a choice either to terminate the pregnancy, to continue it and change the course of identity resolution and the formulation of life goals, or to confront a permanent separation by giving up the child. There is no "good" alternative.

This conflict is of particular developmental significance since it may represent the first time a decision of this magnitude, with life-long implications, must be faced. Even passive acceptance represents a decision to continue the pregnancy. The resolution of a decision about an unwanted pregnancy is often complicated by a regressive response. This is related to the lack of firmly established ego mechanisms, or decision-making capacity, reinforced by family strife (51).

Since denial is a major ego defense of the young adolescent, it is not surprising that acknowledgment of the reality of a pregnancy is often delayed, resulting in the need for a quick decision about termination or continuation of the pregnancy. In addition to denial, inexperience, fear and anxiety play a major role in preventing the teenager from seeking help. Destructive fantasies often increase this anxiety and foster reluctance to seek help. Many adolescents are uncertain about where to turn. Others are fearful, guilty about confronting their parents or overly influenced by peer pressures. At times an adolescent believes that her parents will insist on a course of action, such as abortion, so she postpones telling them of the pregnancy until it is too late to do anything but to continue. The family is then forced to adapt after a decision has been made, rather than to participate in the decision-making process.

In an attempt to separate from her parents, the adolescent may polarize behavior and ideas in order to differentiate herself. She may choose a solution primarily because she feels her family wants the opposite. The family, on the other hand, may be angry and seek to punish their daughter. Since the adolescent most likely will continue to live with her family, it is difficult to help her make a decision without their participation.

The capacity for delay and the tolerance of anxiety may be severely tested with an unwanted pregnancy. In order to reduce the tension, an adolescent may want to avoid counselling, and to reach a rapid decision. This pressure is also a means of denying the implications of the pregnancy and the need to assume an active role in the decision making.

A teenager who has not worked through maturational issues, and who has become pregnant once, is more at risk to repeat a pregnancy. Data have accumulated on the recidivism rate for unwanted pregnancy, and its relationship to non-use of contraceptives. Some authors (48) report that 20-40 percent repeat within three years after a pregnancy. Sarrel (52) reported in a study of teenage pregnancy that of 63 primigravidas who delivered an out-of-wedlock baby, 36 delivered another one a year later. In a follow-up of 100 teenage unwed mothers (13-17 years old) over a five-year period, he found that there was a total of 349 pregnancies and 9 abortions; only five girls did not become pregnant again.

Abortion vs. Continuation

Recent research on the psychiatric risks of abortion generally reveals that the contraindications to abortion are not specific. Some psychiatric sequelae of abortion exist, but they are not major or permanent; they are related to personality dynamics, stress tolerance, and degree of ambivalence (53). In addition, there are indications that fewer problems related to guilt occur when abortion is legal and available than when illegal abortion is the only recourse (53).

Those who choose to carry the pregnancy to term do so out of a desire to have a baby and for other reasons, including the inability to bear the abortion loss, or to make a decision for abortion on religious or ethical grounds. They may be fearful of ostracism by their peer group or family, or they may feel guilty and see the continuation of the pregnancy as a just punishment. The socio-economic

ontext is an important factor. The adolescent who is making a
ecision about an abortion or continuing a pregnancy needs to
nderstand her motivations, explore her ambivalance, and consider
ne alternative solutions as objectively as possible. Discussion about
tture prevention of pregnancy can often be made in the context of
ne experience with an unwanted pregnancy (54, 107). The legaliza-
on of abortion has permitted more careful consideration of the rea-
ons for the choice, and has made it possible for consultation to be an
:tive part of the decision-making process when the psychiatrist
ho does evaluate a woman requesting an abortion is no longer
sponsible for a judgment about whether or not it is indicated, but
e or she as a consultant is helping the woman to make a decision.

A distinction must be made between the woman who is seen in
ounselling or therapy as a consequence of the crisis of the unwanted
regnancy and those for whom a pregnancy is a signal of disturbance
nd who may be referred for psychotherapy with long-term goals.
n the counselling situation there are two primary goals: 1) short-
rm intervention, including decision-making about the pregnancy;
) the beginning integration of the experience, which necessarily
cludes some understanding of motivation and the precipitating
cial and family circumstances. Although pregnancy in a teenager
ay be considered a crisis, it is not in itself either an indication of
ychopathology or a reason for long-term psychotherapy.

It is evident that the liaison between obs/gyn and psychiatry
volves a major teaching and supervisory component. The physician
practice must have the ability to understand complex family
namics and the skills necessary to handle a range of psychosocial
oblems, the majority of which cannot and should not be specifically
ferred to a psychiatrist.

RAPE

Rape has recently received serious attention from medical profes-
onals, who in the past felt that they had little to offer. Profes-
onals shared the popular view that the victim was acting out con-
ious or unconscious sexual fantasies, and therefore was not "really"

a victim. Thus, she could not expect to receive the empathy an understanding usually extended to people in crisis. The increase incidence of rape and changing ideas about it confronted healt professionals with the necessity to become more involved.

The link between the physical and psychological aspects of med cine is particularly emphasized in the approach to the rape victim It is both a medical and psychiatric emergency. In addition to im mediate care, the psychiatrist plays a major role in teaching, super vision and in the development of services which incorporate con siderations of the victim's emotional response together with physica care.

The Rape Experience

Rape is a violent crime which is often misperceived as a sexua experience. The possibility of serious harm or death exists, and th victim's prime concern is to protect herself from injury. The absenc of consent is crucial to the definition of rape. Men are also raped however, the vast majority of victims are women (55).

The presence of unconscious rape fantasies is often seen as evidenc of complicity. While unconscious rape fantasies occur in most people the individual's defensive organization protects him/her from actin out these fantasies which are not equivalent to provocation. The rap victim is confronted with the uncontrolled sadism and aggression o another person, and her own vulnerability. This challenges her self confidence and her ability to function independently.

Rape is best viewed as a stressful situation in which a traumati external event disrupts the balance between ego adaptation and th environment. Since it is an interaction between an extreme environ mental stimulus, and the adaptive capacity of the victim, it is simila to other situations described in the literature on stress, which includ studies of victims of community disasters (56, 57), war (58, 59 60, 61), and surgical procedures (62, 63).

Victims range widely in their initial responses to rape. Som appear to be calm, without overt evidence of fear and anxiety; other react with confusion, agitation and terror. Following the experience as behavioral control and memory are regained, the woman may experience a profound sense of failure and inadequacy if she perceives criticism of her response pattern or mistrust of her story. Retrospectively the victim often blames herself for her lack of perception or attention to danger at the time of the rape.

Affective Responses

Burgess and Holmstrom (64) describe the rape crisis syndrome as an acute disorganizational phase with behavioral, somatic and psychological manifestations, and a long-term reorganizational phase with variable components depending on the ego strengths, social networks, and specific experiences of the woman who confronts this situation. They emphasize the experience of shock, disbelief, and absence of anger in many victims, followed by guilt and self-blame.

Janis (63), in describing surgical trauma patients, offers a partial explanation for this. He states that any threat which cannot be influenced by the individual's own behavior may be unconsciously perceived in the same way as childhood threats of parental punishment for bad behavior. This results in attempts to control anger and aggression in order to insure that there is no provocation of further punishment. Thus, overt anger may be repressed.

Another reason for the apparent lack of initial anger in the rape victim may derive from conflicts about the expression of overt aggression for women in our culture. It is often masochistically turned inward, and appears as self-blame. Identification with the aggressor, as an attempt to gain mastery, is also seen (55).

The suppression of anger during the attack may also be adaptive, since the woman may not have been able to resist. Angry feelings appear later in recurrent nightmares, explosive outbursts, and displacement. Societal support for the idea that she may have, in some way, participated in the rape, encourages repression of anger. The victim also feels guilt and shame concomitant with feelings of helplessness and vulnerability. She may feel that she should have been either more active or more passive in order to have prevented the attack. Inability to resolve the crisis may result in the development of a traumatic neurosis.

The tendency to focus on sexuality rather than violence also supports guilty feelings. Taboos and prohibitions about sexuality make it possible for an unwilling participant to be accused of complicity, e.g., the women in Bangladesh who were raped by the enemy soldiers were unacceptable to their own community afterwards despite their obvious victimization. The popular expression that if a woman cannot avoid rape she should "relax and enjoy it" misconstrues the attack as a sexual experience, which a more sexually comfortable woman would not consider traumatic.

Life Stage Considerations

The single woman between the ages of 17-24 is the most frequently reported rape victim. In this age group, rape victims frequently have prior knowledge of the rapist, who may be a relative or a neighbor. Thus, the victim may reproach herself, feeling that she should have been able to prevent the rape. Her sense of helplessness may reinforce fears of relationships with men. This is especially true for the very young woman whose first sexual experience may have been rape. Parents, friends and relative may invite regression with suggestions that she stay at home or leave school if it is away from home. This reaction often comes from their guilt about not having been protective enough and may not be helpful to the victim.

The gynecological examination may pose particular problems for the young rape victim. Since she may have suffered physical trauma, is susceptible to venereal disease, and may become pregnant, an examination is indicated. The examination may, however, be perceived as another rape, especially by an inexperienced or severely traumatized woman, even though she is also concerned about the intactness and integrity of her body, and needs the reassurance of the examination.

The divorced or separated woman has additional concerns, because her apparent sexual availability makes her more vulnerable. She also may experience rape as a confirmation of her feelings of inadequacy and her inability to be independent. If she has children, she may worry about her ability to protect and care for them. She must also deal with the problems of what and when to tell them, especially if the event is known in the community.

For the "middle-aged" woman, the issues of control of her life and reaffirmation of her sexual identity are important. She may be in a period of reassessment of her role and future goals, particularly as her relationships to her family change. Husbands, in their own mid-life crises, may be less responsive and supportive.

Long-Term Responses

The experience of rape confronts many women with ambivalent feelings about men which may have evolved from past developmental experiences and expectations. The sense of betrayal by the rapist as well as by the husband, father, or lover, who had been seen as potential protectors has a profound effect. Almost all victims describe that they trust men less, for shorter or longer periods of time, following the experience.

It is difficult to predict the long-term reactions or needs of the rape victim, since the experience and the working through of the trauma are so individually determined. Some of the issues which emerge at a later date are:

1) mistrust of men with avoidance or hesitation of contact,
2) sexual disturbances,
3) phobic reactions,
4) anxiety and depression often precipitated by seemingly unrelated events which in some small details bring back the original trauma.

Counselling

Adequate counselling requires an understanding of the victim's life adjustment as well as her ego functions, including object relations, stress tolerance, and adaptive resources. The current life situation of the victim, and the kinds of supports she has available to her are also important.

Initially the rape victim needs reassurance about the way in which she handled the encounter, and her efforts to cope with her feelings following the experience. She may be defensive or displace her anger onto those who are attempting to help, i.e. friends, doctors, or the police. They may react directly to her behavior, often rejecting her without understanding the underlying issues. The more subdued victim may need to be encouraged to communicate her feelings as best she can rather than to be supported for her ability to be "cool" and a "good patient." Rape victims may need to be offered the opportunity for counselling in the future, if they do not want to be seen initially.

Since the psychological issues may be the most critical variables in the ultimate recovery of the victim, they must be given high priority. The anxiety and anger of those who provide the initial care for the rape victim often cause them to focus more on the medical and legal issues, and they may fail to perceive the magnitude of the emotional stress. This is particularly true if the woman has a response in which she attempts to restore self-esteem by being in control. The psychiatrist may function as a supervisor and consultant —to the gynecologist, the nurse, and the counselor—both in the acute care phase and during the follow-up period.

There is considerable controversy about the involvement of psychiatrists, in any role other than as consultants, since their presence may be seen as implying that the response of the victim is pathological. This view, however, fails to consider the diversity of roles for the psychiatrist, and also minimizes the consequences of rape for those women who are severely psychologically traumatized or those women who have already had previous psychiatric problems.

MENSTRUAL FLUCTUATIONS AND PREMENSTRUAL SYNDROME

New information on the female reproductive cycle has thrown into question some established ideas. We will focus on the premenstrual syndrome and menopause. In both of these areas recent critical examinations of existing data, as well as new studies, have indicated that connections between the endocrine and other physiological changes on the one hand and behavioral and emotional symptomatology on the other are not as well established as had previously been thought.

The existence and basis of behavioral and mood fluctuations with phases of the menstrual cycle have been debated for years. The unsuitability of women for important positions was defended on the grounds that they were too strongly affected by these cyclic changes. Although many women experience no changes premenstrually, it is apparent clinically that for others the days before each period are characterized by irritability, lability, or depression. For those who experience it, the symptoms disappear with the onset of the menstrual period.

Premenstrual tension has been made responsible for a wide variety of social behavior and psychological phenomena. Crimes committed (65, 66), suicide attempts, misbehavior of schoolgirls, psychiatric admissions in emergency rooms and walk-in clinics (67, 68) have been related to the premenstrual period. A number of studies of suicidal attempts have indicated that a majority occurred in the bleeding phase of the cycle (69, 70). Suicide and suicide attempts and threats were minimal in the post bleeding, preovulatory phase of the reproductive cycle. Self reports of functioning during the menstrual cycle indicate that a small percentage of women feel their judgment or mental faculties are impaired to some extent, particularly in the premenstrual phase of the cycle (67).

Sommer (67) in a review of studies of cognitive and perceptual-motor behavior in relation to menstruation points out methodological problems in much of the research. The problem of determining the hormonal status of the subjects, the selection bias towards women with regular cycles, the use of self reports, and the compounding of objective with subjective data complicate the evaluation of results. Many studies have not been replicated. A majority of studies using objective performance measures failed to demonstrate significant cyclic fluctuation in performance. Parlee (71) in her review takes a similar position. She has also raised methodological questions about research in this area. Correlational studies do not clearly indicate the relationship between cause and effect.

Sommer (67) concludes "it appears that those instances in which a cyclic effect occurs are those in which responses are mediated by social and psychological factors: Subjects express feelings in interaction with their social environment in ways consonant with their expectations about themselves and about the demands and expectations of the social milieu in which they move. Where social or psychological expectations of menstrual debilitation are altered, the effect disappears." Thus, when a woman expects that her behavior and responses will be affected by her menstrual cycle, and lives in a setting where these expectations are shared, it is likely that her perception of her functioning will reflect this. Nevertheless, the large body of data suggesting some behavioral effects of menstrual phases needs further exploration. Recently there have been some suggestive data that there are EEG responses to varying gonadal hormones (72) which deserve further research (67).

Clinical observations of menstrual variations may reflect responses of the individual to her own and social expectations, identification with important women in her life, or somatic expressions of a wide variety of feelings about herself, her femininity, and her body. Observations of family patterns in menstrual responses (73) indicate a strong tendency for girls to repeat the patterns of their mothers in their premenstrual reactions, dysmenorrhea, and extent of morbidity around the menstrual period.

It is important that the psychiatrist and gynecologist avoid an "either/or" approach to evaluation and treatment of these symptoms and maintain awareness of the individual and social context which may lead to certain patterns of response. The expectation that a woman is likely to have "premenstrual tension" may also lead to relying on this explanation for emotional symptoms, thus closing off further understanding.

MENOPAUSE

In recent years new attention has been paid to the middle years of adult development, an area previously neglected in the psychiatric literature. This has also included reexamination of the menopausal period. Here, also, endocrinological data and social-psychological data (19, 71, 74) indicate that many misconceptions have existed about the nature and extent of the symptomatology directly ascribable to the menopause. In a review of endocrinological data, Perlmutter (75) states, "There are multiple disorders that have been ascribed to the changing hormonal balance and are equated with menopause. In reality, not all the changes that are noted are due to hormonal imbalances. . . ."

Research in this area suffers from methodological problems such as relying on case histories, clinical impressions or analyses of data from selected samples of women under the care of gynecologists or psychiatrists. Those studies which are more reliable show that "psychosomatic and psychological complaints were not reported more frequently by so called 'menopausal' than by younger women (76)."

Vasomotor instability, "manifested as hot flashes, flushes, episodes of perspiration or attack," has been one of the consistent symptoms accompanying menopause. This is present in a large number of women, up to 75 percent reporting some degree of symptomatology (75, 77). McKinley and Jefferys (76) in a review of symptoms of women aged 45-54 in the London area found that hot flashes and night sweats are "clearly associated with the onset of a natural menopause and that they occur in majority of women." The other symptoms which were investigated "namely headaches, dizzy spells, palpitations, sleeplessness, depression, and weight increase, showed no direct relationship to the menopause but tended to occur together."

The etiology of the hot flashes is unclear. Although there is general agreement that estrogen therapy will alleviate the symptomatology in most women, other disease processes in which estrogen levels are low, e.g., stress amenorrhea and anorexia nervosa are not characterized by hot flashes (75). Thus the etiology of the symptoms appears to be more complex than simple estrogen deficit. Psychological factors such as anger, anxiety, excitement, are considered important in precipitating "flashes" in susceptible women, as are activities giving rise to excess heat production or retention such as a warm environment, muscular work, or eating hot food (77). However, the symptoms may arise without any clear psychological or heat-stimulating mechanism.

Another group of changes which do consistently accompany menopause are atrophic changes in skin, subcutaneous tissue, and mucosa. These occur as part of the aging process. The natural moisture of some tissues is lost, accentuating atrophic changes, resulting in dryness of skin and mucosa, and in altered vaginal secretions. This also has some potential effect on the susceptibility to infection, and also on sexual functioning, since vaginal lubrication may be slower to develop. This may create difficulties if the balance of sexual response is very sensitive for a couple. Local estrogen treatment can be highly effective if sexual problems result from changes in lubrication.

Age at menopause varies from the late thirties to middle or even late fifties. This variation supports the tendency to assign a variety of symptoms occurring in these years to a woman's menopausal status. In a study of age at menopause, McKinley, Jefferys and Thompson (78) found that "The median age at menopause in industrial societies now occurs at about fifty years of age and there is no firm evidence that this age has increased at least in the last century, nor any indication of any close relationships between the age at menopause and the age at menarche or socioeconomic status. . . . There is some evidence that marital status and parity are related to the age at menopause, independently of each other (78)."

Many other mid-life symptoms have been attributed to menopause and many menopausal symptoms have been attributed to estrogen deficiency or the hormonal changes. The range of symptomatology considered part of the menopausal syndrome has varied considerably. Insomnia, irritability, depression, diminished sexual interest, headaches, dizzy spells, and palpitations have been considered part of the menopausal period, but they do not occur consistently (76). Neugarten and her co-workers (79, 80) studied 100 women ages 43-53 using menstrual histories as an index of menopausal or climacteric status. They found "climacteric status to be unrelated to a wide array of personality measures." They also found "very few significant relationships between the severity of somatic and psychosomatic symptoms and these variables (79)." Kraines (81) found that menopausal status was "not a contributing factor in self-evaluations of middle-aged women." She also found, as one might expect, that women who had low self-esteem and life satisfaction previously were likely to have difficulties with menopause. This leads to an understanding of menopause as one of the important experiences for women but best understood in the context of their lives.

Thus, women's reactions to turning points in their lives such as menarche and pregnancy are consistent with their reactions to menopause. While this is not surprising, a finding which is more surprising, which is supported by crosscultural data (19), is that it is those women who score high on "motherliness" scales, and those who have invested heavily in their childbearing and rearing who are more likely to experience depression.

This is contrary to earlier ideas, by Deutsch (41) and Benedek (82) who predicted that childless women would have more intense reactions. Women who have not had children actually do not necessarily have the most difficulties at menopause. Many of them have had to come to terms with their childlessness earlier than the biological menopause and have found other ways of organizing their lives. The menopause then represents a less critical event. To some extent childlessness may represent underlying ambivalence about motherhood, which is more readily expressed in contemporary society than was possible earlier, and can be better implemented with effective contraception and abortion.

Social class is an important variable. Middle class and upper class women appear to find the cessation of childbearing more liberating because more alternatives are open to them. Neugarten and her co-workers (83) report that upper and middle class women tended to minimize their reactions compared to lower class women. In this relatively advantaged group, younger women anticipating menopause were more concerned than women who were menopausal. Post-menopausal women generally took a more positive view "with higher proportions agreeing that the menopause creates no major discontinuity in life and agreeing that except for the underlying biological changes, women have a relative degree of control over their symptoms and need not inevitably have difficulties." Other studies (84) confirm that middle class women are less anxious about the menopause than working class women, but generally "menopausal status is not associated with measurable anxiety." Women who have invested heavily in their childbearing role and for whom it has also been an important source of their social status derived from being a mother as well as mothering are more likely to experience depression (19). Cultural factors play a role in determining the importance of menstruating, childbearing, and mothering in the self-esteem and status of women as well as determining their alternatives.

Clinically, the obstetrician-gynecologist as well as the psychiatrist may automatically focus on the menstrual history to explain the presenting symptoms of a middle-aged woman patient. Recent studies have thrown doubt on this inevitable relationship and have stressed the importance of other midlife experiences for women in producing the symptomatology. As in understanding premenstrual symptomatology, rather than automatically focusing on the menstrual history to explain the symptoms of a middle-aged woman, one can understand the experience of menopause by looking more closely at the midlife period. When her major role and source of self-esteem have been perceived as centering around her reproductive life, the ending of childbearing creates a real loss. The concomitant changes of aging and the devaluation of the aged and aging, especially of aging women, leads to lowered self-esteem and to potential depression. However, although depression in women in midlife is an important clinical entity and women are vulnerable to depression, it appears that the group most at risk are married women, but specifically those with young children living at home (74, 85). There is also a postmenopausal rise in energy and activity, possibly deriving from the diminished time and energy needed in caring for children (82). This increase in psychic energy permits a developmental impetus for nonneurotic women whose lives offer them opportunities for growth.

Family experiences of this period are important. The midlife transition for men (86), often the husbands of menopausal women, brings new stresses. This period for men is often accompanied by sexual problems, sometimes leading to affairs, marital disruption, and the abandonment of the women. Adolescent children may be sexually and aggressively provocative, challenging, or disappointing. Children leaving home for school or marriage change the family balance. This has been described generally as loss. However, some women view it as extension or expansion of their parenting to include the wider interests and loci of their children (87). Change and transition do cause stress, require new adaptations, and are sometimes accompanied by symptoms. Bernard (85) in her studies on marriage indicates that marital satisfactions increase as children leave the home. The "empty nest syndrome" appears not to be universal.

The view that midlife symptoms are due to endocrine changes results in treatment of midlife or menopausal complaints with estrogens. The data on effectiveness of estrogen replacement suffer from similar methodological problems as data on other aspects of menopause (75, 76, 78); the greatest agreement seems to concern the effectiveness of estrogens in treating hot flashes. Recent reports of the carcinogenicity of estrogens have raised serious questions about their use. Furthermore, focus on a drug treatment approach also discourages attention to important individual concerns and problems.

The liaison psychiatrist can offer a great deal to the menopausal patient and her gynecologist by helping differentiate the components of her reaction and by avoiding the stereotypes of diagnosis and treatment. Support for her femininity, her continued sexual interest and activity, and the possibilities of new productive directions in her life can follow from the psychiatrist's developmental approach.

SURGICAL GYNECOLOGY

There are several surgical procedures which have particular significance for women since they involve reproductive or sexual organs and hence affect the woman's concept of her feminine identity. Hysterectomy and mastectomy have a major impact on one's body and self image. In addition they are usually superimposed on a serious malfunction. Other procedures such as sterilization or amnio-centesis may be elected for a positive preventive end but at the same time can be experienced as assaults.

A psychiatrist may be called as a consultant to evaluate the impact of these procedures or even to make a decision about indications, such as the proposal for hysterectomy for "intractable pelvic pain."

MASTECTOMY

Breast surgery involves many of the same anxieties about body image, femininity, intactness and mutilation as does hysterectomy.

In response to recent statistics (88), the efficacy of radical mas-tectomy has been questioned. Modified radical surgery, simple mas-tectomy, and even "lumpectomy" for malignancy are performed with good results. For some women, the knowledge that a disfiguring operation is not inevitable has made it easier to seek medical attention for breast masses.

Breasts are important symbolically and realistically to both men and women. For women they represent an important component of femininity, combining nutrient maternal potential with sexual at-tractiveness. Thus, for some women, their capacity to nourish and to give is important not only in their actual functions as a nursing mother or in the role of a lover, but in helping create the sense of worthwhileness and adequacy which underlies self-esteem. Our society idealizes the breasts and their contribution to a woman's sexual desirability. Although changing styles of dress and standards of tastes have affected the degree of visibility and emphasis on the breast, their central importance remains. Since breasts are not part of a child's body but grow in adolescence, their development sym-bolizes the girl's movement into adult womanhood. The breasts are integrated into a woman's image of her sexual attractiveness.

The significance of her breasts to a woman goes beyond realistic considerations alone. For some, the prominence of their breasts as adults may make up for their fantasied anatomic "inferiority" as little girls. For other women an important meaning is the link to mother. The symbolic importance of the breasts remains throughout life.

A mastectomy raises a number of issues. These include the confrontation with a life-threatening illness, the loss of a body part, and specific concerns related to the breast. For the surgeon, the dominant aspect is usually the life-threatening illness. Appropriately, he/she is first concerned with the patient's survival, then with the morbidity associated with both the malignancy and the cure, and finally with the patient's physical and emotional response to the whole experience. Many physicians feel they protect the patient by not fully communicating their concern to her. There may be a discrepancy between what the physician knows and what he tells the patient and family, and therefore what the patient must deal with. There may also be a discrepancy between what the doctor thinks he/she is doing, namely helping the patient and treating the illness, and how the patient perceives this, namely as a helpful procedure for her survival and cure, but also as an attack. The consultation-liaison psychiatrist may be helpful to the surgeon in communicating this double view.

Even if family members are aware of the extent of illness they sometimes cannot confront the patient. A family consultation may be appropriate. The tendency to reassure and play down distress characterizes many aspects of the doctor-patient relationship. In understanding reactions to mastectomy as well as to other surgery, an individual's response to trauma and crisis is important. As noted in discussing reaction to rape, a positive or negative view of how one has coped may affect not only this experience but future capacity to respond to stress.

The individual who has suffered any traumatic experience tends to repeat aspects of the experience in an attempt at mastery. This involves talking about it, reconstructing the circumstances, and exploring alternate responses. However, in an attempt to reduce discomfort, create an atmosphere of optimism, and encourage the patient to feel well, the hospital and staff may promote an environment which reduces for the patient the significance of what is happening to her. The consultation-liaison psychiatrist may be helpful in supporting the staff to permit a patient to express her reactions to the experience.

The acuteness of the situation has considerable effect on the kind of trauma which a mastectomy represents. A sudden change from a state of apparent good health to one in which a major loss has occurred creates greater potential for disorganization. There are psychological advantages to allowing the patient adequate time between diagnosis and surgery, during which she can be prepared. When possible, adequate preparation of the patient and her family is critical. The surgeon is often unable to take this time and may be made anxious by the patient's delay, making adequate preparation difficult. There may be a gap between what the surgeon feels he has explained and what the patient, under conditions of great stress, hears and understands.

A major component of the reaction to mastectomy is a reaction to loss and the restitutive efforts made. Although this is true of other surgery, the visibility of the breast makes it particularly important. The reaction to the loss of a breast may also represent a response to earlier losses which have not been worked through. For instance, excessive grief at the loss of a breast may represent an unresolved reaction to the loss of a mother many years before. A severe reaction to the loss of a breast may really reflect the patient's concern about dying.

The loss of sexual attractiveness is a concern of many women. This is generally assumed to be most prominent for younger women. However, older women may be just as concerned with their sexual desirability as younger women. A menopausal woman who is worried about the effects of aging on her physical attractiveness may be particularly vulnerable to the effects of a mastectomy which further intensify the feeling that she is losing her sexual identity. In the last few years, women have become more outspoken about their sexual feelings and needs. Previous tendencies were to minimize the sexual interest of older women, and to assume that they do not share the concerns of younger women. The physician's support for the legitimacy of these needs can help the woman through this stressful period.

The sense of disfigurement from the loss of a breast may be considerable, even though the absence of the breast may be hidden under clothing. Reconstructive surgery following simple mastectomy in suitable patients may create a positive emotional reaction. It also conveys the physician's belief in her recovery since someone thinks it worthwhile to invest in reconstruction, although sometimes the possibility of reconstruction mobilizes the patient's awareness of the degree of her upset. Goldwyn (89) reports that surgeons show considerable resistance to recommending reconstructive breast surgery. The dispute as to whether this procedure should be considered cosmetic or rehabilitative has affected insurance coverage. For suitable patients it does represent a significant contribution towards restitution and recovery. In Goldwyn's series (89), patients seeking breast reconstruction following mastectomy resembled those who sought simple breast augmentation.

As with hysterectomy, family factors are extremely important in the reaction to mastectomy. The stability of a marriage, sexual reassurance, the capacity of family members to tolerate the truth and the anxiety of uncertainty about the future are pivotal in the amount of support the patient has in regaining her emotional balance.

In rehabilitation of the post-mastectomy patient, the family may thus help or hinder in her acceptance of the loss of the breast and reintegration of a self-image of a person with a changed body but who feels worthy of love. The consultation-liaison psychiatrist may act as a liaison with the family as well as with the surgeon.

HYSTERECTOMY

Hysterectomy has been a much discussed gynecological procedure. The National Center for Health Statistics (92) estimates that 690,000 hysterectomies were performed in the United States in 1973. This represents a higher rate than for any other major operation, and the number is rising. It is performed more than twice as frequently in the United States as in England and Wales, probably for different indications. This suggests that there is no substantial agreement about indications. Thus, the discretion of the surgeon is often decisive.

For women, the experience is psychologically significant for many reasons. The uterus is a symbol of femininity and intactness; although a hysterectomy can leave minor scars or no scars, the sense of mutilation and damage can be profound. Mathis (14) discusses the importance of differentiating conscious from unconscious influences. He cites as an example the apparent relief one would suppose a hysterectomy would bring to a woman who consciously fears further pregnancies; however, the unconscious desire for more babies might produce a post-operative depression. He also states that while this may be an unavoidable response, reactions can be prevented or minimized by pre-operative preparation and post-operative support when the obstetrician-gynecologist appreciates the significance of sterilization as a possible loss to the particular woman. Gynecologists vary in their attiutdes towards hysterectomies. Wright (93) considered the uterus of a woman who had finished her reproductive life a "useless bag"—and better removed, while others are more surgically conservative. The surgeon making a decision to perform a hysterectomy often does not fully consider the alternative nor take into account the impact on the individual or her family. The attitude which is communicated, that a part of the woman is "useless," is also depreciating. In many sociocultural groups men feel the woman is "damaged" and less desirable if she has had a hysterectomy. In part this is because her childbearing status is gone and in part because she is not whole. Consequent rejection may intensify her reaction. Myths about the effect on sexual responses may also affect her and her husband. The loss of the uterus may signal the beginning of the aging process, as does natural menopause. When a hysterectomy is performed in woman over 40, and sometimes younger, the ovaries are often removed as well and surgical menopause is precipitated.

Post-hysterectomy depression is a generally recognized clinical entity. In a number of studies (94, 95, 96) a higher incidence of depression following this procedure as compared with other surgical procedures is reported. Although sampling and methodological problems complicate these studies, they do demonstrate overall vulnerability of women to depression post-hysterectomy. The most vulnerable women are those without organic pathology in the uterus, those who are under age 40, and those whose marital supports have been disrupted. Women with previous emotional disturbance also seem more likely to become depressed. Some of the same considerations important in understanding menopause apply here. Malignancy clearly provides additional stress. The loss of an organ with important unconscious symbolic significance, often with poor preparation by psychologically unsophisticated individuals and at times accompanied by considerable anxiety about the underlying diagnosis, occurs in a context of mythology and superstitution. In addition, the importance of reproductive intactness for a woman's self-esteem is affected by sociocultural values. If her reproductive life is considered as only one component of her femininity and other meaningful life patterns are available and valued by her and society, the reaction to hysterectomy may approach the reaction to other surgery. There are also individual differences in symbolic and unconscious significance. Social recognition of the positive aspects of midlife as a period of potential expansion rather than the beginning of a period of loss and decline can also be important.

STERILIZATION

Another area where changes in patient populations and their problems have brought new issues into focus for the liaison psychiatrist is the increase in sterilization requests by young women. The psychiatrist is consulted only occasionally, since the decision for sterilization generally remains between the patient and her physician. However, if the woman is young and nulliparous, the psychiatrist may be called to evaluate her competence to make the decision and her awareness of its implications, and also to assess her motivation and potential reaction.

Although there are as yet few studies of this group, those which exist indicate that this is a decision based on some thought. Lindenmayer (21), in a small study of nulliparous women in their early twenties seeking voluntary tubal ligation, indicated they had all been considering the decision for a long time and based the wish for childlessness on negative feelings toward children as well as fear of their capacity as mothers and a strong desire for independence.

These middle class, college educated young women varied widely as to psychopathology. Lindenmayer felt it was not possible to explain the decision solely in intrapsychic terms. He noted the importance of assessing the decision making process in these circumstances, determined that there had been no outside pressure or major conflict, and required the agreement of both partners if the woman was married or involved in a stable relationship.

Kaltreider and Margolis (22) studied a group of women under 30 who had decided never to have children. They also found strong internal psychological motivation in those electing tubal ligations. A history of family disruption, fear of motherhood, and dislike of children also characterized this group. Follow-up interviews of these women up to 10.5 months after tubal ligation indicated "no regrets, a sense of increased control in their own lives, and more sexual pleasure." The authors suggest that for this group, "the choice to be barren was multidetermined, persistent over time, and ego syntonic."

For the consultation-liaison psychiatrist, an important ethical and clinical issue arises when confronted with such a patient. The psychiatrist may be aware of the developmental potential of the patient and of the possibility that life events will bring about a change in the balance of her priorities, and thus may be reluctant to agree to an irreversible and possibly self-destructive procedure. However, the studies quoted indicate that at least for some women the motivation for childlessness may be deeply rooted and consistent with other directions of fulfillment. If the patient is fully aware of the implications of the decision, respect for the patient's autonomy and decision making may be in conflict with the psychiatrist's own values.

AMNIOCENTESIS

Recent advances in genetics and medicine have increased our capacity to make prenatal diagnoses and hence to be more involved in reproductive decisions. A number of disorders can be detected in utero with minimal risk to mother or fetus. The availability of amniocentesis has expanded the services provided by gynecologists and increased their responsibilities. While the use of this procedure is relatively restricted at this time, the possibility of future advances has raised serious ethical, social, religious and economic questions. A thorough discussion of these issues is beyond the scope of this paper. However, it is important to emphasize the complexity of the decisions that must be made, i.e., should all women have their pregnancies monitored for chromosomal abnormalities? Should criteria be established for abortion after amniocentesis? Who should be responsible for the decision making about these issues? The current availability of abortion implies that it would be possible to abort for any reason, including the sex or specific genetic makeup of a child. As techniques become more refined, a wider variety of traits and abnormalities may be detectable. What impact will this have on people's decisions? What will be the effect on sex distribution or on other population characteristics?

Some authors have speculated that the choice of genetic qualities and traits will result in the choice of children of a certain sex, or that "gene shopping" will occur to produce children with more desirable traits (97). Clearly these issues will need to be resolved in the near future.

Transabdominal amniocentesis was first performed in 1930 but not widely used until 1965 when it was recognized that the procedure was useful in the management of Rh incompatibility problems (98). In 1968 the technique was applied to analyze amniotic fluid chemically, and fetal cells genetically for certain metabolic errors and chromosomal abnormalities (99, 100).

The procedure is done at between 16-20 weeks gestation and carries a risk of 0.5 percent, which includes all complications, e.g., spontaneous abortion, vaginal bleeding, and fetal injury (101). In 95 percent of the cases the procedures yields favorable genetic results (102). Thus, it represents a significant psychological reassurance to people at risk. While specific prenatal diagnosis is not possible for many congenital abnormalities or genetic disorders, there are a number of important areas where amniocentesis is used, Gerbie and Nadler (103) divide the indications according to degrees of risk. High risk mothers are those who are translocation carriers, carriers of x-linked recessive diseases (e.g., hemophilia or Duchenne's muscular dystrophy where the diagnosis is not precise since 50 percent of men will have the disease) and carriers of inborn errors of metabolism (usually autosomal recessives). The moderate risk group consists of women who become pregnant at age 40 or more, where the risk of a child with a chromosomal aberration, especially trisomy 21 (Down's Syndrome), is greater than 1 percent. The risks of other chromosomal abnormalities are also greater. The low-risk group are those mothers who are between 35 and 40, or those who have had a previous child with trisomy 21. In the latter case, while there is not adequate data on the risk factors, the anxiety of the family about the possibility can be devastating.

Although most families who have a positive genetic diagnosis choose abortion, some elect to continue the pregnancy. Of 115 x-linked carrier mothers undergoing amniocentesis to determine fetal sex (102), 54 women were carrying a male fetus. Of these, 40 women chose to be aborted, while 14 decided to continue the pregnancy. The decision not to abort was based on several factors including: 1) the fact that 50 percent of these male fetuses would be unaffected; 2) religious reasons; 3) inadequate genetic counselling; 4) the prospective parents felt that the disability was not severe enough for them to choose abortion as a solution. Families making this choice clearly require a great deal of support during the pregnancy. In addition, gynecologists may have a point of view which prevents them from being objective or appropriately supportive.

Currently in our own experience requests for consultation related to amniocentesis are rare. However, it is clear that demands will increase as more complex and difficult problems appear. Davis (104) points out that it has already become apparent that the termination of pregnancy may not be warranted when a treatable disorder is discovered, i.e. phenylketonuria, or when there are unknown and unproved risks but strong popular opinion, e.g., XYY fetus. Physicians, she feels, are increasingly concerned that they will be obliged to provide amniocentesis to any patient who requests the procedure, thus raising many medical and ethical questions.

The role of the psychiatrist is similar to his/her role in other liaison areas. However, an understanding of the impact of genetic and/or metabolic disorders on individuals and families must be communicated to gynecologists, genetic counselors and pediatricians in an integrated fashion. The psychiatrist should also be involved in discussions of the ethical considerations, and in the formulation of guidelines for amniocentesis.

CONCLUSION

We have discussed a number of areas where the consultation-liaison psychiatrist working with obstetrics-gynecology has new data to assimilate, has to adapt to changing attitudes, and also has a particular contribution to offer. In all of these areas the psychiatrist optimally maintains his/her identity as a psychiatrist even when the relationships is collaborative. This can best take place when the psychiatrist has the training, the clinical experience, and the point of view that enable him/her to be sensitive to the emotional needs and responses of the patients. He/she must also have knowledge, experience, and interest to become familiar with enough of the content of the obstetrics-gynecology field to appreciate those needs and realities.

REFERENCES

1. LIPOWSKI, Z. J.: Consultation Liaison Psychiatry: An Overview. *Am. J. Psychiatry*, 131:623-630. 1968.
2. LIPOWSKI, Z. J.: Review of Consultation Psychiatry and Psychosomatic Medicine: II. Clinical Aspects. *Psychosomatic Medicine*, 29:3, 1967.
3. HORNEY, K.: Premenstrual Tension (1931). In H. Kelman (Ed.), *Feminine Psychology*. New York: Norton, 1967.
4. FRANK, R.: Hormonal Causes of Premenstrual Tension. *Arch. Neurol. Psychiatry*, 26:1053-1057, 1931.
5. BENEDEK, T. and RUBENSTEIN, B.: Correlations between Ovarian Activity and Psychodynamic Processes (1939). In T. Benedek (Ed.), *Studies in Psychosomatic Medicine: Psychosexual Functions in Woman*. New York: Roland, 1952.
6. LINDEMANN, E.: Hysteria as a Problem in a General Hospital. *Med. Clin. N. Amer.*, May, 1938.
7. RENNEKER, R. and CUTLER, M.: Psychological Problems of Adjustment to Cancer of the Breast. *J.A.M.A.*, 148:833, 1952.
8. HOWELLS, J. G.: *Modern Perspectives in Psycho-Obstetrics*. New York: Brunner/Mazel, 1972.

9. KROGER, W. S. (Ed.) : *Psychosomatic Obstetrics, Gynecology and Endocrinology.* Springfield, Ill.: Thomas, 1962.
10. NORRIS, M. (Ed.) : *Psychosomatic Medicine in Obstetrics and Gynecology.* Basel, Switzerland: Karger, 1972.
11. PASNAU, R. O.: Psychiatry and Obstetrics-Gynecology: Report of a Five Year Experience in Psychiatric Liaison. In R. O. Pasnau, *Consultation-Liaison Psychiatry.* New York: Grune & Stratton, 1975.
12. LIPOWSKI, Z. J.: Psychosocial Aspects of Physical Illness. In *Advances in Psychosomatic Medicine.* Basel: Karger, 1972.
13. LIPOWSKI, Z. J.: Current Trends in Psychosomatic Medicine I and II. *Psychiatry in Medicine,* 5:1974, 6, 1975.
14. MATHIS, J.: Psychiatry and the Obstetrician-Gynecologist. *Med. Clin. N. Amer.,* 51:6, 1375-1380, 1967.
15. LIEF, H. I.: Sex Education of Medical Students and Doctors. In Clark E. Vincent (Ed.), *Human Sexuality in Medical Education and Practice.* Springfield: Charles C Thomas, 1974. pp. 19-33.
16. PARLEE, M.: Psychological Aspects of Menstruation, Childbirth, and Menopause: An Overview with Suggestions for Further Research. Paper prepared for the conference. New Direction for Research on Women. Madison, Wisc., 1975.
17. LENNANE, K. J. and LENNANE, R. J.: Alleged Psychogenic Disorders in Women—A Possible Manifestation of Sexual Prejudice. *N.E.J.M.,* 288:6, 288-292, 1973.
18. GLASSER, M. and PASNAU, R.: The Unwanted Pregnancy in Adolescence. *J. Fam. Pract.,* 2:2, 91-94, 1975.
19. BART, P. and GROSSMAN, M.: Menopause. *Women as Patients,* C. Nadelson and M. Notman (Eds.). Plenum Press. In press. Also published in *Women and Health,* Vol. 1, # 3, May-June, 1976, pp. 3-10.
20. PAYNE, E., KRAVITZ, A., NOTMAN, M., and ANDERSON, J.: Outcome Following Therapeutic Abortion: 100 Cases. *Archives of General Psychiatry.,* 33:6, 725-733, June, 1976.
21. LINDENMAYER, J. P.: Quoted in Roche Report. *Frontiers of Psychiatry,* June 15, 1976.
22. KALTREIDER, N. B. and MARGOLIS, A.: Barren by Choice, a Clinical Study. *Am. J. Psych.,* 134:2, 179-182, 1977.
23. DEFRIES, Z.: Pseudo-homosexuality in Feminist Students. *Am. J. Psych.,* Vol. 133:4, 400-404, April 1976.
24. HERTZ, D. G.: Problems and Challenges of Consultation Psychiatry in Obstetrics-Gynecology. *Psychother. and Psychosom.,* 23: 67-77, 1974.
25. NADELSON, C. and NOTMAN, M.: The Woman Physician. *J. Med. Educ.,* 47:176-183, 1972.
26. FRANKFORT, E.: *Vaginal Politics.* New York: Quadrangle Books, 1971.

27. Boston Women's Health Book Collective. *Our Bodies, Ourselves.* New York: Simon & Schuster, 1973.
28. SCULLY, D. and BART, P.: A Funny Thing Happened on the Way to the Orifice: Women in Gynecological Textbooks. *Am. J. Sociology,* 78:4, 1045-1050, 1973.
29. NOTMAN, M. and NADLESON, C.: Women in Medicine: I. Women as Patients. From the forthcoming *Encyclopedia of Bioethics* to be published by Center for Bioethics, Kennedy Institute, Georgetown University, Washington, D. C.
30. STOECKLE, J. D., et al.: The Quantity and Significance of Psychological Distress in Medical Patients. *J. Chron. Dis.,* 17:959, 1964.
31. BURNAP, D. W. and GOLDEN, V. S.: Sexual Problems in Medical Practice. *J. Med. Educ.,* 42:6, 1967.
32. KAPLAN, H. S.: *The New Sex Therapy.* New York: Brunner/Mazel Publishers, 1974.
33. MASTERS, W. and JOHNSON, V.: *Human Sexual Inadequacy.* Boston: Little, Brown, 1970.
34. WEINBERG, P.: *Dysparenia. Journal of Marital and Sex Therapy,* 1:2, 1974.
35. MEYER, J. K.: Psychodynamic Treatment of the Individual with a Sexual Disorder. In J. K. Meyer, *Clinical Management of Sexual Disorders.* Baltimore: Williams & Wilkins, 1976.
36. NADELSON, C.: Unpublished data, Sexual Dysfunction Section of Psychiatric Out Patient Division, Beth Israel Hospital, Boston, 1976.
37. KAPLAN, H. S.: The Classification of the Female Sexual Dysfunctions. *Journal of Sex and Marital Therapy,* 1:2, 124-138, 1974.
38. BARBACH, L. G.: Group Treatment of Preorgasmic Women. *J. Sex and Marital Therapy,* 1:2, 139-145, 1974.
39. KROGER, W.: Introduction to Chapter on Marriage and Parenthood. In *Psychosomatic Obstetrics, Gynecology, Endocrinology.* Springfield, Ill.: Charles C Thomas, 1962, p. 163.
40. BIBRING, G.: Some Considerations of the Psychological Processes in Pregnancy. *Psychoanalytic Study of the Child,* 14:113, 1959.
41. DEUTSCH, H.: The Psychology of Women. *Motherhood,* Vol. II. New York: Grune & Stratton, 1945.
42. BIBRING, G. DWYER, T., HUNTINGTON, D. and VALENSTEIN, A.: A Study of the Earliest Mother-Child Relationship. *Psychoanalytic Study of the Child,* 16:9, 1961.
43. BIBRING, G. and VALENSTEIN, A.: Psychological Aspects of Pregnancy. *Clin. Obs. Gyn.,* 19:2, 357-371, 1976.
44. DANIELS, R. S. and LESSOW, H.: Severe Postpartum Reactions: An Interpersonal View. *Psychosomatics,* 5:21, 1964.
45. BENEDEK, T.: Sexual Functions in Women. *American Handbook of Psychiatry,* Chapter 37, Vol. I. New York: Basic Books, 1959.

46. BERNARD, V.: Psychodynamics of Unmarried Motherhood in Early Adolescence. *Nervous Child*, 4:25, 1944.
47. MENKEN, J.: The Health and Social Consequences of Teenage Childbearing. *Family Planning Perspectives*, 4:3, 45-53, 1972.
48. MECKLENBERG, F.: Pregnancy: An Adolescent Crisis. *Minnesota Medicine*, 56:2, 101-104, 1973.
49. SCHAFFER, C. and PINE, F.: Pregnancy, Abortion and the Developmental Tasks of Adolescence. *J. Child Psych.*, 14:511-536, 1975.
50. YOUNG, L.: *Out of Wedlock*. New York: McGraw-Hill, 1954.
51. NOTMAN, M. and ZILBACH, J.: Family Factors in the Non-Use of Contraception in Adolescence. Presented at the 5th International Congress on Psychosomatics in Obstetrics-Gynecology, Tel Aviv, Israel, 1974.
52. SARREL, P.: The University Hospital and the Teenage Unwed Mother. *Amer. J. Public Health*, 57:8, 1308, 1967.
53. BUDWELL, M. and TINNIN, L.: Abortion Referral in a Large College Health Service. *JAMWA*, 27:8, 1972.
54. NADELSON, C.: Abortion Counselling: Focus on Adolescent Pregnancy. *Pediatrics*, 54:6, 765-769, 1974.
55. NOTMAN, M. and NADELSON, C.: The Rape Victim: Psychodynamic Considerations. *Am. J. Psychiatry*, 133:4, April, 1976.
56. TYHURST, J. S.: Individual Reactions to Community Disaster: The Habitual History of Psychiatric Phenomena. *Am. J. Psych.*, 107, 761-769, 1951.
57. LINDEMANN, E.: Symptomatology and Management of Acute Grief. *Am, J. Psych.*, 101, 141-146, 1944.
58. GLOVER, E.: Notes on the Psychological Effects of War Condition on the Civilian Population. Part I: The Munich Crisis. *Intern. J. Psychoanal.*, 22, 132-146, 1944.
59. GLOVER, E.: Notes on the Psychological Effects of War Conditions on the Civilian Population. Part III: The Blitz. *Intern. J. Psychoanal.*, 23, 17-37, 1942.
60. SCHMIDEBERG, M.: Some Observations on Individual Reactions to Air Raids. *Intern. J. Psychoanal.*, 23, 146-176, 1942.
61. RADO, S.: Pathodynamics and Treatment of Traumatic War Neurosis (traumatophobia). *Psychosom. Med.*, 4, 362-369, 1942.
62. DEUTSCH, H.: Some Psychoanalytic Observations in Surgery. *Psychosom. Med.*, 4, 105-115, 1942.
63. JANIS, I. L.: *Psychological Stress*. New York: John Wiley & Sons, Inc., 1958.
64. BURGESS, A. W. and HOLMSTROM, L. L.: Rape Trauma Syndrome. *Am. J. Psych.*, 131:9, 981-986, 1974.
65. MARTON, J. H., et al.: A Clinical Study of Premenstrual Tension. *Am. J. Ob-Gynecol.*, 65:1182-1191, 1953.
66. DALTON, D.: *The Premenstrual Syndrome*. Springfield, Ill.: Charles C Thomas, 1964.

67. SOMMER, B.: Menstruation and Behavior: A Review. *Psychosom. Med.*, 35:515-533, 1973.
68. KOESKE, R. D.: Premenstrual emotionality: Is biology destiny? *Women and Health*, Vol. 1, #3, 5/6, 76, pp. 11-14.
69. MANDEL, A. and MANDELL, M.: Suicide and the menstrual cycle. *JAM Med. Assoc.*, 200:792-793, 1967.
70. MACKINNON, H., MACKINNON, P. C. B., and THOMPSON, D.: Lethal hazards of the initial phase of the menstrual cycle. *Brit. Med. J.*, 1:1015-1017, 1959.
71. PARLEE, M.: Psychological Aspects of Menstruation, Childbirth, and Menopause: An Overview with Suggestions for Further Research. Paper prepared for the conference, New Directions for Research on Women. Madison, Wisc., 1975.
72. VOGEL, W., BROVERMAN, D. M., and KLARBER, E. L.: EEG Responses in Regularly Menstruating Women and in Amenorrheic Women Treated with Ovarian Hormones. *Science*, 172: 388-391, 1971.
73. PERLMUTTER, J.: Personal Communications.
74. BARNETT, R. and BARUCH, G.: Women in the Middle Years: Conceptions and Misconceptions. From *Symposium: Toward an Understanding of Adult Development in Women.* Eastern Psychological Assoc. Meetings, April 1976.
75. PERLMUTTER, J.: Menopause from C. Nadelson and M. Notman (Eds.) forthcoming book, *Women as Patients.* Plenum Press.
76. MCKINLEY, S. M. and JEFFERYS, M.: The Menopausal Syndrome. *British Journal of Preventive and Social Medicine*, 28:2, 108-115, 1974.
77. REYNOLDS, S.: Physiological and Psychogenic Factors in the Menopausal Flush Syndrome. In W. Kroger, *Psychosomatic Obstetrics, Gynecology, and Endocrinology.* Springfield, Ill.: Charles C Thomas, 1962.
78. MCKINLEY, S. M., JEFFREYS, M. and THOMPSON, B.: An Investigation of the Age at Menopause. *J. Biosoc. Science*, 4:161-173, 1972.
79. NEUGARTEN, B.: Adult Personality: Toward a Psychology of the Life Cycle. In W. Sze (Ed.), *Human Life Cycle.* Aronson, New York, 1975.
80. NEUGARTEN, B. and DATAN, N.: The Middle Years. In S. Arieti (Ed.), *American Handbook of Psychiatry* (2nd ed.), Vol. 1. New York: Basic Books, 1974.
81. KRAINES, R. J.: The Menopause and Evaluations of the Self: A Study of Middle-Aged Women. Unpublished Doctoral Dissertation. Chicago: University of Chicago, 1953.
82. BENEDEK, T.: The Functions of the Sexual Apparatus and Their Disturbances. In F. Alexander (Ed.), *Psychosomatic Medicine.* New York: W. W. Norton, 1950.
83. NEUGARTEN, B., WOOD, V., KRAINES, R. and LOOMIS, B.: Women's

Attitudes Toward Menopause. In B. Neugarten, (Ed.), *Middl* *Age and Aging*. Chicago: The University of Chicago Press 1968.

84. LEVIT, L.: Anxiety and the Menopause. *A Study of Norma* *Women*. Unpublished doctoral dissertation. University o. Chicago, 1963.

85. BERNARD, J.: *The Future of Marriage*. New York: World Pub lishing Co., 1972.

86. LEVENSON, D., DARROW, C., KLIEN, E., LEVENSON, M. and McKEE B.: The Psychosical Development of Men in Early Adulthood and the Mid-Life Transition. In *Life History Research in Psy chopathology*, Vol. 3, edited by D. Richs, A. Thomas, and M Rott. Minneapolis: University of Minnesota Press, 1974.

87. ZILBACH, J.: Some Family Development Considerations of Mid life. Paper presented at American Psychiatric Association panel. New Look at the Midlife Years, May 1975.

88. TISHLER, S.: Disease of the Breast. In C. Nadelson and M Notman (Eds.) forthcoming volue of *Women as Patients*. Plenum Press.

89. GOLDWYN, R.: Esthetic Surgery in Women. C. Nadelson and M. Notman (Eds.) chapter in preparation for *Women in Context:* *Development and Stresses*.

90. ASKEN, M. J.: Psychoemotional Aspects of Mastectomy: A Re view of Recent Literature. *Am. J. Psychiatry*. 132:56-59, 1975.

91. GIFFORD, S.: Emotional Attitudes Toward Cosmetic Breast Sur gery: Loss and Restitution of the 'Ideal Self'. In R. M. Goldwyn (Ed.), *Plastic and Reconstructive Surgery of the* *Breast*. Boston: Little, Brown, 1976, pp. 103-122.

92. BRAUN, P. and DRUCHNEDER, E. (Eds.): Public Health Rounds at the Harvard School of Public Health. *N.E.J.M.*, 295:264- 268, July 29, 1976.

93. WRIGHT, R. C.: Hysterectomy: Past, Present and Future. *Ob stetrics-Gynecology*, 33:560-563, 1969.

94. BARBER, M. G.: Psychiatric Illness After Hysterectomy. *Br. Med. J.*, 2:91-95, 1968.

95. RICHARDS, D. H.: Depression After Hysterectomy. *Lancet*, 2: 430-433, 1973.

96. POLIVZ, J.: Psychological Reactions to Hysterectomy: A Critical Review. *Am. J. Obstetrics-Gynecology*, 118:417-426, 1974.

97. ETZIONI, A.: *Genetic Fix*. New York: Harper & Row, 1973.

98. FREDA, V. J.: The Rh Problem in Obstetrics and a New Concept of Its Management Using Amniocentesis and Spectrophoto metric Scanning of Amniotic Fluid. *Am. J. Obstetrics-Gynecol ogy*, 92:341, 1965.

99. NADLER, H. L.: Prenatal Detection of Genetic Defects. *J. Pediat.*, 74:132, 1969.

100. NADLER, H. L. and GERBIE, A. B.: Role of Amniocentesis in the

Intrauterine Detection of Genetic Disorders. *New Eng. J. Med.,* 282:596, 1970.

01. DAVIS, J.: Symposium on Amniocentesis. *Am. J. Pediatric.* Washington: D. C., Oct. 20, 1975.

02. MILUNSKY, A.: *The Prenatal Diagnosis of Hereditary Disorders.* Springfield, Illinois: Charles C Thomas, 1973.

03. GERBIE, A. and NADLER, H.: Genetic Counselling. In S. Romney, et al., *Gynecology and Obstetrics: The Health Care of Women.* New York: McGraw-Hill, 1975.

04. DAVIS, J.: Genetic Counselling. In M. Notman and C. Nadelson forthcoming volume, The Woman as a Patient, part of series of *Women in Context: Development and Stresses.* New York: Plenum Press.

05. MENNINGER, W. C.: The Emotional Factor in Pregnancy. *Bulletin of the Menninger Clinic,* 7:15, 1943.

06. PLESHETTE, N., ASCH, S. and CHASE, J.: A Study of Anxieties during Pregnancy, Labor, the Early and Later Puerperium. *Bulletin of the New York Academy of Medicine,* 32:436, 1956.

07. NADELSON, C.: The Pregnant Teenager: Problems of Choice in Developmental Framework. *Psychiatric Opinion,* 12:2, 6-12, 1975.

08. NOTMAN, M. T., KRAVITZ, A. R., PAYNE, E. C. and RUSSELL, J.: Psychological Outcome in Patients having Therapeutic Abortion. In Norris, *Psychosomatic Medicine in Obstetrics and Gynecology.* S. Karger, Basel, 1972.

Part III

THE FAMILY

9

The Family of the Patient

Jerry M. Lewis, M.D. and
W. Robert Beavers, M.D.

The family of the hospitalized patient, an important factor in the patient's experience of illness and hospitalization, is often the most neglected component of the treatment system. The liaison psychiatrist frequently finds himself the person most qualified to clarify for the hospital staff the impact of the family on the patient and the ways in which the hospital staff can assist the family during the crisis of illness. When such clarification does not occur, the family's potential for helpfulness is minimized.

The patient's emotional and behavioral responses to his disease and hospitalization can be seen as part of at least four major systems. First there is the patient as an individual with a specific disease superimposed upon an individual personality (i.e., needs, traits, feelings, and psychodynamic vulnerabilities and strengths). Second, there is the relationship between the patient and his primary doctor—this two-person interaction will have clearly definable characteristics that continue to evolve as the relationship progresses. Third, there is the hospital milieu, which the patient will accept or avoid. (Though often not overtly articulated, an example of the type of value message that may impinge upon the patient is, "On this unit, the patients are strong, and to cry is weak.") Finally, there is the family, for most patients their central psychosocial network, with its tremendous potential for playing either a constructive or destructive role. These four major systems produce much of what may be termed the patient's illness behavior.

Approaches to understanding the patient's behavior from an individual perspective have focused on behavior and attitudes. For example, Cassell (1) has described factors frequently associated with being sick. With some variation from person to person, depending upon the individual's personality or the nature of the disease, many patients experience a pervasive sense of disconnectedness from others. This estrangement is seen as a complex process occurring at many levels of the individual's experience. Cassell feels that hope involves a connection with a social network and that to feel estrangement from one's environment is a factor in the evolution of hopelessness. In addition, many patients feel emotionally vulnerable with a diminished sense of invincibility and impaired thinking about their illnesses.

Cassell's approach to illness behavior is helpful in understanding the patient's dilemma. It provides a useful perspective from which observations about the individual patients can be made. Another way of looking at illness involves the psychoanalytic concepts of regression and defenses against regression. Put simply, illness and hospitalization, particularly if there is threat to life, constitute a serious threat to the individual patient's adaptive capacity. In addition, allowing others to take care of one—experiencing the passivity often required by medical and surgical procedures—is an adaptation to a particular set of environmental demands. Some patients, however, are unable to tolerate any hint of regression without significant anxiety or have difficulty giving up a regressed position when it is no longer useful.

Observations solely concerning the individual patient sometimes grossly underestimate the impact of contextual factors on behavior. To focus only on the behavior of the patient implies that understanding the individual as an isolated psychologic entity is sufficient to guide successful intervention and assist adaptation. We wish to stress that the liaison psychiatrist's capabilities in promoting appropriate adaptation may be less than optimal if any of the interpersonal systems that influence the patient's behavior—the doctor-patient relationship, the hospital milieu, or the family—is not taken into consideration. For example, we suggest that a sense of estrangement from others, an increased sense of vulnerability, a diminished sense of invincibility, and impairment of logical thinking regarding one's disease—cardinal aspects of illness behavior—are quite closely related to contextual factors arising from the variety of interpersonal fields in which the hospitalized patient is participating.

The doctor-patient relationship has definable characteristics that influence the degree of regression and dependency found in patients. Although society gives considerable power and responsibility to the physician, many doctors share it collaboratively with their patients to the extent that each patient and his disease allow; other physicians dominate and control every relationship with patients. The notion that this power differential between patient and doctor can influence outcome is supported by Blum's research (2), showing a positive correlation between the frequency of malpractice suits and the personality characteristics of arrogance and a sense of infallibility in the physician. Some physicians are very sensitive to feelings and appropriately empathic. Others avoid recognizing or responding to the patient's feelings. Many physicians are very clear in their communication with patients, while others are obscure. Such physician characteristics, interacting with patient characteristics, go into the evolution of a relationship system that has a powerful impact upon the patient and his behavior. The physician's behavior is crucial in establishing and molding a relationship that may support the patient's adaptive struggle. To consider the patient's behavior unrelated to the influence of this interplay is to invite erroneous and simplistic interpretations.

The structure of the treatment milieu also has a significant influence upon the patient's behavior. The increasing sophistication of hospital technology can be interpreted by patients in many different ways. Some find reassurance and support in the elaborate instrumentation, while others are frightened or bewildered. Important differences in the psychologic structure of the hospital unit or ward are not so obvious. Among equally efficient units, some are cold and demanding, while others are warm and supportive. Whatever the environmental characteristics, they are assumed by a wide variety of hospital staff and employees. One often hears, "If I were close to death, I'd want to be in hospital A, but for most illnesses I prefer hospital B. Somehow, it's more caring and warm." These system characteristics of hospital environments can represent significant factors influencing the patient in either helpful or harmful ways.

The least appreciated, but perhaps the most significant, interpersonal system in the general hospital is the patient's family. Accumulating data reveal that the family is central to much individual illness. There are at least three types of studies of the family and its relation to physical illness. The most common is descriptive and crisis oriented: an examination of the response patterns of the family unit to a serious illness in a member of the family. Anthony's description (3) of various stages of family adaptation to this stress is representative.

In another approach, family systems researchers report patterns of family relationships and communications that are correlated with a specific disease, frequently one of the classic seven psychosomatic illnesses. This type of investigation searches for specific causal factors within the family system. For example, Jackson (4) found certain commonalities in the families of patients with ulcerative colitis.

A third approach seeks family variables associated with the level of resistance or susceptibility to all illnesses in the total family. One preliminary study within this framework is the family interactional research of Lewis et al. (5), which showed a relationship between the way a family deals with an ambiguous stimulus concerning death, and the overall level of health within the family. Families that discussed death in a personal way (in response to the stimulus) had significantly more days in which all family members were well during the subsequent six months.

As a whole, the results of these studies suggest that family variables associated with individual illness may be predisposing factors, precipitating agents, or important in the course and outcome of the illness.

Despite these significant findings, the staff in many general hospitals pay little attention to the needs of the family, nor do they appreciate the impact of the family upon the individual patient. Attending physicians give widely varying attention to patients' families. Most often, the consulting psychiatrist's function is seen as helping the consultee in finding proper treatment for his patient, or helping the consultee with his particular difficulty with a given patient (6). As such, he may have little awareness of the patient's family. The consensus of opinion at a recent conference for intensive care and coronary care nurses (7) was that an individual patient's family was managed by rigid staff rules that stated, "You may see your ill family member for five minutes every two hours, and do not bother us or him at other times." No attempt was made to help the family deal with the illness, nor was there any suggestion of a specific accommodation to families of varying strengths. This, despite the clinical observation that some families appeared to have a calming and supportive influence on the patient. Other families were clearly upsetting, a circumstance which often could be correlated with changes in monitored physical functions.

Factors Useful in Evaluating Family Functioning

Research data indicate that the patient can be treated more effectively if the liaison psychiatrist helps the hospital staff to understand the role of the patient's family and include family members in treatment plans. To do this, it is useful for the psychiatrist to have a conceptual approach to family systems that can be taught to nonpsychiatric physicians and nursing personnel.

As with individual patients, a comprehensive understanding of the family's level of competence is essential to effective intervention. Even though the situation is complicated by the impact of the acute stress generated by the family member's hospitalization, it can be accomplished if one obtains the clinical data with some grasp of family systems. The psychiatrist needs a theoretical, structural framework—a cognitive roadmap—to guide him in the evaluation of family strengths and difficulties. We offer here a method based upon interactional research that can have practical clinical applications.

The basic process of obtaining useful family data differs from interviewing, whether it be of each member of the family individually or of the family as a group. In most such interviews, the psychiatrist plays a directive role, and the family orients itself to the presence of an authority figure. In contrast, during an evaluation of family functioning, it is important to encourage the family to be involved in conversation, with the psychiatrist playing an unobtrusive and, if possible, inactive role. This approach is much more likely to reveal significant aspects of the family's organizational structure, strengths, and areas of difficulty. In the general hospital setting, this may be accomplished by giving the family a task which is appropriate for the situation and then intervening little, or not at all, as they work together. For example, the task might be for the family to discuss what changes their member's illness necessitates and how they might go about making these changes. This approach will allow the family, as a unit (excluding the individual patient only if his or her illness mandates), to begin a family conversation around a realistic problem. Such a process allows one to make observations about the family's success or failure in achieving the goals of their discussion. If the family tries to draw the psychiatrist into the discussion, he may suggest by a shrug that the family go ahead. Rather than focusing on the entire gestalt of the family during their verbal exchange, the liaison psychiatrist makes observations in regard to discrete family communication variables. We have found (5) that judgments in regard to 12 to 15 variables functioning in concert discriminate between various levels of family competence. For general clinical purposes, however, the liaison psychiatrist needs to assess at least the following four specific variables as he is observing the family conversations: 1) the overt power structure or pattern of interpersonal influence, 2) the degree to which the family encourages autonomous functioning, 3) the family's feeling tone and mood, and 4) the ability of the family, as a group, to negotiate and solve problems.

In describing a continuum of overall family competence, we have selected arbitrarily three points on this continuum (designated "severely disturbed," "midrange dysfunctional," and "healthy") and will characterize the expression of the four variables at each of the levels of competence.

Overt Power. A major factor in determining the effectiveness of a system is the way in which power is distributed. To function well, any human system must have a person or persons who provide leadership when necessary for integrating information and directing. This directing function requires interpersonal influence and, when one observes families, power differences among members are usually clear. In the severely disturbed families, however, the differences in power are not obvious. The parental coalition is weak, and frequently leadership seems almost nonexistent. The members communicate their goals, wishes, and opinions poorly, and obscuring, covert processes substitute for clear direction.

In the midrange dysfunctional family, individuals struggle to gain power, and *control* is the watchword. Parents consider that controlling their own impulses and those of their children is crucial. Two strikingly different styles of midrange families occur: those in which the control generally succeeds and those in which the control chronically fails. In the former, the parental coalition is relatively good, and one parent (often the father) exercises more influence than the spouse, and the children are controlled with little concern for their opinions, needs, or particular view of the world. In the latter style, where control fails, the parents are in a continual, unresolved competition for power. There are obvious maneuvers between the parents and between parents and children to control others, but discipline is relatively ineffective, and bickering is constant.

In healthy families, the parental coalition is strong, with only modest differences in power, if any, between the father and mother. Each member respects the subjective reality of all other family members, and there is freedom for choice. The clear family structure reveals differences in power that are modest in degree and used to lead rather than control. Most differences respond to good-humored negotiation rather than covert operations or naked power plays.

The Encouragement of Autonomy. Autonomous functioning is not possible in severely disturbed families. Interpersonal boundaries are blurred, individual thoughts and feelings are seldom expressed clearly. The symbolic invasion of living space by speaking for others is common in this group, and seldom occurs at better levels of function. Indirect and confusing mechanisms, such as evasiveness, strategic silence, sarcasm, and irony, are used to express feelings. These ways of communicating evolve relationships that are ambiguous and irresponsible.

Midrange dysfunctional families encourage a significantly greater degree of autonomy than do the severely disturbed. Family members generally express their thoughts coherently and, within rather narrow limits, they take responsibility for subjective reality and behavior. The acceptance of separateness—husband from wife, parents from children—is genuine, if reluctant.

Recognition of the boundaries between family members is not sufficient, however, to make autonomy easy or gratifying. In the midrange dysfunctional families where control is successful, much that is human and emotional is unacceptable and submerged, either individually repressed or systematically denied by the whole group. As a consequence, resentment and unresolved conflict pervade their lives. In those midrange families that fail in establishing a stable hierarchy of power, blaming and hostile attacks on others limit the growth of autonomous functioning.

In healthy families, the open expression of individual feelings and opinions occurs in a climate of respect for the differences in individual subjective reality. An optimistic belief in the essential decency of all family members greatly reduces the need for the continuous control efforts so limiting to the growth of autonomy. The increasing capabilities of children are met with enthusiasm, and individual competence is generally considered to be valuable (rather than threatening) to others in the family.

The Family Feeling Tone and Mood. The important point is that even in the presence of an ill family member, there are differences in feeling tone that correlate with family functioning. In severely disturbed families, pessimism, cynicism, and distancing maneuvers promote apathy, quiet despair or, occasionally, unbridled rage.

In midrange dysfunctional families, a variety of chronic, painful feeling states occur: depression, anxiety, intermittent or continued hostile wrangling. Successful control encourages quiet acceptance of interpersonal disappointment; unsuccessful control results in mutual attacks.

In healthy families, even in times of great stress, there is hope, warmth, and mutual support in facing the uncertainties of a loved one's illness. Openness prevails in the expression of painful feelings, such as sadness, fear, frustration, and anger.

Negotiation and Problem Solving. Severely disturbed families are extremely poor at responding effectively to tasks presented them. Their lack of clear leadership, the murkiness of diffuse interpersonal boundaries, and inability of family members to express their feelings and opinions coherently make negotiation impossible and problem solving starkly inadequate.

Midrange dysfunctional familes solve problems better than severely disturbed families. More often than not, however, their effectiveness is clearly related to the capability of the most powerful individual in the family. As a consequence, frequently these families can accomplish specific tasks despite obvious deficiencies in the ability to negotiate with each other. In such instances, the dominant individual arrives at a solution to the problem without taking into consideration the thoughts, feelings, and wishes of the other members of the family.

In healthy families, problems are solved effectively and promptly with consideration of each member's needs and feelings. If the task set by the evaluator seems relevant and sensible enough to induce cooperation, even during times of grief, the family characteristics of leadership, organization, and autonomous differentiation will allow for impressive shared competence.

The determination of the basic level of competence of the family is an important step in assisting the family to care for their ill member. Both the severely disturbed families and many of the chronically conflicted midrange dysfunctional families often require a firm and clear directiveness on the part of the clinician. This relatively authoritarian stance would alienate a healthier family. With a severely disturbed family, the liaison psychiatrist may have to select a single member and assign him or her the responsibility for getting things done for the patient, because there may be one member who is more effective alone than the family is as a group. He may find it advisable to suggest to the treating physician that because of the lack or weakness of leadership in the family, the treating physician would do well to adopt a firmer, more direct role with the patient as well as with the family. Occasionally, in the presence of chronic, severe conflict, authoritarian assignment of responsibility is necessary in midrange dysfunctional families. It would, of course, be counterproductive in dealing with healthy families.

The material presented here offers the liaison psychiatrist a useful approach to evaluating clinically the general level of competence in the patient's family. It is also important to address the impact of the family member's illness upon the family. It is necessary for the clinician to be able to distinguish those acute and responsive aspects of the family from their basic level of competence.

THE EFFECTS OF ILLNESS UPON THE FAMILY

There is mounting interest in the impact of physical illness on family life, but the research studies (3, 8, 9) have had varied samples and methods of study; with such heterogeneity, generalizations about these are difficult. Of course serious illness in a family member poses a strain for all the family. The degree and quality of the family's response appear to be associated with the general level of competence of the family, the role of the sick person in the family and the nature of the illness, the individual patient's style of adapting to the illness, and the family's capacity to deal with ambivalence and the threat of loss.

More competent families deal better (on average) with the crisis of serious illness. Even with extremely competent families, however, successful adaptation requires earnest and stressful work. Koos (8), for example, has found that well integrated and organized families cope better with illness than other families. However, it is important to emphasize that the family's level of overall competence is, in itself, not an accurate predictor of the family's ability to deal with a particular stress. Other variables are involved also.

There are those who posit that any enduring social system undergoes a more-or-less typical change in response to severe stress. Moss (10), for example, suggests a four-phased process of invalidation, exploration, innovation, and habituation. In this scheme, a family would experience the stress of severe illness initially as something which invalidates a basic premise: that is, the family is going to remain for some period of time essentially as it was prior to the development of the serious illness. Following this stressful period of invalidation, there is a period of exploration in which the family searches for accommodations to their dilemma and then moves to some new or innovative, stable state. This new and stable state then may become the family's more-or-less typical organizational format.

Anthony (3) has borrowed Toynbee's historical hypothesis and suggests that illness in a family member is a challenge. This challenge leads to a period of breakdown which then is followed either by a creative reintegration or a disintegration. Anthony's clinical descriptions of these stepwise processes are similar to the characteristics of families described in the second section of this paper: Well functioning families demonstrate distinct, effective organizational structure with considerable flexibility, allowing the family to respond adaptively to differing situations; at a lower level of competence, the family's structure is rigidly organized and is unable to deal effectively with change; at the lowest level of family competence, the family's organization appears chaotic and there is little effective problem solving. Anthony speaks of another type of continuum with flexibility, rigidity, and chaos—that of phases through which a family may pass in response to the challenge of serious illness. He believes that, though the probability of recovery of family function is related to its pre-stressed competence, a typical family, during the phase of breakdown, becomes less productive and more given to authoritarian controls. The family loses cohesiveness and may take up a hostile posture in relation to the outside world. If the family does not reintegrate from this less competent level of functioning, it may, at this point, move toward distintegration. At its worst, disintegration is characterized by deteriorated relationships within the family, almost complete alienation from the outside world, and an alarming sense of drift and aimlessness. These family structures become blurred and roles seem undifferentiated. The phases of breakdown and disintegration are strikingly similar to the rigid, midrange dysfunctional families and the severely dysfunctional or chaotic families we have studied.

Koos (8) has pointed out that the process of family regeneration may return the family to its pre-illness level of functioning, to a level that appears to stabilize at less than pre-illness level or, in a few families, to a level higher than the pre-illness level.

Another factor in the impact of illness on the family is the role within the family of the seriously ill person. In general, there is more stress for the family if the patient is a parent in a family containing young children. Although the stress for the well parent and total family may be blunted by the extended family and close friends, it remains a potent force. When the nuclear family, bereft of the support of all but the most intense of kinship bonds, faces illness, its terrible vulnerability raises questions about our major reliance upon the family as the sole supportive network. Other institutions, including the hospital and its staff, are desperately needed to reach out to this fragile group.

Parsons and Fox (9) have offered a general format for evaluating the impact upon the family of serious illness in different family members. They indicate that the nature of the resulting family stress, although high for serious illness in any family member, has a different quality if the sick member is the father, mother, or adolescent child. They suggest that illness in the mother may be the most distressing of all because it subjects the family to under-support at a time of very high demand. Serious illness in the father may threaten the economic position of the family and impose stress in this way. Often the wife's concern and attention are unavoidably drawn more intensely to her husband, and the children suffer double loss and feel threatened and alone.

In general, the response of the family to serious illness in a family member will be more intense if the sick person has fulfilled a special role within the family and if that specialness is seen as exclusively the sick person's. Both the specialness of the role and the rigidity of the role assignment, then, combine to intensify the stress. Families which see a parent as all powerful or a child as the only creative or successful member are examples of this type of rigid, special role assignment that makes family adaptation more difficult.

Both the seriousness and the nature of the illness may influence the family's response. In general, illnesses that carry the threat of death or severe disfigurement are most disturbing. Even here, however, there is considerable variation between families, and idiosyncratic responses will often be seen in severely dysfunctional families. Even midrange and healthy families may intensely cathect particular traits such as physical beauty or athletic competence. For them, an illness that affects such a specific and highly valued family characteristic can be more disruptive than a more serious one that does not.

The issue of potential loss of family members present in most serious illness severely taxes the strength of the family. In working with research volunteer families (5), we presented them with a stimulus in which death or dying was explicit. Only one in five families could discuss death openly in personal terms. Even competent families appear to have difficulty with this charged issue. Families that can deal openly with anxiety about death have the advantage of sharing with each other this central concern. In families that cannot, individual members must bear the burden alone.

We speculate that this capacity to deal openly with the possibility of loss is related to the acceptance of ambivalence as a part of all human relatedness. Families vary tremendously in the degree to which they allow the expression of all feelings, including, of course, those that reflect normal ambivalence.

The family's reaction to a serious illness in a family member is influenced directly by the amount and quality of support received from the hospital staff. If the family members are more or less isolated in a waiting room, they may feel alone and even more frightened. If the staff is ambiguous or vague, family anxiety is apt to multiply. Too often physicians and nursing personnel are unaware that their warmth, support, and clarity can be crucial for the family.

Hofmann, Becker, and Gabriel (11), in describing the complicated adjustments required when an adolescent is hospitalized, observe that staff members have a natural empathy toward those for whom they care, "often functioning as advocates and defenders of the patient in opposition to his adversaries." As adolescents may see other members of their families as adversaries, the staff may unwittingly become over-protective of a patient and hostile or rejecting of the family.

Our observation is that families with a strong and shared transcendent value system often deal more effectively with the threat of loss. With some exceptions, those who can turn naturally to their God find a source of strength and support. For these families, the treating physician should bear in mind that the presence and support of their pastor will play a helpful role.

The Effect of the Family on the Patient's Illness and Behavior

The family of a sick person has a significant role to play in the progress or resolution of most serious illness. This role may have a cumulative impact (which can be either positive or destructive) upon the patient. It is not possible, however, for the clinician to separate clearly the effect of the family on the patient from the effect of the patient on the family. Perhaps it is more reasonable to think of these effects as reverberating forces within a field. For example, a patient with a myocardial infarction can be dealing with a great deal of underlying fear and anxiety about his illness. The family's level of anxiety may be so severe that it increases the patient's anxiety. This, in turn, is communicated to the family and escalates the total stress of an already complex and threatening situation. In this schematic example, it is evident that what is an effect one moment is a cause the next.

Anxiety

Perhaps more than any other single variable, the level of family anxiety and the way the family deals with its anxiety and concern about the ill member impinge upon the patient, his illness, and his behavior. It is useful to think of a continuum of family concern: At one end is complete denial, in the middle is appropriate concern, and at the far end is over-concern. Either extreme of this continuum can have a destructive impact on the patient. If the family is, for example, denying the gravity of the illness, the patient is apt to wonder and doubt his own reality testing. If, on the other hand, the family demonstrates a grossly inappropriate over-concern, the patient may come to question whether or not the physician and the hospital staff are being open and honest with him about his illness. In addition, the patient's way of dealing with the anxiety about his illness also influences the family. It is useful to think in terms in a patient's response to his illness as involving either excessive denial, appropriate concern, or excessive exploitation. Though some denial in the acute phase of severe illness may be adaptive and desirable, the patient who seeks to deny the seriousness of a prolonged or life-threatening illness presents a significant problem for all of those caring for him. He is very likely to be uncooperative and impede treatment efforts.

> A 47-year-old physician was admitted to the hospital with substernal chest pain. Physical examination and a variety of studies led to the diagnosis of a myocardial infarction. The physician-patient refused to accept the diagnosis as valid. He would not stay in bed, continued to smoke, and paced the hospital corridors.
> His wife and brother refused also to accept the fact of his myocardial infarction. They encouraged him to leave the hospital and were openly antagonistic to the nursing staff who attempted to enforce the prescribed treatment. On the fourth hospital day he left against advice. Two days later he died suddenly while mowing his yard.

In this instance, the patient's denial was compounded by a general family denial of the seriousness of the patient's illness. The complications were, of course, profound. The treating professionals had no ally within the family, and treatment could not be instituted.

If the patient's excessive use of denial is incongruent with the family's, other problems are presented. If the patient has been very powerful within the family, the family is caught between the conflicting points of view of the powerful family member's denial and the physician's and staff's need to base treatment on an adequate assessment of the seriousness of the illness. For the family, this sense of being "in the middle" can add much anxiety and fear to that which the illness has incurred. If the excessively denying patient has not been seen as extremely powerful, there is nevertheless the difficult problem of dealing with a family member who is unable to perceive realistically his dilemma, and this level of denial may lead the family to a cycle of increasing efforts to convince him, subsequent frustration, anger, and guilt.

The family's over-concern and encouragement of dependency may not only sabotage recovery, but also be quite inconsistent with the patient's wishes. An alert hospital staff may need to intervene to protect the patient's desire to remain as capable as possible. Hoffman, Becker, and Gabriel (11) described an 18-year-old young man hospitalized for severe, recurrent osteomyelitis. Psychiatric examination revealed clinical depression. The parents were extremely solicitous, and one of them was always with him during waking hours. Finally the patient, exasperated with this babying, asked staff assistance in both keeping his parents away more and in arranging visits with his girlfriend, who felt awkward at visiting in the presence of his parents. With this done, he become less depressed and coped much better with the episode.

In the general hospital setting, patients who exploit the sick role are seen frequently. They deal with the anxiety and fear incurred by illness by regressing to a position of excessive child-like dependency. Such patients are often held in contempt by the staff as being baby-like or "whiners." The family may identify with this regressed state and support it with the development of a struggle, usually subterranean, between the family and the staff. Often in such a situation, both family and patient see the staff as uncaring, whereas the staff see both family and patient as excessively demanding. Vigorous intervention on the part of the liaison psychiatrist may break up this escalating tension; if the family can be enlisted in encouraging the patient to reach obtainable goals in convalescence, the strain is greatly reduced.

If the family disapproves of the patient's regressed position, a conflict may develop in which the staff and family appear to be aligned against the patient, who feels increasingly disconnected from two very important interpersonal support systems in his life. Intervention here requires making the family's desire for the patient to become more autonomous a source of strength rather than a liability.

The impact of a patient's family upon the development and progression of his illness, and his response to treatment, is only beginning to be recognized. Cohen et al. (12), for example, investigated the impact of family interactions upon the response of schizophrenic patients to phenothiazines. Although this example involves a psychiatric rather than a "physical" illness, it highlights the influence of a family system upon an individual family member's response to a pharmacologic preparation. These investigators found that chlorpromazine significantly decreased the schizophrenic patient's aggression if the patient was living in a family of low-level tension and conflict. The chlorpromazine-treated patients from high conflict and tension families responded no better than to a placebo. They interpreted their results as indicating that this potent psychopharmacologic agent will significantly reduce a patient's aggressive behavior if that behavior is dissonant with family interactional patterns, and will be less effective in those situations in which aggressive behavior is consistent with family interaction patterns.

Attitudes

Families vary tremendously in the degree of closeness offered an ill member. Some families see illness as an immoral evasion of family problems, and they may treat the patient in a way which compounds his problems in an already threatening and lonely hospital environment. On the other hand, the ability of some families to accept and adapt to the necessarily changed circumstances attendant with a family member's illness can effectively reduce the anxiety, despair, and guilt which may be a part of the individual patient's response.

Hopefulness in families is of great importance in the management of physical illness. Seligman (13), a psychiatrist who works with burned children, lists the parents' degree of hope as one major factor in assessing prognosis. Time spent with family members in helping them develop enough trust and understanding to have reasonable hope is often very therapeutic.

Responsiveness

Families vary greatly in their capacity to accept the unpleasant, painful feelings of an ill member. Those families which are fearful of or unable to accept such feelings may inadvertently precipitate the patient's becoming depressed or his illness being unduly prolonged. A team treating burned adults has learned to stress the importance of instructing relatives that the patient's recovery would be augmented by his ability to express feelings and to cry if so disposed (14). This direct and clear way of assuring the families of such patients may pay many dividends in promoting the patient's and the family's acceptance of the variety of regressive, unpleasant feelings that are to be expected during the course of recovery.

Family Roles

The role that a patient plays in a family can have a profound influence on his morale and recovery possibilities. If there is no semblance of the family's need for the patient to resume his role within the family—if, in effect, the family appears to do quite well without him —the possibility of depression increases (13).

One can get some idea of the hidden but potent influence of role assignments and conflicts within a family on disease processes in family members from the work of Minuchin and his co-workers (15). They reported a study in which the blood levels of free fatty acids in all family members were monitored. The family included two sisters, aged 12 and 17, who had diabetes mellitus. Researchers observed the sisters relating in different circumstances to their parents, first watching their parents converse through a one-way mirror, and then entering the room and relating to them face-to-face. The 17-year-old daughter was trapped in the conflict between her parents, with each parent trying to establish a coalition with her. The younger sister experienced no such tug-of-war, since she was not a target of these competitive demands. Free fatty acid levels, considered by the investigators to be an adequate measure of emotional stress, were elevated in both children during the observation period when they observed and listened to their parents' dialogue from behind the one-way mirror. When both daughters entered the room with their parents, their free fatty acids increased further. At the completion of the family dialogue, the younger girl's free fatty acids promptly declined to baseline levels. In the older daughter, the target of the parents' competitive demands, the free fatty acids remained high for a much longer period of time. This girl, an extremely labile diabetic, had experienced multiple episodes of ketoacidosis and hospitalization.

Inevitably, there is some degree of role change associated with being seriously ill. The willingness of both the patient and the family to accept an altered role for the ill member is an important factor in successful recovery. It is also important for the family to be able to tolerate a resumption of the patient's usual family role as he recovers. Koos (8) has presented data suggesting that in some families containing a markedly dominant parent, serious illness results in a loss of this dominance, and the family then actively refuses to let the control return to this now deposed power figure. Such loss of power may encourage unnecessary invalidism.

The Quality of the Family's Relationship with the Hospital Staff

The family of the hospitalized patient is engaged in a powerful and significant relationship with the hospital staff. This is true regardless of the intensity of contact; even a lack of contact between the two represents a choice by family or staff that speaks volumes to the ill patient. Occasionally, the staff routine and morale may be seen to crumble before the social power of the relatives of a "very important patient." More commonly, however, the family is frightened and intimidated by strange people, rules, and ambiguous expectations. Trouble arises when the family is seen as an unnecessary interference rather than a potentially valuable ally. The nature of the relationship between the family and the hospital staff may greatly influence the patient's response to his surroundings. Capable and well-informed family members can perform a badly needed liaison between physician, staff, and patient.

Seligman (13) movingly reports her appreciation and respect for the father of a severely burned child, who took the agonizing responsibility to tell her of her mother's death in the same fire. He stayed with her and gave support in many ways. Seligman was conscious of this father's ability to relieve the physician's load and concern about the patient.

At the other extreme, however, confused, frightened family members who are given little information and small respect can find no part to play and can add to the staff's burden in a variety of ways ranging from verbal attacks on hospital personnel to hostile, dependent, passive, or obstructionist behavior.

The Many Roles of the Liaison Psychiatrist

The liaison psychiatrist can play a valuable, helpful role in regard to the family of the patient. In order to do so, however, he must have the willingness and competence to deal with complex social systems. Some liaison psychiatrists, by virtue of training, focus solely on the individual patient and are unable or unwilling to deal in any significant way with the patient's interpersonal milieu. Occasionally, of course, there are clinical situations in which contextual factors are relatively unimportant, and focus on the individual patient represents optimal treatment. In most situations, however, inattention to the interpersonal context will result in less-than-optimal treatment for the patient.

Under the best circumstances, the liaison psychiatrist is capable of directing intervention efforts to the individual patient, the patient's family, the hospital staff, and the primary doctor-patient relationship. If the liaison psychiatrist is sensitive to all of these possibilities, he can focus on the point at which his leverage may be greatest. In many situations, this will be the individual patient, but in others it will be the family, staff, or doctor-patient relationship. In some situations, the psychiatrist will need to be concerned with all of these systems. Hackett's paper presented in this book (16), focusing on liaison in intensive-care settings, describes what might be called the "compleat" liaison psychiatrist. He emphasizes the need to be clear with the patient and family as to what may be reasonably anticipated. Support should be offered directly and in an optimistic way.

Hackett also stresses the need to recognize the crucial role of the staff. Nurses, in particular, play an important role, and he stresses the educative, consultative, and problem-oriented role of the liaison psychiatrist. He indicates the freedom of the psychiatrist to intervene in the primary doctor-patient relationship as exemplified by the psychiatrist's insuring that burn patients receive adequate analgesia for their pain. The family can also be helped through group meetings, education, arranging for frequent contacts with the patient if such is advisable, and formal family therapy if indicated. In addition to a focus on multiple systems, Hackett's description of liaison work emphasizes the importance of multiple or pluralistic intervention techniques (from group singing to auto-hypnosis). The value of anticipation, clarification, and warm support is stressed.

We would emphasize also the role of the liaison psychiatrist as a specialist at the interface between all systems. His capacity to detect conflicts among the complex relationships (patient, doctor, family, and staff) and to intervene and resolve them may be crucial. Judgment regarding the focus of intervention is one of the many ways in which the liaison psychiatrist is an educator for other staff. In most general hospitals, the overwhelming bias is to focus on an individual patient. If his behavior seems inappropriate, it follows automatically that something should be done for or to him. The psychiatrist can demonstrate, however, that intervention may more appropriately be directed at staff, the attending physician, family, or at conflict-resolution among them. Such intervention presumes a broadly ranging competence along with appropriate responsibility and authority. Curiosity and knowledge concerning family dynamics, theory of groups, and contextual variables, in addition to knowledge of individual psychodynamics and one-to-one psychotherapeutic skills, are most important to the compleat liaison psychiatrist.

For many patients and families, hospitals are not repositories of hope, but places where individuals die and families experience painful loss. Assisting family members in dealing with death or severe loss is an appropriate function for the liaison psychiatrist. He will be aware of the painful memories and fears that can be precipitated by the family member's admission to a hospital. This experience may, for some, reawaken incompletely mourned earlier losses, and sensitivity to this possibility allows the psychiatrist to help them convert a reaction of over-concern to one of appropriate concern. Paul and Grosser (17), for example, have written extensively about the terrible toll of psychopathology from incomplete grief work and the importance of helping people experience and share grief over painful losses. Little (18) presents a clinical vignette of a 42-year-old woman's years of neurosis and mistrust of physicians, which he believed arose from the gross mishandling of her father's death when she was 12. "No one helped Susan properly mourn for her father; no one tried to find out how she felt about his death. . . ." He makes a passionate plea for physicians to assist family members, especially children, in coping with the trauma of death in the family.

We have described the family of the patient as the most frequently overlooked factor influencing the patient's illness and behavior. To correct this deficit is important work. Ideally, the psychiatrist is able to assess clinically both the basic level of family competence and the impact of the patient's illness upon the family.

The Liaison Psychiatrist and the Family

The suggestions made in this paper may be impossible to carry out in many current medical settings that present obstacles to effective liaison psychiatry. The resistance to people-oriented care is often great, the struggle of concerned psychiatrists is continuous, but it is our belief that an increasing emphasis on family involvement will result in better patient care and improved ward morale.

In addition to the direct assessment and intervention in the life of the patient's family, the psychiatrist has the opportunity to educate the hospital staff to the importance of the family in the patient's response to illness and treatment. This can be done in many ways: staff conferences, case conferences with a special family focus, and inclusion of other staff, particularly nurses, in one's interviews with the family. In our experience, medical personnel are generally eager to learn and use an evaluation of family competence.

The liaison psychiatrist deals daily with crises. Crises may be resolved successfully and produce learning and growth. If not resolved, the ensuing distress may become chronic and increase disability. For this reason, the liaison psychiatrist must have a strong commitment to preventive work. His efforts to understand and assist the patient and family deal with the crises of serious illness may play a crucial role in the prevention of subsequent difficulty.

This chapter suggests a clinical approach to the evaluation of family competence that is based upon careful research. It offers some clinical and theoretical guidelines for estimating the family's response to the acute stress. Throughout, the emphasis is that these judgments have practical usefulness. Whether one intervenes with a family as an authoritative expert providing structure to a distintegrated, chaotic family, or appoints one family member as the family leader in what appears to be a chronically conflicted family, or gently supports a competent family's consideration of the changes necessitated by the illness of the family member, essentially one is basing intervention upon clinical judgment of the strengths and liabilities of a particular family. Such an individualized, data-based approach to families not only reflects the best that psychiatry has to offer, but also offers protection from either gross inattention to families or the indiscriminate application of standard procedures to all families. In this way, the liaison psychiatrist can be a force for the humanization of patient and family care in a setting frequently dominated by technology. Though technology often saves lives that would have been lost in simpler times, it does so frequently at the needless cost of lack of respect for the vulnerable people served and their sense of human connectedness.

REFERENCES

1. CASSELL, J. T.: *The Healer's Art: A New Approach to the Doctor-Patient Relationship.* Philadelphia: Lippincott, 1976.
2. BLUM, R. H.: Report to National Malpractice Commission. HEW, 1974.
3. ANTHONY, E. J.: The Impact of Mental and Physical Illness on Family Life. *Am. J. Psychiat.*, Vol. 127, 138-146, 1970.
4. JACKSON, D. D. and YALOM, I.: Family Research on the Problem of Ulcerative Colitis. *Arch. Gen. Psychiat.*, Vol. 15, 410-418, 1966.
5. LEWIS, J. M., BEAVERS, W. R., GOSSETT, J. T., and PHILLIPS, V. A.: *No Single Thread: Psychological Health in Family Systems.* New York: Brunner/Mazel, 1976.
6. CAPLAN, G.: Types of Mental Health Consultation. *Am. J. Orthopsychiat.*, Vol. 33, 470, 1963.
7. LEWIS, J. M.: Psychosocial Aspects of Heart Attack. Presented to the American Association of Critical Care Nurses, Beaumont, Texas, Oct. 29, 1976.
8. KOOS, E. L.: *Families in Trouble.* New York: King's Crown Press, 1946.
9. PARSONS, T. and FOX, R.: Illness, Therapy, and the Modern Urban American Family. *J. of Social Issues*, Vol. 8, 31-44, 1952.
10. MOSS, G. E.: *Illness, Immunity and Social Interaction.* New York: John Wiley & Sons, 1973.
11. HOFMANN, A. D., BECKER, R. D., and GABRIEL, H. P.: *The Hospitalized Adolescent.* New York: The Free Press, 1976.
12. COHEN, M, FREEDMAN, N., and ENGELHARDT, D. M.: Family Interaction Patterns, Drug Treatment, and Change in Social Aggression. *Arch. Gen. Psychiat.*, Vol. 19, 50-56, July, 1968.
13. SELIGMAN, R.: A Psychiatric Classification System for Burned Children. *Am. J. Psychiat.*, Vol. 131, 41-46, Jan. 1974.
14. ANDREASEN, N. J. C., NOYES, R., HARTFORD, C. E., BRODLAND, G., and PROCTOR, S.: Management of Emotional Reactions in Seriously Burned Adults. *New England Journal of Medicine*, Vol. 286 (2) :65-69, 1972.
15. MINUCHIN, S.: *Families and Family Therapy.* Cambridge Mass.: Harvard University Press, 1974.
16. HACKETT, T. P.: Liaison in Intensive Care Settings. This volume.
17. PAUL, N. and GROSSER, G. H.: Operational Mourning and Its Role in Conjoint Family Therapy. *Community Mental Health Journal*, Vol. 1, 339-345, 1965.
18. LITTLE, R. B.: The Family in Distress. In *Stresses in the Single-Parent Family*, Vol. II (3) *Excerpta Medica*, 1976.

Part IV

THE STANLEY R. DEAN
AWARD LECTURE

10

The Management of Schizophrenia in the Community

John K. Wing, M.D., Ph.D.

INTRODUCTION

The title of this paper requires explanation. In the early part of the nineteenth century, such care as people with schizophrenia received was given "in the community," not in hospital. Attitudes toward institutional and community psychiatry have changed over the years. The first psychiatric hospitals were set up, both in Britain and in the United States, in reaction against the appalling conditions of "community care" then prevailing (1, 2). They were small, with a high turnover, and in the best of them the staff fostered a family atmosphere, with emphasis on moral treatment, the ideals of which were not altogether dissimilar to those fashionable during the past 20 years, and took pride in the fact that they used no methods of physical restraint. Since then, the balance of advantage to the patient, of receiving care inside hospital compared with receiving care outside it, has swung both ways, but it has never been an absolutely clear-cut decision as to which was preferable; there has always been something to be said on both sides. The psychiatric hospitals, in both our countries, went through a prolonged period in which patients experienced pauperism, neglect, institutionalism,

427

restraint, and occasionally cruelty. This was the "custodial" era. Whether conditions outside would have been any better at that time is rarely discussed.

As late as the 1930s, in England, a patient admitted for the first time with a diagnosis of schizophrenia had only one chance in three of discharge within two years. After two years, the discharge curve reached a plateau, and the only chance most people had of being taken off the books was by dying. There was, of course, a large excess mortality. The English Mental Treatment Act of 1930 was the first substantial movement back of the pendulum for half a century, since it allowed patients to be admitted voluntarily instead of by commitment. When a fresh influx of psychiatrists entered the mental hospital service after the second world war, full of high social ideals and pioneering spirit that was characteristic of that time, they found large numbers of patients whose psychiatric condition did not justify being in hospital. This was the time when new concepts of social treatment, offering alternatives to long-term hospitalization, were introduced: the therapeutic community, social and vocational rehabilitation, sheltered work, after-care, day centers, hostels, domiciliary supervision, crisis intervention, pre-admission screening (3). In hospitals such as Mapperley, in Nottingham, the numbers of beds were being drastically reduced long before reserpine and chlorpromazine became available (4).

The combination of social and pharmacological treatments was astonishingly successful. Large numbers of patients were discharged and the expectation became that single or multiple admissions to hospital would rarely result in a prolonged stay. Since the mid-1950s, the number of occupied beds in mental hospitals has gradually been decreasing, and it is still going down. Because of the marked improvement often occurring in patients who had previously spent long years in hospital, some psychiatrists began to think most of the symptoms and the disability found in long-stay hospital patients were actually caused by being in the institution. If people could be prevented from coming into hospital, much of this morbidity would be prevented altogether. At the same time, sociologists were showing that, in some areas of the United States, people were being admitted to hospital and given a diagnosis of schizophrenia although their problems appeared to be social rather than medical, and the functions of the hospital seemed custodial rather than therapeutic (5). Some of the seeds of the anti-psychiatry movement were actually planted by psychiatrists themselves. The very success of psychiatric efforts seemed to show that psychiatry was unnecessary, at least so far as the functional psychoses were concerned. In some parts of the United States it became as hard to get into a hospital as, in former days, it had been hard to get out of one.

We have passed through a similar period in England, though not perhaps quite so extreme as in some States here, but there is general agreement that the time has come for a reappraisal of the situation. This is due to two factors. The first is that many patients quite clearly continue to be disabled, and vulnerable to relapse, even though they have spent only a brief time in hospital, or no time at all. The other is the rediscovery that "community" (that is, non-hospital) *care* also has deficiencies, sometimes quite as great as those of hospitals. The conditions most involved are the major psychoses, dementia and mental retardation, but outstanding among them is schizophrenia, so much so that we can use it as an acid test against which to measure the success of services.

From now on, when I use the term "community care," I shall assume that it includes the services provided in hospitals as well as those provided outside. Three principles of service organizations have evolved in different parts of the world, and are now accepted as being fundamental, although they have been applied with very varied degrees of thoroughness. First, there is the principle of district responsibility. This means that it is possible to identify, in any geographical area, who is responsible for providing the service and who, therefore, is responsible if the service is ineffective. It means that the service is geographically accessible to the local population. The main danger is that rigid insistence on geographical boundaries could limit choice. It is important, therefore, that this principle, like the others, should be applied flexibly and in the interest of the consumer. The second principle is that a sufficiently broad range of services, both medical and social, should be provided to cover all contingencies. The third principle is that any service which provides a wide variety of social and medical agencies needs to be properly coordinated, so that there is adequate communication between agencies and no block or delay when a patient moves from one part of the service to another. These three principles are conveniently summarized as the provision of a responsible, comprehensive, and integrated community service (6).

However, important as these principles are, there is one that is considerably more fundamental. The chief aim of the health services is to decrease or contain disease, disability, or distress—first, in the patient; second, in the patient's immediate family; third, in the community at large. Each service agency has a combination of diagnostic, therapeutic, rehabilitative, and preventive functions. Prevention is better than cure. Primary, secondary, and tertiary preventive methods are used to stop disease occurring in the first place, to detect it at an early stage, to limit development of chronic disabilities following acute disease, and to prevent the accumulation of harmful secondary reactions, if chronic intrinsic impairments are unavoidable. This is what is meant by the "containment" of morbidity.

The concept of *"management"* is basically the same as that of containment. In spite of the bureaucratic sound of the word, it is a useful one and connotations of officialdom and authoritarianism should not be read into it. In the rest of this presentation, I shall try to summarize the knowledge that has accumulated during the past 30 years that enables us now to help, by treatment, counselling, provision of services, and the fostering of self-help, to minimize and contain disabilities that were once regarded as carrying a virtual sentence of institutionalization for life. I shall need to discuss the definition of the acute and chronic syndromes, their prevalence and course, their social reactivity, the influence of adverse secondary reactions and extrinsic disadvantages, and the attitudes and expectations of people in the immediate and more remote social environment. It is only on the basis of this knowledge that we can begin to *plan services rationally* and hope to give the most effective individual help to affected individuals and their families.

THE ACUTE SYNDROMES OF SCHIZOPHRENIA

The *concept of schizophrenia* has been expanding and contracting like a concertina ever since it was invented. Kraepelin himself merged the *démence précoce* of Morel, Hecker's *hebephrenia,* and Kahlbaum's *catatonia,* into one concept of *dementia* praecox, leaving the *paraphrenias* and *paranoia* as separate entities. Bleuler ended this uncomfortable separation; however, by insisting that all schizophrenias were based upon only two *fundamental symptoms,* neither of which was easy to define (flatness of affect and loosening of associations), he opened the door so wide that some clinicians were able to diagnose virtually anyone as schizophrenic. Berze's suggestion that a general lowering of "psychic activity" was the key factor was even more vague. Psychodynamic formulations, based on the recognition of primitive or infantile types of thinking, have to be interpreted by experts, and none has ever shown that the judgments involved can be made reliably. Gruhle, Jaspers and Kurt Schneider did something to redress the balance by emphasizing the processes underlying delusions and hallucinations, but Kleist and Leonhard took the process of differentiation to lengths that bordered on the absurd.

The upshot is that several *diagnostic schools* have evolved in different parts of the world: in the USSR, in France, in the UK, in Germany and other parts of Europe, and in the U.S. The *lifetime expectancy* of schizophrenia calculated from data in the Rochester (New York) *case register* is three percent, compared with an estimate of just under one percent derived from the similar register in London, England. This three fold difference must bedevil any attempt at generalization unless we keep it firmly in mind, and it is therefore worthwhile considering in some detail what is involved.

Morton Kramer compared age-adjusted *first admission rates* to public and private mental hospitals in the U.S. with equivalent rates in England and Wales (7). The American rate in 1960 was 24.7 per 100,000 total population compared with 17.4 for England and Wales. The rates for the major affective psychoses, on the other hand, were 11.0 and 38.5 respectively. Table 1 shows the one-year *prevalence*

TABLE 1

One-Year Prevalence of Schizophrenic and Depressive Disorders
in Three Urban Areas Covered by Case Registers

Diagnostic category	Rates per 100,000 local population, age 15 years and over, in:			
	Baltimore, USA Non-white	White	Aberdeen, Scotland	London, England
Schizophrenias	722	685	246	317
Manic-depressive psychoses	59	135	225	377
Other depressions	80	134	338	519

Adapted from Wing, Wing, Hailey, Bahn asd Baldwin (8)

rates (based on the unduplicated statistics of psychiatric services
during 1964) in three urban areas covered by *case registers*—Aberdeen, Scotland; Baltimore, Maryland; and London, England (8).
Schizophrenia was diagnosed markedly more often in Baltimore than
in the other two localities, in both sexes, and particularly between
the ages of 25 and 64. Depressions were commoner at all ages in
Britain but were particularly common in women.

That much of the differences is accounted for by cross-cultural
diagnostic biases is suggested by results of the US-UK *Diagnostic
Project* in which a standard clinical technique (the *Present State
Examination*) was used to interview patients admitted to hospitals
in New York and London, usually with acute and severe psychiatric disorders (9). When hospital diagnoses were compared, the
higher frequency of schizophrenia in New York and of affective
disorders in London was confirmed. When standardized diagnoses
were compared, there was very little difference between the two
series. In other words, American psychiatrists were using broader
criteria to diagnose schizophrenia than their British colleagues.
However, the project did not help to determine which of these
biases was correct.

Another large-scale international comparison was carried out
under the auspices of the *World Health Organization—the Interna-*

tional Pilot Study of Schizophrenia (IPSS) (10). Nine centers took part, chosen for the cultural diversity of their populations and the divergent schools of psychiatric thought represented. They were: Aarhus (Denmark), Agra (India), Cali (Colombia), Ibadan (Nigeria), London (England), Moscow (USSR), Prague (Czechoslovakia), Taipei (Taiwan), and Washington (USA). In this study, in addition to the standard techniques of examination used in the U.S.-U.K. Diagnostic Project, a standard classification procedure was also used, which produced a reference "diagnosis" based on the standard ratings of symptoms classified according to rules laid down in a computer program (known as CATEGO), thus eliminating variations in subjective judgment (11). If 9 percent of cases are omitted because insufficient information is available for a reference classification, there is a substantial degree of agreement (in fact, almost an identity) between three of the major CATEGO classes* (S, P and O) and a center diagnosis of schizophrenic or paranoid psychosis. This was true of all nine centers. However, the same was true of concordance between a clinical diagnosis of affective psychosis or neurosis and the equivalent CATEGO classes (M, D, R and N) only in seven of the centers, while in the other two, there was a major amount of discrepancy. The latter two centers were in in Moscow and Washington. The data are summarized in Table 2. What this means is that virtually all the cases placed by CATEGO into classes S, P and O, purely on the basis of PSE symptoms, were given a diagnosis of schizophrenic or paranoid psychosis, but that psychiatrists in the Moscow and Washington centers also included many of the cases that were regarded elsewhere, and by the reference classification, as affective. This confirms the result of the U.S.-U.K. Project but shows that a broad concept of schizophrenia is not confined to the U.S.A.

The amount of disagreement should not be overemphasized. Out of 801 cases diagnosed as schizophrenic or paranoid psychoses, 726 (90.6 percent) were also in classes S, P and O. This provides an

---

* For convenience, the major CATEGO classes are listed in Appendix 1.

TABLE 2

Concordance Between Center Diagnosis and Reference
Classification in Two Groups of IPSS Centers

CATEGO classes	Moscow and Washington N	% concordance	Seven other centers N	% concordance
S+, S?, P+, O+	114	*96.5*	642	*96.0*
M+, D+, R+, N+	90	*48.9*	191	*84.8*

(Omitted: 94 cases with diagnoses other than schizophrenic, paranoid, or effective
disorders, and 71 cases in uncertain CATEGO classes)
Adapted from WHO (10)

empirical way to describe the symptoms and syndromes present
during the acute psychosis. The syndrome profiles of these three
major classes are presented in Appendix 2. By far the largest of
the three is class S (67 percent of all cases diagnosed as schizophrenic or paranoid psychosis in the IPSS). The main symptoms
involved are thought insertion, thought broadcast, thought com-
mentary, thought withdrawal, delusions of control and alien pene-
tration, and certain kinds of auditory hallucinations. Most are
among the *"symptoms of the first rank"* described by Kurt Schneider (12). Whenever they are present, there is almost always a
wide range of other symptoms as well. The profile in Appendix 2
demonstrates, for example, that 85 percent had depressed mood,
31 percent a hypomanic syndrome, 32 percent grandiose delusions,
and so on.

Experiences of this kind are likely to be interpreted differently
by different people. The temptation to develop delusional explanations, in terms of ideas which otherwise seem to come straight from
science fiction, is obviously great. Suppose, for example, that someone hears his own thoughts being echoed or repeated or spoken
aloud in his head, so loud that he feels that anyone standing nearby
must be able to overhear them. Suppose that the experience goes
further—that some of the thoughts have a distorted quality and do
not appear to be his own, or that they seem to come from outside,

i.e. are heard as "voices." We are dealing here with a disorder of the most characteristically human experience, "internal language." It is entirely comprehensible that the affected individual will consider all sorts of explanations, including hypnotism, telepathy, radio waves, spirit possession and so on, depending on his cultural background. This effort of the imagination can help us to understand what is happening in the early stages of schizophrenia. In addition, we can see why fear, panic, and depression are so common, and why judgment is so often distorted.

Experiences like these can occur after taking *amphetamine* or in *chronic alcoholism* or as part of the aura in *temporal lobe epilepsy*. Evelyn Waugh gave a vivid description, in *The Ordeal of Gilbert Pinfold,* of a hallucinatory state due to chronic intoxication by *bromide* and alcohol. When there is a known organic cause of this kind, the condition is not usually called "schizophrenia" and is excluded from most types of research project, though they might well give very useful information if studied comparatively.

The second major *CATEGO* class is class P, which contains cases with delusions other than those specific for class S but without predominantly manic or depressive delusions: 17 percent of all diagnosed schizophrenic or paranoid psychoses fell into this group. Only in one center (Taipei) was there a good concordance between a diagnosis of *paranoid psychosis* (as contrasted with schizophrenic) and class P and it seems that many psychiatrists do not have very clear criteria for making the distinction. It may or may not be useful but, unless the distinction is made, we are unlikely to be able to discover whether it has any value. Conditions in class P included cases characterized by a single "delusion"—for example *morbid jealousy,* or a conviction that the patient's teeth were too protruberant, or that he gave off an unpleasant smell, or that other people thought him homosexual—as well as more florid clinical pictures with widespread persecutory or religious or grandiose delusions. There were also conditions that seemed specifically *subcultural.* There was, however, no case of *"paranoia querulans."*

Finally, there is class O, accounting for only 6 percent of the schizophrenic and paranoid psychoses diagnosed in the IPSS. The syndrome profile in Appendix 2 is characterized mainly by behavioral abnormalities: catatonic symptoms, excitement, retardaiton, bizarre behavior, and so on, in the absence of more specific delusions or hallucinations. These conditions were commoner in the developing countries. Once again, the class is heterogeneous. Some conditions might have had an organic origin, such as encephalitis, some might better be classified as *Asperger's syndrome,* or the later manifestations of *early childhood autism* (13), and some (e.g. acute excitements without other identifying features) might better have been regarded as specific *subcultural* states. Yet others were simply chronic *residual conditions,* following previous more typical episodes of schizophrenic psychosis.

We have seen earlier that yet other conditions than those described in classes S, P and O may also be described as schizophrenic, particularly within certain schools of psychiatry. Anyone who wishes to discuss the causes, treatment, management or prevention of "schizophrenia" must somehow come to terms with this diversity. Every generalization must have so many exceptions that it may seem pointless even to make the attempt. Nevertheless, I shall hope to show, paradoxically, that some useful statements can be made if we first recognize that we must set limits to generalization. For the moment, I shall be concerned mainly with patients who have experienced the central schizophrenic syndrome (class S), and the paranoid syndrome (class P), since these are the largest and the most easily definable groups. Both can, of course, persist for months or years, and can therefore be regarded as chronic as well as acute syndromes. But before considering the environmental factors that precipitate or maintain them (which might provide a basis for rational intervention), it is necessary to give a good deal of attention to the other chronic syndromes associated with schizophrenia.

THE CHRONIC SYNDROMES

Whatever theory of schizophrenia is adopted, it is common ground that acute psychotic attacks characterized by symptoms of the first rank are frequently preceded, accompanied, or followed by more long-lasting impairments, which can be summarized in terms of Bleuler's two *fundamental characteristics*—flatness of affect and loosening of the associations. The first of these chronic syndromes may be called the "chronic poverty syndrome." It is characterized by flatness of affect, poverty of speech, slowness, underactivity, social withdrawal, and lack of motivation. These traits are highly intercorrelated and can be reliably measured, in long-stay patients, by means of *behavior scales* (4). Together they constitute a useful measure of the severity of one kind of chronic impairment. The social withdrawal score is highly correlated with work output at simple industrial tasks, and also with measures of central and peripheral *arousal* (14, 15). It also represents quantitatively the individual's ability to *communicate* using verbal and non-verbal skills. The most severely impaired person conveys little information through his use of facial expression, voice modulation, or bodily posture, gait or gesture.

In addition to these chronic negative symptoms, there may be *incoherence of speech* and *unpredictability of associations*. The individual does not seem to be able to think to a purpose but goes off on a sidetrack because of some unusual association to a chance stimulus and thus gives the impression of confusion, incoherence, and incompetence. Occasionally this may give the impression of creativity, but usually the syndrome is constricting and handicapping. Most of the creative people who have been afflicted with schizophrenia have had their creativity abolished, not enhanced.

These two kinds of chronic syndrome are not unrelated. Social withdrawal, for example, could in part be a reaction to an individual's experience that his attempts at communicating with other people were received with a more or less polite brush-off. Attempts at communication may actually be painful. However, this is by no means the whole explanation of social withdrawal or slowness. It is generally accepted that both types of impairment can be manifested in childhood and adolescence, long before the first onset of a recognizable acute syndrome (16). Certainly, they are often the most characteristic features of the chronic state.

Table 3 shows that the type and severity of chronic syndromes in schizophrenia may vary markedly according to the setting in which the study is being carried out. A serious methodological difficulty in comparing the results of therapeutic trials has been that the composition of the series has not been specified with sufficient clarity to make generalization feasible. The three series described in Table 3 comprised: (a) long-stay schizophrenic women selected at random in three mental hospitals in 1960 (4); (b) long-stay schizophrenic men selected for a trial at an industrial rehabilitation unit (17); (c) a group of chronic schizophrenic patients who had not been in hospital for at least a year but who had been unemployed throughout that time (18). The reliability and use of the method used to classify type and severity of syndrome have been described in detail elsewhere (13). The aims of these three studies were quite different and their conclusions can only be applied to the specific group selected. It is clear that a wide range of type and severity of chronic syndromes can be present and that generalizations about chronic schizophrenia must therefore be applied with great care.

Chronic impairments contain a component that is "intrinsic" and a component that is reactive. From a purely practical point of view, an *intrinsic impairment* is one that will not go away, no matter what biological, psychological, or social factors are brought to bear therapeutically. Of course, we can never be certain, in theory, that we have tested the limits of treatment, and circumstances sometimes change in a way that surprises even the most astute clinician, so that it is never wise to give up hope of improvement. But to deny that severe and chronic intrinsic impairment can exist must do more harm than good. It is only by recognizing and studying disabilities that it is possible to find ways of compensating for them.

The Importance of Diagnosis

The relationship between the acute and the chronic syndromes has long been a matter of controversy and confusion. Some theorists have thought that specific kinds of delusional experience were primary, while others have regarded the affective flattening and

TABLE 3

Severity and Type of Syndrome Present in Three Series
of Chronic Schizophrenic Patients

Type and severity	Series A* %	B** %	C*** %
No evident syndrome	11	42	20
Moderate severity only	18	22	37
Severe flatness of affect, otherwise only moderate syndromes	5	—	7
Coherently expressed delusions predominant	11	4	22
Severe incoherence of speech	15	—	4
Severe poverty of speech	26	—	7
Mute	15	—	2
Total number in series	(273)	(45)	(54)

* Series A. Random sample of long-stay schizophrenic women, aged 18-59, in three mental hospitals (4).
** Series B. Long-stay schizophrenic men selected for course at industrial rehabilitation unit (17).
*** Series C. Schizophrenic men and women who had lived outside hospital at least a year but had been unoccupied (18).
Adapted from Wing, Wing, Griffiths and Stevens (18)

thought disorder as fundamental. A *multigene theory,* together with the action of a variety of environmental precipitants (somatic, psychological and social), could comprehend both points of view, and also link the dimensional with the categorical approach. The main point about a diagnosis, however, is to suggest to the clinician theories that might be helpful when applied in practice, i.e. theories that will predict a useful form of treatment or prevention or management or, at the very least, suggest a prognosis. None of the concepts of schizophrenia at present in vogue is firmly grounded in a set of linked and tested theories in the way that diabetes mellitus, for example, is, although there are many analogies between the two concepts and we may hope that, one day, our knowledge of schizophrenia will equal our knowledge of diabetes. It is therefore necessary to proceed to some extent empirically.

We know that the acute syndromes usually respond to *phenothiazine* treatment whereas the chronic syndromes respond less well. We know that the acute syndromes, particularly when precipitated by organic factors such as amphetamine or alcohol, are less likely to be preceded or followed by the chronic syndromes. We know that social withdrawal often accompanies chronic depression, mental retardation, chronic physical disability, and severe social deprivation. Moreover, mild degrees of affective blunting or of "thought disorder" cannot be recognized reliably. These are good empirical reasons why any theory linking acute and chronic schizophrenic syndromes should not be applied in practice, except with great circumspection. In particular, the supposed presence of chronic syndromes should not lead to a regime of treatment suitable only for the acute syndromes if the latter are absent, and especially if they have never been present. Terms such as simple, pseudoneurotic, pseudopsychopathic, latent, or sluggish 'schizophrenia" should not be made to carry too much therapeutic meaning. Still less should the "spectrum" concept be used clinically. Failure to understand this basic distinction has contributed, in my view, to practices that can indeed be criticized. There is a close analogy here with diagnosis of severe mental retardation. The functions of differential diagnosis —for example, between mongolism, phenylketonuria, epiloia, and so on—are different from the delineation of the pattern of impairments that determine the kind of medical, educational, and social help needed by the child and family. There will be a degree of overlap since the diagnosis can, to some extent and in some cases, lead to a prediction of what the pattern of impairments will be. But two essentially different models of "diagnosis" are involved.

Much sterile controversy has stemmed from the fact that this distinction has not been recognized, and absolutist schools have grown up that altogether deny the applicability either of disease concepts or of concepts of chronic impairment. At the most nihilistic, some schools have even denied both.

In the sections that follow, I shall deal separately with the empirical evidence concerning social influences on both acute and chronic syndromes, in order to prepare the ground for a rational discussion of management, which must, of course, include consideration of the problems that occur when both types of syndrome occur, as they often do, together or in alternation.

SOCIAL DISABLEMENT AND THE COURSE OF SCHIZOPHRENIA

So far, we have been considering, in a rather cross-sectional manner, the acute and chronic syndromes that make up the clinical picture of schizophrenia, and have not dealt with their effects upon the individual's level of social functioning. Two other factors need to be dealt with first: extrinsic disadvantages and secondary adverse reactions.

The term "extrinsic" is taken from physical medicine and it cannot be applied to psychiatric disorders without qualification. The basic idea is straightforward—extrinsic factors would be disadvantageous whether or not the individual had become ill. Someone born in a large family in a poor area, with inadequate housing and high unemployment, is socially disadvantaged. If he has few assets in the way of vocational skills, intelligence, social attractiveness, family support, and so on, he is not well prepared to cope with chronic illness of any description, let alone schizophrenia. However, the socially disadvantaged are more at risk of developing all sorts of diseases, schizophrenia being one of them. There has been a long discussion of whether socially disadvantageous conditions are likely to cause schizophrenia, or whether the high rates observed under such conditions are due to a preexisting *drift*. Intrinsic impairments often precede the first acute attack. In such cases the prognosis is less likely to be favorable. The balance of the epidemiological evidence at the moment is in favor of the view that much of the association noted between the onset of acute schizophrenia and factors such as social class, marital status, migration and social isolation is due to selection rather than stress (19). On the other hand, it is also clear that a disadvantaged background has an adverse effect upon the course because of the lack of social support (20). This is why an attempt to increase the number of assets, by social skills and vocational training, by the creation of a graded series of supportive social environments, by counseling in methods of self-help, and so on, is of such importance.

The other type of factor is the reaction of the handicapped individual to the combination of intrinsic impairments and extrinsic disadvantages that he or she has experienced. An example from physical medicine may make the distinction clear. Compare the violinist who injures the little finger of his left hand with the laborer who suffers the same injury. The implications and the effects are quite different in the two cases. Compare also an individual who suffers a severe coronary thrombosis, recovers, and is back at work within three months as though nothing had happened, with someone who experiences a mild chest pain and thereafter becomes a "cardiac invalid." We are dealing here with self-attitudes, confidence, expectations, and personal habits, not only in the affected individual but in the people who are important in that individual's social environment, and upon whom his well-being may depend. Whether a man who has had a leg amputated makes a success of his rehabilitation may depend as much upon his wife as on him. Such factors are particularly important in schizophrenia, as we shall see later.

These three types of difficulty—intrinsic impairments, extrinsic disadvantages, and adverse secondary reactions—do not vary independently of each other; how severely each type affects everyday life and social performance depends on a somewhat different group of determining factors. Each individual shows a unique pattern of difficulties. The overall result, however, is that the individual is handicapped from achieving some personal goal; this condition may be called *"social disablement." Management* (which includes rehabilitation, training, the realization of potential assets, and the provision of sheltered environments when necessary) is most rational when it is based upon a thorough knowledge of the various types of handicapping factor that produce social disablement, and of the way they can be influenced for better or worse. Having identified the unique pattern of impairments, disadvantages and reactions that is responsible for an individual's disablement, a plan is constructed jointly with him or her, which consists of trying to increase the number of options that are realistically available, so that there is a greater choice of paths forward. The more evident that movement along a particular path will be rewarding, the greater the motivation to take it.

Before coming to a consideration of the social reactivity of the acute and chronic syndromes, and of the adverse secondary reactions, it will be useful to consider the *course of schizophrenia* as it has been determined statistically in various follow-up studies. Mayer-Gross followed up, sixteen years later, patients with early schizophrenia admitted to the Heidelberg Clinic in 1912 and 1913 (21). Harris and his colleagues followed, for five years, patients admitted to the Maudsley Hospital in London for insulin coma treatment, between 1945 and 1948 (22). Brown and his colleagues examined, in 1961, a group of patients first admitted for schizophrenia to three English mental hospitals five years earlier in 1956 (23). The figures are not strictly comparable because of variations in mortality and numbers followed up, and because standard methods of defining and selecting the cohorts were not used, but they do provide a basis for approximate comparison.

The proportions of patients in the three series who were alive, out of hospital, functioning well socially, and without major psychotic symptoms, at the time of follow-up, were 35, 45, and 55 percent. The proportions who were alive, out of hospital, but unwell or unoccupied, were 3, 21, and 32 percent. The proportions in hospital or dead were 62 (two-thirds of whom were dead), 34, and 13 percent. A more detailed comparison of the two English series is shown in Table 4.

A considerable improvement in *prognosis* is suggested, part of which seems to have taken place before the new era in pharmacological and social treatment had begun. But even among schizophrenic patients first admitted in 1956, over one-quarter were in hospital (and had been there for more than six months), or were severely disturbed in the community, five years later. Another 16 percent were outside hospital but unable to work or maintain a

Table 4

Comparison of Two English Series of Schizophrenic Patients
Followed up for Five Years

	Maudsley 1945-48 (Insulin patients)	Three hospitals 1956 (First admissions)
	%	%
Patient independent: moderate or no symptoms	45	56
Patient dependent: moderate or no symptoms	12	16
Severe disturbance	9	17
In-patient	34	11
No. followed up	123	94
Dead	1	3
Not followed up	1	14

Adapted from Brown, Bone, Dalison and Wing (23)

home, although their symptoms caused only moderate social disturbance. However, 55 percent could be said to be *"social recoveries,"* if we include a number whose adjustment was rather precarious. Neurotic symptoms were common among this group. Of patients who had been in hospital before 1956, and were readmitted in that year, only 38 percent were working and reasonably well in 1961.

Perhaps the most remarkable follow-up study of recent years is that carried out by Manfred Bleuler, who had published a detailed account of a personal series of 208 patients admitted in 1942 and 1943 to the Burghölzli clinic in Zurich. He concludes that, after 20 years, between a quarter and a third of the patients are severely handicapped, and that the prognosis has improved during this time (24).

It is a reasonable working hypothesis that the prognosis can be improved still further by the application of knowledge that is already available. The next three sections will therefore deal with the social reactivity of the acute and chronic clinical syndromes, and of the adverse secondary reactions, by way of introduction to a discussion of the ways in which management can be improved.

THE SOCIAL REACTIVITY OF THE ACUTE SYNDROMES

The most convenient way of initiating the scientific study of the social reactivity of the acute syndromes of schizophrenia is to investigate the social concomitants of relapse. Stone and Eldred, for example, described the reemergence of delusions in two patients, shortly after they had been transferred to a special ward for intensive treatment, who had been free of such symptoms for many years while living in the sheltered conditions of a mental hospital (25). We observed the same phenomenon in six out of 45 moderately disabled patients during the first week of a course at an industrial rehabilitation unit (17). The course entailed traveling from the mental hospital to the rehabilitation unit by public transport and mixing with a group of people most of whom were physically rather than psychiatrically disabled. It therefore entailed a very considerable change in routine and demanded the exercise of skills that there is not always an opportunity to practice in mental hospitals. In fact, 21 of the 45 patients came from a hospital where social conditions had only recently improved, and there had been very little preparation for the rehabilitation course. Of these 21 patients, five relapsed with delusions and hallucinations that had not been present for years. The other 24 patients came from another hospital which had pioneered methods of social and vocational rehabilitation and only one of these relapsed. More patients from the former hospital were receiving *phenothiazines* (and in higher doses) than patients from the latter, so that this factor cannot explain the difference.

More recently Goldberg and his colleagues found that social casework and vocational rehabilitation hastened relapse in patients who had more severe clinical symptoms at the time of discharge from hospital, while it seemed useful in patients who were asymptomatic at discharge (26).

The significance of these studies will be discussed later, but we can already hypothesize that social pressure can lead to relapse, even when it is applied with the best of intentions by professional helpers. A different kind of social precipitant was described by Brown and Birley who found that there was a marked increase in the frequency of occurrence of certain events, compared with control groups, during the few weeks immediately before the first onset or an acute relapse with florid schizophrenic symptoms (27). Excluding events that could have been the result rather than the cause of a recrudescence of symptoms did not diminish the extent of the association. Some of the events would be expected to have been experienced as pleasurable, others as unpleasant: becoming engaged to be married or receiving a promotion at work, for example, compared with hearing about the death of a relative or being involved in a traffic accident. Nearly all the events were familiar ones, in the sense that most people would expect to be affected by them during the course of their lives. People who had previously had attacks of schizophrenia seemed more vulnerable to common stresses than most people. The relapse was usually characterized by the same sort of florid schizophrenic symptoms that had been manifested in earlier attacks.

There has long been a theory that the relatives of people with schizophrenia are in some way implicated in the original causation of the disease (28). Very few empirical studies have been carried out to test this hypothesis and, in any case, the methodological problems are immense. Studies of identical twins brought up together or apart provide little convincing evidence (29). The best work methodologically is that by Wynne and his colleagues, suggesting that *communication deviances* are common in the parents of patients with schizophrenia, though this has no necessary bearing on origins in childhood (30, 31). However, this clear-cut result has not been replicated in a recent very careful study in England, and it may be that the reason, at least in part, is that the criteria for diagnosis in the two series were quite different (32). As for the really passionate advocates of various forms of the early environment model of causation, it is difficult to understand where the strong motivation to believe such theories springs from, in the absence of any substantial body of evidence in favor.

There are, however, several recent studies that seem to show that factors in the family might be responsible for precipitating the first onset or relapse of acute schizophrenia. The most recent study, by Vaughn and Leff, used the same design and method as an earlier one and yielded very similar results, thus providing one of the rare examples of replication within the field of social psychiatry (33, 34). Series of schizophrenic and depressed patients were examined shortly after admission to hospital, using a standard technique to describe and classify their symptoms and to ensure that the processes of clinical selection were unambiguous. A key relative was interviewed while the patient was still in hospital and ratings made of hostility, emotional overinvolvement and criticism. Of these three factors, the last proved most important and could be measured very reliably in terms of the number of critical comments made about the patient during the interview (35). All three factors were combined into one index of *"expressed emotion."* This index was associated with previous work history and with the amount of disturbance in behavior during the three months before admission. It was also highly significantly related, but quite independently, to relapse rate during the nine months after discharge. Two other factors were important in predicting relapse. One was the amount of time that patient and key relative spent in face-to-face contact with each other (itself affected by whether the patient was working or attending a day center); the other was whether the patient was taking *phenothiazine* drugs.

Thus a hierarchy could be set up in terms of risk of relapse. Those at most risk (over 90 percent) were living at home in constant face-to-face contact with highly involved relatives and not protected by taking phenothiazine drugs. If they were taking medication or if they had little contact with the involved relatives (another protective feature), the risk was much lower (40 to 50 percent). If both protective features were present, the risk of relapse (15 percent) was the same as if they had returned to a low-emotion family. Approximately half the families came into the high-emotion and half into the low-emotion category. The association of high emotional expressiveness in the relative with previously disturbed behavior and poor work history in the patient suggests that, at least in part, there was a vicious circle effect of patient and relative on each other. Further light is thrown on this by Vaughn's analysis of the content of the criticisms made about patients by relatives (36). Less than a third of these were concerned with symptoms of the florid attack; these criticisms were usually not associated with a poor previous relationship between patient and relative. Over two-thirds of the criticisms were directed at longstanding personality traits which had been present before the first onset of florid symptoms. These traits were mainly lack of sociability, communication and affection. So far as could be judged, such earlier indications of negative impairments were not found only in patients whose relatives were critical about them, but the measurement of *previous personality* is notoriously difficult, and the relatives were the main source of information. The question of cause and effect must therefore remain open.

It is difficult to see a single common factor underlying all these situations associated with relapse, except the very vague one of "stress." One possibility is *social intrusiveness;* i.e. an environmental agent (whether an eager therapist, an accidental contact, or an over-involved relative) that does not allow a sufficient degree of protective withdrawal, so that an individual with inadequate equipment for communication is forced into interaction in a social situation and an underlying cognitive disorder becomes evident.

Data concerning the level of psychophysiological *arousal* in schizophrenia are relevant to this explanation, but discussion will be reserved until after the social reactivity of the clinical poverty syndrome has been considered.

THE SOCIAL REACTIVITY OF THE CHRONIC SYNDROMES

A great deal of attention was given by psychologists between the wars to the nature of *"psychological deficit"* in schizophrenia. Jung had pointed out in 1906 that patients with *dementia praecox* showed a "passive registration of events which are enacted . . . but all that which requires an effort of attention passes without heed (37)." He quoted Stransky's experiment in which subjects were asked to talk at random on a given topic for a minute without giving any attention to what they were saying. The result recalled the incoherence of dementia praecox. These two features, *lack of attention* and *incoherence of speech,* which were regarded by Eugen Bleuler as *fundamental,* were usually investigated separately and few further attempts were made to link them theoretically. Clinicians tended to regard *deterioration* (deficit increasing with time) as inevitable in schizophrenia. Babcock thought that deficit began in childhood and that she could trace it through its course, but her conclusions were based on cross-sectional surveys of verbal and performance tests (38). Most subsequent workers agreed that her conclusions did not follow from the data. Kendig and Richmond, for example, showed that there was a genuine intellectual impairment, but no tendency for it to increase over time (39). Foulds and Dixon later confirmed this (40). Many other psychologists described experiments in which it was demonstrated that the performance of schizophrenic patients could improve with practice and that there were ways of motivating them to perform better (41-47). This large body of work on psychological deficit succeeded in more precisely describing and measuring the two components of impairment identified by Kraepelin and Bleuler but not in suggesting practical methods of rehabilitation.

Subsequently, a distinction was made between *"paranoid"* and *"non-paranoid"* patients, who tended to react in different ways, and studies were made in realistic workshop conditions using more global measures of *social performance* (48-50). One interesting observation was that the improvement due to practice, which would be expected, by analogy with normal people and even with the severely mentally retarded, to be negatively accelerated, tended in schizophrenia to be slow and linear. One workshop experiment gave more encouraging results than the others, perhaps because patients were encouraged to perform better by well-known and trusted nurses rather than by giving artificial rewards reminiscent of a laboratory setting (51). This study demonstrated that active social supervision could considerably increase output in an experimental group but that the response was sharp and immediate, rather than taking the expected form of another *learning curve,* and that as soon as the extra *social stimulation* was withdrawn, output fell at once to its former level. Moreover, output in the control group (who were situated in the adjoining workshop and were aware that they were *not* getting extra attention) fell and then rose again in a mirror image of what was happening next door. The improvement in output was reflected in a decrease in aimless wandering and fidgeting, or simply sitting staring into space, but this change in behavior was not generalized to other times of the day. The patients involved were all very severely impaired, but they were living in a resocialization villa in a hospital with an excellent reputation for *social therapy,* so that the improvement was not simply due to the fact that they had previously been neglected. It appeared that the extra social stimulation provided a source of motivation that needed to be kept up continuously, since the improvement disappeared at once when it was withdrawn. It could be said that the supervisors were passively exercising functions which the patients were unable to exercise actively for themselves, in the hope that the functions would eventually return. This is an excellent and fundamental principle of rehabilitation.

A larger-scale survey, in which samples of long-stay schizophrenic women in three mental hospitals were interviewed, was designed to test the hypothesis that the social environment in which the patient lived had a measurable influence on the severity of the *clinical poverty syndrome* (4). There were marked social differences between the three hospitals which could be summarized in terms of the degree of *"social poverty"* characterizing them. The measures used were the number of personal possessions owned by patients, the attitudes of nurses toward them, the amount of contact with the world outside, the restrictiveness of ward regimes, and the amount of time spent by the patient doing absolutely nothing. This last measure proved particularly crucial. At the first hospital, it was 2 hours 48 minutes per patient per day, on the average. At the third it was 5 hours 39 minutes, on the average. All the indices used showed equivalent dif-

TABLE 5

Social Environment of Samples of Long-Stay Schizophrenic
Women in Three Mental Hospitals in 1960

Index	Hospital A (N 100)	Hospital B (N 73)	Hospital C (N 100)
Hours spent doing absolutely nothing	2h.48m.	3h.15m.	5h.39m.
Patients possessing a comb	89%	69%	30%
Nurses who thought patient could do useful work in hospital	76%	52%	26%
Mean ward restrictiveness score	27	40	60

Adapted from Wing and Brown (4)

ferences. Thus 79 percent of the subjects owned a handbag at the first hospital, but only 42 percent did so at the third. This revealing item shows how useful simple indices can be; the ownership of items such as a handbag tells us a great deal about how the role-performance of hospitalized women is affected by administrative policy. Table 5 illustrates the differences between the hospitals on selected measures.

Having demonstrated differences between the hospitals, it was possible to proceed to a first test of the hypothesis that there should be equivalent clinical differences. In fact, these were also marked and followed the predicted pattern. Symptoms such as blunting of affect and poverty of speech, rated at a standard interview with each patient, and social withdrawal, independently rated by nurses, indicated a much higher level of impairment at the third hospital than at the first. Table 6 shows the clinical condition of patients at the three hospitals. Of all the social indices used, the one most clearly correlated with clinical condition was length of time doing nothing.

Since the groups were followed up at the three hospitals over an eight-year period, during which time the social conditions improved and then to a varying extent fell back again, it was possible to test

TABLE 6

Clinical Condition of Sample of Long-Stay Schizophrenic
Women in Three Mental Hospitals

Clinical condition	Hospital A (N 100)	Hospital B (N 73)	Hospital C (N 100)
	%	%	%
No evident syndrome	10	15	8
Moderate severity only	21	19	13
Severe flattening of affect, otherwise only moderate symptoms	9	5	2
Coherently expressed delusions predominant	17	8	6
Severe incoherence of speech	17	14	15
Severe poverty of speech	20	25	32
Mute	6	14	24

Adapted from Wing and Brown (4)

this hypothesis fairly rigorously, but it was not possible to disprove it. An increase in social poverty was accompanied by an increase in clinical poverty, and social improvement was accompanied by clinical improvement. Moreover, the least impaired patients were most likely to be discharged, so that improvement did mean something in concrete terms as well.

Thus the conclusions of the earlier experiment were confirmed on a larger scale. A socially rich social environment tends to minimize the development of negative symptoms in schizophrenia. These are symptoms that have been regarded as *fundamental* and immutable. However, in many cases they did not disappear entirely even when active rehabilitation was maintained over many years. This was particularly evident in a series of rehabilitation studies, some of them experimental (17, 18, 52). Long-stay schizophrenic patients who appeared very little impaired while in hospital seemed slow, lacking in initiative and unsociable when working alongside physically disabled people in an industrial rehabilitation unit or a sheltered factory. Nevertheless, they were not unfriendly when approached and their work, though plodding, reached an acceptable standard. It was shown that many long-stay schizophrenic patients could achieve a stable resettlement outside hospital, particularly if sheltered working conditions were available.

All the studies so far considered in this section were focused on large mental hospitals. They showed that *"social treatment"* was not merely an empty phrase. It may be questioned, however, whether the results could be applied to conditions outside hospital. In fact, there is considerable evidence that the principles of social treatment can be applied more generally. It has been found that schizophrenic patients are vulnerable to *social understimulation,* whether this is found in hostels, hotels, group homes, day centers, sheltered communities, centers for the destitute, in lodgings, or in a patient's own family. In one five-year follow-up study it was found that, among those who were unemployed at home, the length of time spent doing absolutely nothing was of the same order as in long-stay inpatients in a hospital with a poor social environment (23).

A careful study was made in Camberwell, a predominantly working-class area in southeast London where psychiatric services are reasonably good. The purpose of the study was to find all the patients known to the local case register who had not been in hospital for the previous year although they had been given a diagnosis of functional psychosis, were of employable age (18-54), and expected to be in employment, but had been out of work for at least a year (18). There were 75 such people, most of whom were schizophrenic, a rate of 44 per 100,000 population. Many of these people were socially isolated and, as the results of an experimental evaluation of a rehabilitation workshop demonstrated, in need of protected living environments. Other studies, of the "new long-stay" patients still accumulating in English mental hospitals (though at a much slower rate than hitherto) (53, 54), and of the alternative residential accommodation now available (55), indicate that social withdrawal and social isolation remain a problem even when patients are no longer in hospital.

Thus there are two major problems: one the reduction of an excessive level of social withdrawal and associated behaviors by enriching the social environment, without at the same time provoking an acute relapse with florid symptoms; the other, the maintenance of these impairments at a minimal level by providing the appropriate kinds of protected environments.

OPTIMUM CONDITIONS FOR DRUG AND SOCIAL TREATMENT

The work discussed in the previous two sections suggests that many patients who experience an attack of acute schizophrenia remain vulnerable to social stresses of two rather different kinds. On the one hand, too much social stimulation, experienced by the patient as *social intrusiveness,* may lead to an acute relapse. On the other hand, too little stimulation will exacerbate any tendency already present towards social withdrawal, slowness, underactivity, and an apparent lack of motivation. Thus the patient has to walk a tightrope between two different types of danger, and it is easy to become decompensated either way. The difficulty in thinking and the inability to communicate, verbally and non-verbally, will be most evident in interactions, for example with close kin, and will be exacerbated in conditions of anxiety and high arousal. Families might provide protective or provocative settings; there is no general rule. The same is true of non-family environments. However, the first onset usually occurs within a family setting and there is a natural tendency on the part of relatives towards normalization, which can lead to further intrusion, particularly if the patient withdraws in natural reaction. The patient may try to explain the abnormal experiences in terms of hypnotism, thought transfer, witchcraft, or other subculturally acceptable ideas. The more intrusive the environment the less the patient is able to withdraw and the more the symptoms are perpetuated and provoked. Being admitted to hospital, or wandering off alone, may provide relief simply by reducing the degree of social stimulation.

After several attacks, the patient may come to terms with his experiences and find (whether he consciously formulates this or not) that a degree of withdrawal is protective. Relatives, too, may learn for themselves just what degree of stimulation is permissible, so that a working solution is arrived at. Patients usually do not wish to be entirely alone, but they do like to remain in control of the intensity of contact. The *role of the relative*, however, is a very difficult one since it is unnatural to acquire the degree of detachment and neutrality required; it is much easier for professional people to adopt such a stance. The relatives of handicapped people may easily become overprotective and overinvolved. In the case of schizophrenia, this overinvolvement has specific effects in increasing the liability to further breakdown. When this shows itself in symptoms such as violence, noisiness at night, refusal to eat, or delusions involving the relative, a circular effect is set up. The relative expects such reactions on future occasions. This is a much more likely explanation of the findings than is the assumption that the original cause of schizophrenia is somehow familial.

The alternative temptation for the patient is to withdraw altogether into contemplation of private experiences. When a patient is allowed to do so in the understimulating conditions of some large hospital wards, or in badly run hostels, or in reception centers, or even in an attic at home, the negative impairments become more and more obvious.

If *phenothiazine* drugs work, at least in part, by reducing a high level of arousal (56), they should be most effective in conditions of social overstimulation, and there is some evidence that this is so (33, 34). It has been suggested that patients who live in low-emotion families can avoid relapse (except for the operation of accidental stresses) even without taking preventive medication (57). Tarrier has recently shown that schizophrenic patients, sitting quietly by themselves in their own homes, have a high arousal level as measured by skin conductance (58). If a "high-emotion" relative enters the room, there is no change in arousal level. If a "low-emotion" relative enters, the high arousal habituates towards normal. The work needs to be repeated but, if it holds true, it suggests that some relatives have a calming and supporting effect, similar to the protective effect of a good hospital or hostel. The evidence that phenothiazines are useful for long-stay patients is conflicting but it may be hypothesized that the more optimal the social conditions provided, the less the need for medication. Most studies of the effects of medication do not give sufficient information to assess how protective, or how *overstimulating* or *understimulating*, the social environments of patients are, but on the whole it appears that medication is less necessary when the patient is living in optimal social surroundings (56).

To generalize: The *optimal environment* is structured, with expectations geared precisely to the level of performance that the patient actually can achieve, or perhaps a little above, but with supervision that is not emotionally involved. Complex decision-making is particularly difficult for patients and tends to rouse their anxiety or their withdrawal. Control of the level of social stimulation must be left to some extent in the patient's hands. A relationship of trust and confidence, whether with relatives or with professional staff, is most likely to develop when these conditions are optimal.

A great deal remains to be explained about the acute and chronic syndromes. The mechanisms whereby *first rank symptoms* such as thought echo or "thoughts spoken aloud," which are direct descriptions of basic experiences with very little elaboration, can be explained, in terms of over-arousal, of phenothiazine action, or of cerebral pathology, remain obscure. Recent advances in pharmacology and biochemistry are so promising that it is clear that links will have to be made. Meanwhile, the formulation put forward here has obvious relevance to problems of management. Before considering practical issues of application, one further area of handicap needs to be explored, one where there is also a useful body of empirical work.

ADVERSE SECONDARY REACTIONS

Relatives, employers, workmates, friends, and professional people reflect back to the person handicapped by *intrinsic impairments* or *external disadvantages,* or a combination of both, an indication of their opinion of his social status and worth. If they think he is less of a man because of his illness, he will tend to think so too. If he is helpless, he may have no choice but to depend upon his environment to help him. A congenitally deaf child must rely on others to teach him to talk and to help him communicate. The more severe the intrinsic impairment, the more inevitable is the development of secondary impairment as well.

Handicapped people have to (or wish to) opt out of certain social responsibilities. Therefore others must take them on. If the others are professionally trained for the job, there tends to develop what Goffman called a staff-client split, each side taking up rather stereotyped attitudes toward the other (59). The longer the client experiences *dependence*, the more he will tend to prefer it. Staff, in turn, may exaggerate the severity of intrinsic impairments, and thus a vicious circle is set up, with unnecessary dependence developing as well as that which is unavoidable. The acceptance by the handicapped person of limitations which are not actually necessary is the essence of secondary reaction.

The most obvious example of adverse *secondary reaction* in schizophrenia is *institutionalism,* at the heart of which is a gradually acquired contentment with life in the institution which culminates in the individual no longer wishing to live any other. Institutionalism is thus caused partly by a reflection back to the handicapped person of his own altered status as a human being. He is seen as a patient, rather than as an employee, a father, a customer, or a companion. The patient role is a constricted one, replacing many others which he might have been able to undertake. Partly, however, institutionalism results from forces in the patient—his own previous experience of illness, his self-confidence, his potential for developing alternative skills, and his determination to achieve independence (4, 60).

Table 7 illustrates the process occurring in the three mental hospitals described earlier (see Tables 5 and 6). In spite of the marked social differences between them, patients in all three tend to adopt attitudes of indifference or of desire to stay the longer they have been resident. This remains true when the most severely impaired patients, who were mute or so incoherent that their answers to questions were incomprehensible, were omitted. Other factors, such as age, sex and social environment, are also related, but they do not

TABLE 7

Attitudes to Discharge of Sample of Long-Stay Schizophrenic
Women in Three Mental Hospitals: by Length of Stay

Length of stay	Hospital A (N 100)	Indifferent or wish to stay Hospital B (N 73)	Hospital C (N 100)
	%	%	%
2 to 10 years	40	53	50
11 to 20 years	58	58	75
21 years or more	75	82	83

Adapted from Wing and Brown (4)

much reduce the very strong association between attitude to discharge and length of stay.

Other attitudes and personal habits are affected in the same way.
The patient loses any ability he might originally have retained to
play a wide range of social roles; he does not replenish his stock of
useful current information (such as how much a postage stamp
costs); he does not practice traveling on public transport, or shopping; he gradually ceases to make plans for the future, or he simply
repeats some vague formula if he is asked about them. Visitors, of
course, also begin to fall off, and even if he is allowed to go outside
the hospital, he will tend to do so less and less.

It was mentioned earlier that hospitals tend to differ markedly
in the social conditions they provide. Although exposure to a socially
impoverished environment is not necessarily associated with increased
negative impairments, with the major exception of an imposed idle-
ness, it is fairly obvious that *social poverty* is likely to encourage the
development of adverse secondary reactions. Thus institutionalism,
pauperism, and neglect contribute to the *disablement* of hospital
patients as well as to their discomfort.

Once attitude change has taken place, as in institutionalism, it is
very difficult to remedy. Festinger's early work on reference groups
provides a possible theoretical approach. It may be that the success

of rehabilitation units is attributable to the improvement in attude and *self-confidence* which comes about when a handicapped person is exposed to a social group in which confidence and self-reliance are valued and are visibly being acquired by other physically handicapped people. The evidence of a study carried out among 212 entrants to such a unit certainly pointed that way (61). Moreover, those who acquired confidence were more likely to be employed two months after leaving the unit than those who remained unconfident. Unfortunately, however, there was a group of people with idiosyncratic motivation or with very little motivation at all who did not wish to join the more conforming group. Their self-confidence did not change, and they were not very successful. Most of those with schizophrenia were in this group.

Probably attitudes toward discharge or toward work outside the hospital can be changed in schizophrenic patients only by methods designed specifically to effect such a change. Thus in one of our studies, we successfully changed the *attitude toward work* by getting moderately handicapped long-stay schizophrenic patients to go to an industrial rehabilitation unit outside, after adequate preparation. We found that those who improved did in fact find jobs (52). What we did not anticipate was that there was no change in their attitude toward discharge. Even those who began working out still wanted to live in. These attitudes are very specific.

Although this analysis of secondary reactions has been based mainly on the problem of institutionalism, it is of course true to say that nowadays far fewer long-stay patients are accumulating in hospitals. Nevertheless, there are *"new" long-stay* patients in hostels, day centers, and sheltered communities, and it is important to remember that the principles of the development of institutionalism are most unlikely to be different in kind for these people than for the *"old" long-stay* patients in mental hospitals. Indeed, in some respects the problems are more difficult. Mann and Sproule, for example, found that after only two or three years in the hospital the "new" long-stay patients already wanted to stay where they were (53). This is what one would expect as the process of selection focuses to a greater extent on those with more severe intrinsic impairments and extrinsic disadvantages, and as the "hospital" becomes more and more a sheltered community.

Even those who spend most of their time at home and do not have to remain in sheltered environments of various kinds are still at risk for developing secondary handicaps other than institutionalism. Brown and his colleagues found that 20 percent of their schizophrenic patients admitted to the hospital in 1956 left home during the subsequent five years and did not return (23). Divorce is much commoner among schizophrenic patients than in the general population. The secondary problems arising from unemployment, solitary living, poverty, and even destitution are important causes of an attitude of indifference or despair. Once you are down, you tend to be ground further down; handicapped schizophrenics are no exception to that rule.

Even among those who stay at home, there are some who have outstayed their welcome. There tends to be a discrepancy between the attitudes of relative and patient, the former seeing the patient as disabled and often a bit of a trial to live with, the patient himself regarding his circumstances with a touch of complacency (62). We have heard a good deal about the effect of relatives upon patients but much less about the reverse.

THE MANAGEMENT OF SCHIZOPHRENIA

The *management* of schizophrenia needs to be considered from three different points of view: those of the patient; the patient's relatives and others in the immediate social environment on whom his livelihood may depend; and the professional people, administrators and politicians who provide, plan, or control access to services. Each group sees a different set of problems and often fails to appreciate the difficulties faced by the others. It may therefore be useful to look through the eyes of each group separately.

Self-help

Every individual has to learn to live with himself, warts and all. Everyone is handicapped in some way. But those people who are severely impaired in their *inner language* and in their ability to *communicate* with themselves have very little chance to achieve a satisfactory solution unless others help them. Fortunately, most people with schizophrenia are not as severely impaired as that. The central problem is still, however, one of *"insight."* The acute symptoms of schizophrenia carry a peculiar conviction to most of those who experience them, which cancels out the skepticism of their relatives or professional helpers. Given that many have always been somewhat detached from social opinion and that the first onset often occurs during the rebellious teens anyway, it is not surprising that patients find themselves at odds with their relatives and unwilling to take advice from them. Sometimes it is only after prolonged experience and suffering that patients begin to understand some of the factors that make matters better or worse for them.

The following list of factors that are at least partially under the control of patients contains some of the major keys to self-help:

> Whether to take medication
> Recognition and avoidance of triggering situations
> Specific and restricted social withdrawal
> Methods of dealing with primordial symptoms
> Finding work within competence
> Finding companions who are not intrusive
> Helping others to understand the condition

In every case, much depends on others as well. At the moment, misunderstanding of the nature of schizophrenia is common, among specialists as well as among relatives and the general public. Nevertheless, some people do, by trial and error, discover that they can help themselves. They discover, for example, that *medication* controls the acute symptoms and that discontinuing medication brings them back. They also discover the side-effects and then have to balance the advantages against the disadvantages. Three highly intelligent professional people, who contributed to a volume of essays on experiences of schizophrenia, each said that they found phenothiazines dampening and depressing, although each one found the acute symptoms intensely distressing and was grateful for the relief that medication brought (63). Studies of long-term medication in conditions such as tuberculosis, parkinsonism, epilepsy, and diabetes have shown equivalent problems, and the fact that up to one-third of patients with schizophrenia do not persist with their medication is not extraordinary (64). Serious attention given to explanations about the type of drugs available, the use of other drugs to minimize side-effects, the effects of varying the dose, the value of doing so in anticipation of stressful occasions, and the consequences of discontinuing medication may prove very helpful, particularly if it matches the patient's own experience.

Some patients learn eventually to recognize situations which make them feel worse and which might trigger episodes of relapse. One said: "There is a sensitivity in myself and I have to try to harden my emotions and cut myself off from potentially dangerous situations. . . . When I get worked up I often experience a slight recurrence of delusional thoughts." He avoided arguments on topics that made him emotionally upset. Another found that sometimes, when sitting in a subway train, he noticed the eyes of another passenger begin "to radiate." Then he would deliberately turn his attention to something else; in fact, he had evolved a relaxation technique in order to deal with such occasions. Another only experienced hallucinatory voices last thing at night, when his attention began to wander before he went to sleep, but he knew that he would not act on them and quite enjoyed them. A very bright girl chose her men friends among people who were not her intellectual equals because she did not get so involved with them and found she could control the situation better.

Social withdrawal is a technique that can be consciously manipulated by patients and used in a specific way to avoid situations they find painful. It is important that they know the dangers of going too far, since understimulation carries its own risk of increasing morbidity. A degree of external social stimulation is necessary for ordinary social functioning. Nevertheless, being withdrawn is often found preferable to being forced into unwanted social interaction. Work that is within the patient's competence and not too socially exacting is a great help but other people do not always recognize how exhausting many patients find a full-time job, even of this kind.

The degree of *insight* required to use these techniques sensibly is uncommon and some patients take them too far. Many never attain this degree of control; severity of illness is an important factor and it can vary independently of the quality of the social environment. Many could achieve more insight but are given very little help. Many meet with difficulties that are outside their competence to deal with: an over-involved relative who uses the emotional relationship to intrude upon the patient and force him into unwanted interaction; a lack of protected environments such as day centers, sheltered workshops or group homes; a critical attitude from friends or employers; an unrealistic professional helper who does not understand the impairments; accidental stresses such as can occur to anyone.

Most patients are not highly intelligent and articulate. Those who are have to speak for their fellows. The less capacity an individual has to recognize and cope with his own intrinsic impairments, extrinsic disadvantages, and personal reactions, the more important become the sympathy and the help of those with whom he or she has to live.

The Problems of Relatives

A study of schizophrenic patients admitted to three English mental hospitals in 1956 showed that, on discharge, 40 percent went to live with parents, 37 percent (mostly women) with a spouse, 8 percent with some other relative or friend, and 15 percent went to lodgings, rooming houses or residential jobs (23). By the time of follow-up, 5 years later, only 29 percent were living with parents; there was less change in the other groups. Few separations from parental homes were due to disturbed behavior, which parents tolerated with remarkable fortitude. A third were due to the death or ill-health of a parent and a third to positive reasons for leaving. Parents often made very little complaint even when they felt great distress and some developed very skillful methods of managing disturbed behavior. Three-quarters of the parents were over the age of 60 and 40 percent over the age of 70.

There was a *high divorce and separation rate,* probably three times that in the general population. It was particularly high among men. Although a much smaller proportion of the men had married, the rate of separation was nearly double that of the women. Disturbed behavior was responsible for nearly all the separations during the follow-up period. Other studies have emphasized the difference in the types of *social problem* experienced by parents and spouses (33, 36, 65). If neighbors come to call, it is fairly socially acceptable for a mother to say that her son is sick, by way of explanation of the fact that he dashes for the safety of his room as soon as he hears the doorbell ring, and does not come down until the visitors have gone. Such behavior by a husband or wife is much more difficult for the other partner to explain, particularly if there are children about.

As time goes on, there is no doubt that patient and relative, if they stay together, come to acquire a tolerance which neither might have had earlier. The relative, however, does so at the expense of restricting his or her life (66). Often the parents of unmarried schizophrenics are elderly widows who are glad to have some companionship, to have someone to do a bit of shopping if they are physically disabled, and who are not too worried by not being able to live a life of their own. Under such circumstances, even a patient with a turbulent history of frequent breakdowns may eventually settle into a routine. It is another kind of *institutionalism*, less expensive, of course, and less demanding of the patient than a good hospital with workshops, leisure activities, and socialization programs would be, and sometimes a good deal more restricting on the activities and interests of relatives. Few, however, complain. The major problem raised by relatives articulate enough to be able to make a point is worry over the patient's future (65). One father called it the WIAG ("when I am gone") syndrome.

However, this contented, if restricted, outcome for family life, at least for the unmarried patient, is sometimes only reached after what is, in some cases, a lengthy and profoundly distressing time, during which the patient's condition is constantly unstable and the relatives do not know what will happen next. It is not surprising that many patients find themselves homeless and drift to common lodging houses or reception centers. There do not have to be very many patients from each area each year to account for the large numbers found in Salvation Army hostels and shelters for the destitute (67, 68).

Since relatives are almost as much in the front line as patients, so far as living with schizophrenia is concerned, it is surprising that there have been so few informed surveys of their views on the subject. Much work appears to have been carried out with the major object of selecting quotations that fit the author's preconceptions of the pathogenesis of schizophrenia. Relatives do, of course, acquire considerable experience of *coping with difficult behavior* but their methods are inevitably trial and error. Some learn not to argue with a deluded patient; others never learn. Some discover just how far they can go in trying to stimulate a rather slow and apathetic individual without arousing resentment. Others push too hard, find their efforts rejected or that they make matters worse, and then retreat into inactivity themselves. Some never give up intruding until the patient is driven away from home.

A recent survey of the experience of relatives was undertaken with the deliberate objective of learning from them what could be done to help people with schizophrenia (65). Fifty patients were living with relatives who had joined a newly-formed voluntary organization, the National Schizophrenia Fellowship, and another 30 were selected from those known to specialists in an area of southeast London where services were reasonably good. The two groups therefore formed a marked contrast, since it was to be expected that relatives who joined the Fellowship would be articulate and responsible, but also that they would have particularly marked problems. Between the two groups it was possible to form a clear impression of the difficulties of families. Table 8 shows the kinds of problem mentioned. It is hardly necessary to illustrate them since they are so obvious. A few examples will suffice.

Altogether two-thirds of the 80 patients were reported as being markedly or somewhat underactive. However, even those who had some activity, tended to adopt some ritual way of spending the time, for example by brewing tea continuously or chain smoking. One relative explained graphically that, "in the evenings you go into the sitting room and it's in darkness. You turn on the light, and there he

TABLE 8

Behavior Problems Encountered by the Relatives of
Schizophrenic Patients

Characteristic	Fellowship (N 50)	Camberwell (N 30)	Total (N 80)
	%	%	%
Social withdrawal	76	70	74
Underactivity	60	50	56
Lack of conversation	54	53	54
Few leisure interests	54	43	50
Slowness	34	70	48
Overactivity	54	20	41
Odd ideas	44	17	34
Depression	38	27	34
Odd behavior	44	17	34
Neglect of appearance	38	17	30
Odd postures or movements	38	3	25
Threats or violence	32	7	23
Sexually unusual behavior	6	10	8
Suicidal attempts	6	—	4
Incontinence	—	10	4

Adapted from Creer and Wing (65)

is, just sitting there, staring in front of him." Some relatives used
the word "uncanny" to describe this kind of behavior. One mother
said her son spent most of his time closeted in his room, only
coming out at night when everyone was in bed. Usually he was
talking to himself and moving about, but every few weeks there would
be complete silence for a few days. "After that has been going on
for a day or two, I sometimes wonder whether he is dead."

Relatives had various theories to explain the periods of total inactivity and the long hours spent in bed. Many felt that it was because ordinary everyday living and contact with people was simply an unbearable effort to the individual suffering from schizophrenia—he had to withdraw and "recharge" himself frequently. As one mother put it, "He just can't bear *people*—even to be in the same room as another person." One patient himself explained that he had to have the time lying on his bed that he did, because he was "all fizzing up inside." Some relatives feared that if they allowed too much underactivity, the patient would get worse, and therefore insisted that the patient should perform certain household tasks, even though they had to stay in the room with him to make sure he did them and even though the pace at which he worked was often painfully slow. Others decided this kind of thing was too exhausting. "I'd sooner not ask him to wash up," one said, "because it only means he uses cold water or forgets to use any washing up liquid, or leaves half the food on the plates." Some people tried to keep the patients active by keeping them entertained as much as possible—taking them out in the car, for walks, etc. But this was usually very draining emotionally.

About a third of the patients had odd ideas of various kinds—for example, that the neighbors were plotting against them or that some particular relative was at fault. The latter could be very distressing for the relative concerned. The odd ideas often concerned agencies or organizations whom the patient believed to have power over him or to be planning to harm him. Relatives found it difficult to know what to do when a patient expressed this kind of idea. If he said he had just been pursued up the road by a secret agent, ought they to accept what he said and pretend to believe it, or should they tell him he was imagining it? Many relatives feared that if they used the former approach they were encouraging the patient to lose touch even more with reality. But if they took the latter course, would the patient lose his confidence in them?

Patients tended to develop sudden irrational fears. They might, for instance, become fearful of a particular room in the house. Maybe they would tell the family the reason for their fear. "There's a poisonous gas leaking into that room" or "There are snakes under the bed in that room." At first relatives are baffled by this. Some admitted they had grown frustrated with a patient's absolute refusal to abandon some idea, despite all their attempts to reason with him, and had lost their temper. But they found this only resulted in the patient becoming very upset, and in any case the idea continued to be held with as much conviction as ever.

Several patients talked or laughed to themselves, but did this only in their own rooms, and not in front of their family. "If you stand outside his room you can hear that he's keeping up a more or less constant monologue in there." "Sometimes I hear shrieks of laughter coming from her room." Others, however, would sit throughout a meal laughing to themselves, regardless of who was there. Some would occasionally cry out in great distress in reaction to hallucinatory voices. A few relatives had been able to persuade a patient that he must not behave in this way in public. If he forgot and started to do it when others were present, a discreet reminder from the relative would silence him, or else he would go off somewhere alone until he had finished his muttering.

Innumerable examples like these could be given. One of the major complaints by relatives was that when they asked for advice from professional people as to the best way to react, they received no answer at all, or the question was simply turned back on them and their own amateur answers received with polite disdain. Perhaps their advisers had no better idea than they and were doing their best to conceal their ignorance?

A particularly important and distressing problem concerned compulsory admission to hospital. Relatives at the end of their tether and concerned for the long-term welfare of the patient are less inclined to argue the ins and outs of the civil rights issue than those who do not have to live in the situation, although I have met very few who are not distressed by the necessity. Relatives very rarely have advocate lawyers to argue their case for them.

Other difficulties concerned the administration of medication, the lack of sheltered work, the non-availability of hostels or homes where the patients could go when the relatives needed a break, and the difficulty of obtaining welfare support when the patient was unwilling to claim it for himself. Relatives were often under strain themselves—depressed, anxious and guilty. Sometimes there was division within the family as to the best way of proceeding. There was also the agony of not knowing what to tell children.

It is extraordinary that so many relatives do manage to find a way of living with schizophrenia that provides the patient with a supportive and non-threatening home. Some of the factors that are to some extent under their control are as follows:

Creating a non-critical, accepting, environment
Providing the optimal degree of social stimulation
Keeping aims realistic
Learning how to cope with fluctuating insight
Learning how to respond to delusions or bizarre behavior
Making use of whatever social and medical help is available
Learning to use welfare arrangements
Obtaining rewards from the patient's presence
Helping patient's attitudes to self, to relatives, to medication, to work

General Factors in Management of Schizophrenia

Part of the peculiar difficulty in managing schizophrenia is that it lies somewhere between conditions like blindness which, though severely handicapping, do not interfere with an individual's capacity to make independent judgments about his own future, and conditions like severe mental retardation, in which it is clear that the individual will never be able to make such independent judgments. There is frequently a fluctuating degree of insight and of severity. In some cases the fluctuations appear to follow no obvious pattern. They are then quite unpredictable and environmental circumstances seem unrelated. The fact that the impairments are invisible makes the problems even more difficult, since neighbors and friends, and even unfortunately some professional advisers, deny their existence altogether.

Nevertheless, a good deal is now known about the social and pharmacological reactivity of the acute and chronic syndromes and of the way adverse secondary reactions develop. This means that it is possible to influence the course of schizophrenia for the better. Indeed, in a great many areas, some part of the service already operates effectively to minimize impairment, maximize assets or relieve burden. If it were possible to put together a service that was effective in all its parts, instead of in only some of them, a great deal of illness, handicap, and suffering would be prevented. Such a service would have to include a range of sheltered day and residential environments. The elements of a responsible, comprehensive and integrated service are well-known on both sides of the Atlantic.

One further point requires emphasis, because it has been insufficiently recognized hitherto. This is that the relatives are nowadays the real primary care agents. They and the patients deserve better *counseling*. Our attitudes to cancer have changed fundamentally during the past decade. Opinion leaders are willing to say that they have been treated for it and that they can live with it. This is not yet true for schizophrenia. Doctors themselves are still frightened of the word. Because the most effective methods of management, and the services to back them up, are not yet universally available, known or applied, it is rare for the condition to be frankly and realistically discussed. Public opinion remains ill informed and prejudiced. But just as the results of treatment have dramatically improved during the past quarter of a century, so the application simply of our present knowledge could produce a further substantial step forward. We would find that public opinion moved forward with us.

Perhaps the most important and most difficult requirement, for patient, relative and therapist alike, is to be realistic. If the therapist expects too much (endeavoring, perhaps, to fit the patient into the straightjacket of some untested theory), he can very easily make the patient worse (17, 25, 26, 70). It may seem reasonable to submit the patient to an intensive regime of social skills training, or rehabilitation, or social activation, on the theory that invisible impairments need not be considered, but although it will sometimes work, it often will not. It should always be remembered that there is a noteworthy suicide rate in schizophrenia (18). If the patient has severe intrinsic impairments, they will usually be obvious and it may, for example, be worthwhile to accept work in a sheltered setting where only part of the social role need be adopted. A neutral (not over-emotional) expectation to perform up to *attainable* standards is the ideal. This rule, if difficult for the specialist to adopt, is a thousand times more difficult for relatives. Nevertheless, we should be humbled to recognize that a large portion of relatives, by trial and error, do come to adopt it, without any help from professionals. The patient will have the greatest chance of acquiring insight if those around him, in spite of everything, are realistic. This is why skilled counseling (which means much more willingness by professionals to learn from relatives and patients) is the essence of good management.

I have concentrated attention on the severely handicapped patient with schizophrenia for obvious reasons, but most make a good social recovery. With the application of all that we now know, many more could do so.

APPENDIX 1

The Major CATEGO Classes

Class	*Diagnostic equivalent (approximate only)*
Class S	Central schizophrenia
Class P	Paranoid psychoses not classified as S, M or D
Class O	Non-paranoid and borderline psychoses not classified as S, P, M or D
Class M	Manic psychoses
Class D	Depressive psychoses
Class R	Retarded depressions not classified as D
Class N	Neurotic depressions
Class A	Anxiety states
Class B	Obsessional neuroses

Each of these classes has a more certain form (S+, P+, etc.) and a less certain form (S?, P?, etc.).

APPENDIX 2

Syndrome Profiles of Three Major CATEGO Classes

(IPSS data)

Syndrome	Class S %	Class P %	Class O %
1. Nuclear syndrome	82	—	—
2. Catatonic syndrome	10	—	58
3. Incoherence of speech	31	19	53
4. Residual syndrome	22	7	55
5. Depressive delusions	19	1	3
6. Simple depression	85	77	39
7. Obsessional symptoms	15	8	2
8. General anxiety	66	51	42
9. Situational anxiety	19	17	6
11. Affective flattening	51	32	65
12. Hypomanic syndrome	31	11	29
13. Non-affective auditory hallucinations	74	1	—
14. Delusions of persecution	64	69	3
15. Delusions of reference	64	52	5
16. Grandiose and religious delusions	32	13	11
17. Fantastic delusions	78	72	16
18. Visual hallucinations	51	26	5
19. Olfactory hallucinations	17	7	3
20. Overactivity	10	2	24
21. Slowness and underactivity	36	25	76
22. Non-specific psychosis	69	50	71
23. Depersonalization	41	17	11
24. Guilt and self-depreciation	42	24	8
25. Agitation	20	11	32
26. Self-neglect	19	6	40
27. Ideas of reference	68	52	10
28. Muscular tension	72	58	23
29. Lack of energy	42	29	19
30. Worrying	88	87	37

Syndrome 10, and syndromes 31-38 omitted.
For details of the symptoms making up the syndromes, and the glossary of definitions, see Wing, Cooper and Sartorius (11).

ACKNOWLEDGMENTS

I have drawn largely on work carried out by members of the MRC Social Psychiatry Unit at the Institute of Psychiatry in London during the past twenty years. Full details of those taking part in the International Pilot Study of Schizophrenia are given in volume one of the publication (10).

REFERENCES

1. JONES, K.:*A History of the Mental Health Services.* London: Routledge, 1972.
2. DEUTSCH, A.: *The Mentally Ill in America.* New York: Columbia University Press, 1949.
3. WING, J. K.: Institutional Influences on Mental Disorders. *Psychiatric der Gegenwart, Band III 2 Aufl.* Berlin: Springer Verlag, 1975.
4. WING, J. K. and BROWN, G. W.: *Institutionalism and Schizoprenia.* London: Cambridge University Press, 1970.
5. SCHEFF, T. J.: *Being Mentally Ill.* Chicago: Aldine, 1966.
6. WING, J. P. and HAILEY, A. M. (Eds.): *Evaluating a Community Psychiatric Service: The Camberwell Register,* 1964-1971. London: Oxford University Press, 1972.
7. KRAMER, M.: Some Problems for International Research Suggested by Observations on Differences in First Admission Rates to Mental Hospitals of England and Wales and of the United States. *Proceedings of the 3rd Wld. Cong. Psychiat. 3.* Montreal: McGill University Press, 1963.
8. WING, L., WING, J. K., HAILEY, A. M., BAIIN, A. K., SMITH, A. E., BALDWIN, J. A.: The Use of Psychiatric Services in Three Urban Areas: An International Case Register Study. *Soc. Psychiat.,* 2:158-67, 1967.
9. COOPER, J. E., KENDELL, R. E., GURLAND, B. J., SHARPE, L., COPELAND, J. R. M., and SIMON, R.: *Psychiatric Diagnosis in New York and London.* Maudsley Monograph No. 20. London: Oxford University Press, 1972.
10. WORLD HEALTH ORGANIZATION: *The International Pilot Study of Schizophrenia.* Geneva: W.H.O., 1973.
11. WING, J. K., COOPER, J. E. and SARTORIUS, N.: *The Description and Classification of Psychiatric Symptoms; an Instruction Manual for the PSE and Catego System.* London: Cambridge University Press, 1974.
12. SCHNEIDER, K.: *Clinical Psychopathology.* Fifth edition. Trans: Hamilton, M. W. New York: Grune and Stratton, 1959.
13. WING, L. (Ed.): *Early Childhood Autism: Clinical, Educational and Social Aspects.* New York: Pergamon, 1976.
14. CATTERSON, A., BENNETT, D. H., and FREUNDENBERG, R. K.: A

Survey of Longstay Schizophrenic Patients. *Brit. J. Psychiat.*, 109, 750, 1963.

15. VENABLES, P. H. and WING, J. K.: Level of Arousal and the Subclassification of Schizophrenia. *Arch. Gen. Psychiat.*, 7:114-9, 1962.

16. WATT, N. F. and LUBENSKY, A. W.: Childhood Roots of Schizophrenia. *J. Cons. Clin. Psychol.*, 44:363-75, 1976.

17. WING, J. K., BENNETT, D. H. and DENHAM, J.: *The Industrial Rehabilitation of Long-stay Schizophrenic Patients.* Med. Res. Council Memo. No. 42. London: H.M.S.O., 1964.

18. WING, L., WING, J. K., GRIFFITHS, D., and STEVENS, B.: An Epidemiological and Experimental Evaluation of Industrial Rehabilitation of Chronic Psychotic Patients in the Community. In J. K. Wing and A. M. Hailey (Eds.), *Evaluating a Community Psychiatric Service.* London: Oxford University Press, 1972.

19. COOPER, B. and MORGAN, H. G.: *Epidemiological Psychiatry.* Springfield: Thomas, 1973.

20. COOPER, B.: Social Class Prognosis in Schizophrenia. *Brit. J. Prev. Soc. Med.*, 15:17-41, 1961.

21. MAYER-GROSS, W.: Die Schizophrenie. In O. Bumke (Ed.), *Handbuch der Geisteskrankheiten. Band IX.* Berlin: Springer, 1932.

22. HARRIS, A., LINKER, I., NORRIS, V., and SHEPHERD, M.: Schizophrenia: A Social and Prognostic Study. *Brit. J. Prev. Soc. Med.*, 10:107-14, 1956.

23. BROWN, G. W., BONE, M., DALISON, B. and WING, J. K.: *Schizophrenia and Social Care.* London: Oxford University Press, 1966.

24. BLEULER, M.: *Die schizophrenen Geistesstörungen im Lichte langjähriger Kranken und Familiengeschichte,* Stuttgart: Thieme, 1972.

25. STONE, A. A. and ELDRED, S. H.: Delusion Formation During the Activation of Chronic Schizophrenic Patients. *Arch. Gen. Psychiat.*, 1:177-9, 1959.

26. GOLDBERG, S. C., SCHOOLER, N. R., HOGARTY, G. E. and ROPER, M.: Prediction of Relapse in Schizophrenic Outpatients Treated by Drug and Sociotherapy. *Arch. Gen. Psychiat.* (to be published), 1977.

27. BROWN, G. W. and BIRLEY, J. L. T.: Social Precipitants of Severe Psychiatric Disorders. In E. H. Hare and J. K. Wing (Eds.), *Psychiatric Epidemiology.* London: Oxford University Press, 1970.

28. LIDZ, T., FLECK, S. and CORNELISON, A. R.: *Schizophrenia and the Family.* New York: International Universities Press, 1965.

29. ROSENTHAL, D. and KETY, S. S.: *The Transmission of Schizophrenia.* New York: Pergamon, 1968.

30. WYNNE, L. C.: Methodologic and Conceptual Issues in the Study of Schizophrenics and Their Families. In D. Rosenthal and S. S. Kety (Eds.), *The Transmission of Schizophrenia*. London and New York: Pergamon, 1968.
31. WYNNE, L. C.: Family Research on the Pathogenesis of Schizophrenia. In P. Doncet and C. Laurin (Eds.), *Problems of Psychosis*. Excerpta Medica International Congress Series, No. 194, 1971.
32. HIRSCH, S. R. and LEFF, J. P.: *Abnormality in Parents of Schizophrenics: A review of the Literature and an Investigation of Communication Defects and Deviances*. London: Oxford University Press, 1975.
33. BROWN, G. W., BIRLEY, J. L. T., and WING, J. K.: Influence of Family Life on the Course of Schizophrenic Disorders: a Replication. *Brit. J. Psychiat.*, 121:241-258, 1972.
34. VAUGHN, C. E. and LEFF, J. P.: The Influence of Family and Social Factors on the Course of Psychiatric Illness. *Brit. J. Psychiat.*, 129:125-37, 1976.
35. VAUGHN, C. E. and LEFF, J. P.: The Measurement of Expressed Emotion in the Families of Psychiatric Patients. *Brit. J. Clin. Soc. Psychol.*, 15:157-65, 1976.
36. VAUGHN, C. E.: Patterns of Interaction in Families of Schizophrenic Patients. In H. Katschnig (Ed.), *Schizophrenia: the Other Side*. Vienna: Urban and Schwarzenberg, 1977.
37. JUNG, C. G.: *The Psychology of Dementia Praecox*. Trans. A. A. Brill. Nervous and Mental Diseases Monographs, 1936. 1960.
38. BABCOCK, H.: *Dementia Praecox: A Psychological Study*. New York, 1933.
39. KENDIG, I. and RICHMOND, W. V.: *Psychological Studies in Dementia Praecox*. Ann Arbor: Michigan, 1940.
40. FOULDS, G. A. and DIXON, P.: The Nature of Intellectual Deficit in Schizophrenia. *Brit. J. Clin. Soc. Psychol.*, 1:199, 1962.
41. GATEWOOD, L. C.: An Experimental Study of Dementia Praecox. *Psychol. Monogr.*, 11:2, 1909.
42. KENT, G. H.: Experiments in Habit Formation in Dementia Praecox. *Psychol. Rev.*, 18:375-410, 1911.
43. PEFFER, P. A.: Money: a Rehabilitation Incentive for Mental Patients. *Amer. J. Psychiat.*, 110:84-92, 1953.
44. PEFFER, P. A.: Motivation of the Chronic Mental Patient. *Amer. J. Psychiat.*, 113:55-59, 1956.
45. PETERS, H. N. and JENKINS, R. L.: Improvement of Chronic Schizophrenic Patients with Guided Problem-Solving Motivated by Hunger. *Psychiat. Quart. Sup.*, 28:84, 1954.
46. PETERS, H. N. and MURPHREE, O. D.: The Conditional Reflex in the Chronic Schizophrenic. *J. Clin. Psychol.*, 10:126, 1954.
47. GARMEZY, N.: Stimulus Differentiation by Schizophrenic and

Normal Subjects Under Conditions of Reward and Punishment. *J. Personality*, 20:253, 1952.

48. CARSTAIRS, G. M., O'CONNOR, N. and RAWNSLEY, K.: The Organization of a Hospital Workshop for Chronic Psychotic Patients. *Brit. J. Prev. Soc. Med.*, 10:136, 1956.

49. O'CONNOR, N., HERON, A. and CARSTAIRS, G. M.: Work Performance of Chronic Schizophrenics. *Occup. Psychol.*, 30:1-12, 1956.

50. O'CONNOR, N. and RAWNSLEY, K.: Incentives With Paranoid and Non-Paranoid Schizophrenics in a Workshop. *Brit. J. Med. Psychol.*, 32:133-143, 1959.

51. WING, J. K. and FREUDENBERG, R. K.: The Response of Severely Ill Chronic Schizophrenic Patients to Social Stimulation. *Amer. J. Psychiat.*, 118:311, 1961.

52. WING, J. K.: A Pilot Experiment on the Rehabilitation of Long-hospitalized Male Schizophrenic Patients. *Brit. J. Prev. Soc. Med.*, 14:173, 1960.

53. MANN, S. and SPROULE, J.: Reasons for a Six Months Stay. In J. K. Wing and A. M. Hailey, (Eds.), *Evaluating a Community Psychiatric Service*. London: Oxford University Press, 1972.

54. MANN, S. and CREE, W.: 'New' Long-stay Psychiatric Patients: A National Sample of 15 Mental Hospitals in England and Wales, 1972/73. *Psychol. Med.*, 6:603-16, 1976.

55. HEWETT, S., RYAN, P., and WING, J. K.: Living Without the Mental Hospitals. *J. Soc. Policy*, 4:391-404, 1975.

56. WING, J. K., LEFF, J. P., and HIRSCH, S. R.: Preventive Treatment of Schziophrenia: Some Theoretical and Methodological Issues. In J. O. Cole, A. M. Freedman, and A. J. Friedhoff (Eds.), *Psychopathology and Psychopharmacology*. Baltimore: Johns Hopkins University Press, 1973.

57. LEFF, J. P. and WING, J. K.: Trial of Maintenance Therapy in Schizophrenia. *Brit. Med. J.*, 3:599-604, 1971.

58. TARRIER, N., VAUGHN, C., LADER, M. H., and LEFF, J. P.: Bodily Reactions to People and Events in Schizophrenia. To be published, 1977.

59. GOFFMAN, E.: *Asylums: Essays on the Social Situation of Mental Patients and Other Inmates*. New York: Doubleday, 1961.

60. WING, J. K.: Institutionalism in Mental Hospitals. *Brit. J. Soc. Clin. Psychol.*, 1:38, 1962.

61. WING, J. K.: Social and Psychological Changes in a Rehabilitation Unit. *Soc. Psychiat.*, 1:21-28, 1966.

62. WING, J. K., MONCK, E., BROWN, G. W., and CARSTAIRS, G. M.: Morbidity in the Community of Schizophrenic Patients Discharged from London Mental Hospitals in 1959. *Brit. J. Psychiat.*, 110:10, 1964.

63. WING, J. K. (Ed.): *Schizophrenia from Within*. London: National Schizophrenia Fellowship, 1975.

64. HIRSCH, S. R., GAIND, R., ROHDE, P. D., STEVENS, B. C., and

WING, J. K.: Outpatient Maintenance of Chronic Schizophrenic Patients with Long-acting Fluphenazine: Double-blind Placebo Trial. *Brit. Med. J.*, 1:633-637, 1973.

65. CREER, C. and WING, J. K.: *Schizophrenia at Home.* London: National Schizophrenia Fellowship, 1974.

66. STEVENS, B. C.: Dependence of Schizophrenic Patients on Elderly Relatives. *Psychol. Med.*, 2:17-32, 1972.

67. TIDMARSH, D. and WOOD, S.: Psychiatric Aspects of Destitution. In J. K. Wing and A. M. Hailey (Eds.), *Evaluating a Community Psychiatric Service.* London: Oxford University Press, 1972.

68. WOOD, S. M.: Camberwell Reception Center: A Consideration of the Need for Health and Social Services of Homeless Single Men. *J. Soc. Pol.*, 5:389-99, 1976.

69. WING, J. K.: *Reasoning About Madness.* London and New York: Oxford University Press, 1977.

70. STEVENS, B.: Evaluation of Rehabilitation for Psychotic Patients in the Community. *Acta. Psychiat. Scand.*, 49:169-180, 1973.

Epilogue

Peter A. Martin, M.D.

This volume should help the reader become current with the latest relationships between psychiatry and the remainder of medicine. The papers by Brodie on Central Control of Endocrine Systems, Weiner on Psychobiology of Human Disease, and Reiser on Psychosomatic Illnesses are iconoclastic; they push borders aside, broaden viewpoints, and make the terms psychosomatic, liaison, and consultation psychiatry woefully inadequate or usable only if redefined by current concepts.

These papers demonstrate the tremendous increase in knowledge accumulated about brain metabolism through years of research in America. The complexity of knowledge of the neurobiology of the endocrine system as presented by Brodie is so great that even the relatively sophisticated audience of the College was impressed with how much knowledge they would have to absorb to stay abreast of these developments.

To place this explosion of new knowledge in an historical perspective, one must recognize that up until 1952, we did not even have a viable brain concept. Prior to that time, the brain was conceptualized as a relatively simple switchboard. Then newer conceptualizations of the brain, based on psychoanalytic research and accumulating knowledge of brain chemistry and metabolism, began to appear. Early concepts of psychosomatic medicine were developed (under the stimulus of Franz Alexander, Flanders Dunbar, and the other

479

pioneers referred to throughout this volume) which opened new avenues for the flood of research which followed. In research laboratories, techniques have been developed to study brain metabolism. The history of a science is the history of its techniques. The technological advances allowed for better collection of vital data on brain chemistry. The accumulated data allowed for more sophisticated conceptualizations of the multiple factors involved in sickness and health.

This meeting of the College reported no one great discovery, but maturely presented concepts of illness and health based on sound data. Based on a superior depth of information, our thinking can now be more incisive. Nevertheless, this is still but an intermediate report of the metabolism of the brain. We still are handicapped by incomplete knowledge and are making tentative formulations and conceptualizations of disease entities.

We anticipate, in the future, a definitive report of metabolism of the brain. This anticipation is, however, qualified by another observation brought about by this meeting. The awesome accumulation of data presented involves scholarly reviews of past work which are reflections of the golden age of the American psychiatric culture following World War II, when funds and resources for research seemed unlimited for a quarter of a century. The ascendency of this subculture seems to be coming to an end. The political-economic world in which we live exerts decisive influence. The current mental health research program of the United States is being threatened, as is all government supported research. Even more serious is the fact that because research cannot be separated from the goals of service and training, the success of the total mental health program in the United States depends on resolving the current research support crisis. Many psychiatrists, having lived through and participated actively in the Golden Age of funding for mental health, mourn its apparent loss under present and future socioeconomic and political conditions. Changes, such as loss of the rotating internships and transition from four-year to three-year medical schools, are seen as disastrous.

The examination of liaison and consultation psychiatry opens up economic, political, and sociological aspects of psychiatry, as well as the question of the relationship of psychiatry to the body of medicine.

The phenomena of resistance among medical psychotherapists against maintaining touch with the main body of medicine and the resistance of the rest of medicine to psychiatrists, interested in liaison and consultation psychiatry are significant. In addition, the recent attacks from within psychiatry predicting its demise, the difficulties in clarifying the differences between medical and nonmedical psychotherapists, and the difficulties experienced in defining what a psychiatrist is have quickened concerns for psychiatry's future relationship to medicine. However, some positive signs are appearing on the current scene.

Recent surveys of psychiatric practice show an increasing merging of psychiatrists with the rest of the medical community in terms of models of patient management, therapeutic intervention, somatic therapies, and joint therapeutic intervention. Advances in medical technology have created new problems that have brought the psychiatrist to dialysis centers, coronary care and intensive care units, and burn centers—not, however, without resistance from our medical colleagues, as noted above. These resistances vary in intensity, as does the degree to which psychiatrists have become accustomed to their expression. Moreover, advances in the study of psychopathology of common complaints and of behavior therapy have led psychiatry into areas such as the treatment of pain, obesity, and other metabolic disorders.

A certain amount of the time of most psychiatrists is devoted to diagnosis and treatment of minor medical ailments that are not seen by other physicians because the patient refuses to go to them or because of other practical considerations. Furthermore, the conception of psychiatric disorders and their clinical picture has come to resemble ideas predominant in other fields of medicine. The psychiatrist's expertise increasingly refers to common disorders with discrete clinical pictures and relatively well-known course and prognosis.

Psychiatry's relation to the rest of medicine has been further strengthened by the current emphasis on primary care physicians.

There is almost total agreement that the field of psychiatry has an essential and special role to play in the education of all primary care professionals. Francis J. Braceland presented the keynote special lecture of the 1976 American Psychiatric Association annual meeting entitled, "A Bicentennial Address: Benjamin Rush and Those Who Came After Him." He suggested that it was time for psychiatry to move back into the mainstream of medicine, retaining, of course, mastery of psychotherapeutic techniques and knowledge of psychodynamics. He added that this move can best be accomplished by employing the principle of complementarity, the art of encompassing different approaches to problems and utilizing the essentials of each to arrive at workable solutions (1).

The fields of liaison and consultation psychiatry appear to be the most likely way of achieving this goal. These fields are important but, as yet, their future is unpredictable, since they depend on potential technological advances. Their future may be that they will be the essential representatives of all psychiatry to the public or continue the current picture of small gains against great resistance. The hospital-based psychiatrist may become what is understood as psychiatry, while the psychotherapist will be the one who does not practice in a hospital. These are provocative ideas and are easily debatable.

The present excitement is not about liaison and consultation psychiatry, but about the recognition of the potential explosion of psychosomatic medicine and of the possibility that liaison psychiatry may become synonymous with psychosomatic medicine or may be only its practical arm. The reason for this is that, *if* progress in research on brain chemistry continues to a successful discovery of underlying mechanisms of disease processes, then, for the first time in the history of medicine, we will have a comprehensive theory of health and disease. As Weiner so clearly postulates, the only branch of medicine that has a comprehensive view of disease is psychosomatic medicine. It is psychiatry then, through psychosomatic medicine, which has retained and nurtured its roots in medicine and biology. It is psychiatry then which not only attempts to deal comprehensively with problems of mental health and disease, but which reminds the rest of medicine of its responsibility to do likewise. To quote from Reiser's chapter and to underscore it as the exciting keynote to the "happening" at the seminar: "Undoubtedly, the answers on the relationship of mind/body/illness will be derived from the understanding of the brain as it controls and integrates the biological, psychological, and social environment." When that day comes, artificial distinctions in treating parts of the patient will give way to truly holistic approaches.

This meeting of the American College of Psychiatrists gave a glimpse into the future with full recognition of the tiresome, tedious, grinding type of intensive and extensive work necessary to achieve this millenium. Future techniques gathering even newer and more sophisticated data will be needed to achieve the goal. A society which financially supports the ideal of a high quality of life would nurture such research.

The excitement of the meeting did not lie in reports of the success of liaison psychiatry to educate other physicians so that, by their attending to and treating the psychological stresses of their patients, they could ameliorate symptoms and affect the course of the patients' illnesses. Rather there was recognition that technological data collection offered the hope of eventually understanding the underlying mechanisms at work. This is psychosomatic medicine. This would bring psychiatry back into the field of medicine and biology. The term "psychosomatic" as used here does not imply a dichotomy between mind and body—indeed, just the opposite. Alexander stated this in 1950, but it has been often ignored. The major focus of his research of the "holy seven" diseases did not express an intent to limit the concept of psychosomatic medicine to a small group of diseases. Psychosomatic indicates a method of approach—the simultaneous and coordinated use of somatic and psychologic concepts and methods. "Theoretically, every disease is psychosomatic, since emotional factors influence all body processes through nervous and humoral pathways (2)." The emphasis established by Alexander on a general approach to all illnesses remains the view of psychosomatic medicine and liaison psychiatry. Understanding states of health and illness involves understanding of biological, psychological, and social parameters and understanding of the complex interaction of biopsychosocial processes.

Understanding psychosomatic medicine and the promise of things to come rekindles the hopes for a scientifically based theory of illness and health which is central to the practice of holistic medicine in general and to the psychological care of the medically ill.

Instead of wondering whatever happened to psychosomatic medicine, the new question was, "What is going to happen to liaison and consultation psychiatry?" The terms liaison and consultation have been used almost conjointly up to this point. The distinctions between the two entities must be made to give recognition to the different responses of the participants. Of the two, consultation psychiatry, whose primary function is to alleviate acute psychiatric symptomatology in the individual patient and the assumption of major responsibility for psychiatric care of the patient, seems to be marking time without making greater inroads into medicine's utilization of psychiatrists as members of the team approach to treating patients' illnesses. Consultation and referral models pose the threat of fragmentation of services and ineffective total patient care.

It is liaison psychiatry which seeks to enhance the psychological status of all medical patients through primary prevention and tertiary prevention. It is liaison psychiatry that is closely allied with and promoting the resurgence of psychosomatic medicine.

In addition to the conceptual schema of the common psychosocial reactions of the medically ill patient to illness and hospitalization, the liaison model promotes the continuing collaboration of the internist, social worker, and psychiatrist in the assessment and formulation of the interrelationships of psychological, social, and physiological factors within the patient.

Having elevated liaison psychiatry to this level of importance, we must now ask, how effective are these efforts?

I am going to make these predictions of things to come, more because they will summarize and clarify the points I have made, than because of any feeling of assurance of the accuracy of my predictions. Also, these predictions will have two different qualifying "ifs."

Psychiatry and medicine cannot be separated from the society in which we live. If the present trend of limiting resources for research and training continues, if we are a civilization in its descendancy, then progress will slow and the intermediate state of knowledge of medicine in which we live will continue for generations to come. What is psychiatry? There isn't one psychiatry, there are many psychiatries. Economic psychiatry is central to what is going to happen. We do not have an information overload. Within five to ten years, higher levels of generalization will be reached and we will be in need of new information. The new information will undoubtedly be sparse and slow in coming if quality of life is no longer an ideal of our government and funding to achieve it is no longer possible in our country.

If this occurs, then we will see a continuation of the present picture of liaison psychiatry. Liaison psychiatrists will continue to be missionaries who do the daily grinding labor of trying to educate, convert, and do battle with the ever-present phenomenon of resistance to change present in human nature and which impedes the progress they seek.

Wing's chapter on "The Management of Schizophrenia in the Community" is an example of an holistic approach to a disease which has so far remained resistant to all our research efforts. This mysterious, devastating, and tragic disease has little known about its pathophysiology even though progress is being made in understanding something about its etiology, pathogenesis, and treatment. If research funds are not available for continuing effort to solve the mystery of its pathophysiology, a gloomy prediction is in order for this disease and for psychiatry as a branch of medicine.

Now for a more optimistic prediction. Based on the tremendous progress in research in brain chemistry which this meeting demonstrated as compared to the early days of psychosomatic medicine, continued research in biochemistry and molecular biology in the next 50 years will lead the path of medicine toward a workable theory of illness and health. This will bring psychiatry to the forefront of medicine. Knowledge of the functioning of the brain is within the province of psychiatry and, not only will it be integrated with medicine, but psychiatry will be the leader in holistic medicine. Comprehensive psychiatry and comprehensive medicine may then become synonymous.

PETER A. MARTIN, M.D., *President,* 1976-77
American College of Psychiatrists

REFERENCES

1. BRACELAND, F. J.: "A Bicentennial Address: Benjamin Rush and Those Who Came After Him." *Amer. J. Psychiat.*, Vol., 133, No. 11, 1251-1258, Nov., 1976.
2. ALEXANDER, F.: *Psychosomatic Medicine—Its Principles and Applications.* New York: W. W. Norton & Company, Inc., 1950.

Name Index

Included are those authors cited by name in the text as well as referenced.

Subject Index

Boldface page numbers indicate material in tables, graphs, or illustrations.